HUMAN RIGHTS AND HUMAN WRONGS

HUMAN RIGHTS AND HUMAN WRONGS

A Life Confronting Racism

COLIN TATZ

© Copyright 2015 Colin Tatz
All rights reserved. Apart from any uses permitted by Australia's Copyright Act 1968, no part of this book may be reproduced by any process without prior written permission from the copyright owners. Inquiries should be directed to the publisher.

Monash University Publishing
Matheson Library and Information Services Building
40 Exhibition Walk
Monash University
Clayton, Victoria 3800, Australia
www.publishing.monash.edu

Monash University Publishing brings to the world publications which advance the best traditions of humane and enlightened thought.
Monash University Publishing titles pass through a rigorous process of independent peer review.

www.publishing.monash.edu/books/hrhw-9781922235688.html

Series: Biography

Design: Les Thomas

Cover image: Colin Tatz at Oribi, Pietermaritzburg, 1952. From the author's personal collection.

National Library of Australia Cataloguing-in-Publication entry:

Creator:	Tatz, Colin, author.
Title:	Human rights and human wrongs : a life confronting racism / Colin Tatz.
ISBN:	9781922235688 (paperback)
Series:	Biography (Monash University Publishing)
Notes:	Includes index.
Subjects:	Tatz, Colin.
	Racism.
	Race relations.
	Ethnic relations.
	Social justice.
	Aboriginal Australians, Treatment of.
	Australia--Race relations.
	Australia--Ethnic relations.
Dewey Number:	305.8

Printed in Australia by Griffin Press an Accredited ISO AS/NZS 14001:2004 Environmental Management System printer.

The paper this book is printed on is certified against the Forest Stewardship Council ® Standards. Griffin Press holds FSC chain of custody certification SGS-COC-005088. FSC promotes environmentally responsible, socially beneficial and economically viable management of the world's forests.

In memory of
Edgar Harry Brookes (1897–1979)
a great South African
whose humanism and intellect nurtured my search for social justice.

CONTENTS

Thanks ix

Part I: Pre-Natal. 1

    Chapter 1   We Three 3

    Chapter 2   Chickens and Eggs. .10

    Chapter 3   Daventry Calling 28

    Chapter 4   Pygmalion. 44

Part II: Natal 61

    Chapter 5   Green to Black. 63

    Chapter 6   Extra Lessons. 78

    Chapter 7   Shadow and Substance. 93

Part III: Post-Natal 111

    Chapter 8   A Pair of Holdens .113

    Chapter 9   Gulliver 130

    Chapter 10   Centre Forward 150

    Chapter 11   The Representative. 165

    Chapter 12   Race Matters 183

Part IV: The Middle Ages 199

    Chapter 13 Rustic and Hectic............................201

    Chapter 14 Radio Activity 220

    Chapter 15 Oscar Nomination 237

    Chapter 16 Romans and Jews..........................253

    Chapter 17 Obstacle Races...............................273

Part V: Pre-Mortem 291

    Chapter 18 Groucho..293

    Chapter 19 Breathless.......................................310

    Chapter 20 Seldom Softly.................................327

    Chapter 21 Fourscore 344

Appendix: Author's Published Books...........................361

Index...363

THANKS

This book began as a family memoir, informing children, grandchildren and close friends about aspects of my life of which they knew between little and nothing. It was printed privately in what is politely called a limited edition, under the title *The Lion's Feathers: How I Think I've Lived*. Electronic copies of that version are held in the libraries of the universities where I have taught.

Initially, Michelle Webster asked me to write an essay for her on *shmaltz*, literally, chicken fat, and this is what turned out. Years later, Graeme Ward prodded me into this exercise. Friends Douglas Booth, Winton Higgins, Elizabeth Kuiper, Graeme Ward and Ruth Wilson read drafts, offered comments and suggested a slimmer publication for a wider audience.

The enabling factor, of course, is Sandra, my wife of almost six decades. She supported me unselfishly in this venture as she has done in everything else in my life, always there with love, care, advice, comments, literary and technical help, and medicaments. How else does one make it to 80?

Thanks to my children Paul, Karen and Simon and my grandchildren for their friendship, encouragement and help with memories and pictures. On some matters they have better recall than I have. My sister Pam guided me on Jewish history and rituals and shared very mixed family memories. Shelley Kenigsberg has been so professional, warm and sensitive in her editing. Lesley Yee listened intently. Libby Raichman vetted my Yiddish usage and spellings and Christine Winter watched over my dubious German.

Amanda Bresnan, Shirley Cook, Bob Harding, Konrad Kwiet, Bob Melson, Promund Obel, Michael Phillips, Jan Richardson, Kylie Simpson and Anna-Louise Shapiro helped with photographs. Joan Brookes and the Alan Paton Centre and Struggle Archive in Pietermaritzburg gave permission to use the Tito Field portrait of Edgar Brookes; and Alan Moir made a gift of his cartoon. Michael Phillips, especially, gave generously of his time, care and skill in arranging the images.

Nathan Hollier, Joanne Mullins and the staff of Monash University Publishing took on this venture with ease and grace. Maryna Mews compiled a meticulous and comprehensive index.

Part I:
Pre-Natal

Chapter 1

WE THREE

> We three, we're all alone
> Living in a memory,
> My echo, my shadow, and me.
> We three, we're not a crowd
> We're not even company
> My echo, my shadow, and me.

It was soon after the start of World War II, early 1940, when I first heard the famous Ink Spots sing the words that were to capture the cadences, the highs and lows, the rhythm and blues of my life. The echoes are from a once-was Lithuanian Jewish world; the shadows are cast by domains that are oppressively black and cruelly white; and me, not quite a crowd—Jewish, alienated, migratory, and deeply troubled by food.

Not enamoured of autobiography, I half agree with Yehuda Bauer, my mentor in Holocaust history, adamant that he will never write his memoirs. He says that when historians have nothing left to say they start writing about themselves. Hollywood movie mogul Samuel Goldwyn felt no one should write their autobiography until they were dead. (Good thinking, Sam.) Yet here I am, writing about the variables and coefficients in my life's equation—historical, spatial, familial, parental, marital, professional, nutritional especially, and often enough accidental. Some are explicable, some unfathomable, some remain unknown.

I haven't the fiction-writing skills to even think of imitating, let alone emulating, writers like Saul Bellow, Joseph Heller, Bernard Malamud, Phillip Roth and my favourite, Mordecai Richler—men who spent lifetimes explaining themselves and their Jewishness to themselves (and sometimes to the wider world), with humour and pathos, enlightening and always entertaining. One needs Richler's Montreal–Jewish upbringing *and* his creative imagination to portray the Inuit poet Atuk who thought the whole world was Jewish, and the cunning and unscrupulous Duddy Kravitz, and the obsessed St Urbain's horseman, and the haplessly dementing Barney Panofsky, and the complicated writer who is Joshua (*Then and Now*), and then the wandering Jew, Solomon Gursky.

Such fictional characters were real in my life. I experienced many of their fantasies, sharing with Richler's very urban Uncle Joey the yearning to ride a heroic horse into the Paraguayan jungle to bring to justice the monstrous Nazi medical experimenter, Dr Josef Mengele. But I didn't have the *chutzpah*, the effrontery, to even think of portraying them in fictive print. A solemn and serious scholarly book is so much easier to write than an item of delicious fiction, a field where you can fiddle with character and time, indulge in flashbacks and flash forwards, where you can invent, conjure, digress, add layers, and play all manner of games. What's more, you can have fun. We academics, on the other hand, '-ise' for a living: we conceptualise, hypothesise, theorise, surmise, verbalise, synthesise, philosophise, and analyse evidence for our advocacies. At times we even plagiarise.

I want to write about my interaction in events of greater significance than my small or possibly largish role in them. This, then, is less of a memoir in the conventional sense and much more an account of a professional life spent chasing down the rights and wrongs in race relations.

Exactly one-third of my life was in South Africa, two-thirds resident in Australia. Clearly, the tenors and rhythms change—from the recollections of a lonely, insecure, bewildered and discordant kid to the chronicle of a critic with a sense of capacity and confidence. Yet the matter of being an insider or an outsider (or both simultaneously) remains unresolved: an emigré South African Jew of Lithuanian origins, I found that I belonged at some levels and was very much the stranger at so many others.

The inner dynamic of my life, the foremost factor, is my version and interpretation of my Jewishness. I comment with pleasure and lament with degrees of pain on its joys and jests, its perplexity and perversity, its dissonance and bloody-mindedness in general. In 1991, Dagmar Strauss produced a six-part television series for the then Australian Broadcasting Corporation (ABC). I was one of her six 'characters'. She wanted to call the program 'Torah Australis', a nice touch, but the ABC dubbed it 'Thinking Jewish'. In that 55-minute interview I came to see just how much this Jewish thing has suffused my life. Inevitably, it has led to studying, teaching, writing and talking a great deal about genocide and the Holocaust especially.

A related if not conjoined propulsion is the quest for social justice, hence a lifelong devotion to matters of race and racism, confronting the sometimes well-intentioned policy aims but mostly bad practices of several nations towards their native peoples and 'coloured' immigrants—South Africa, Canada, New Zealand, Australia, Israel, the United Kingdom and the United States. Much of my life has been about efforts to produce or effect change, always an individual activist, never a herdsman in a crowd or a company.

Early exposure to the bizarre deaths of a synagogue beadle and a great-uncle led to a search for the insoluble riddle of suicide, especially among Australian Aboriginal youth. I look for what psychoanalyst James Hillman calls 'the soul of the suicide', and never find it. (Nor does anyone else.) As a migrant, the mostly good and the less bad aspects of that experience loom large. To counter the gloom of these domains, my escape has been into sport, evolving a love-hate relationship with it. I use it as a metaphor for many things, understanding that students learn, and learn more, if they can relate their subject matter to a framework they like or at least know about. Explaining Aboriginal history to Australian university students through the prisms of their sporting achievements is far more effective than explaining Aboriginal history. How, indeed, did Aborigines manage to play cricket during an era of frontier killings by settlers and murderous squads of special Native Police units?

* * *

In 1967 Stephen Birmingham published *Our Crowd*, an admiring and critical account of the arrogant nineteenth-century German–Jews who made good in New York, the crowd that scorned, indeed excoriated, the *Ashkenazi* or Central European Jews, especially the Poles, Lithuanians, Latvians, Bohemians and 'other rabble'. They lobbied the American government to keep them out. Mind you, at the start of World War II the Anglo-descended Australian Jews took the same action to exclude *Ostjude*—an insulting term for Jews 'from the East' who were regarded as 'foreign' Jews. And when they did arrive in smallish numbers they were met at the docks with a written admonition from the Jewish authorities: 'Above all, do not speak German in the streets and trams. Modulate your voice. Do not make yourself conspicuous anywhere by walking with a group of persons, all of whom are speaking loudly in a foreign language.'

So much for Jewish unity, a culture and a faith riddled with conflict between Orthodox and Reform, Conservative and Reconstruction in between, *Ashkenazim* (Europeans) versus *Sephardim* (Spanish and Portuguese descendants), West Europeans opposing East Europeans, Lithuanians and Poles disdaining German Jews, secularists against assimilationists, *misnagdim* (the sceptical and learned ones) up against *chassidim* (the ecstatic and joyous ones), Zionists polarising anti-Zionists, Israelis versus Diaspora Jews and so on. Theodor Herzl, the famed Zionist leader, said 'we are a people—one people'. As viewed from without by the rest of the world, that may be so. But assuredly not so felt and enacted from within. Oneness may have advantages when it comes to external threats but divisiveness often creates calamity within communities, even when faced with such threats.

My crowd were *Litvaks*, Jews originating in Lithuania as were 90 percent of South Africa's 120,000-odd Hebrews. All were odd. We, the world of *us*, were the centre of the universe. *Them*, the Polish Jews, were very different, in names and in Yiddish locution. American scholar Dovid Katz explains that standard Yiddish has drawn upon three major East European dialects: Polish, Ukrainian and Lithuanian. Standard Yiddish pronunciation, he concludes, is far closer to that of the centuries-old cultural capital, Vilna (Vilnius). One up for *Litvakia*.

The German-speaking Jews, the *yekkes*, were quite beyond them and us, untouchables. To me, as a child, they not only sounded different, they looked different. They were disparaged by anyone even though it was their forebears who gave birth to Yiddish in the thirteenth century.

That language has been described as 'an eclectic mish-mash of manners, speech, and a cultural and emotional collectivity of things Jewish'. Better still is the description by Nobel Laureate Isaac Bashevis Singer: Yiddish captures a 'frightened and hopeful humanity'. UNESCO describes it as a 'definitely endangered' language. In 1948, Israelis chose Hebrew as the language of the new state, eschewing—even condemning, certainly disdaining—Yiddish as the quintessence of the ghetto world, the small village (*shtetl*) world of oppression, doom and death. A story: an Israeli sees a granny teaching her grandchild Yiddish. 'Why are you doing *that*?' he admonishes. 'I want him to remember he's a Jew', she replies. It is a language that constantly reminds me too.

As important as Yiddish is to the Lithuanian saga, so too is the philosophy that shapes that ethnic identity. In the main, *Litvaks* were *misnagdim*, opponents of the *chassidic* popular, pietist, religious, social movement of the eighteenth century. *Misnagdim* were both wary and sceptical about the rise of a movement that seemed to be an extension of an earlier messianic sect—that of the false messiah Rabbi Shabbatai Zevi (1626–1676) that didn't end all that well (when he was forced to convert to Islam).

Ecstatic prayer, emotional music and a direct personal relationship with God were the early hallmarks of the *chassidim* rather than the scholarly, rational, Talmudic studiousness of the *misnagdim*—people who were regarded as smart, inquisitive, learned, but quintessentially sceptical. They were so clever, it is said, that they prayed for forgiveness before they sallied forth to sin.

I turned out to be a *misnagged*: questioning, critical, dubious, hesitant about conventional explanations of the world around me. Yet, for many of my South African compatriots, something went awry in the migration process to Africa—very few indeed pursued an intellectual life, with the great majority opting for careers in the professions and in business.

'Beneath every history', wrote novelist Hilary Mantel, 'another history'. Yes, most things are here, things underneath things are here, echoes and shadows, and some of me certainly. What is not here is a 'regular' memoir. In my breathless rush to complete things, to chew through racial agendas, I have found little time for cogitation, for reflection, for analysis of how I felt about the issues I confronted. Nor have I managed a highly personal account of my rich life with Sandra and my children. I want to explain the factors that made up my early socialisation because they help unravel the dilemmas and doings of an immigrant humanist, a political liberal, frustrated by what he couldn't say or do in South Africa but found he could accomplish in Australian society. South Africa was always a place of can't and don't; from what I read, it still is. It is a long voyage of transition from life in a transposed Lithuanian *shtetl* in race-riven Africa to the outback and metropolitan worlds Down Under. It is also an exploration of alienation of several kinds, many of which produced the adrenaline needed for action. According to sociologist Émile Durkheim, alienation can lead to suicide but it can also be a most effective spur to creativity and achievement. If being Jewish is the 'x' in my equation, alienation is the 'y', and food the 'z'.

WE THREE

Jewish characters in Lithuania in the nineteenth century, courtesy Vilna Gaon Jewish State Museum, Lithuania.

Chapter 2

CHICKENS AND EGGS

When one is descended from an embattled immigrant community, luck is certainly an element in one's birthplace. Economically forlorn and politically intimidated, Lithuanian Jews left in hordes between the latter half of the nineteenth century and the first two decades of the twentieth. They landed, as if by lottery, in England, the United States and South Africa—better luck indeed than arriving in Germany, Poland or Hungary. Unaccompanied husbands as exploratory scouts and, sometimes, whole families found their way to Odessa, thence to Southampton and from there to wherever a convenient boat was heading.

Does birthplace, accidental or chosen, matter all that much? Does place in and of itself produce a reflexive and indelible patriotism, a sense of 'birthright', an implacable value of 'my country-right-or-wrong'? Not for me it doesn't. But a native land is a place of nurture, early education and the slow accretion of values. South Africa, then, was the place of my echoes and shadows, my chickens and eggs.

***

The Clarendon, a private nursing home in Berea, a bourgeois Johannesburg suburb, was where, on 18 July 1934, I was born. Eight days later I was circumcised by the *mohel*, Reverend Glass, dubbed by the nurses as Rev Cut Glass. Despite human rights hysterics about the barbaric bodily harm of such rituals, I don't feel mutilated, even physically. The Glass work was to be the subject of serious examination 28 years later.

Old before my time, I always claimed I was two when I was born. At five I felt even older and had to act that way in a household of eight adults. For five years before that ménage I lived with my parents in a block of apartments owned by my paternal grandfather, Kivel Tatz, *Zeide* as grandfathers are called. He was the well-to-do owner of a dairy, fish-distribution centre and ice-works downtown; our apartment was in nearby Pritchard Street, the lively (and dead) centre of Johannesburg city.

Maurice and Bessie Tatz (neé Isaacson), Johannesburg, 25 May 1933.

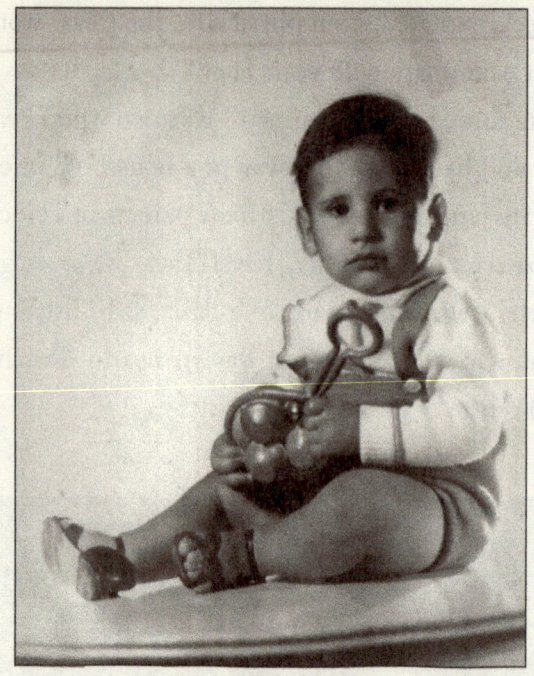

'I was two when I was born.'

Two memories of two women: Katherine (Katie), a White nanny, a hitherto unheard of and quite shocking social and domestic phenomenon, followed by Daisy, a conventional 'non-White' in the South African idiom, adorable, loving, my foremost mentor. Katie lived with us, befitting her colour; Daisy had to share a room, as did all 'non-Whites', in the purpose-built servants' quarters on the roof-garden.

Toddlers become attached to and hug such constant mother figures: but I recall when Daisy and I were asked not to kiss each other. The age of innocence ended early in that country and this prohibition was to be but one of the many 'marvels' of South African socialisation. I was still allowed to hug Mr Khourie, owner of the greengrocery downstairs. He was a different kind of 'different'—a Lebanese Christian migrant.

Mother Bessie went back to work at the Jewish Guild when I was six weeks old. She was administrative secretary of that flourishing social, cultural, sporting and match-making body in the heart of the city. There she had met my father, Maurice, who sang exquisitely in Guild musicals and light opera by night and delivered ice for his father by day. Said my dominatingly diminutive mother to my diminutive and gentle father: 'I will *not* be married to an iceman'. So Maurice opened his men's outfitting store close by. He stopped singing (in public). But his versions of the songs that end the Passover *seder* service are still memorable; even today, I can hum those lyrical tunes, sing them in poor voice. Maurice said few words to me in my life but he did sing for me once a year.

In 1939 we moved from the city into a rented house in Honey Street, Berea, joining my maternal grandparents, *Bobbe* and *Zeide* Isaacson, two of Bess's unmarried brothers, her young sister Babs (Barbara), always my friend and only joy in youth, and after she married, her husband as well. Babs was what Swiss philosopher and psychologist Alice Miller calls an 'enlightened witness'—someone who understands what you are enduring, who doesn't have to *do* anything but simply lets you know in one way or another that he or she *knows*. A shrug, nod, raised eyebrow, a rolled eye is enough.

Aunt Babs (Barbara) Isaacson, always a joy in my childhood and adult life (here with husband Gerald Goldstein), 1944.

The Isaacson family had lived in Smit Street, Braamfontein. Berea, then a pinnacle of social aspiration, was a serious advance from the semi-detached ghettos of Doornfontein and Braamfontein, the first points of settlement for the migrant *Litvaks*. Hillbrow, Berea, Yeoville, no more than two to five kilometres respectively from central Jo'burg, were the places to be. Houghton, Hyde Park, Morningside and Sandton would be the next rungs in the geographic and social ladders, places that didn't end in '*fontein*' (fountain) and sounded grander with their Anglo syllables. From Braamfontein to Berea was a short distance but an immense social graduation; from there to Houghton signified true arrival.

I was the solitary and only child until the age of ten. For five or six years I spoke a Yiddish of sorts to *Zeide* and *Bobbe*. *Zeide* graduated from running a small bagel and milk store to selling eggs wholesale at the Johannesburg municipal markets. Short, strong, cropped but grizzled grey hair, he looked old even when relatively young. He bartered his wares for poultry and fish and every Friday afternoon he'd come home with two dozen dead or alive chickens, unplucked and uncleaned, a turkey or two and an occasional goose, a duckless domain.

I had to help pluck and de-gut the dreadful things, feed yards of hideous intestines (*kishkes*) to four malevolent cats, remove the unborn eggs with care, cut off the chickens' feet, scald these with boiling water, peel off the flaky yellowy outer skin, clip the nails with pliers and ready them for the chicken soup. (All this because we had 'only' two servants.) I would hide in the extra outdoor toilet while the kosher slaughterer plucked a few neck feathers of the live ones, and cut their throats. You know the rest.

Most of these now 'fully-dressed' creatures were gifts to his children who attended Friday night Sabbath dinners. Our remaining chickens were always boiled, never roasted, my father's abiding *bête* (or bird) *noire*. I can't explain why I eat them. Perversely, *dafke* (pronounced *duff-keh*), I love chickens' feet, but only the Chinese version. Cathie, a waitress at my favourite yum cha restaurant, lights up when she sees me. 'Ah, welcome, Professor Chicken Feet!'

CHICKENS AND EGGS

* * *

Taciturn, a forbidding man, *Zeide* had few likes and many dislikes. Every night but one he and *Bobbe* played a crazy card game called *zeks und zechtzig* (66), spiced with animus, antagonism and muttered maledictions. I liked the imprecation 'have a healthy cholera in your belly' or 'may God give you a new soul'. The grandparents never called each other by name or endearment. Mine was hardly a tactile or an outwardly loving mob. *Zeide* retired at nine every night with a tray of eight very hard-boiled eggs (yolks turned turquoise, sometimes mauve, after 50 minutes), ten to fifteen grams of salt in a huge cellar with its single hole widened to over a centimetre all the better to pour it with, and two jugs of cold water all the better to wash it down with. His other bed companion was chronic phlebitis, inflammation of the leg veins, a condition he and the family claimed had nothing whatever to do with the nocturnal eggs or the surfeit of sodium. (For me, 20-minute eggs are just fine.)

He hated the *shul* cantor, Shlomo Mandel, this man of exquisite voice and an undertaking business on the side. On *Shabbes* he prays for us to live, growled *Zeide*, on Sunday for us to die. He resented the men we came to know as Bwitish wabbis, often Jews' College and Oxford men or the locals who imitated the mannerisms of these exotic men. They preached fire, bwimstone and banality, never mentioning the hideous social and political vortex outside the front door: a raging world war, civil strife between the pro- and anti-war forces, between English- and Afrikaans-speakers for political power, violent antisemitism in a country rife with fascist movements, the seeming calamity for Jews when the Nationalist Party came to power in the late 1940s, the fear of rising racial tensions of the 1940s, 1950s and beyond. I was awkwardly aware of the thunders outside; if not the details, then certainly the darkening shadows and the tangible tensions.

Bobbe was very short, very stout, with powerful forearms, massive hands, stubby fingers. She wore her hair short and in a manly style (oiled with

Vaseline or liquid paraffin and with an occasional broad comb for 'going out') and she always dressed in self-knitted one-piece dresses, hairs everywhere. When she cut bread it was with the loaf against her bosom in a sideways sawing motion towards her torso. One got used to eating bread, butter and angora fluff. She hoarded every length of string she could find and could have answered the philosopher's conundrum: how long is a piece of string? She salvaged 0.6 million ill-matched buttons and collected an array of pencil stubs too short for sharpening—in case! These bizarre items were housed in old Mazawattee tea tins; their contents were my early toys and treasures. My sister Pam still collects such containers and she didn't know her grandmother. Tin genes?

'The worst of ours are better than the best of theirs,' was *Bobbe*'s daily pontification about the Jewish–*goyish* divide. She had no non-Jewish friends or even acquaintances; nor did my family generally, yet their sermonising

Maternal grandparents, Zeide Morris-Behr Isaacson, Bobbe Faiga-Ita (Levine), 1940s.

suggested vast experience about 'them', the *goyim*, the gentile world. At that age I visited the homes of non-Jewish school friends and knew better. As to the Blacks, she would implore the heavens as my family embraced every facet of not just having but having to 'handle' the constant procession of live-in servants in their backyard quarters. 'They' were the ones whose first names were often allocated solely to suit the diction capabilities of the 'master' and the 'madam', who seemed not to have surnames, who appeared to be without husbands, wives or children. Four or five times a day she (and many thousands like her) would complain to *Der Aybeshter*, the lord above, about the gross imperfections, brain deficiencies, genetic deformities, the stupidity, laziness, cussedness and marble-hearted ingratitude of these black Africans: 'how can one live from such people?'

Later generations of White South Africans exemplified such humiliating attitudes by having refrigerators with Yale locks built into both freezers and main compartments: 'They'll eat you out of house and home, you know!' In a strange way they were honest: they said these things to their servants' faces, not just behind their backs. One came perilously close to not wanting to be Jewish: dismay not so much at my (and their) misshapen Jewishness but horror and much shame at the dissonance, hypocrisy, sanctimoniousness, materialism and empty ritual of their existence.

Most of my family, many of my friends and their families knew no Hebrew to speak or write, only enough to read in prayer. Our earlier prayer books didn't have translations. With upward mobility came American rather than Lithuanian editions with English alongside the Hebrew. Not that the English words are inspiring; much is repetitive and often quite banal. Yet these Orthodox minions prayed with such outward fervour, having conversations with God in a language most couldn't understand. Do you know what you're asking forgiveness for? I'd ask. *Shah*, shush, *He* knows!

Perhaps others of my enclosed world had a different upbringing. Perhaps they were suitably prepared, as Jews, for life in an essentially hostile, non-Jewish mainstream. I question seriously whether their schools and *shuls*—

both there and here in Australia, both then and now—gave them the armament with which to be confident Jews, both within their milieux and outside of them.

Many friends sustained themselves because they huddled. Huddling is a protective device, a tortoise-like carapace, especially if you never move away from that protection physically, socially or culturally. I was never a serious or even semi-serious huddler. Being a semi-loner, often alone, I had no such ammunition or armour, having to forge it in an environment of racial hatred that was often enough inimical to confidence about any set of human relationships. There was not one elder to answer my questions and curiosity except by way of facetious comment—spurred by the *Litvak* love of *chochmes* (jokes, gags, puns)—even when perchance only one in a hundred works.

I desperately wanted to know about my family origins. I asked, no one listened, no one answered. My grandparents and elders refused to talk about *der heim* (home), about what happened or didn't happen in the *shtetls* in Tsarist-controlled Lithuania (1795–1918) and then briefly an independent state until 1940. All the *Litvaks* I knew hated Russia and Russians, but I still see so much affectionate Russianism, perhaps only things culturally Russian, in their descendants. Why would an 'old country', even a hated one, be so off limits? I settled for book knowledge and, later, the memoirs that flowed from Holocaust survivors and from a visit to *der heim*.

The *Litvaks* were close-knit *landsleit* (fellow-dwellers, kinsmen): Lithuania is smaller than Tasmania and the *shtetls* were never more than 200 km apart. Society in general was very formal and all adults were Mr and Mrs but a degree of intimacy was afforded by calling adults uncle and aunty even if unrelated. This was *Gemeinschaft*, a real sense of communalism and community togetherness.

Arriving in South Africa about 1900, my forbears spoke Russian and Yiddish, with English of sorts in between. Men often came well ahead of wives and children. I once asked my *Bobbe*'s elder sister about the eleven-year gap between her Lithuanian-born daughter and locally-born son. She smiled: 'Colinke, it was very, very difficult.' Never a mention of occupations. Eventually I found hints of a sisal patch, a broom factory, a cow and a small dairy, but little else. I imagined we stemmed from peasants, but if so then they were in fact lower middle-class ones, literate in Russian and Yiddish. A few sepia pictures survive, very *shtetl*, very grim and prim.

Berea was always a midway, middling and medium place, *mittel* in most things: *mittel*-culture—Bing Crosby, Enrico Caruso, Benjamino Gigli and dozens of recordings of cantorial singing in the same collection; *mittel*-style—kitchen-dressers and brass samovars from Kovno and moquette settees (with antimacassars) from upmarket furnishers; *mittel*-cuisine—crustless, triangular sandwiches skewered by a toothpick alongside a lump of quivering, coarse, pickled brisket with a massive ridge of white glistening fat, hot mustard and sauerkraut; *mittel*-modernity—with deliveries of the English dailies and the Yiddish weekly newspapers, the latter always printed in brown ink.

Berea *Shul* in Tudhope Avenue was always poorly lit and the downstairs area (for men only) was permeated by the effluvium of one of the worst urinals in the one part of Africa claiming to be civilised. Some of the older men, decked in large black and white prayer shawls (*talaysim*), were funny; most were frightening. We had nicknames for many: one, Bertzik Kaufman, 132 cms tall, we called 'Bonecrusher'—that's what he did for a living. He dominated the congregation, forever barking instructions to be quiet and handing out a sniff of snuff (a *shmek tabak*) to a favoured few, including me on occasion. Decorum is not what one finds in Orthodox prayer houses.

Behind the *shul* was the *cheder*, the Hebrew school we were compelled to attend after normal school four days a week plus Sunday mornings. A pedagogic disaster, a catastroscope as comedian Jimmy Durante would say. It was part of our 'traditional' education but I went for ten hours a week for at least eight years, learned to read but never to write or comprehend, let alone speak Hebrew. When you asked the teacher, 'why are *tefillin* (prayer phylacteries) black?' 'Because', he would say amid slaps and smacks, 'tefillin must be black!' I'm past caring about black leather but I am still astounded at the pedagogic style.

One Sunday, the *shammes* (the rabbi's assistant and ceremonial officer) was on fire. Literally. Our teacher caught the whiff just as we did: something was burning. The *cheder* side door abutted the back door of the *shul*'s internal back staircase that led to the choir room one floor up (putting men perilously close to the possibly menstruating women upstairs). I was one step behind the teacher and one step was enough: there lay the *shammes* a-smouldering, his long heavy black gown still sparking after he'd doused himself with methylated spirit and lit the match. The purple spirit (used for *yohrzeit* or death-anniversary lamps) had a stronger smell than the burning beadle. He survived, only to try again and again.

Thus my first confrontation with suicide, a subject that absorbed me for much of my later life.

* * *

'Tell me what you eat and I will tell you what you are,' said epicure Jean Brillat-Savarin. He knew nothing about the *shtetl* food cooked by my grandmother or its effects on my psyche and circulatory system. Our particular *Litvak* ingestion and indigestion (rather than *cuisine*) essentially comprised boiling or braising, using lots of rendered chicken fat (*shmaltz*) to cook with—for taste and afterglow. An unintended but common side effect was cardiac disease. Braised food was a notch more sophisticated than boiling but not yet as exotic as roasting. *Goyim* roasted.

Jews are enjoined to eat kosher food. This is not only a selection of foods according to strict dietary laws but also the manner of animal slaughter. Making meat kosher after humane killing meant rough-salting it to draw out all blood. Perhaps twice a year a piece of steak appeared. Usually a cheap cut, served modern-style, it had the crap and everything else, like flavour, beaten out of it with the back of a soft-drink bottle—Berea *schnitzel*, bloodless and totally distant from its battered relative in Wiener. No pig products, of course, no fish without scales, no scavengers, a life without mussels. Beef and lamb hindquarters were barred (dirty places), hence no rump or true fillet. But our God allows oxtail. The first-born generation, like Bess, always hankering (certainly hungering) for modernity, served 'macon', mock bacon—smoky and curly slivers of mutton, a little fatty and vaguely like the real thing. The pinnacle of style and ritual defiance was mock crayfish cocktail, delicate white fish flakes sitting in false pretences in a posh pink sauce.

So, Monsieur Brillat-Savarin, what I am is perhaps what I didn't, wouldn't or couldn't eat. The grandmother presiding over my childhood insisted I had to be the brightest, best-mannered and best-fattened of her grandchildren. Much of her fare couldn't be swallowed or held down for very long. The variations of lumpy porridge were coercively consumed and all returned soon after. Her ultimate stratagem was to sieve out the gluggy lumps, liquefy the residue and make me drink it from a pint glass with a straw. It ended up where these things always ended up—the kitchen or laundry sink, the alternative outdoor toilet or the drain underneath the outdoor tap. Ever vigilant, she'd lift the drain grid and like an experienced caver would shine a flashlight into the murky water in search of tell-tale dairy products. Each failure to retain 'nourishment' brought the inevitable whacking across the face, neck and head with a *kochelefel*, a wooden cooking spoon. I'd show my mother the bruises; like all mothers in movie scripts and child welfare interviews, in denial she'd say I must have fallen, hurt myself at soccer or gotten into a fight that was my fault. Each ingestion of *gersht* (barley) or *farfl* (small pasta pellets) in soup, or of milk soup with lentils floating like magnetic mines, or tea with milk boiled so a skin (the *plefke*) formed, had the same short life and the same wooden response. Of all the sights and textures of my life, *plefke* remains the ultimate evil.

Holidays were my worst daymare. They were taken in Warmbaths, a mineral water, sulphurous mudbath and spa resort north of Pretoria, described in some advertisements as South Africa's 'hidden secret'. Some secret. I went with *Bobbe* for a *bod*, a bath, every morning, another with *Zeide* in the afternoon. Twice a day I was doused, soused, wrinkled, turned pink and then swaddled with bath sheets large enough to dry a soccer team (and the reserves). Seated on wooden benches in the bath cubicles I would be fed apples, oranges and pieces of *snoek*, a tasty smoked fish. I have searing recollections of ageing bodies, pendulous breasts, triple stomachs and a gigantic two-chambered protuberance, aka a scrotum, unlike anything I'd seen in the family copy of *Gray's Anatomy*.

What a contrast my world was to that created by Milt Gross, a Bronx cartoonist and humourist. In 1927 he published *Nize Baby*, a compendium of Yiddish-inflected English dialogue (Yinglish) stories about a Lower East Side tenement where a reluctant boy would be seduced into eating *his* inedible menu. 'Nize baby, itt up all the Chucklit Pudding, so momma'll gonna tell you a Ferry Tail from Jack witt de Bean-stuck.' And later, if baby will only ingest the proon-jooze, farinna, rize witt milk or cheeken zoup, she'll tell him a nice 'sturry' from 'Weeliam Tell, soch a moxman witt bow' or the Pite Piper from Hemilton or Rad Ridink Hoot or Romplesealskin. I got the bolley zoop, rize witt milk, tea witt *plefke*, all without a hint of a ferry tail.

Public shaming was another agony. Our free-standing claw-legged bathtub had a small, dark space between the wall and the toilet, large enough to deposit the eternally grey vegetables, stringy stew, boiled fish, stale bread, dry chicken breast and the even drier *klops* (meat loaf). After several years she discovered the fossilised midden. She also caught me rifling the Jewish National Fund blue box, a charity tin. On tram rides to the city she informed all within (and without) earshot that her travelling companion not only denied food to the starving children of Europe but stole the funds that could have fed them. Bullying and beating were bad enough but this kind of demeaning was something else.

Stern and taciturn as he was, I had a softish spot for *Zeide*. When *Bobbe* locked me in a bedroom for a foodless day or two for not eating 'properly', he would call me to the laneway window and through the metal burglar-proofing (standard fittings on all White households) he'd pass me an apple, his pocket-knife, buttered bread and, God help him, pieces of unkosher *biltong* wrapped in brown ink newspaper. He didn't say a word.

It took another forty years for an attentive psychologist to tell me I was a battered child—a shock because while I knew that other kids were battered, that sort of thing simply never happened in our crowd.

A brighter side. Three of my mother's brothers travelled to Pretoria and other Transvaal country towns on their respective business visits. I was allowed day trips with each of them and occasionally an overnighter. With Black drivers, an uncle and me on the front bench seats of their panel vans, the vehicle was loaded up after a quick stop at Segal's Butchery and the Crystal Deli for *kosher* polony (*vursht*), pickled cucumbers, sliced smoked beef, sliced stuffed turkey, smoked salmon, *snoek*, hard-boiled eggs, and rye bread with caraway seeds. The drivers weren't offered any and I would ask why not? '*They* prefer their own food.' This travelling picnic was both my revenge menu and a chance to meet a wider world. Sipping tea in little cups in dark, carpeted dens in incensed Indian business houses opened both eyes and sesame. Tamil Indians had been imported as sugar-cane labourers in the 1860s and promised repatriation—which never happened. Facing immense discrimination as non-natives and non-citizens, the small non-servant group struggled in small businesses in the Transvaal and Natal provinces; all Indians were disbarred from the Orange Free State. To meet Indians in a non-servile environment was rare and I came to admire their ability to sustain a reasonably normal life in what was an otherwise seriously abnormal society. I also learned that White South Africans could be civil to 'people of colour' when a serious business deal was to hand.

Uncle Louis was a special mentor. He said that if I behaved (ate nicely), he would take me to his private zoo to see the hephimoflunts, the hippono-sauruses and the lion's feathers. On drives with him I would look out the back window and ask what happened to the roads at night. The night-time *shvartzes* (the Black ones) rolled them up, he said, and stored them in a big shed, then the early-morning *shvartzes* rolled them out each dawn. Irritating and outrageous in so many ways, he was always fun. Apart from these commercial trips to different horizons, there was a shortage of fun in my life.

This was the age of the whispered words: 'big C' and other taboo words like divorce, affair and miscarriage, of which my mother had four before sister Pam was born. Given the *Litvak* diet it was remarkable that any of them were healthy. *Bobbe* and *Zeide* both died of heart attacks, she at 64, he at 74; four Isaacson uncles had eight between them; Bessie had one, possibly two; one uncle suffered from both emphysema and vascular problems; Babs is 93 as I write. I've managed one heart attack as well as emphysema and adult diabetes. Two uncles and Maurice had *thromboangiitis obliterans* or Buerger's Disease, clotting in the legs and groin, requiring surgery. *Zeide*'s phlebitis was attended, variously, by the cupping guy, the leeches man, and his wife. His legs were wrapped in bandages made from torn sheets (left over from Warmbaths) dipped in a mixture of glycerin and ammonium bituminosulfonate, producing either *ichthyol* or *icthammol*, a reddish brown goo that reeks of ammonia, fresh bitumen, old vinegar, fetor and other unearthly vapours. It may have done some good for psoriasis and other skin malfunctions but I don't believe it got anywhere near his inflamed vascular system. Coming home from school often meant knowing several blocks away that *Zeide* was in pain and the house rendered uninhabitable.

* * *

Zeide and I worked together making Passover wine each year. In an unused back bathroom he would have me trample the baskets of grapes in the tub (I was a requisite Jewish Orthodox male, albeit under thirteen) and then help him stir the mix in the oak barrel with a newly bought broom handle. This overly sweet, cloying liquid was served as a three-week-old vintage, considered suitable for benedictions (it was red enough). While God, through Moses, had imposed ten plagues on the Egyptians, this brew could have been the eleventh.

My *Bobbe*, as one would expect, was replete with *bobbe-mysehs* (old wives' tales, nonsenses). For any medical complaint below the navel, the regimen was either liquid paraffin or castor oil; between the navel and the neck region, a wintergreen embrocation or a gooey, green herb balm called Zambuk; for earache, hot liquid paraffin poured into the orifice, a poison akin to the one used on Hamlet's daddy; for sore eyes, an eyebath of boracic powder; for anything laryngeal or bronchial, an egg-flip (*gelchl*), a hot egg-shake of boiled milk, *plefke* on top, butter, honey and brandy. *Bobbe-mysehs* weren't a Jewish preserve. In 1945, at the height of one of many poliomyelitis epidemics, the Health Department decreed that every single schoolchild wear a lanyard attached to which was a red metal locket with a small circle cut out of it, the inside (prophylactic?) substance just visible: camphor wax! We can be thankful that science progresses and that we can learn.

On Friday evenings, at the house we had moved to in Houghton in 1945, the Sabbath table groaned with food and an attempt at delicacy by having finger bowls complete with floating flower or rose petal. This was the site for Uncle Louis' heart attack number three. In one of the more memorable evenings he keeled over at the table. I ran for our GP who lived about 50 metres down the road. The doctor put down his bag, glanced at the patient laid low, called an ambulance and inspected the repast: the first course—still on the trolley in case someone felt peckish—of chopped liver, chopped herring, pickled herring, fried sole, fried *gefilte* fish, boiled *gefilte*, flanked by the essential condiments of pickled cucumbers, red horseradish, two mustards, two vinegars, tomato salad, beetroot salad; two loaves of *challeh*, that half-brioche-half-cake Sabbath bread South Africans called *kitke*; followed by two huge white platters, three or four storeys high, one for flank, brisket, soup meat and boiled meat dumplings quivering, with huge, brimming marrowbones posted like sentinels; layers of chicken giblets, gizzards, necks, wings, feet (*fieslech*), carcasses aloft and unborn chicken eggs for decoration (and ingestion) in the other; two pyrex dishes of *petsha* (brawn), one with garlic, one without, one with sliced hard-boiled eggs inserted under the top layer of a grey-brown gelatinous mess, the other without (to distinguish the garlic one). The platters accompanied the soup and its inserts, to be followed by the main course, usually a roll of beef and vegies, roast chicken for those who didn't want meat, the desserts still to come.

'Bess', said the learned doctor, 'you really must watch what you people eat'. Bess levitated one or two metres and in her voice of unalloyed, unparalleled scorn, replied: 'Max, I'll have you know that we *only* eat plain food in this household.' Food indeed to die from, and most of them did.

A pair of enigmas. The first arose from *Bobbe*'s younger sister and her husband. They had a grocery and fish store in Mayfair with its cool wall sign, 'Fresh from the C2U'. Their 'delivery boy', Cyril, would bring provisions fortnightly. Eagerly greeted by *Bobbe*, he was invited to sit at the kitchen table and drink tea with her in a porcelain cup brought all the way from Russia. They would talk for an hour or so, the other servants fuming at having to serve a fellow African, and me straining to grasp the dialogue. Cyril spoke fluent Yiddish and mine was mediocre. Did that make him 'human'? In which case, the world should learn what may now well be a languishing language.

The other puzzle was the 'Egg Man'—a bogeyman afflicting adults and children alike. He had no name that anyone knew of, was the spitting image for the late Yasser Arafat yet Jewish in every caricaturish way: big goitred and hooded eyes, stubble beard, as hunched as the guy from Notre Dame, braces, pants at half-mast, sleeves rolled and a big basket on each arm. He'd ring the doorbell, stand and simply say, '*Broch eyer*'. Not a word else. Broken, cracked eggs is what he offered for sale. He never named a price or suggested a quantity, just stared with those ghastly eyes until you handed over any amount just to be rid of him for another month. My grandmother feared him although she did sometimes talk to him, and my egg-merchant grandfather would never supply him with any of *his* broken eggs. Nobody bought Egg

Man's wares and so fresh stock was never a problem. He was said to have owned slabs of Berea and Hillbrow real estate. Problem: unlike Cyril, he didn't present as human but his language was also Yiddish.

Instinctively I must have been a survivalist. At every chance, some I manoeuvred, I would escape to relatives for weekends. At one uncle's home, I learned about beautiful flowers with euphonious names like columbines, ranunculus and sweet Williams, and how lovely canaries were reared. At the home of Uncle Abe, my Dad's eldest brother, I found a much more liberal environ. He would take us to the city to buy very unkosher Perks' curry pies and his wife Helen demonstrated the finest art of roasting crispy-skin chicken.

Their daughter, cousin Brenda, about three years my senior, was already in school: she taught me to read and write before I entered Grade One, giving me a head and shoulders start. She was dead at 52 of Alzheimer's, widow of a suicide, a son dead at 21 of muscular dystrophy, and two remaining children later dead by their own hands.

Mine was to be a better start and finish.

Chapter 3

DAVENTRY CALLING

Films and books tell us much about children in war-time, about bombing, shelters, rations, absent enlisted fathers and munitions-worker mothers, evacuations, even to foreign lands. War in a safe land has little sense of imminent harm but it still has a fair-to-middling impact on a young psyche.

In the context of a global conflict, the one that eminent historians have defined as 'the war against the Jews', my junior years were beset by my own wars—against *Bobbe*, mother, family, empty ritual, solitariness, school bullies, street thugs, boxing opponents, Nazi hat-makers, and something I came to know as social injustice.

The war year of 1939 began with my attending Yeoville Boys' School, still five years old. Day one I asked my mother why she wasn't dressed and ready to take me to enrol. She gave me a sixpence, told me to board the Number 1B Yeoville tram and ask the conductor to put me off at the school where I'd hand in the paperwork. 'How do I get home?' I wailed. 'Same 1B tram' she replied. 'Get off at the Berea *Shul* tram-stop… you know how to get home from there.' If this was self-reliance, then, as Socrates would have said, I had an instinctive notion of what it was.

At seven, I begged to be taken to Muizenberg, the famous Indian Ocean beach resort near Cape Town, a place where my friends spent holidays. Bess had to help Maurice in the shop but she solved the problem. At Johannesburg Station she paid the train conductor £5 to look after me. Deposited in a second-class compartment with five adults, he watched over me during the 956-mile (1,538 km) two-day-one-night journey. Met by relatives, driven to

Muizenberg, I was installed in my own hotel room. Uncle Louis's wife was also in residence and instructed to supervise me for a month. This lazy lady from Leeds left me alone while I battled loneliness and some disdain from the other children in residence who saw me as an orphan. The return journey was by car with another uncle. We stopped overnight at a hotel in Colesberg in the Karoo desert where, acting the grown-up, I ordered *hors d'oeuvres*, including something white I'd never seen before. I liked it but learned that eating forbidden crayfish, especially mid-desert, equalled a week in hospital with ptomaine poisoning. This first fight for liberation of various kinds ended in a painful draw.

The war years confronted me with vivid deaths. First, my *Zeide* Tatz, a short, barrel-chested, handlebar-moustached man who would carry me under his arm around his dairy, often taking me down a ladder into a cavernous vat of cream cheese and buttermilk, foul, floating, yellowy icebergy things. I recall this same man later, then thin, frail, white-haired, sitting on the verandah of his large home in Parktown with a sweeping circular driveway and a full-size billiard table. The White housekeeper Marie attended him as he died, wisp-like and slowly, of lung cancer.

Next, the expiration of my *Bobbe*'s brother, great-uncle Dotke Levine. Despite his dignified, poetic manner, his pince-nez glasses and goatee, Uncle Dotke sold grain, mainly corn for chicken feed—bought on 90-day credit and sold on 30-days credit. My *Zeide* Isaacson sold eggs by the gross (twelve dozen), packed into wooden crates. The layered eggs were separated by sheets of thin, light-grey, wartime-quality cardboard. *Zeide* taught Dotke to fold the cardboard concertina-style to use as ledgers. Dotke licked his indelible pencil and used the resulting mauve to enter the precious numbers. One day, aged about seven or eight, I was given the news that Uncle Dotke was dead. 'Dead! How?' I asked. 'He stopped breathing'. This information-rich answer from Uncle Louis was my first face-to-face lesson in life extinguishment. Years later, Dotke's nephew, my Uncle Harry, explained: as executor of the will he had found a note. Now, either great-uncle D wasn't all that literate or he was bad at arithmetic or, most likely, his 'ledger' pages became confused in their unfolding. He thought he was bankrupt—too much in the 90-days account, too little in the 30-days column. Whereupon he headed for the barn where he suspended himself by his braces from a sturdy beam. Comfortably solvent, he nonetheless contrived to stop breathing. He was the first of at least ten suicides in my close family, a grim raw number, and an absurd rate in two smallish clans.

The third indelible death was my *Bobbe* in November 1944. A Friday afternoon, a dozen cars outside, family wailing, explanations about both heart and breathing having stopped. I tiptoed to the verandah from where I could look into her bedroom bay window. I wasn't curious so much as wanting to reassure myself that this woman I so dreaded was indeed *dead* (in English), *tayt* (in Yiddish). I checked, too, that the *vacher*, the paid body watcher (needed until she was safely buried on the Sunday) still had a job to do.

What would she be remembered for? To her seven children she was a godly and saintly figure, feared yet adored, a sage, a woman of philosophy, a fine *balleboste* or family manager. All she ever taught me was dread, grief and adversity—an unusual (and *dafke*) role reversal: Jewish grandmothers are supposed, foremostly, to dote on their grandchildren.

***

For me, the war was about blackout curtains, food shortages, rationing, but also about a locked cupboard of luxury items like Libby's giant white asparagus, tins of Crosse & Blackwell pink salmon, herrings in tomato sauce, Portuguese sardines in oil and tins of condensed milk. These tins would be the finest accompaniment as my friends and I walked to the large botanic garden called The Wilds. We'd climb the *koppies* (hillocks) and sit smoking and sipping cans of Nestlés condensed milk.

Petrol was available by scarce coupons, rice wasn't to be seen and bread was grey. To make the desired white flour, Maurice made a sieve in which I hand-stirred the bran-filled flour until enough white stuff came through. The leftover brown stuff was for my breakfast. *Bobbe* would add a dozen eggs to the 'bread' mix, ensuring that we ate cake and butter every day. She would implore God to strike her down if she ever put eggs in the 'bread'. I waited for *Avinu* to act, but He took His time. The whites left over from the bread eggs were placed in a huge jar and used for white egg omelettes, ten centimetres thick, thirty across, frisbee or discus-shaped, ready to be flung (when possible) over the high wall between us and the antagonistic household next door. Their baleful black hound Trigger died, said the vet, of what sounded to me like chronic eggtoplasm.

Shortages produced intrigues. Uncle Louis had rice, flour, silk stockings, cosmetics, golf balls and a thousand other 'goodies' stashed away. Until the

Uncle Louis Isaacson.

outbreak of war he had been in partnership with a group of Japanese engineers making South Africa's only source of interlock cloth, used mainly for underwear. His skills included blackmailing his brother Harry to be 'nice' to him—Harry was desperate for some saleable goods in his grocery shop; threatening Bess that if she wasn't 'nice' to him she'd get no stockings, rouge or lipstick. After some years of nagging, Louis relented and gave Maurice and Uncle Ian (always known as Itz) a dozen Wilson golf balls, beautifully wrapped in crinkly red cellophane. I was with Itz at Killarney golf course when members crowded round him, offering up to £10 a ball, well over $200 in today's money. I watched him hit a great drive down the first and as we approached the place where the ball should have been, we found a neat pile of sawdusty powder and slivers of thin rubber windings. Golf balls perish in fairly quick time and these had been hoarded for more than a decade. Another notch in the belt of brotherly love.

My bedroom was a tiny space in a passageway. After the servants were 'off' after 7 p.m. I became the chore boy. One night-time duty was to fill glasses with water and powdered Steradent, a cleaning and anti-discolouration product ready to receive family dentures. Maurice had been told that the cure for his headaches was removal of all his teeth. His new set clicked in at age 29. My grandparents arrived toothless in Africa and the creatures that grinned at me from the glasses every night seemed to have lives of their own; when tea was taken, the half-slide began—the bottom rack slid forward, a cube of sugar or a teaspoon of satsuma plum jam was placed on the inner surface, and the dentures slid back again, the drink siphoned through the sweetener. The full version after a meal was more elaborate: the pink and white horror was tongued forward enough to allow a finger in to scrape out all that adhered, then the *tseiner* clicked back in. I look after my teeth very carefully.

Chores included filling cigarette cases for the five heavy smokers in the house (50 plus per day each), fetching deadly analgesics for the ubiquitous and chronic headaches, and playing the shellac 78 records that needed a new or re-sharpened needle for each side. Our music miscellany included Bing Crosby, the Andrews Sisters, the Mills Brothers, Glenn Miller, Nelson Eddy and Jeanette Macdonald (a cloying duo), and the serious operatic arias by Amelita Galli-Curci, Enrico Caruso, Benjamino Gigli, Jussi Björling and Zinka Milanov—but not what my family called the 'scratchy music' of violins, cellos, piano concerti or symphonies.

A large double glass-door bookcase in the hallway exposed me to everything from *Gray's Anatomy* to a miniature Yiddish–English dictionary. Between, a bound set of Leslie Charteris' Saint books, *Pears' Cyclopaedia*, a maroon-covered *Consolidated Encyclopaedia* in ten volumes with lots of annual updates; Herman Rubin's 1933 volume with the dare-I-look title *Eugenics and Sex Harmony*; a dozen cigarette-card albums on everything from war planes to South African flora and fauna.

Not readers of good non-fiction, the family went through hundreds of thrillers by Agatha Christie, John Dickson Carr, Ngaio Marsh and Ellery Queen. No zest for the worlds of private eyes, the more literary worlds of Dashiell Hammett and Raymond Chandler. Their real world was conveyed by such magazines as *Look*, *Life*, *Cosmopolitan*, *Esquire*, *The Illustrated London News* and a local weekly, *Outspan*. With only one big radiogram in the house, those books become my friends. I read the whole bookcase, repeatedly, indiscriminately, almost eating *Pears'*. The Rubin title was my first encounter with the word eugenics, and it wasn't to be my last. Later years would be consumed with 'scientific racism', race purity and regimes of *Über* and *Untermenschen*.

My family wasn't learned. Of the fourteen Isaacson and Tatz siblings, one was an almost-doctor, two were doctors, one a pharmacist and one an elocution teacher; of their 26 progeny, my first cousins, six became teachers of various kinds. Bess' brother Harry, the eldest, studied medicine for just on five years, then quit before his finals. He married and became a grocer, betraying the parents' sacrifices to send only the eldest son to university. Uncle Louis (somehow) became a pharmacist and later (somehow) an industrialist.

My father's half-brother, Koppel, trained in England as a doctor, became a dermatologist, later in life Johannesburg's most renowned pimple doctor. In Edinburgh he took twelve years to do the six-year course because his mother had said she'd support him as long as he was a student, so student he remained, amid much leisure and pleasure. He returned to South Africa in his British army captain's uniform before war's end, presenting me with my first watch (with gorgeous Roman numerals) and taking me to a matinee to see Disney's *Pinocchio*. I adored him.

Uncle Koppel Tatz.

At Yeoville Boys' we played war games: Allies and Axis were just another version of cowboys and Indians. We drooled over the names of planes, always uttered in full to savour the flavour: the British-made de Havilland Mosquitos and Vampires, Bristol Blenheim bombers, Handley-Page Halifaxes, Supermarine Spitfires; the American P-51 Mustangs, Grumman Wildcats and Avengers; the Nazi Messerschmitts, the Junkers Ju 87 Stuka dive-bombers, the Dorniers and Heinkels; the Japanese Zeros; the Russian Yakovlev Yak-9s.

My family were not distinguished soldiers. Maurice, deemed unfit for army service, was a member of a local civilian defence unit. One uncle served in Abyssinia (Ethiopia) and Kenya; another, a lieutenant in the Red Cross in peacetime, joined the Medical Corps, was captured in Italy and was in a POW camp there when catastrophic telegraphic news came that he had been hospitalised! An arm broken playing soccer. Bess spent the war commandeering cigarettes from business houses and taking them weekly to the Cottesloe military hospital. She would also take the socks and scarves knitted on giant wooden needles by *Bobb*e. On many a visit with her, I would talk to the convalescents in their light-blue denim outfits, men ever ready to talk about their experiences. I learned something about war from them, but nothing like what was to come.

* * *

Each evening at six o'clock we'd hear 'Daventry Calling', the Empire Service from a BBC radio station in Northamptonshire. On Saturday afternoons we went to the 'bioscope' (cinema) to see musicals and B-grade war propaganda movies. The afternoon's programs included a Batman serial, a Disney or Heckle and Jeckle cartoon, an occasional Wurlitzer and sing-along session, also one or two newsreels: The March of Time, British Pathé News and Gaumont British News. These newsreels helped pry open what was, for us, a relatively safe and certainly a quasi-cloistered world. Early in 1945 a loud but hidden voice hushed the cinema audience, urging children under twelve to leave the cinema for ten minutes or to place hands over their eyes. We stayed and peeked through fingers—at the first Bergen–Belsen footage. This was incomprehensible: how could people be so skeletal? Were they human? Were they us?

I understand now how the strength of early influences, one or two episodes, events or sights become such a defining fixative in one's mind and personality. As an adult, that first footage remains even fresher, more affecting than the many subsequent viewings of the same scenes.

Bobbe and I connected emotionally in two contexts (apart from the matter of the wooden spoon). As Daventry called, she would ask me to show her where the Nazis were. '*Vay iz mir*' she'd cry out: 'they're gone', as I opened the maps in my precious *Pears' Cyclopaedia*. How does a nine-year-old understand one's family as *gone*? Much later I recognised her astonishing prescience: if Holocaust scholars only began deciphering mass death in Europe well after it had occurred in 1942 and 1943, how could she have known about *gone* as gone was happening? My morbid obsession with genocide had begun.

Primary school was filled with St George Orphanage boys, most of them not really orphans but children whose fathers were in the army and mothers in munitions factories. Hungry bullies, they used a variety of standover tactics. I learned that there were other people besides 'us'—people with broken or dislocated families who were White, poor, angry and hungry. At least 500,000 Afrikaners (mainly) in a population of just on four million Whites lived on or below the breadline, yet even they tended to have one servant. While these Whites lived below the poverty line, most Blacks lived below the subsistence line, a very South African (and all too real) distinction. The Carnegie Committee on the 'Poor White Question' reported in 1932 and it was Dr DF Malan's Nationalist Party platform to eliminate 'poor Whiteism' that helped him win the 1948 election. He did that very quickly by reserving jobs held by Blacks for Whites only.

Any form of difference was noticed by schoolchildren too. I quickly learned not to wear my school blazer, cap and tie because most boys didn't have any uniform items. I was a puny youngster and developed my survival instincts early by paying for protection. The racket consisted of supplying rye bread sandwiches, with *shmaltz* and kosher polony laced with piccalilli, to hungry kids. I would tell *Bobbe* that I needed double sandwiches every day; it was the only time she beamed at me and the second instance of our connecting. When the sandwiches lost their lustre the new demand—mostly from Morris Belnick, my once chief tormentor and (in my eyes) the image of Charles Laughton in the Hunchback movie but now my senior bodyguard—was for condoms. I had no idea of their significance but was forced to acquire some.

The source was Uncle Hymie. He was married to one of my Dad's sisters and they lived near us in Berea. His son, my cousin Mervyn, was my mate and mentor, older and ahead of his age and time with cigarettes, booze, girls, street smarts. He was at the smaller end of delinquency and taught me to smoke, shoplift (comics and tins of sardines mainly), steal hubcaps, tell dirty jokes, stop worrying about early morning erections and the words missing from my dictionary. He also introduced me to Uncle Hymie's storeroom, brimming with the dozens of products he sold as a commercial traveller. One corner held cartons of condoms, gross boxes (twelve dozen = 144 tins times three prophylactics in each = 432 frenchies in all) called 'Goldstein's Five Star Specials'. We swiped boxfuls. Mervyn knew what to do with them. I had a different use: I would go to a friend's flat overlooking Nugget Street Hill, the steepest street in Africa, and watch cars, all manuals and without synchromesh gears, battling to get to the top in first gear, often stalling. We would release the water-filled condoms onto their bonnets—our orgasmic experience.

Mervyn tried very hard to teach me the value of money. I was a poor pupil. I once stole a £5 note from Bess's purse, took myself to the city and bought a medical corps badge for my scout belt. Badges on belts was big time. This one cost two shillings and sixpence (25 cents) and I was terrified by the sight and feel of the goodly sum of £4.17.6 ($9.75) change bulging in my pocket. Between the tram stop and home I dribbled the money under bushes, leaves, and cracks in brickwork fences. I told Mervyn, who spent about ten days tracking the trove. He never forgave me, and I never learned what people call 'the value of money'.

The bottom end of Honey Street was a laneway that housed the fire brigade, a place of danger and caution because it was the lair of the toughest kids in town. Word was that all the firemen's children were illegitimate. When I was told this meant they had no mothers, it was beyond my understanding. If so, how could they *be*? Everyone knew that bees pollinated mothers who swelled up and bore children. The leader, Herbie Baker, was everyone's and my ultimate bogeyman, complete with facial knife scar at twelve. He once hung me from my braces in a jacaranda tree at the Bedford football ground opposite our school. My sobs were heard by an African delivery man who needed to stand on another man's shoulders to cut me down. This, and Uncle Dotke's manner of death, ensured I never wore braces again. Herbie did teach me to ride a bike, how to read a street, to sense and smell trouble and avoid it. Several years later when I saw him ravaged and savaged by his life, he told me he was proud of me, one of 'his boys' making good.

Yeoville Baths in Raleigh Street was the place to swim. Tough guys abounded, mainly the Jewish water polo players. One or two went on to serious crime and names like Effie Levy made one quake. (Morris Belnick was always there for me, in case.) Mervyn, stick-like and hollow-chested, had had enough of the school and neighbourhood bovver boys and decided to take up boxing. We both joined Joe Rosella's Gym downtown, a dingy, sweaty, jock-strappy place suffused with wintergreen, and inside it a ring, punch bags, skipping ropes, the occasional exercise mat and a pissoir to match the one at Berea *Shul*. Tuition was simple: day one Joe laced huge 16-ounce (0.45 kg) gloves on me and pitched me into the ring with the local champion. Another lesson: the deep end of everything is the bloodier end.

Over the years I fought three bouts in the Southern Transvaal junior championships, all against Cyril Vincent in the quarter-finals. In the first I pushed him, his head hit the unpadded ring pole from which his concussion ensued. In the second I ducked and his flying elbow caught me smack on the temple, from which my concussion ensued. In the last I tripped him, his head hit the rim of the galvanised-iron spit bucket the ref had forgotten to remove, and you know what ensued.

We both quit the fight game but I was left with a love–hate relationship with what the brilliant American writer AJ Liebling called *The Sweet Science*. I bought and read every monthly *Ring Magazine*, the *Esquire Annual Book of Boxing* and every poorly written book by the *Ring* editor, Nat Fleischer. I learned about the rise of the Black boxers, including Jack Johnson, West Indian Peter Jackson, Sam Langford, Hurricane Henry Armstrong, Joe Louis, Archie Moore and the legendary Sugar Ray Robinson, a man who once sent me a posed picture of himself signed 'To Colin, Yours in sport'. This was also the golden era of Jewish fighters, of brothers Max and Buddy Baer (only vaguely Jewish but who wore a *Magen David* (Star of David) on their trunks), 'Slapsie' Maxie Rosenbloom, Barney Ross, the incomparable Benny Leonard and Louis 'Kid' Kaplan. My favourite was not Jewish, Puerto Rico's first world champion, bantamweight Sixto Escobar. I loved the euphony of his name and the fact that he had an extra digit on one or both of his feet.

The mostly pleasant pugilism at least offset the excruciating elocution lessons my mother insisted on. It may have been because I had taken to speaking like the comics I read. Hiding these lessons from soccer and street mates was a strategic triumph as talking posh, or properly, was almost top of the stigma charts. My instructor understood my reluctance as she taught me that Betty bought a bit of butter but found the butter bitter so she bought a bit of better butter to make the bitter butter better. She also taught me to read Rudyard Kipling, Charles Dickens and Stefan Zweig, and enough to get a senior certificate from the Trinity College of Music in London. The final exam was administered by a visiting, goateed English gentleman resident in India. 'Do you enjoy doing this stuff?' he asked. I told him I did not (as eloquently as I could with my new vowels). 'Well then, let's just get this over with and you can then go fight or play soccer.' An official letter—with A grades for elocution and speech therapy—arrived soon after.

Speaking in confidence in public, even a very small public, was put to an early test. In his 1987 *Radio Days* movie, Woody Allen presents a lovely scene where his aunt Bea, edgy about her evening date, is ready hours earlier but gets Woody to tell the sweating suitor—white suit, two-tone shoes, matching tie and kerchief, Panama hat—that she's not quite ready. A year older than Allen, I got there before him, acting as a receptionist, telling the beau to take a seat on a cane chair in the front parlour (the 66 arena) because Aunt Babs wasn't quite ready. She'd been ready since three o'clock, having changed four times. We all have to learn sociability and this was my apprenticeship at eight or nine, discussing the state of the world for half-an-hour with alpha, beta and a few gamma males. I had a feeling they resented me.

The Yeoville school principal, Mr Krige, was a fine man, youngish enough to have enlisted but with two fingers missing from an accident and therefore ineligible. Most teachers, it seemed to me, had funny names: the music teacher was Drummond Bell, which we thought was priceless. One senior male was Mr Piccardy (born Piccarsky) which was also hilarious (no songwriter would have written a classic melody called 'Roses of Piccarsky'). We had two younger and good-looking women, Misses Niewenhuizen and Oosthuizen. Such was our sexual expertise, we believed that if a woman had reddish marks at the back of her knees and upper calves she had had sex the night before. We waited eagerly for each of the *-huizen* ladies to stand up, write on the blackboard, and ogle the telltale signs. School dictionaries were of no avail: no 'f' words, no 's' words and the only 'r' word we could find was rape—and that turned out to be some kind of seed which produced some kind of oil, or a vinegary substance left over from squeezed grapes. So why were people jailed for *that*?

I learned the three Rs well enough. I skipped a class and was a very young, small and insecure ten-year-old, turning eleven in final year of primary school (there were seven years in primary). These years were full of local tensions. A large percentage of the (then) 2.4 million White Afrikaner population were opposed to South Africa's entry into what they considered a purely European war. Much of their sentiment and sympathy blended well with fascist and National Socialist ideas on race. Afrikaner youth were given to attacking soldiers in uniform especially at military bases in country towns like Potchefstroom. Bombs exploded at big festive occasions like the Rand Easter Show in Johannesburg. On a few occasions we needed paid guards to escort us home from *shul* on Sabbath eve. Sabotage abounded and the death penalty was mandatory under emergency regulations for anyone carrying arms or explosives. Fascist and pro-Nazi organisations flourished: the Blackshirts, Greyshirts, *Ossewa Brandwag* (the Watchers of the Ox Wagon or OB for short) who were the ultimate bogeymen, the more intellectual New Order of politician Oswald Pirow, the Gentile Protection League and the South African Gentile National Socialist Movement.

What people called 'nice South Africa' wasn't so nice, certainly not for Jews, African Blacks, Indians and Cape Coloured people.

The European war ended in early 1945. A new deputy-principal, Major Phil Green, arrived. He'd not yet been demobbed, wore full uniform and ribbons, and we begged him to tell us about the war, the Allies versus the Axis, the Spitfires versus the Messerschmitts. But instead of *Boy's Own* heroics, he assailed us with his first-hand account of the bastardries that men perpetrate on men in the name of race. He had been in North Africa, Sicily, Germany and had seen a camp liberation. Now the Pathé newsreels, *Pears'* maps and Daventry broadcasts were making sense. It was, though, still incomprehensible.

Green changed my life. The embodiment of life learning rather than book learning, he took us through prisoner-of-war camps, death camps, refugee camps and through South African military camps where local Blacks were in uniforms but still servants. General Smuts, he explained, had told Winston Churchill that he couldn't 'arm the Natives' for fear they would one day turn on the White man. Here was another lesson: there is simply nothing better than an inspirational teacher in the flesh. My first lessons in injustice, inhumanity and the width and depth of moral divides came not from family or Judaism but from Phil Green.

Towards the end of 1945 I witnessed an accident outside the Yeoville school fence. A car driven by a White man turned right into a main street, ignoring the stop sign and collided with an African delivery man on his bicycle. I volunteered a statement to the attending police. Some weeks later a detective arrived at our new Houghton home. He wanted me to rewrite my statement, suggesting the Black cyclist was more at fault or at least as much at fault. The driver, he said, was a 'good man' with a wife and children. I refused; I may even have exaggerated the driver's actions. I never found out what happened, but this was a Rubicon moment—the knowing of what was so wrong in that system.

Between Green and that accident another defining moment was born: the treatment of Blacks at home, at a personal level. My life was starting to fractionate, to become nasty every time a servant was berated, demeaned or dehumanised. Never in my family or in friends' families did I hear the words 'please' and 'thank you' to a servant. My indignation arose *within*, perhaps instinctively, but certainly viscerally.

Solitude led to many conversations with myself and I knew, at ten, that my outlook was quite different from those of my family and most friends. I belonged but wasn't an insider who shared their perceptions. Our family, Bess especially, were much given to the notion that we were 'our kind of people', that is, not only in relation to the wider context of society but also among fellow immigrant Jews, our kinsfolk. The way we thought, ate, prayed, mourned, held rules dear, chose which charities to help, was *unser veg*, our special pathway, the one always better than anyone else's. A common enough foible. My problem was that I knew their world was so *shtetl*-ingrained that they knew nothing or very little about the ways others did things.

I had more than a glimmer of what death was, of what genocide might mean; I had a vague idea about suicide and more than an inkling of race hatred, vilification, humiliation. It was a sense of what I later understood as empathy and an experience of the physical and confrontational faces of fascism, Nazism and antisemitism. Learning about such things may well have been part of growing up, but my growing began at an inordinately young age.

Outwardly I may not have been that different, but I sure as hell felt different.

Chapter 4

PYGMALION

Whatever little innocence was left over from primary school soon dissipated in secondary school. I attended the unremarkable and mediocre government high school, King Edward VII (KES). It had all the puffed-up pretensions of the few posh private schools of the period. Mid-schooling, my *bar mitzvah* year was to be initiation into adulthood and its responsibilities, a graduation into the beliefs, practices and responsibilities of Judaism. KES was also an initiation into a number of South African 'values'.

Most boys who'd attended Yeoville Boys in primary graduated to KES. In 1946 there were four first forms; of the 35 in my 1D class, all but four or five were Yeovillite–Israelite. We were kept truly apart from other first formers until form IV with no explanation or justification. My schoolmates accepted this divide, but I couldn't and didn't.

The school ethos was gung-ho sport, team sport, macho masculinity. 'Swots' played chess, debated and played in the school band. I wasn't a swot, but in a world of team games, 'team spirit' and the usual British-derived crapitude about sport as moral education, my choice of sprinting and playing tennis was considered selfish.

In form I, the principal addressed the school assembly, asking Jewish boys to stay behind: 'All of you people try to avoid cadets or look to join the medical orderly team. Why is that?' How did he know who 'you people' were or how many such people were in the medical corps and how many were not in the regular military cadets program? Paranoid questions? Perhaps, but I recall a helpful definition of a paranoid as someone who is aware of all the facts.

PYGMALION

***

When people ask why Jews are smart, they start with the wrong premise. Jews are not any smarter than others: it's just that they have millennia of literacy behind them. Jewish youngsters are not alone in confronting the holy books but they face footnotes like no other pubescents.

In 1947, my *bar mitzvah* ceremony included reciting a portion from the Prophets in the Old Testament—Isaiah, Chapter 40. Eight lines of one verse were allocated sixteen lines of footnotes, one of which read:

> These words of the Prophet are 'like balm upon a wound, or like a soft breath upon a fevered brow' (Graetz). The Hebrew language and genius are seen in the Book of Isaiah at their perfection—this has naturally had its effect on the English translators of the Bible, whose Version nowhere perhaps rises to such beauty as in this Book (Matthew Arnold).

At a tender age I was introduced to such improbable sounding men like Heinrich Graetz, 1817–1891, Bible scholar and author of *Monatschrift für die Geschichte und Wissenschaft des Judentums* and to that astute but sometimes pompous litterateur, Matthew Arnold. How many cultures can match *that*?

The *bar mitzvah* celebration wasn't my best memory. On the Saturday night of the Shabbat morning performance I was allowed to take four friends to the cinema. On the Sunday night my parents had 300 guests in a huge marquee in our ample garden. I was allowed six. My mother was daring enough to think of engaging the Manhattan Brothers to play, then emerging as one of the best African jazz groups in the country. I was ecstatic at the prospect but Bess abandoned the idea because she thought it mightn't sit well with the guests. There was little to redeem the night.

Most of my presents were cheques, totalling £350 (sterling), a tidy sum in those days. Later, when I needed the money for university fees, my father told me he had needed it the more. I have since come to hear of several such appropriations of *bar mitzvah* money and so my once lone grievance is no longer lonely. A gold-topped Parker '51 fountain pen, a gorgeous brown leather travelling wallet and a copy of the Reverend Cobham Brewer's *Dictionary of Phrase and Fable* are the only surviving artefacts.

I didn't like living in Lower Houghton, the well-to-do suburb to which we had moved mid-1945. It was outside my Dad's means but Bess was keen and when Bess was keen… It was leafy, spacious, pretty, with big houses on large tracts, usually an acre, sometimes two. Luxury was very evident and in our street of only ten homes there were three clay tennis courts and three swimming pools. The KES old boys' club, Old Edwardians, was an eight-iron away and in the enormous grounds I aimed a lot of golf balls between the rugby posts, venting anger and frustration. A dark youth, perhaps a black one, there was much to vent.

My main friends were the Witkin brothers, Aaron, Isaac and Jacob (Jacky). We acted out our version of socialism by shooting out municipal street globes with an airgun, forcing potatoes up luxury car exhausts, pouring sugar into the petrol tanks of swanky cars, screwing out expensive brass house numbers and reversing them and driving golf balls from our manicured nature strip into busy Central Avenue down below. But I hankered for Berea, taking every opportunity to go back to the Honey Street home we had vacated. The Harry Isaacson family had left Brixton to take over the rental of that house.

***

My Holocaust mentor, Yehuda Bauer, is now (2015) translating his latest work, *The Impossible People*. The Hebrew word in his title is *mehutzaf*—from which the word *chutzpah* derives. It means, variously, impertinent, insolent, rude, cheeky, but which he translates as impossible. For me, Jews are the *dafke* people, the perverse ones whose behaviour is so often contrary to expectations. A *dafkenik* has dozens of choices but *dafke*, contrarily and perhaps with a tinge of spite, has to pick the one either not available or not remotely suitable.

I found the world of *Yiddishkeit*, the Jewish way of life, of looking at life and death, sometimes frightening but mostly warming, vibrant, funny. It was hardly the religious ritual that engaged me but the ethnic humour, the self-deprecation, the constant neuroses, the complaining or *kvetching* about everything from Hitler to herrings, the alternative and sometimes upside-down view of the world.

One Houghton activity did appeal in a funny way: every seventh Sunday night my father hosted the regular seven-man poker game. They gathered in the lounge and the wives played rummy in another room. Maurice would let me set out the coloured chips, stored in a magnificent leather and velvet-lined case. I was allowed to stay up till midnight to help serve the whiskies and the mid-game 'snacks'. One player, the very foreign-sounding Oscar Fruman, was a pre-war refugee in the (big) business of selling commercial and industrial scales. He told *Nize Baby* stories. One night, Harry Cohen (wholesale groceries) leaned across the table and started ribbing him. 'Oscar' he said, 'tell me how exactly did you make your money during the war?' 'By giving it hallocution lassons' was the instant phonetic reply. I loved it and so began a lifelong reading of books about invective and abuse and the gentle art of making enemies.

Courtesy of one of Dad's customers, I worked at the Crystal Deli in what was still heavily Jewish Doornfontein. It was near a Jewish aged home, and as I passed by the old people (men mainly) would call me over and give me ten shillings to buy a bottle of brandy. Though under-age, I could buy from a liquor store if I had an 'adult note'. Unkempt, unshaven, untoothed liars and cheats, these old men were wondrous storytellers. They adopted me as a mascot. The Crystal soon enough promoted me from bagels to *oogerkes*, pickled cucumbers. On my first day an old lady came in demanding a pound of them. I reached into the glass container mounted under the counter and pulled out four or five. *Dafke*, 'I vant dose vuns, not dese vuns,' she said, pointing to the 'vuns' at the very bottom of the tank. The brine suffused everything, and my resignation was swift. In the age of the disposable glove I might have had another career.

A Macquarie University friend visited the city of Cochin in Kerala, South India, once the home of a thriving Cochin or Malabar community of Black and White Jews, now almost bereft of such a presence. Bob Stern was shown around by the keeper of the early *shul*. 'So what's it like to be a Jew in Cochin?', he asked. '*Nu*, so what's it like to be a Jew anywhere?', was the answer. Younger generations don't have that sardonically fatalistic view of life, embodied in the phrase *es is shver zu zein a Yid*, it is hard (heavy) to be a Jew. Only the older generation use the word *Yid*, the antithesis of the modern generations who tend to cringe at that way of life (and history).

The sound of Yiddish, once described as the music of a lamenting harp, was present in my house, in my life, in many ways. I wanted to spend time with the older generation much more than to be with my parents and their friends who were in a transition zone.

* * *

Friday nights were baiting nights, occasions in which many (not all) the assembled family would take turns putting me on the rack: 'Why haven't you had a haircut, the haircut is too short, why did you fail arithmetic, tuck your shirt in, where are your table manners, I hear you missed *cheder* last week, why weren't you at *shul* last Saturday?' There were usually eight to ten interrogators. Maurice, as ever in my life, said nothing. Bess appeared to go along with it.

There was a strange attitude to children among this generation: progeny seemed more a duty than a joy; encumbrances that occasionally gave *naches*, proud pleasure, but who seemed nonetheless to be interrupting journeys to social mobility and voguishness. By thirteen I'd had enough. I can't remember my verb but I told them all, with clear diction and choice words, to bugger off and never, ever, to bully or berate me in that way again. I well recall my first elocuted declaration of independence. They took some fright and thereafter 'wary' is a good way to describe my family relationships.

In adolescence I actively hated them. In later life I have come to treasure aspects of family and recollect, even savour, some few moments of pleasure (and many more of pain). A smidgin of sentimentailty surfaces. Years later Bess would say she couldn't understand where all this aggressive individualism came from. She might have started her analysis with recollections of the 1B Yeoville tram as I neared six or the train to Cape Town at seven or her failure to defend me on the holy nights of my inquisition and stake-burning.

* * *

The fights were not just in our home. In 1946, Eric Boon, British lightweight champion, came to Johannesburg to battle Laurie Stevens, South Africa's small White Hope. Boon, who had the widest shoulders and smallest waist I have ever seen, came into Dad's shop where I often worked after school, on Saturday mornings and during most school holidays. I sighed, oohed and pestered him for autographs and boxing stories. After crushing Stevens in three rounds that year, he was training to fight Alf James (South African welterweight champion, once my instructor, and Jewish) in 1947. I would collect Boon's dry cleaning, buy flowers for his girlies and do anything he asked. One day the request came for French letters. This twelve-year-old had sage advice from friends that if you went into a pharmacist, said nothing, but flipped a coin on the counter, he (and only a he) would know what you wanted. In the Raleigh Street Chemist, Yeoville, I flipped the biggest coin the mint produced, a half-kilo half-crown silver alloy piece. I flipped and flipped. Eventually I cracked the glass counter and fled. Twenty years later I saw the pharmacist socially in Melbourne, his new domain as a big-time financier. Introduced, he said 'Don't I know you from somewhere?' I said we'd met.

Then, I remembered Uncle Hymie's storeroom.

After his fights, Boon, in a nice twist, took the lead in a Clifford Odets play, *Golden Boy*, about a talented violinist who turns to prize-fighting in the American Depression. His leading lady was a young redhead named Gay Gibson. Boon gave me tickets and cousin Mervyn and I went to adore him at a Saturday matinee at the old, wooden Standard Theatre. There were four other people in the audience.

Late in 1947, headlines screamed that Miss Gibson was dead—aboard the *Durban Castle* sailing to London, her body pushed through a cabin window, in a case forever known in criminal lore and literature as 'The Porthole Murder'. A steward, James Camb, was arrested at Southampton and tried, dramatically, in the absence of a body. During his vividly reported trial, evidence emerged that Camb's defence of consensual sex may have been well founded. She was known to be sexually very active said Camb's barrister, evidenced by the twelve tins of condoms (three in each, remember) in her suitcase, all with a strange name: 'Goldstein's Five-Star Specials'. Camb claimed she invited him, they indulged in things I'd never heard of and couldn't find in any dictionary, she died *en passant*, he panicked and pushed her, post-*passant*, out the porthole.

Fearing arrest as an accessory of some kind, I hid under the bed until the trial was over. Camb got death, commuted to life, was paroled in 1959 and then, after a series of sexual assaults on young girls, spent the rest of his life inside. Two morals: if you have to steal frenchies, make it a generic brand; second, keep away from British lightweights.

***

The cultural offset to this saga was in 1948 when Ivor Novello, the much-applauded actor and composer, notably of 'We'll gather lilacs in the spring again/ And walk together down an English lane', brought his musical *Perchance to Dream* to South Africa. He came into Dad's shop wanting bathers. I fitted him with bright yellow Jantzen elasticised briefs designed to come well below the navel. Mr Novello insisted they come up to his armpits, which meant they squeezed him rather tightly downstairs. 'Never mind' said the maestro, 'wrap 'em'. He did give me two tickets for *Perchance* at His Majesty's Theatre, a night to remember.

My salesmanship for Dad was, at times, selective. In those days almost all men wore hats. We sold many, especially to Black men. The popular brands were the Italian Borsalino, the American Biltmore and the British Battersby. Even at that young age I refused to sell anyone a Battersby: one scion of that family, James Laratt Battersby, was a Nazi and the leader of the League of Christian Reformers. He published *The Holy Book of Adolf Hitler* in 1952. I was already politically aware.

The lyrical and sentimental mood of Novello was sharply contrasted by the politics of the time. The 'Purified' Nationalist Party of Daniel François Malan, doctor of theology, came to power in 1948, essentially on a platform of greater segregation of the four 'races'. Whites (or Europeans, as they always styled themselves) were at the top, then came the remaining three categories, always called 'non-Whites'. They were the Cape Coloured people, usually known as Coloureds, originally descendants of mixed unions between male Dutch East India Company officials, local farmers, soldiers, settlers and local Hottentot and Bushman women. Next in social status were the Indians, originally indentured Tamil labourers. At the bottom of the totem pole the great majority, the Bantu-speaking, indigenous Africans, known variously as 'Kaffirs', Natives, Bantu, Blacks.

The incumbent United Party of General Jan Christian Smuts went to the election toying with a greater liberalisation of what had always been *apartheid* (apart-ness) laws, regulations and customs as far back as the 1770s, counter to the commonplace but misplaced doctrine that apartheid began with Malan (or ended with Mandela).

A 1939 speech encapsulated Malan's form of antisemitism: 'We have, moreover, the Jewish problem which hangs like a dark cloud over South Africa. Behind organised Jewry stands the organised Jewry of the world. They have so robbed the population of its heritage that the Afrikaner resides in the land of his fathers, but no longer possesses it'. Malan wasn't an aberration. In the mid-1930s, South Africa stopped all German migration of any ilk but Jews in particular. After the war General Smuts refused to take Holocaust survivors, telling a UN agency that 2,000 orphans would be better off in Palestine (as they probably were). Given this pre- and post-war physical absence of European Jews, one can say that the major impact of the Holocaust passed South Africa by. Malan had always cuddled and coddled the various Shirt movements and the *Ossewa Brandwag* in particular. On Malan's ascension, a few of my Afrikaans-language teachers said, 'Why don't you guys go back to Palestine,' and so on.

Gym was compulsory throughout high school years. Our Scottish gym master insisted that gym ball games be played as Jewish A versus Christian A, Jewish B *ad nauseam*. Some teachers addressed every Jewish schoolboy as Lazarus or Moses. Many Old Edwardians tell me they don't remember any of this, but many of my compadres exhibited much wilful amnesia about those years. It was true enough for me.

In form IV, Roy 'Mango' Corbett—the senior maths teacher later to become headmaster—would single me out as Lazarus and use a thick elastic ping on a bare thigh when I refused to answer unless called by my name. I reported him, in my aggrieved 14-year-old personage, to the Transvaal Education Department. Soon after I was called to a meeting with Corbett in the office of the headmaster St John B Nitch. The incident was explained away as a 'tribal'-but-friendly in-joke that needn't go any further. The behaviour did stop. Several decades later, when visiting South Africa, Corbett heard I was in town and asked if I—as one of only four or five old boys in 80-odd years to have become a full professor—would address a school assembly. By then I'd found the 'f' word in a proper dictionary and had it conveyed to him.

In forms IV and V, a group of us started running night classes in the assembly hall for African servants in the Upper Houghton neighbourhood. Attendance was massive, between 300 to 400 people. Africans always had (and have) a thirst for education, seeking something better than the demeaning regimen of domestic service. A handful of enlightened teachers—Frank Puxley, Teddy Gordon, Ray 'Rusty' Barker, Cecil Williams—encouraged and helped us until the government forbade the classes as 'disruptive of normal race relations'. (In contexts like this, one can say that four teachers can make a bad school a better one, even a goodish one; and in the case of Yeoville, one was enough.)

Early in 1950, the headmaster became ill and the deputy took charge. On opening day he ordered every boy to attend sports practices, cripples included. Sport alone, he declaimed, maketh the man. This kind of nonsense left me with a critical and mostly jaundiced view of sport in my later life. I was fifteen, turning sixteen midway through my final year. Some 50 of the 120 matriculation candidates failed that year, I among them. I failed well in Latin, physical science and maths, passing comfortably enough in English, Afrikaans and geography. Sport maketh very little.

I admit to a total lack of interest in that kind of learning. All I wanted was a job, probably in Dad's shop, to earn enough to take girls to the movies, to buy them the chocolates required as bribe or barter for a bit of a kiss or a feel and to buy the cigarettes that I could no longer steal with impunity from the family. My best friend Glynn Evans and I were together in Cape Town when the exam results came out. Sitting on the top of Table Mountain, his local cousin Ronnie Horwitz expressed disdain for my constricted vision. He was going to England, he said, to become famous in the theatre. Sir Ronald Harwood did, indeed, became famous on stage and screen. I never saw him in person again but much later helped him, by mail, with some Holocaust lessons for his play-turned-film, *Taking Sides*, on the interrogations of the famed conductor Wilhelm Furtwangler for his Nazi connections. I had never encountered such singular determination and goal setting in a 16-year-old.

My mother said I had to go back to school, until I was 35 if need be, to matriculate. Under school-leaving age, I wrote (she wouldn't) to King Edwards seeking readmission and a repeat year. Nitch said he'd consult his staff. He did and told me that they had rejected me by 33 votes to three. The trio I saw as humanists supported me, but the near-unanimous verdict was that I was lazy, pure trouble, a bum, a deadbeat, a no-hoper who should get a job in the post office as a clerk or letter sorter. Bess half-concurred, insisting that though I was still misusing and confusing personal pronouns like 'I' and 'me' and saying crampons for croutons, I should at least be a matriculated and grammatically correct no-hoper.

No regrets: I hated the place and its values—the cant, the pomp, the play-play soldiering at cadets, the overt prejudices, the laziness of so many of the staff, the cliques, the compulsory Saturday afternoon attendances to cheer the rugby players. I came to despise the heavy drinkers and the one or two pathetic men who offered money to have a student beat their bare buttocks with a brush. Bryce Roberts, a year older but a class below me, became Bryce Courtenay (taking his mother's name), described very similar feelings in his novel *The Power of One*.

I have always despised smugness, especially of a group, a society, a clan that exudes a self-satisfied belongingness which feels best, knows best and is best. By now I understood the concept of alienation, both of outsideness and of antipathy, an important force in my life, not negative but a spur akin to adrenaline. I also started to learn that two seemingly contradictory phenomena can be true in the same space and place, that my school experience could be (and was) the antithesis of the boy at the desk next to me.

Did I learn anything? Yes, some humanism from men like Teddy Gordon, Frank Puxley and Cecil Williams, the last a troubled soul who returned from the war, helped found the Torch Commando, a body of some 250,000 ex-servicemen dedicated to stopping the attempts to abolish all Cape Coloured political representation. He would scream if we called him Sir, a fascist word in his eyes. He validated my feeling that we lived in an abnormal society.

Puxley gave me some insight into TS Eliot, an appreciation of Shakespeare, CS Forester, George Bernard Shaw (*Pygmalion*, a major metaphor in my life) and HG Wells. I came to a love of geography, especially the human variety rather than climatology. But in the end, for me school was essentially about antagonism, cruelty, crude and cheap politics, a place of unjoy.

That trio's humanism (and mine) was, of course, at one immense physical remove from the realities that they were being human about. No White South African ever toted a barge, lifted a bale, planted 'tators or cotton, bent their knees or bowed their heads or slaved till they were dead. No one emptied a bin or a fireplace, collected garbage, polished a floor or silverware, swept or dusted or cleaned, washed laundry, nappies or a car, built rockeries or roads, painted a wall, thatched a roof, delivered a parcel, hauled bricks, mixed cement, laid sleepers or pavements, mowed lawns, caddied, rolled clay courts or fetched anything except their children from school.

Was I a misfit, a non-fit? Yes, in that I had an instinctive sense of not having a place. I didn't fit in with what English author George Calpin called 'the South African way of life'. I didn't really belong; on the surface, yes, but more a sense of toleration and toleration by virtue of being considered, but only barely, part of the 'White race'. Later, studying South African history, my instinct was confirmed by examining the ideologies of both Black and White intellectuals, leaders and opinion-makers. Jews wanted to belong, hankered to belong and expended great energy trying to prove why they should belong, forever talking up their 'contribution' to South African society. They still do, with increasing desperation.

But their belongingness was (and is) but a paper-thin tolerance. Today's South African Jews belong there even less than in my younger days, many of them huddling in Orthodox, gated communities, at formal prayer at least twice daily. I don't belittle their devotion but feel truly sad about where they are and highly critical because they should (or could) be somewhere else. They really don't belong any more, and some senior figures in South African political life keep telling them so today. I admit to tiring of their laments about having nowhere to go. When they say they can't afford to migrate what they mean is that they can't afford to re-locate and replicate their lives of convenience and material comfort. In my lifetime I have watched Jews not *wanting* to move but *having* to move—from much of Europe, parts of Asia and South America.

Paradoxically I still had (and occasionally still have) a strong sense of pride in South Africa, relishing the artistic, medical, scientific, literary and sporting achievements. The art of Alexis Preller, Irma Stern, Tinus de Jongh, Sidney Goldblatt and Gerald Sekoto is exceptional. I believed then and now in the liberalism suffusing the writings of Olive Schreiner and Sarah Gertrude Millin, particularly the latter's book on the Cape Coloured people, *God's Stepchildren*. Today, the Coloureds, now ten percent of the population, are increasingly converts to militant Islam, filled with jihadist hate and violence, especially towards Cape Town's remnant Jewish population.

In an international radio quiz show—really heavy, serious stuff—the home side comprised the renowned astronomer Arthur Bleksley, journalist and anti-apartheid activist Owen Townley-Williams and Eric Rosenthal, famous historian and author. They were inspiring models who led me to become a junior quiz kid on the South African Broadcasting Corporation radio for a while.

The performances of cricketers were a joy, despite the near-misses in Tests. In rugby I rooted for the Springboks against the All Blacks in 1949, sitting in the grandstand at Ellis Park after a pre-match stint of ushering (a favour given by the acting headmaster as a reward for typing his correspondence with a brown ribbon). I was ecstatic at the fortunes of flyweight boxer Jake N'Tuli, a Zulu man who wasn't allowed to fight at home but who won the British Empire title in London in 1952. Maurice took me to see the Vic Toweel *v.* Jimmy Carruthers bantamweight world title fight in 1952; I yelled at him to watch as he fussed with his cushion, drink bottles and cigarettes. He never saw the fight: the Australian hit Toweel 110 times in less than two minutes and that was IT.

On occasion Maurice took me to the professional wrestling. My favourite was Sky High Lee, a Canadian giant who always beat the hell out of local hero Willy Liebenberg, a serious lapse in patriotism. He once lifted Willy into the overhead floodlights, burning him to a half-crisp. I had the luck to watch Gorgeous George, born George Wagner, a psychiatrist who dressed more camply than Liberace, with platinum blond hair in curlers and silk-embroidered, sequined gowns. Later, when writing about sport, I discovered that he 'invented' purgation theory: get the crowd to hate you enough, to vent all their spleen at the stadium so that they felt purged enough to treat their womenfolk kindly at home. Fat hope.

I revelled in the great golfing achievements of Bobby Locke, winner of four British Opens and leading money winner in the United States in 1947 against the likes of Sam Snead, Byron Nelson and Ben Hogan. (I learned to play golf from Nelson's golf manual). Gary Player and I played in an under-15 rugby team and we played our first round of golf together at Observatory course with some of my Dad's spare clubs. I then watched with great glee as he became a winner of nine majors and a genuine legend. I used to think that Gary was my closest brush with fame, but I've met more than a few erudite others since then.

***

There were some quite memorable but brief episodes of Samaritanism. The adult night school at KES was one. Another was the response to an appeal for blood after a devastating tornado struck Albertynesville near Johannesburg in 1952, injuring 500 Africans and killing 30. I couldn't get near the Hillbrow Blood Bank (with my rare group) because the (White) queue to donate was so long. And in the same era, when the Putco bus company raised Black fares by a penny a journey, some 60,000 Alexander Township workers walked thirteen kilometres to work—whereupon thousands of White families drove out of their way to give them rides into and from the city.

But pride in such people and events was all too often challenged by hearing and reading stories of the gross inequalities in that society. In early teenage years I began to take angry notice of the separate racial facilities: red buses and trams for Whites, green ones for Blacks, each with its own stops; separate ambulances; separate elevators in buildings; separate queues in post offices; different hospitals; all-White schools (we didn't even know where Black children went to school); all-White cinemas, concerts; separate and much smaller stands for Blacks at sports events; separate entrances and exits in buildings and businesses; *Blanke* and *nie-Blanke* signs on public benches and public toilets. Churches were segregated in the sense that Whites and Blacks attended in separate shifts; Blacks usually at the earliest possible time slots and Whites at the most convenient ones.

All Black men (but not Cape Coloureds and Indians) had to carry a 'pass' as well as a 'special', a note saying that the servant was on a chore like buying milk or delivering something for the 'master' or the 'madam'. 'Specials' became so necessary that the Central News Agency (CNA) sold printed pro forma tear-off booklets with spaces for names and dates to be inserted and a place for a signature—including mine often enough.

I was always called 'Master Colin' or, when older, addressed as 'Boss Collie' by all Black people, no matter their age. There I was, at ten, writing notes in a good hand, for the 50-year-old 'boy' to be abroad in the streets. I spent much of my evening time in the servants' quarters, teaching some reading and grammar and listening to comments about White society that one would not otherwise hear. The matter of their absent families was a taboo: they wouldn't allow that kind of discussion. At that age I didn't know what a conjugal right was but I knew enough to know that people were supposed to be married, have parents and children.

I began learning about a quite separate life in townships like Alexander, Orlando, Pimville, Sophiatown and then Soweto, from Amos, one of my father's delivery men. Amos was quiet, strong, political, a Rhodesian illegal, but he would show me both licit and illicit newspapers and pamphlets that illuminated, vividly, how the rest of our world had to live. He was astute, good at evading the labour bureau and the police and I regret I didn't learn more from him.

* * *

My first re-matriculation choice was to go to Damelin College, a non-denominational private 'cram' school in the city, mostly for second-chance students like me and in part for students who wanted to get a good matriculation. My mother insisted on a second option, so I met Dr Benjamin Damelin, the founder of the original Damelin College in 1943, who was now running a new venture called Regis College. A small, dapper, mesmerising man who lived on coffee and cigarettes and taught every subject bar Afrikaans. In the face of his personality I opted for Regis, but in March that year the good doctor attended a Passover dinner and ate (or over-ate) *matze-ball* soup: to medical astonishment, his shrunken stomach actually burst, resulting in peritonitis.

By May, after nearly two months of waiting for his return and after endless games of snooker at the nearby parlour, I was smart enough to recognise I was going nowhere. I went to the college that bears his name and that was certainly another momentous change in life. I met, admired and later befriended Isaac Kriel, Max Witt, Asher Israel (the three owners), interesting, passionate, persistent teachers, driving students to achieve (and so ensure new college enrolments). I had come in late, had to switch certificates to the Joint Matriculation Board (JMB) exam, changing subjects and passing mathematics for the first and only time in my life.

Despite much rote learning, 'spotting' of likely exam questions and learning cramming techniques, these men opened up vistas I'd not encountered. Isaac especially, left me with a mission to achieve even one tenth of his knowledge. The maths moment was a truly significant one and remains the subject of

Dr Isaac Kriel (1927–1988).

a recurring nightmare (especially as I write this). I still have dreams about failing that maths exam, hence the entire matriculation; about the consequent imprisonment in the Johannesburg Post Office, still sorting the mail if not yet replaced by an affirmative action Black lady. About not finding my one and only wife Sandra, no Australian children, no university, no migration, no life, no career, just golf and void.

In Houghton I started breeding Rhodesian Ridgebacks, once entering them at a kennel show. My veterinary interests included cycling to a clinic in fairly distant Rosebank, treating middle-class pets in an upper middle-class suburb, clipping nails, giving distemper shots, removing ticks, soothing or smoothing ruffled budgie feathers. I was the owner and avid reader of such dense books as the *Diseases and Surgery of the Horse* and ditto the Dog. These works never said anything about maths or physics, so a vet I was to be, a profession with a very short half-life.

Part II:
Natal

Chapter 5

GREEN TO BLACK

Somehow I matriculated and headed for Natal University in Pietermaritzburg, described by an American visitor as half the size of New York cemetery and twice as dead. Then very much 'Sleepy Hollow', it would become the country's most violent city in the mid-1970s during the phase of the Inkatha Freedom Party. The Zulu nation—descended from the empire so cruelly forged by Shaka, the extraordinary *genocidaire*, in the early nineteenth century—was accustomed to independence and aggression.

Natal had campuses in Durban, 'Maritzburg, and Wentworth, the site of a politically embattled and geographically separated 'non-White' medical school. Two factors underlay my choice of 'Maritzburg: to do the first few years or the whole of a BSc Agriculture as an entry into the elite veterinary school at Pretoria University; and to get as far away as possible from my mother, within reason.

Noon on a 38°C February day was a sight or, rather, an unsight. Nothing moved, no cars, no people, only dazed horseflies flitting occasional flits. Oribi, the men's residence, was an ex-army, out-of-town convalescent facility, rows of bungalows, eight rooms to a block, corrugated iron roofing, no ceilings, no fans, whitewashed walls, polished concrete floors, coir mats, naked bulbs, single wardrobes, desks of a kind, no bookshelves, coir mattresses of a sort, top and bottom swing doors as in horse stables. The main dining room—a hangar-like version thereof—had a few listless fans on the bare beams above.

Attendance was required at three of the five formal dinners each weeknight. Wednesday night, the one with boiled pork and ostensible apple sauce, was compulsory. The Master of Oribi was Oswald Black, also the Dean of Arts and the University Counsellor, a one-time bearer of the grand title 'Psychologist to the Government'. He disliked me from opening day, calling me *'n slim Jo'burg Jood* (a slick/cunning Johannesburg Jew). This young *Jood* either ate the pork or went hungry since the soup always had things in it and the dessert was lumpy once-yellow custard—served by an *impi* (squadron) of Zulu men in white starched uniforms, white gloves, the seniors distinguished by red cummerbunds.

The best was to come. Dr Black changed his policy of having a weekly rotation of students to recite the meal prayer and chose me to intone it, in Latin, *every* formal dinner night for a year. For about 141 nights I delivered the 'Bless us O Lord, and these Your gifts which You have given us', *'Benedictus domine nos et donator...'*. There were some 250-plus in the throng, nearly all 'Agrics' doing a four-year degree. Nine were Jewish but I was to be the only one in a handful of Arts students, a group treated for the most part as queers: real men drank warm beer, pulled udders and shoved fists up bovine bums.

An outsider, sorely afraid, I stepped into this un-Jewish domain, dealing with a different society and culture, confronting a first-year curriculum of physics, chemistry, botany and zoology. I was confident about the botany I had recently learned, but then had to look real animals—not middle-class ones—in the eye. I was addled, as always, by physics and chemistry.

In week one, Miss Beulah de Villiers presented each of us with a frog. This, she demonstrated, is how you cut it open, lay the skin back, pin it and start looking for the spine. In the fifth week she raced down the aisle and demanded to know why my frog was still intact when all others were well past rats and onto dogfish. I hadn't the stomach for the guts, I explained; true enough but surprising given my chicken history. She made me cut, whereupon I screamed that my frog was bad, full of black bubbly things. A lady frog, what else? A tough lady Miss de Villiers, she suggested counselling.

Smirking at my discomfort, Dr Black administered a series of tests of the 'would-you-rather-address-a-roomful-of-people-or-drive-a-combine-wheat-harvester' variety. The usual anagrams, geometric patterns and puzzles followed. Having learned cryptic crossword puzzle techniques as a kid, the anagrams were a breeze. *Ja, seker*, yes, certainly, exclaimed the doctor in his, and my, eureka moment, I think you should talk for a living. So that's what I did.

I switched, albeit pretty late, to a BA (Law), majoring in English, political science and Roman Law. Somehow I lasted nearly three years at the depressing Oribi, mainly because it provided the cheapest bed, bacon and powdered eggs in town.

In my first-year cell at Oribi, Pietermaritzburg, 1952.

Towards the end of first year I went back to Johannesburg for a few days. My father quietly informed me that he had no money and couldn't afford the lavish lifestyle (five servants) or my university costs. Stunned, or more accurately mortified, at the pretences and pretensions of all those years in high-end Houghton, I said I'd pay my own way. I was angry that despite this state of affairs Maurice continued playing weekly poker where he won or lost sums two or three times greater than my total annual university costs. Family admonished me, saying this was Maurice's only outlet in life. Later I came to some appreciation of desperation poker when I found myself playing for food in my belly.

Money was always a problem for me. Before university days Bess gave me a meagre pound-a-week pocket money and I earned about £10 ($20) a month working in Dad's shop, double that in university vacations. Dinah, our cook, was a smart business lady and she and I had an arrangement. She was a grog-runner in a society that outlawed alcohol for Blacks. She didn't do the usual thing of running a *shebeen* (illicit grog shop) which served *skokiaan*, that impossible brew of every living vegetable that could ferment; she bought real booze, mostly brandy, from Chinese suppliers, diluted it, sold it by the pannikin and then, with my protection, she would hide the stash in the metal bread-bin in the pantry. Since I was the only person in the house who went to that container, it was safe. Police had the power to raid servants' quarters, the outhouses in backyards but not the White household. For my guardianship she either gave me or loaned me the extra money I needed.

At that time I was approached by Mr Desai. He and Mr Dehru owned the Delhi Fruit Market where my parents were lavish customers. Mr Desai bought clothes from Dad and I often attended to him. Childless, he offered to sponsor me to study in Delhi or Bombay—medicine if I chose. My parents choked at the very notion: apart from the obvious 'colour considerations', this was a time of very fraught relations between India and South Africa, essentially over the treatment of all the indentured Indian labourers who were never repatriated or compensated despite Mahatma Gandhi ensuring that the very first item on the agenda of the newly-created United Nations was the treatment of Indians in South Africa.

I passed everything and won a gold medal for philosophy. But money continued to be scarce. I worked the midnight-to-dawn shift on what was then a racist, rigid and parochial newspaper, the *Natal Witness*. There, in a disused stationery cupboard, I found reams of war-time antisemitic pamphlets, minus the printer's logo required by law—*Witness* productions. The paper changed both tune and tone over the years and is now one of the few remaining bastions of democratic thought and free speech in the 'new' South Africa.

My job was to operate the switchboard and telex machines. I did some sub-editing when the regular sub was wiped out on gin and cordial. I earned a few bob extra as the paper's film critic: three cinemas, each with two movies a week, quite a feat, though critic isn't the right word for 'this is good family entertainment'. A few quid came from playing snooker and darts for money at (Jewish) Barney Froomberg's pub, festooned (inexplicably) with Nazi military insignia. There I wrote letters for illiterate (White) railway workers seeking promotion from Wheeltapper Number 2 to Wheeltapper Number 1. I wouldn't take money but did agree to an occasional box of cigarettes or a brace of brandy-lime-and-water. I gave the same help to male nurses from the city's mental asylum, Fort Napier. My Olivetti 22 ex-army typewriter's brown ribbon seemed to impress people.

An old and trusty standby was the 32-card game called *klaberjas* (pronounced clubby-yuss), said to be of Dutch origin but of Hungarian favour. I had some tough contests but a few easy marks kept me afloat. The easiest source of money was playing Scrabble against Agrics. A fairly recent invention, the game was a craze. Language wasn't a talent of those majoring in porcines, ovines, caprines, equines and bovines. I was also allowed into the Sunday night poker school as a freshman, a move Dr Black insisted was yet another instance of a Jew subverting good order, discipline and governance. The game's convenor was Peter de Villiers Booysen, then head student and later an esteemed Vice-Chancellor of Natal University. Towards the end of each year Black threatened me that if I failed *any* subjects I was out of Oribi. Some threat.

Easy money beckoned, very briefly. In Durban one weekend with a girlfriend and her parents, I met a nice Jewish doctor who was also the medico for dockworkers, Customs and immigration officials. The illicit or undeclared goods confiscated by Customs from ships and passengers were wrapped in grey parcels and sold at blind auction: the doctor 'knew' the contents and became a very rich man. An Indian colleague at the *Witness* asked if I would visit a Mr Soni who owned a 'gold bought and sold' shop. I called in. Did I travel to and from Durban? Did I know Dr S—? Yes and yes. Would I care to deliver some small sealed parcels to and from him? My services would earn a percentage of the value, which value I had to trust to his integrity.

Mates egged me on—to liberate us all from poverty and Oribi. But I envisioned myself, in the middle of a course in criminal law, in the witness box later pleading I was but an innocent messenger unaware of the consequences of my actions.

I left Oribi of my own accord late in third year, moving into a large upstairs room in a two-storey heritage-type house close to the university. The landlady Marie was a trim 40-something. I came home late one night and in the dark knocked over a bottle of full cream milk. I cleaned up, unaware of ill-fitting floorboards. At breakfast she was tearful and miserable. I can't understand it, she said, I woke up at three, nightie all wet, sticky and a bit smelly, but surely, surely not! *Not*, I assured her in the professional tone of one who knew all about these things, you are *not* lactating, you've simply had a wet dream.

A positive aspect of this sojourn was that the unpregnant landlady allowed me a one-plate stove on which I began life as an aspiring cook. The menu was relentless: sharing corn flakes or rice bubbles with my room-mate for breakfast, foodless at lunch and for a few nights a week, but with a one-shilling slab of lamb leg chop which I cooked with tomato and onion gravy on the other nights.

Giving up cigarettes and brandy-lime-and-water never entered my mind. A female colleague's mother took me in for one good meal a week and my (new) girlfriend Val Rosen's delightful parents, Percy and Bess, provided another. That Bess I loved and she cosseted me with goodies, introducing me to pork as it was meant to be, a roast shoulder of sweet succulence, complete with crispy, crunchy crackling. Those few meals aside, hunger is neither a good nor a salutary experience.

* * *

The Arts Faculty was relatively small but there were several outstanding staff, including Geoffrey Durrant in English, Edgar Brookes in political science and Arthur Keppel-Jones in history. They were humanists, true liberals—in the South African sense—anti-apartheid and anti-authoritarian in a near-totalitarian landscape. The majority of the Agriculture faculty were Afrikaners who supported the traditional South African value system. The law staff were odd or frightened or both. As law upon law was being suborned, subverted and transformed by the new government, so they evaded the issues. Even major attempts to amend the constitution by trickery were banned as a topic in class or tutorial discussion.

Edgar Brookes was my mentor, friend and idol. This brilliant man began as a segregationist, pushing a separate but equal philosophy akin to that endorsed by the American Supreme Court from 1896 onward. Remarkably, perhaps uniquely, he had been plain Mister, Reverend, Doctor, Professor and then Senator Brookes (representing the Africans of Natal). After heart trouble he came to Pietermaritzburg to run the Political Science department. Keppel-Jones was famous for *When Smuts Goes: A History of South Africa from 1952 to 2010, First Published in 2015*, written in 1947, believing the Nationalists would come to power in 1952. That happened in 1948 but what looked like satire in 1947 became almost the template and textbook for what followed even down to the very titles of statutes. Keppel-Jones predicted just about everything, except that he, like me and a number of other race relations historians, wrongly saw the end as massive conflagration and Armageddon. I asked him if he was a seer, a man of prescience. No, he replied, I'm a good historian and I simply follow the tramlines of history all the way to their various termini. A good lesson; I still follow the trams, especially in the field of Aboriginal history, as we will see.

I was fortunate to hear lectures from Leo Kuper, then Professor of Sociology at the Durban campus; his later influence as the founding father of genocide studies at Berkeley in California was immense. Geoffrey Durrant was a different influence. His school of literary criticism was tough: he scorned 'scholarship' in literature; it didn't matter what Wordsworth's real relationship was with his sister or what the poet ate for breakfast, what mattered was the literary quality of his poems. He taught me to appraise by assessing a thing's intrinsic value. Much later I became an inveterate 'contextualiser', assessing value or non-value but *always* in context. Then immature, insecure and uncertain of myself, I learnt from Durrant to make judgements and to be decisive, one of my key maturing points.

I gained a place in the university golf team. We played our first inter-varsity at Houghton Golf Club in Johannesburg, a course I knew well and I did well. Scottsville was our home course and I became the university golf club secretary. Later, and in that capacity, I wrote to Pietermaritzburg Country Club seeking block membership for some 30 students of that prestigious outfit. It was, too, the prejudiced club dating back to 1886, one which had never admitted a Jew—until they got me in 1953 (they presumed this infusion of young blood would fit their social criteria). Perforce they had to have me; it was a good course and fun while it lasted. This was the first of several instances of my being a little like and a little unlike Groucho Marx— willing to join clubs that wouldn't have people like me as a member.

***

I never considered myself a waif but others seemed to see me that way. I was befriended, sometimes pampered, certainly wined, by some memorable childless couples in 'Maritzburg. I'm not sure even now whether they were couples in search of a child or I was the child in search of parents—probably both. I have fond memories of Jack and Jane Heath, he the Professor of Fine Arts, she the ceramicist, he the marvellous cover illustrator of my first book, *Shadow and Substance in South Africa*. Jack argued that Jews made good art, music and literary critics but had no creative instincts or talents. I would head for the library and come back with screeds about Camille Pissaro, Marc Chagall, Jozef Israëls, Jacob Epstein, Max Lieberman and Amadeo Modigliani. We learned nicely from each other.

The notion of critic, as raised by Jack Heath, has since fascinated me, especially after reading Jewish historian Cecil Roth. Jews, he wrote, are the eternal *protest*-ants, that is, protesters, never satisfied with the status quo in anything, always seeking improvements, always *kvetching*. Michael Wex, in his *Born to Kvetch*, asserts that Jews *kvetch* (criticise, carp and complain) about the problem and they *kvetch* about the solution. Wex records the long history of *kvetching*, going back to Exodus: Moses sent twelve spies to check out Canaan—Caleb and Joshua said it was okay but the other ten didn't like the fruit that grew there nor the 'giant' *goyim* who dwelt there. So they sat in the desert for another 37 years, complaining. It can be irksome and infuriating but it is also a wonderful spur to creativity.

Completing a legal BA and contemplating that profession I opted to work in the Office of the Master of the Supreme Court as an examiner of insolvent and deceased estates. I was better at the deceased estates than the insolvencies, especially in dealing with Letters of Administration, the submissions legally required from attorneys as an accounting for their handling of estates. We returned about 99 percent of them for resubmission. I loved being dined by lawyers asking me what the mistakes were, answers I was forbidden to give on the Master's orders. 'They earn more in a week than I do in a year,' he said, 'so let them figure it out'. The Master took me for coffee one day, asking me gently if I intended a career path in the Department of Justice. I said no, to which he replied he was pleased to hear it because it was no place for me (an English-speaking Jew) and wouldn't be for him as an English-speaker soon enough. This was my introduction to the politicisation of a whole society, the none-too-gradual but effective process of Afrikanerising the public service, of making what were legitimate practices, beliefs, mores and idioms illegitimate, and vice versa. In later studies this was a useful lesson in how relatively easy it is to transform the value system of whole societies by establishing a 'state ideology' and using draconian laws to cajole and shape a people whose basic desire is to conform. In Nazi Germany it lasted but fourteen years; in South Africa, more like half a century.

Instead of further study to complete a Bachelor of Laws for legal practice, I opted to do the Honours year in political science, the only student in that discipline to do so. For a brief moment I enrolled in the Diploma of Education required for professional certification. The professor, an ex-Cambridge don, said on the second day, apropos of nothing, that Jews could never make good teachers because of their constricting and constipating faith. That kind of alienation was then, and remains, a spur; and I quit, still resolving to become a teacher.

The Honours curriculum comprised five courses: a topic from each of political philosophy, public administration, international relations, and constitutional history, plus a European language other than English or Afrikaans. Having Brookes and Keppel-Jones to myself for a year was an exceptional, formidable, defining and possibly a unique experience. I learned a great deal about Anglo-American relations since 1900; much about St Thomas Aquinas and natural law; the nature of bureaucracy; the machinations in South Africa's underlying efforts to subvert constitutional precepts; and very little about German. That professor thought I had a cute southern German accent and speech pattern, which I later admitted to her was Berea Yiddish of sorts. She wrote a testimonial saying she was certain I could readily read German texts. *Nein*.

I did some original work, tracing a continuum of ideas and even of wording about natural law and human rights. The public administration segment led me to specialise in health. Edgar Brookes took me to Polelo forestry reserve, at the base of the Drakensburg Mountains, to meet Dr Sidney Kark, then the influential pioneer of community health centres. He and his wife were training Blacks to go out among their people as health educators, especially dealing with venereal disease and tuberculosis. Here was a magnificent project combining and integrating promotive, preventive, curative and rehabilitative health services. The Karks took this system to Israel; later, I tried to take it to Aboriginal Australia, only to be met with incomprehension, rank conservatism and mistrust.

On one of these visits I met an irate Professor of Bantu Languages from Durban. He was deeply concerned at the erosion of standard or 'deep' Zulu in favour of urban Zulu, replete with anglicisms. He called to see the chief, protesting at the corruption of traditional words like *ihhashi* for a horse and *idada* for a duck, the first letter *i* pronounced as *ee*. Holding up a photograph of a domestic feline, he indignantly told the chief that people were calling this animal *ikati*, pronounced ee-kaa-tea. 'Chief, what would you call it?' he asked. The unforgettable reply—*ipussy*.

At the outset I had no money for this, but there was an Honours bursary that covered the year's tuition fees. When I applied, Dr Black informed me, very quietly, that people like me had to get 15 percent higher marks than the next guy to warrant a chance. At the end of first term tests when I achieved a 20 percent edge, the Doctor of *Sielkunde* (soul science) gave me the bursary and smilingly told me that he was simply teaching me some of life's lessons (he did) and that I'd do well.

Amid family angst about not finishing an LL.B, I was rescued by Uncle Harry Isaacson. Becoming a teacher, as I clearly intended by then, is a *mitzveh*, a blessing, he said. As the executor of *Zeide*'s estate, I had £250 coming to me at 21. He would advance me the money and reimburse himself later. That was a cosmic sum in those days. I moved into the Central Hotel downtown, shabby and seedy but not Oribi, and there ran up tabs for at least three mates who were then worse off than I was. Dining on steak, chips and green peas at the Plough Hotel once or twice a week was a graduation from eating horse steak and onion sandwiches from the 'Pie-Cart' behind the Town Hall.

One afternoon, still at Oribi, I had a visit from Uncle Jack Zulman, one of several brothers of my step-grandmother Annie Tatz. A rich baker and confectioner in Vryheid, his wife Ann had died badly of cancer, childless. He invited me for a drink at the Imperial Hotel, the best in town and the place where students liked to imbibe. Downing two whiskies-and-milk, which quite boggled my mind, he got to the point. Had he had a son, he said, he would have wanted him to be a doctor, and since I was the only relative who seemed to have any brains, he'd pay for me to study medicine anywhere in the world. But it had to be *yetzt*, now, not later. I said I'd do it but I wanted to finish my Honours year. No, he said, and left me to pay for the drinks.

***

'Maritzburg was the birthplace of the Liberal Party, which in the South African context had very different connotations from 'Liberal' politics in Britain or Australia. It preached 'one-man-one-vote' and a place in the political, economic and social sun for all adult South Africans. It was, at best, radical in the domains of Black voting and equal wages but it was never a truly revolutionary party. Founded in 1953, its short life span ended in 1968.

Initial founders included renowned humanists. Several, especially Peter Brown, were harassed by the security police but Edgar Brookes and Alan Paton were not placed under house arrest or similar restrictions. Paton was already too famous—his novel, *Cry, the Beloved Country* had been published in 1948. Brookes, a deeply-committed Christian, had taught most of the Nationalist Cabinet members at Pretoria University when he was in his 20s and had a special place in their eyes, despite his liberalism. I was invited to join. I'm not sure where the notion sprang from but I instinctively answered that I wasn't a joiner. I am still not. Perhaps it was all those years as an outsider looking in, of not really belonging and possibly being too scared to belong. I would be a recorder, transcriber of minutes, a possible historian of the movement, but nothing more.

I was friendly with David Paton at Oribi and he invited me to one of his father Alan's house parties in the well-to-do area of Kloof. There I observed a different kind of hypocrisy. A 'mixed' party was under way, men downing cane spirit and orange juice to stoke up the courage to ask a Black or Indian woman to dance—considered a dangerous prelude to inter-racial sex then outlawed by the *Immorality Act*. The dancing didn't bother me, but four Black men did: dressed in full white livery, with red sashes and red caps, white-gloved, they carried silver salvers offering 'master' or 'madam', the conventional idiom of servitude, a canapé, a cucumber sandwich, a cocktail sausage, toast and fish roe and toothpicked cheese cubes. Dissonance, dialectical contradictions and very unsettling ambiguities were staring at me.

Such inconsistency was to surface in the infamous Rivonia Trial in 1963 in which six Whites (all Jews) and eight Blacks (including Nelson Mandela and Walter Sisulu) were tried for sabotage, prosecuted (vigorously) by Dr Percy Yutar. At the time of their arrest in a four-bedroomed house on a 20-acre farm called 'Liliesleaf', they had eight Black servants (who were arrested with them). Fourteen freedom fighters to eight servants was a good South African ratio.

Another dissonance confronted me in 1953. In July I drove my mother, sister, Uncle Louis's wife and daughter to Southern Rhodesia. We visited the sight-of-a-lifetime Victoria Falls on the border between Northern and Southern Rhodesia and then took part in two celebrations. The first was the Cecil John Rhodes centenary, with much cultural activity and a chance to see both the Sadler's Wells ballet company and John Gielgud in *Richard II*.

The other was the birth of the teratogenic Central African Federation, a joint venture in geopolitics between Northern Rhodesia (Zambia), Southern Rhodesia (Zimbabwe) and Nyasaland (Malawi). Based on a system of A and

B roll voters, A-rollers were the minority Whites returning the majority of seats and Bs were the Blacks electing a minority of seats. I'm not sure what made us think this was *avant garde*, a pointer to a brighter future for southern Africa, but we young liberals believed (briefly) in what looked like Africa's great experiment. It lasted a mere decade, a longer life than it deserved. The notion that the second prime minister of that 'nation'—Sir Roy Welensky, who described himself as 'half-Jewish, half-Afrikaner and 100 percent British'—was some kind of saviour, was a moment of serious aberration but it looked a good deal better than the South Africa of that time.

My good mates were doing Honours in history or in English. They teased me, saying that as Professor Brookes's pet he would give me an A for B class work, a B for C standard and so on. I achieved first-class Honours, *cum laude*. I started to believe the tease and that left a near lifelong niggle that I was *always less* than my results, always less deserving of the praises that came my way. A little assurance came when I was told that all my Honours papers were externally examined by a fierce Scottish historian at Rhodes University and she had concurred within a mark or two of the internal examiners. Another lesson perhaps: try not to be someone's pet and have as much independent assessment in life as one can find. There is a third perhaps: take appraisal and approval at their full face value.

The University of KwaZulu-Natal (as renamed) today boasts its equalitarian policies and practices. But never mentioned in all the glossy magazines and alma mater newsletters was the era of strict segregation. During my Honours year I was invited to give a few tutorial classes at the Durban campus. I would give a class from, say, 10 till 11, then race off to give the same discussion at Sastri College, the place for 'people of colour'. Sastri began in the mid-1930s on the basis of 'separate is better than none at all'. The difference in student attention and enthusiasm was palpable.

* * *

After Honours exams I headed back to Johannesburg to live with my parents. I did overhear my mother—forever on the phone (a particular South African social disorder)—telling assorted relatives and friends that I had passed well but she couldn't quite see to what end. I could. Earlier I had written to Isaac Kriel at Damelin asking for a job. Yes, he said, you're welcome. For him there was kudos in an ex-pupil becoming staff. For me the motive was crystal clear: that College had *pygmalioned* me and I wanted to return that favour, the one that had taken Colin Doolittle and turned him into a seeker, preacher and teacher of knowledge, fast approaching more than a tenth of what Isaac knew.

As my wife reads these chapters, she comments that I seem to be filled with nostalgia for this South African side of my life. Perhaps. I see it rather as an exercise in deconstruction, trying to find out the factors that have produced such phobias and *meshugassen*, as well as a strong survival instinct, alienation, anger, angst, energy, will, creativity, boldness and above all a critical eye—of both self and the world I live in. There is much pain but there is comedy in all this, Chaplainesque sad–funny people and places with a touch of Evelyn Waugh, Groucho, Joseph Heller and Mordecai Richler.

Best of all, what I once cried over I can now reflect on and laugh at.

Chapter 6

EXTRA LESSONS

'What should I be doing', I asked Isaac Kriel on my first day at Damelin College. Walk into the Form III classes and teach them some geography, he replied. With no formal instruction in pedagogics, I was nervous. The deep end usually answers such questions: you instinctively find what to do. I said hello to 36 students, a dozen of them Chinese, and it was plain sailing from there, with never a day's troubles, punishments, detentions or a raised voice.

My discovery and theirs was that I taught with passion rather than simply more knowledge. Yes, it is just possible to convey some excitement about the Drakensberg and Outeniqua mountains, the Brahmaputra and Mekong rivers, though Australia's Hay and Narrandera irrigation schemes were somewhat less evocative. And if not excitement, at least enough verve to hold student attention. Synthesising context and relevance helps greatly.

Learning how to *act the teaching* became my specialty—to listen to the sound of what I was saying, to inflect, to raise and lower the temperature of the voice, adjust the rhythm of a talk, to read an audience in a classroom or lecture theatre. I was able to project myself outside myself, to get as far back as the third or fourth row and hear what I was saying, to watch for boredom or incomprehension and to adjust. Teaching in this way, without notes and gadgetry, was and is my *shtik*, my 'thing'. Comedians and actors do it, so why not teachers?

Something else emerged. There are two Colins (in addition to the echo and the shadow). There is the *manual* one who has to grind out the reading and research, assemble the lesson or lecture, frame the article or chapter. The *automatic* one doesn't have to think or rehearse. He opens his mouth and his fountain pen and the stuff flows. Whatever this dual mechanism is, it works.

Soon enough I was taking senior English, geography, commerce and mercantile law, subjects in the matriculation curriculum. Students loved the law material and were much taken with the mysteries of cheques and other negotiable instruments, stuff they realised would soon be part of their [pre-plastic and electronic] lives. I liked the variation of subjects and the need to intersperse rivers and mountains with a diversity of themes and ideas. I learned to appreciate holism, the relationships between the parts, and the parts and the whole, an approach as applicable to life's situations as it is to teaching and research.

I was given Joint Matriculation Board (JMB) English classes on language and grammar, also Dickens's marvellous *Great Expectations*. I relished the student eagerness to acquire knowledge rather than simply looking to pass exams. Chinese students weren't admitted to government high schools but could attend places like Damelin and a few church-run private schools. They were a joy and delighted in turn when I included them on excursions outside of their worlds, such as to gold and coalmines and to that amazing facility, Sasolburg in the Orange Free State. There they learned how the Nationalist Afrikaners had foreseen the day when they would be subjected to international sanctions. Sasol produced oil and petrol from their limitless coal; vast quantities of fuel were processed, sold for marginally less than ordinary petrol but at a tenth of the cost of crude oil products. The Nationalists borrowed from Exodus, storing for the seven and even the seven times seven lean years.

I found post-school jobs for some of the Chinese girls whose parents were not keen on their undertaking tertiary study. A cousin had a large scrap-iron business and I recommended a Chinese lass to him. She was appointed to an upfront receptionist position, a bold move in those days. (Chinese weren't considered 'non-White', but they weren't considered White either.) She stayed for over a decade with the cousin keenly persuading other business colleagues to employ young Chinese.

A shared staffroom led to a strong friendship with Mike Hall, two years ahead of me at KES. We played about a thousand games of snooker that first year and travelled enormous distances around South Africa and the two Rhodesias on his Featherbed Norton motorbike. I never learned to ride but became a first-class pillion passenger, albeit without helmet and leathers. Many miles were spent in taking 35 mm slide pictures of geographic items for the students. There was no television at the time (or until 1976) which meant no documentaries.

I got to know the 'office boy' Johannes Mokwane, a resident of Soweto township, and the College's typist of typists ASK Joomal who did all the Gestetner wax stencils for the voluminous course notes. Well paid and hard worked, he became a well-known expositor of Islam, well before that faith consumed much of the Cape Coloured population. A little warily he introduced me to aspects of that belief system. The one sour note was when the Damelin directors bought an American mail-order doctorate in Johannes's name—an enormous, heavily decorated and tinselled certificate framed very visibly on his door—an unseemly swipe at Benjamin Damelin's doctoral qualifications and Johannes's dignity.

One day Mike suggested that in a particular class I should look at the 'doll' in the last right-hand row, third from the front, dark-haired, blue-eyed. I did and was smitten, smote, beguiled. I must have stared a lot because the following week she approached my desk and genuinely (and coyly) asked me the meaning of 'jejune'. I know now—it's simplistic or naïve—but I didn't know then, mumbling something that sounded right. I was 21, Sandra Melmed still 16.

We thought the romance was a secret because we sat in dim cafes wearing dark glasses and held hands under tables. The dark glasses and cafes didn't work. Isaac called me in to say he knew what was going on and if Sandra failed her JMB exam I'd be fired; he couldn't afford the scandal of a student failing because of a relationship with a staff member. No one sweated more over someone else's exam than I did. She passed well enough, this bright, lovely and very young lady, still with me nearly 60 years later.

She had lost her mother at a young age, in December 1954, and lived with her father Ben and brother Eddie. Ben was a doctor in what was called a 'Native practice'. Doctors had either Black or White practices; if mixed, they were in separate consulting rooms in different parts of the city. Ben seemed less enamoured of me, or at least me as a teacher with no seeming future, but Sandra's aunts and uncles were friendly enough. In all my family connections, apart from Uncle Harry, the notion of 'a future' meant earning medium to big money. Teaching, as they understood it, couldn't possibly do that.

My mother took to her and they became good friends, but Sandra took a while to get used to the aggregation of family *farribles* (fallings-out, grievances) and the food fads. Early on I asked her if she'd consider going to the end of the earth with me, she said yes and later she did. For me, 1956 was a momentous year: I had found a partner for life, a good pal in Mike, a vocation and my very own snooker cue with its own cute case, carried everywhere on the Norton.

* * *

In July Mike and I went to Victoria Falls in his father's gift to him, an Austin A40. Mike owned the little car but didn't have a driver's licence at that time. I drove the 1,000 km, half of them on the notorious strip roads. At the miserable mining town of Wankie at the border we stopped at the general store for drinks and cigarettes. My neck was profoundly sore, tilted alarmingly from controlling this rigid-frame vehicle meant for English lanes where people gathered lilacs. The storekeeper gave me two pills: swallow these, he said, they'll help. At the fabulous Victoria Falls Hotel—where, incredulously, prime steak and roast pheasant were on the breakfast menu—I went to the loo and starting peeing blood. Frantic, because I knew enough about bilharzia, a dreaded African waterborne disease where little flatworms called *schistasoma* lodge in either bladder or bowel, lay their eggs and slowly destroy you, blood the telltale symptom. I phoned Uncle Bernie, Dad's medical half-brother in Bulawayo and screamed my concern. Shh, shh, he said, did you stop at Wankie? Yes. Did the guy there give you some pills? Yes. How's your neck? What fucking neck! I cried. Aha, said the learned Bernard, you have swallowed harmless pills with a purple dye and you've discovered acupuncture of the mind (and neck).

The following year was to be very different. Always in a hurry because I had a *meshugas* (a quirky, nonsense notion) that I wouldn't live to 30 (or later 40, 50 and so on), I accepted an offer from two civil engineers to help start a new college, Yale, in the city centre. A half-floor was ample for the initial 20 matriculation students (as opposed to Damelin's 250-plus). I taught English, history, geography, commerce and mercantile law in the National Senior Certificate curriculum. It was tough but my aspiration (and horizon) then was to get a stake in the business, something I had hoped would happen at Damelin, from whom I'd had a polite rebuff when I'd approached them on the matter. I borrowed some money to put into the Yale business. All this was an immense leap from selling non-Nazi hats or sorting letters in the post office.

On 31 May 1957 I told Bess that Sandra and I were engaged and the announcement would be in that evening's Johannesburg *Star* personal columns. What ensued was her very highest dudgeon (she was a world-class dudgeonist): first, this didn't give her time to ring the relatives with the news before they read it in the paper, bringing her shame, chagrin and likely loss of family esteem; second, how dare I, pipsqueak that I was—a nobody teacher at a nothing school—sully and despoil this gorgeous, charming, wonderful 'girl in a million'.

At every turn my Jewish family life was the essence of *dafke*, the reverse (or perverse) of everything in the literature: teaching was a dumb thing to do despite a *Litvishe* veneration of secular and intellectual pursuits; my grandmother belted and berated rather than doted on me; and my mother said her unprecious son simply wasn't good enough for this rare treasure. Many children in life have to contend with adversity; my lot was to overcome perversity.

Shortly before, Sandra's father Ben, then 51, asked us to meet Elsa, a widow of 41 with a teen daughter Lily, originally from Rhodes island, then controlled by Italy. Auburn-haired, chic, she spoke fluent Turkish, Italian, French, Greek, Spanish and something not quite English. Both sides of Ben's family wanted him to wait until Eddie finished medical school at the end of that year and for Sandra to be married. Ben simply couldn't wait and they married privately in Port Elizabeth.

When it came to our wedding fifteen months later, Sandra and I, who had no money, asked for a small, mid-week morning ceremony with few family and friends. We suggested that our families' gifts be the money that would have been spent on a lavish affair. Elsa, coiffed head down and determined not to be seen as the wicked stepmother, insisted on the best event in town. The Blue Moon, a basement nightclub, was the venue, a Monday night wedding in formal dress, trimmings plus trimmings, the inevitable smoked salmon entrée, chicken-in-a-basket for main course, a bottle of whiskey on each table. Some 200 guests were chosen with blood and disembowelments on each side between Elsa and Bess as to how many invitations each could have, and with the bridal couple allowed four friends (plus the Damelin and Yale directors).

Our choice of best man was Mike Hall, of course. But he was considered a problem (wrong religion) by the family and so I asked Promund Obel, then in final year of his medical internship, to do the honours. I'd met him when we were both on a junior radio quiz team. We were married under a *chuppe*, the traditional four-pillared canopy. Mike was considered safe enough to be a pole holder; cousin Ben Isaacson officiated at Berea *Shul* with great passion and genuine love. Accompanied by Ben Melmed under the canopy, he murmured, 'You sure you know what you're doing? It's not too late: she's spoiled rotten, immature, she's pretty difficult.' Another inversion: I wasn't good enough for Sandra in my mother's eyes, she not good enough for me in her father's. They were both so very wrong and perhaps that's why, after we had migrated, our parents became such good friends, in-laws and in-flaws, especially in Bess's failing years when Ben was so attentive to her.

Berea Synagogue, Johannesburg, 9 December 1957.

Promund had married another Damelin 'product' a week before we did and we agreed to meet in the Cape after our weddings. Ben gave us Eddie's 'old' car, a black 1951 or '52 De Soto Deluxe manual (with a reconditioned motor and Eddie's photo mounted in the grille). We drove to the Van Riebeeck Hotel in Gordon's Bay, a 45-minute drive from Cape Town. The Obels went to another hotel which was just as well because there was constant bickering between the couples. I was able to show Sandra the adjacent town called the Strand, a vacation place where I had spent some holidays as a child. I remembered well an Apostolic sect that massed every Sunday morning at the beach; they prayed fervently, then jumped up to search for Jesus under the upturned fishing boats and in between the wooden supports of the pavilion and pier. They just knew that the only place He would hide was at the Strand.

On our return to Johannesburg we moved into one room in a residential hotel in Berea. I befriended Patrick and Elkanah, the two switchboard operators, both ambitious and keen to matriculate. At that time Sandy worked for a company that published the white and yellow pages. I continued at Yale with one slight change. I relented to the nagging from Bess and Ben to finish a professional law degree and went to Witwatersrand University as a part-time night student.

Not many academics are radicals or even adventurous. These law professors avoided any discussion of the calamitous constitutional crises of the time. The Nationalist Government wanted to tear up parts of the constitution but the Appellate Division (the highest Court) denied them; they then sought to have Parliament become the constitutional court, a crass effort in turn struck down. Not just an elephant in the lecture theatre but a crash of rhinos and a bloat of hippos.

My mate was the brilliant Mike Schneider, a scholarship student whose English migrants parents ran a garage in Brakpan, a Reef town. Being poor, he hankered to be rich and from time to time would ask me to join a few others in selling booze to Blacks or forming a consortium to lend Blacks money for housing at exorbitant interest because in those days neither banks nor building societies would lend them money. I was appalled and remain so at the thought of these *shlente* projects.

We had about eight Black students in the class: they huddled together in this so-called liberal environment, always well outside the circle. Cape Town and Witwatersrand were the only two 'mixed' universities in those days. Natal was segregated, Rhodes in Grahamstown had a nearby University College for Africans called Fort Hare. Pretoria, Potchefstroom, Orange Free State, Stellenbosch and later Rand Afrikaans, were Afrikaans-speaking institutions for Whites only.

Mike and I invented a new society which we named the *Grobberbond*, our take on that malevolent Afrikaner secret society the *Broederbond*, the band of brothers founded in 1918 by Afrikaners determined to wrest political, economic and cultural power from the hated English-speakers and, as ever, 'the Jews'. They did for the most part, controlling every aspect of life in the country until their membership lists started leaking a little in the late 1950s and their pivotal secrecy and power waned. There was an inverse pyramidal power structure: the higher-ranking members of the *Bond* were more powerful than the prime minister, for example, and only one man reached both pinnacles—FW de Klerk, the man who later released Nelson Mandela and paved the way for Black government. For Mike and for me the *Grobberbond*'s membership rested on who was the most *grob*—lacking in couth, ill-mannered, racist—as a qualification for admission into our secret phantom society. You didn't have to be Jewish, though most members were. The membership was oversubscribed and so we disbanded the organisation.

Our entertainment included foreign movies and lots of censored films. The 90-minute *St Louis Blues* on the life of composer WC Handy was reduced to 39 minutes because all scenes showing 'mixed' social settings—such as between Nat King Cole, Eartha Kitt, Cab Calaway and White characters—were excised. We ate out (cheaply) a great deal and spent many a night at Res-Doc, the medical residence where the Obels were housed. The officially named 'Non-European Hospital', adjacent to the Johannesburg

General Hospital, was close by and so was the Anatomy Lab, a strange choice of venue for ferocious games of *klaberjas* with Promund and fellow doctors. There would often be bizarre additions to our games: a detached arm placed at the table by the medical students who suggested we might have room for another hand. The humour was missing entirely when I attended Saturday night emergency sessions at 'Non-E' with Promund who was then doing his surgery internship: axe wounds, disembowelments predominant, stabbings with sharpened bicycle spokes in the spine often causing paralysis. A place of carnage. To see this kind of disregard for one's fellow beings shattered my already battered sense of normality. More battering was to come. Johannesburg, at high altitude, was always restless, short of breath and serenity, a landscape of death. It still is.

Mid-year I received a phone call from Mark Obel, Promund's father and part-owner of Circle Court in Hillbrow, then the world's most densely populated centre outside of Jakarta. He had an apartment for us in his rent-controlled building on Clarendon Circle. At £18 a month for a two-roomed flat plus a glassed-in verandah, this was a huge lift up. We decided to be servantless, a topic that turned tongues. But we all forgot, or chose not to notice, that with the rent came the building's 'flat boy', in this case 50-year-old Moses, uniformed in calico shorts and shirt, sandals made from tyre rubber, who cleaned the bathroom, toilet, stove, the windows, removed the garbage and polished the floors. Family and friends held us in esteem for this 'brave' piece of social conscience.

Towards the final law exams I realised that I didn't want to live in that society; that a South African law degree heavily into Roman-Dutch and Roman Law wouldn't be recognised abroad; that I wanted to teach and not practise law. Amid family headshaking I quit. I never regretted the legal BA at Natal or this extra year of study: legal and social justice prisms were to become the cornerstones of my research and writings.

Yet another *meshugas*—that I wanted to live in Sao Paulo. Professor Keppel-Jones contrived to get me a job there with UNESCO, difficult because

UN bodies were already boycotting White South Africans. I had taught Sao Paulo in geography and thought it idyllic. I had private-lesson pupils, including a man sent to me by my Dad's Portuguese-speaking partner. Some eight years my senior, Carlos Pereira de Lemos was a land surveyor working on the Limpopo River schemes in Mozambique. He had developed a tropical illness and came to Johannesburg for treatment. He could say three words in English, 'hello' and 'thank you'. We did a deal: I'd teach him English and help him matriculate in South Africa, both of which eventuated, and he would teach me Portuguese. Today, Carlos, a good friend, is the honorary Portuguese Consul in Melbourne and has a street named after him in the city of Warrnambool in Victoria.

Extra lessons had their moments. As a youth I had read the hysterically funny book, *The Education of H*Y*M*A*N K*A*P*L*A*N*, written under the pen-name Leonard Q Ross in 1937 when Leo Rosten was a poor sociology student in the United States. He taught night class English for immigrants and three of his books are uproarious accounts of K*A*P*L*A*N—who always printed his name in capitals and with coloured-crayon asterisks in between—of Miss Mitnick, Mr Norman Bloom, Mr Perez, Mrs Moskowitz, Miss Gidwitz and Mr Parkhill, the principal of the American Night Preparatory School for Adults. Mrs Moskowitz would write to her husband Oscar in 'Miame, Floridal' that 'the pussy should get every morning milk'. Kaplan produced his homework on nouns and plurals. He wrote: house makes houses, dog makes dogies, library makes Public Library and cat makes Katz; the opposite of milk is cream, life is debt and dismay is next June. He liked to read Hawk L Barry Feen and Toms Oyer and Julius Scissor, a great play written by an Irishman named MacBat.

My very own Kaplan was Mrs Slotkin. She and her husband had a store and eatery, with 'spayshil bacon eggs, cripsy' for me and Schneider. Large, we dubbed her 'Battleship Potemkin', her prow provoking that image. Our joy was to hear her yell at her husband in the back, 'Slotkin, forvard, shop' when a customer entered. She called into Yale and asked me to teach her the language she'd been murdering for 30 years. Expensive, I said, retreating from both torso and tuition. 'Expensive, who cares?', she said, 'Let's do it, ve start now.'

Within weeks the staff and half the class would stand behind my office door, panting for the next venture into the land of Shakespeare and Dickens, the world of degrees of comparison, alliteration, hyperbole, oxymoron, personification and punctuation. She did her homework every night and insisted that she read her efforts aloud to me: I move, I can move, I can have moved and so on. For each recitation she had an interrogative tone, as Jews often do. '*I could be moving?*' led her to stop and say, 'Vy? Vy should I be moving, I like my house'. She was outraged when I suggested we go through *Nize Baby* so that she could actually see what she was doing to the language. She insisted on 'proper' books. And so the denouement was her sight-reading a passage from *The Pilgrim's Progress*, that very *goyish* novel by John Bunyan. She recited: 'And the party slowly progressed up the hill towards Edinburgh, to the accompaniment of fifes…'. '*Zog mir*, tell me, Mister Colin', she asked, gravely, '*Vos is fifes?*' The lesson ended as the teachers (both Colins) could no longer contain themselves.

This snippet in my life reminded me of one, and one only, conversation with *Bobbe* Tatz. She gave me a small cheque for my *bar mitzvah* and soon after she asked me to visit her. She wanted to know where she could buy a gun for her favourite child Bernie, but since she didn't want stepson Maurice to know what she was paying for it she had to shop elsewhere. I knew what she meant and I sent her to Levinsons, owned by a former partner of Dad's. She asked Issy Janit what guns he carried. He told her to go to Bree Street, about six blocks away, to a shop called Rosettenstein and Falk. She told Mr Rosettenstein what she wanted. Producing an array of Colts, Brownings, and Smith and Wessons, he asked if she had a licence. 'Fool', she yelled, 'I'm vanting a morning gun, a dressing gun!' So much for Yinglish.

HUMAN RIGHTS AND HUMAN WRONGS

***

One more memory from Yale—an urgent call to rush to the Johannesburg General Hospital where Uncle Louis was dying and said he wished to see me. I took the trolley bus and met cousins Charles and Ben at the bedside. Louis was dead, blackish-faced, cyanotic-lipped, tubes every which way. The nurse said he'd gone a few minutes earlier. We talked about his foibles, his food intake, his cellar hoardings of everything under the sun.

I looked away and down, only to see an eye open in the darkened head. I'm not sure if I screamed but Charles (a pathologist) felt his carotid and pronounced him alive. The family duly arrived, Uncle Harry already saying prayers, Uncle Benny fuming that Louis still owed him money, Bess and Babs saying how wonderful he was (after a lifetime dedicated to bagging him) and so on.

Whereupon, a propped-up Louis proceeded with a declamation that he had passed over into the next world, seen Ma and Pa, and they had messages for the immediate family: Uncle Harry was nothing but a *kashrut* (dietary law) and ritual fanatic who wanted Louis to die so he had another reason to say *kaddish*, the prayer for the dead; Benny was a money tightwad without a *neshomme* (soul); Itz should have been married years ago (he never did marry); Maxie was a *gornisht*, a nobody; and Bess, well Bess who thought she could succeed Ma as managerial matriarch simply couldn't and who, what's more, ruined every one of Itz's marital prospects (she did); Babs was Bess's puppet and had surrendered her life to her sister. Charles, Colin and Ben, he murmured between tubes, were the only *menschen*, the only decent people in the whole clan. An occasion to savour as they listened in half-belief. I think Louis lived another five years and by then I was out of the country.

Mid-1957 my father finally sold the Houghton home and moved to a luxury apartment in Parktown with me (for a few months), Uncle Itz and my sister Pam. Maurice had liquidated his business because his partner wanted out and there was no money to buy him out. He took a temporary job and then moved on to be manager of the men's floor of a wholesale firm. He was near Sandra's work place and they met every day for lunch with Maurice especially attentive during Sandy's pregnancy.

Our son Paul was born amid some drama on 1 October 1959. Sandra lost a great deal of blood that midnight and Dr Norman Shapiro sent me to the Hospital Hill Red Cross blood bank, run by his brother Maurice, a renowned haematologist, to collect the two or three pints awaiting. Sandra couldn't understand why the Rev Cut Glass kept calling at Circle Court, nor could I until someone explained that a *mohel*—the circumcision guy— neither negotiated a fee nor sought one. The *bris* is a blessing and one was supposed to 'make a donation'. Mine was whopping, nearly a month's salary.

With much pressure from both sets of parents, we agreed to employ a maid. Christina Zungu was about 23, smart, with a child in her mother's care in a remote rural town. Our conversation on hiring Christina went: 'How much would you like as a salary?' Shrug. 'Is £10 a month okay?' 'Yes.' Do you want our meat or servants' meat? (alongside 'dog's meat', this was how butchers categorised their wares). 'Yours'. 'You will have to share a room with another maid on the roof-garden.' Shrug. Our parents would visit and have a *chammime* (akin to body and organ spasm) as they watched Christina knitting at the kitchen table while I fried steaks for the three of us. Unheard of. (Besides, isn't that where Communism starts?)

When Paul was a few months old we had a social visit from Mark Obel, a former member of the Communist Party (CP) and Sonia Bunting, the building's superintendent. Mrs B was the widow of SP Bunting, founder of the CP in 1921 and mother of Brian, author of the condemnatory book, *The Rise of the South African Reich*. Mr Obel asked Christina to go to the local shop, then opened the discussion. Were we paying Christina £10 a month? Yes. Well, the conventional rate is £6. We'll pay what we please, I said. No, he replied, not in this building you won't, you're upsetting the building's economy. So much for the CP and its boast that it never wanted to see the overthrow of the government or a Black republic (as Moscow was demanding) but only a place in the economic sun for the masses of the exploited and the poor. We discussed it with Christina: she said she understood, that she couldn't figure how we arrived at the figure of £10 in the first place and agreed to take the £6, with the balance in goods, books and tuition for her child.

We encouraged Christina to aim higher; after we emigrated, Bess arranged a position for her with a businesswoman where she became the third of the city's Black women to get a driving licence. Later in life, Miss Zungu became a *muti*-lady, dispensing medicine and often caring for the soul as well as the body; she was one of Soweto's most sought after and richest witchdoctors (shamans). *Muti* (pronounced mooty) must never come free, said Ben Melmed; Black patients want to and must pay for a bottle of something (in addition to vaccinations or injections) if they are to get better. The something was often diluted alcohol with a coloured dye.

I often had Patrick and Elkanah coming in for grammar lessons or tutorials on *King Lear* or the Napoleonic Wars. I met Patrick on a return visit to Johannesburg some five years later. He seemed successful enough; Elkanah matriculated, studied further and became a health inspector in neighbouring Lesotho. Circle Court was opposite a huge apartment block called Groot Drakenstein, reputed to be a high-rise department-store brothel. On a few occasions, busybodies opposite would report us for consorting or conspiring. Why else would two Blacks and two Whites be sitting in lounge chairs? Maurice put up curtains for us, but life was becoming very difficult on the racial front.

Chapter 7

SHADOW AND SUBSTANCE

By now I had developed a serious purpose in life—to be a teacher and a scholar. Teaching was fine but I wanted something more.

I discussed an Honours Master's thesis with Professor Brookes. Author of *The History of Native Policy in South Africa (1830–1927)*, he had always had a hunch that there was a strong connection—back to the late nineteenth century—between the 'non-White' franchise and land available to Blacks. Few explicit historical references existed that related the two but direct connections emerged shortly before the unification of the four colonies in 1910. This land–vote connection needed intense scholarship.

I liked the theory and eagerly took on the detective work. This was to be a very *manual* exercise, excavating, gouging evidence for a relationship. And there I was, working closely with a stellar intellectual, an experienced parliamentarian, a deeply Christian man, a humanist confronting racism. Before the era of electronics, drafts were written or typed, scissored, sticky-taped and pasted, then sent by slow mail. I commuted to 'Maritzburg every two months.

The work cemented what Brookes and a few others had already recorded: that from the eighteenth century onward a consistent ideology of racial superiority was the basis of South African society. It had three foundations: British imperialist doctrines and dogmas, the 'scientific racism' that began to emerge in the eighteenth century, and more importantly, Dutch Reformed Church Calvinism, fervent and fundamentalist.

South African 'Native Policy' remained essentially unchanged from the 1830s to the 1990s. Three religio-racial cornerstones were embedded well before the commonly misdated era of *apartheid*, so mistakenly said to have begun in 1948. First, a determination to retribalise an already largely detribalised people. The common view, then and now, is that ethnic loyalty is the same as 'tribalism' and tribalism is the same as barbarism. Second, maintaining a permanent (God-given) system of Black migratory labour to service and sustain White-owned agriculture, manufacturing, mining and domestic servitude. Third, removing any potential Black influence on White politics. (Later, the government would decree that only Whites could partake in the activity called politics.)

Not many people knew of or could see this consistent pattern running through a century and a half of White governance. For me there was exhilaration in dissecting out the ingredients of White supremacy, racial segregation or *apartheid* as it came to be called in 1944. This exercise helped develop an ability to vivisect as one lived amidst an ongoing system, to be a social historian of the present tense.

The research was laborious at times but it was a revelation to read all of the country's parliamentary debates (Hansard) from 1910 to 1960. The land–vote nexus remains crucial to an understanding of the pillars of *apartheid* (and its aftermath) and here I need to outline the deep roots of the racial ideology that underpinned and sustained so much of the overt and obvious *social* racism.

Blacks and Coloureds in the Cape colony enjoyed a municipal vote from 1836, an era that became known as 'Cape liberalism'. There was social segregation and economic disparity but the Cape Colonial parliamentarians genuinely believed in universal political rights, formally established in 1852. The other three colonies—Natal, the Transvaal and the Orange River Colony—were dead set against any rights of any kind for *nie-Blankes*, people other than White and Christian. When negotiations for a united South Africa began after the Boer War (1899–1902), a special commission drew up a set of racial policies for the future union. Too fearful of racial turmoil to entrust a new nation state to a federal system, as in Canada and Australia, South Africa chose a strongly centralised form of governance.

South Africa is full of racial myths. That commission illustrated one of them—that Afrikaners are the 'baddies' on race, the English-speakers the 'good guys'. (In 1961, when I had a brief meeting with Australia's Prime Minister Robert Menzies, he told me that his government was waiting for the election that would return the 'nice' Englishmen and depose the evil Dutch descendants.) The commission, almost exclusively of English-speakers, recommended territorial segregation as the only answer to the 'Native Question', with separate lands to be 'dedicated and set apart' for the Whites and for the Natives [the terminology of the times]. Maps would be drawn to settle the boundaries of what were to become the 'Bantustans': they were not invented in the 1950s and 1960s but way back in 1905.

Importantly, the Black and Coloured votes at the Cape were a potential danger: while Whites (then) formed 84 percent of the electorate, the other sixteen percent could in time and by sheer fecundity come to sway if not dominate political life. Their vote should be abolished and in their new 'dedicated' lands they could establish their own political systems. This land-in-exchange-for-a-franchise was the truly dominating force in race politics until the Mandela reign began in 1994. A misinformed and commonly held belief was that 'petty *apartheid*' issues—the world of separate social facilities for example—were at the heart of things.

Union came about in 1910. The preceding National Convention had come to grief over the Cape's liberal views. Cape delegates said they'd never join a union that didn't extend the vote to Blacks and Coloureds across all colonies (the provinces to be) and the so-called 'northern colonies' said they wouldn't join a union that even considered a vote for people they perceived as *schepsels*, a Dutch (and Afrikaans) word meaning creatures.

A compromise was reached—the status quo by which the Cape would keep its liberal system, the others their rigid antipathies. The Cape African vote could only be removed by a two-thirds majority of both Houses of Parliament in a joint sitting, a safety device believed unachievable. The new Union constitution, however, barred 'non-Whites' from being elected to or sitting in Parliament. Meanwhile map-drawing began when the *Land Act 1913* banned Black purchase of land until the maps were completed. That landscape was finally defined in 1936, allocating thirteen percent of all South Africa's land to nearly 90 percent of the population. That was the very essence of South African racial arithmetic.

Generals Louis Botha, Jan Christian Smuts and JBM Hertzog were Boer War heroes. Hertzog broke away from Botha and Smuts in 1914 and formed the country's first Nationalist Party, determined to abolish the Cape's colour-free franchise. Hertzog came to power in 1924 and from then until 1936 he campaigned feverishly for a land-for-franchise swap, claiming that Blacks (not Coloureds) should give up the shadow of the vote for the substance of the land. To achieve his goal, his party merged with Smuts' South African Party and the United Party (UP) was born. A very small group of Afrikaners broke away from the new UP, calling themselves the 'Purified' Nationalist Party, led by Dr Daniel Malan. Only twelve years later that rump became the government that ruled so brutally until 1994.

The 1936 deal abolished the Cape Black vote by the necessary two-thirds majority, kept the Coloured vote and agreed to allocate land in special Native Reserves. Hertzog promised that that land would be bought by government within five years; it took until the early 1980s to come about. These were the areas the later Nationalists came to call the 'Bantu Homelands' and 'Bantustans'. Hertzog's peculiar but interesting sense of justice determined that in return for the lost franchise, all Blacks (not just Cape Blacks) in the country could elect, on a separate voters' roll, three White House of Assembly representatives and four White Senators to look after their interests.

When World War II began on 1 September 1939, Smuts as Deputy Prime Minister insisted the country join Britain. Despite the lingering Boer War bitternesses, Smuts was an Empire man. Hertzog viewed the war as a purely European one. (Even at five, I recall my joy at South Africa joining the war.) A vote was taken in the Assembly and by a mere thirteen votes the Smuts motion for war was passed. The Governor-General asked Smuts if he had the numbers, which he had, and he duly became Prime Minister, until 1948. This schism was very much reflected in the fascist politics of the time, with splinter groups not simply anti-war and fascist but avowedly supportive of a Nazi victory, even to the extent of sending an emissary to Germany to negotiate the South African spoils when Hitler triumphed. (One of them was Robey Leibrandt, a former South African heavyweight champion who later joined German Intelligence and the Nazi Party. I remember my disappointment that it was a boxer who turned traitor.)

My work analysed the history of race relations, racial laws and African reactions from 1910 to 1960, effectively continuing Edgar Brookes's major treatise. To be this great man's successor was momentous, especially when looking back at what and where I was a mere eight years earlier. Sadly, apart from my wife, my family couldn't see any import in any of this—until they were able to write to me in Australia as Dr Colin Tatz. The research helped me unravel how and why governments consistently justified official racism by keeping the distinctions clear between people who were 'civilised' and those who weren't; to comprehend the wide disparities in wages, occupations, services and facilities; to understand the enormous gaps in social indicators like life expectation and mortality from communicable diseases; to fathom the horrors of migratory labour and the separation of families for such long periods. The work also taught me how lore and custom can be as tough and as painful as legal statutes and how social expressions of disdain and disregard are most often legitimated by law.

The thesis was awarded *summa cum laude* and one of the examiners urged me to publish a slightly amended text, which I did in 1962 as *Shadow and Substance in South Africa*. The book was well received and even *Die Burger*, an avowedly Nationalist Afrikaner newspaper, described it (in translation) as 'nice research spoiled by too much liberal propaganda'. Brookes was excited at the work and suggested it be considered for a doctorate. South African universities didn't allow jumping from Honours to a doctoral enrolment, and if it had been accepted that would have meant not only foregoing the MA but also the (soon-to-be) Australian doctoral scholarship, my precious ticket out of there. I declined, with thanks.

The book became a standard text in history and politics courses, even in Afrikaans universities. That sat very well with me: it was a huge undertaking, completed in short time; it broke ground and had practical application. In August 1960 the UP declared that it had never had a land-for-franchise deal for Blacks and hence the party could repudiate 'Bantustans'. My thesis was a total refutation of that mischief and the newly-formed Progressive Party (later to be led by the renowned Helen Suzman) used my work to validate their existence.

Much of my research was at the remarkable South African Railways Library, a block away from Damelin. During World War I, the parliamentary proceedings known as Hansard were not printed for austerity reasons. Nothing was available on debate and legislation from 1914 to 1919—except transcripts taken from shorthand reporters working for the *Cape Times* newspaper. This library had albums of these precious news cuttings for the crucial years. While working there I met two eminent Afrikaner historians, DW Krüger and FA van Jaarsveld, men who had a profound understanding of Afrikaners and their politico-religious nationalism. Far too many English-speaking historians have ignored their insights, and far too few South Africans, of any colour or creed, have ever really understood Afrikanerdom.

Krüger, author of *The Making of a Nation* and *The Age of the Generals*, was a professor at the Potchefstroom University for Christian–National Education. Teaching there meant you had to be White, Afrikaner, a member of one of the three branches of the Calvinist and deeply fundamentalist Dutch Reformed Church and a dedicated *apartheid* man. I found Krüger to be simply a White, dedicated Afrikaner but liberally-inclined and quite isolated. He encouraged me a great deal while asking me if his work was worthy! Sad in many ways to be a mid-twenties junior scholar giving some kind of succour, counselling and friendship to such a senior figure in South

African history. He sensed that I would one day have the tools to get out of there and he had nowhere to go.

Floris van Jaarsveld was no less remarkable. The author, among other works, of *The Afrikaner Interpretation of South African History*, his was an insider's view of what made his fellows tick. The most prolific and controversial of all South African historians, he taught me that these men were not mere calculating opportunists but true believers in a fundamentalist God, a deity who had cursed forever Noah's Black son Ham and his descendants. The curse was that they would be 'hewers of wood and drawers of water', a perpetual servant class, but more importantly they could never achieve true spirituality with the White man no matter how many doctorates they earned or how Christian they believed themselves to be. Much later he was physically attacked by the dreadful Eugene Terre'Blanche, leader of the Afrikaner Resistance Movement. van Jaarsveld was literally tarred and feathered for his 'blasphemy on sacred Afrikaner symbols'.

Making a contribution like this to South African history, albeit ugly history, felt uplifting. I didn't see myself in the same company as Brookes and Krüger but the very thought of being an apprentice in their arena gave me a sense of worthiness and belonging to something.

I learned much about a South Africa that I didn't know, and there is much I still don't know. It always amazes me how little even fervently jingoistic and patriotic people know about the societies they hold dear. The Australian experience has been no different. Australians know less about their dark history than South Africans know about their country's appalling past. Admittedly, many Afrikaners—certainly the intellectuals, clergy and most politicians—were steeped in their history: in their eyes, history was the nation and the nation was history, albeit one of constant warfare against the British, against the Blacks, against modernity and Satan of course. South Africa was one of the last Western states to have television: this devilish 'vehicle of foreign ideologies' was finally permitted in 1976, a full 20 years after that innovation came to Australia.

Sandra typed the thesis on our green manual Hermes machine, using wax stencils. It was laborious and she helped enormously; she always has. It was duplicated on a Roneo machine by Johannes and me working back late at Damelin. I would drive him home to Soweto, he more terrified than I was that police would stop us and question why a Black man was being driven by a not-Black man at night—unless for a nefarious purpose. In those days, if you drove your Black babysitter home she had to sit in the back seat as there could only be one reason why a 'mixed' pair would be sitting together in front. Insane, yes; paranoid, yes; demeaning, certainly, but accepted by all as a norm.

Earlier I discovered a quirk of eye or brain. I found I could read two lines almost simultaneously or a sentence on one page would lead me to jump ahead and pick up names, even ideas, further along. I got through books quickly but this, I believe, led to something else: it was a metaphor of a quirky soul, one that made me start the next phase or project even before the previous one was concluding. Getting to Australia as soon as possible was one example of 'arriving early'. These fast-forward decisions didn't mean I was better than my talents (or anyone else's); simply that I could arrive at a conclusion often well ahead of when it could normally be expected. This has been a lifelong source of success at some things and of major frustration in others. And it is doubtless connected to my manner of rushing through life because I was destined for a short one (that is turning into a long one).

***

By 1959 I had decided, with Sandra, that we would leave the country by the end of 1960. The intention was to go to Israel, with Sao Paulo a distant, over-populated, heavily polluted and now bad notion. The Israeli emissary at the South African Zionist Federation told me I'd never make it: I'd need three jobs, he said, to make ends meet and my wife would have to work, child or no child. An academic job, which I mentioned as an aspiration, was not advisable because rich American professors who taught eight months in their year were free to volunteer their vacation services and they occupied all positions. Pretty shaken at the rejection of what I believed was young and willing talent, we were at a loss. Part of me still tells me that we should have persisted and that Israel was the emotionally sensible place to be.

I left Yale with my stake returned to go back to Damelin in 1960, teaching the usual subjects but with many more senior English classes, adding *King Lear* and modern English verse. Damelin now paid me much more and I had a battery of private students, the money needed for the intended migration. Mike Hall went to Australia early in 1960. He explored the possibilities of our starting a Damelin in that country but his letters weren't encouraging. The idea of a college partnership was fading and the prospect of an academic career was far more exciting.

A competition occurred at this time between Isaac Kriel and me. As he watched my progression he asked me what was involved in a Master's by thesis and said he would also embark on such a degree. He did, most successfully, and later took joy in having a splashy column in a Damelin newsletter showing the two of us clutching our graduation certificates. When I left for Canberra to enrol in the doctoral program, Isaac decided also to enrol in one. Later, his joy and publicity were even greater, with 'twin' teacher and pupil doctorates on display. Nice for both of us.

In a library I spotted *The Commonwealth Universities Handbook*. Finding an entry for the Australian National University (ANU), I wrote to Professor Leicester Webb, head of Political Science in the Research School of Social Sciences (RSSS), asking whether I could undertake a doctorate while I taught in a Canberra high school. He asked for some thesis chapters and within weeks sent me an offer of a doctoral scholarship, complete with airfares, married student accommodation and a stipend. I had also approached Oxford where I was offered a scholarship for a DPhil, but enough only to sustain me. When I said I had a wife and child, they conveyed their sympathies for such a pitiable condition but insisted it was a single student stipend.

I asked Webb if an academic career would have a better prospect with an Oxford rather than an Australian degree and he huffily replied that I should come to Australia. At that point Edgar Brookes rang to say there was a two-year temporary lectureship in political science at Natal and he'd like me to take it. Dream of dreams. I telegraphed Webb about deferring the scholarship for two years, evoking a sharp response that I needed to come right now. He was right, of course, and he explained his reasons on arrival: he was fully aware of the dangers inherent in any criticism of the regime and he feared for me.

The reasons were really pretty obvious. The Pan African Congress (PAC), beginning in 1959 under Robert Sobukwe, had separated from the African National Congress (ANC), more strident in its determination to throw off repressive laws, especially the labour and movement control laws—from way back in the nineteenth century—which made it compulsory for all Black adult males (and later females) to carry a document called a 'pass', production of which dictated who would be allowed to work in which regions, in which industries and in which capacities, when and for how long. (The 'pass' was the key document to domicile and work: the 'special' referred to earlier was merely to allow the servant to be away from the home premises that day.)

The PAC organised a pass-burning and a demand-for-increased-wages exercise on 21 March 1960 at Sharpeville, near Vereeniging in the Transvaal. Intended as non-violent in nature, the pass-burning resulted in the police using dum-dum bullets that killed 69 Blacks and wounded 180. This was the seventh major pass-burning incident since Union and hardly the first episode of racial violence in the century. History shows an almost annual 'riot' of one kind or another, with greater frequency at election times—a time for a government to display its capacity to maintain 'law and order'. But this time the word Sharpeville reverberated around the world and became the quintessence of the *apartheid* evil. Even the Afrikaner Nationalist press proclaimed that 'South Africa is now the polecat of the world'.

A state of emergency was declared and the government demonstrated that, despite claims in textbooks about the impossibility of arresting public opinion, it could do so. More than 11,000 people were detained without trial, often as a result of vexatious denunciations about being 'Commies', subversives, and worse—'liberals'. Derick Marsh was among them. Arrested very early one morning in 'Maritzburg, he was released after his solicitor secured his freedom on a technicality. He knew he'd be re-arrested and when the police arrived he took with him a ream of paper and a copy of Shakespeare's complete plays. Imprisoned without trial for about ten weeks, he wrote his doctoral thesis on Shakespeare's last cycle of plays, later published by Natal University Press at the same time as they published my *Shadow and Substance* book. His remarkable dedication was to FC Erasmus, Minister of Justice, 'who kindly provided the time and place for this research'.

Friends like Derick were going down like ninepins. We were advised to have a suitcase to hand, the car parked in the street and the petrol tank full, ready to travel to Basutoland (renamed Lesotho in 1966), a neighbouring and landlocked British protectorate. Several men and women I knew were in hiding. Others had been incarcerated or bailed during the infamous Treason Trial. Starting in 1956, 156 people were indicted, many charges were withdrawn and by March 1961 the remaining 28 accused were acquitted.

I knew the (later) famous Father Trevor Huddleston, an Anglican priest (later bishop) whose remarkable *Nought for Your Comfort* had a worldwide audience. His order made him return to Britain. I also knew Bishop Ambrose Reeves, head of the Anglican Cathedral located near Damelin. I would meet him for an occasional tea and he would lament the poisonous letters from congregants left on the pew seats. Reeves was (ill) advised to flee to Britain after Sharpeville.

The Jews played it straight, except for Chief Rabbi Louis Rabinowitz and his assistant, my cousin Ben Isaacson, at the large Wolmarans Street *Shul*. Their sermons were vigorously anti-*apartheid*, Ben's perhaps the more so. On Friday nights he would start his sermon with the usual need to obey the rules of ritual and to avoid inter-marriage, whereupon the very obvious Special Branch guys would leave and Ben would continue the political and moral lessons. Dr Percy Yutar, the chairman of the *shul* board and the Transvaal's notorious Attorney-General, would threaten Ben (physically as I once witnessed) for 'desecrating' his place of worship. I spoke with Yutar once about studying law: he told me that unless I practised commercially I'd wind up as an academic or a public servant like he was, both professions clearly less than ideal in his mind. When Ben gained his own parish in Krugersdorp, he and his (then) wife Ann gave haven and comfort to the children of those who had to hide or flee, and to political prisoners in Pretoria Central. After a while he was refused such pastoral prison visits. (Like Reeves, both rabbis received anonymous hate messages left by congregants at Wolmarans Street *Shul*. An ecumenical society!)

Jewish formal organisations were abysmal at this time, ducking for cover, keeping *shtum*, but worse, castigating those who were opposed to the system, decrying them as 'non-Jews', apostates, traitors. Rabbi Rabinowitz was moved to say in a 1959 *Yom Kippur* (Day of Atonement) sermon:

> There are some Jews in the community who do attempt to do something… and when, as a result, they fall foul of the powers that be, the defence put up by the Jewish community is to prove that these are Jews only by name, that they do not belong to any synagogue… Have Jewish ethics ever descended to a more shameful nadir? … I have practically abandoned all hope of effecting any change in this matter.

Jewish attitudes and behaviour had reached rock very bottom. There was community applause when a Hungarian Reform rabbi in Port Elizabeth, Andre Ungar, was deported for his 'liberal' views, and when journalist and writer Ronald Segal had to take his excellent journal, *Africa South*, to Britain where it became *Africa South in Exile*.

My friend, Israeli scholar Gideon (Gidi) Shimoni, wrote his *Community and Conscience: the Jews in Apartheid South Africa* in 2003. There was nothing in this behaviour that deserved moral pride, Gidi wrote, but it was a phenomenon of 'self-preservation, performed at the cost of moral righteousness'. I am a lot more judgemental than my former South African colleague and persist in castigating not their 'self-preservation' and their seeming silence but their active and conscious adoption of all forms of racial supremacy. One should also add their disgraceful denunciations of fellow Jews.

We were advised to apply for the £10 assisted passage scheme available to Poms and 'British subjects'. One afternoon a detective arrived at Circle Court. I panicked because my desk was a mass of OB, Blackshirt and other eagle-emblemed pamphlets, together with a few Communist Party papers. To hide them, I recall placing year-old Paul, complete with wet nappy, on these precious documents. He had come, said the policeman, to check whether I had a criminal record. The Australian Embassy, he explained, wanted some information, specifically that I had a clean record and was White. 'These bladdy countries', he concluded with disgust, 'they're not like our democracy.'

Democracy it wasn't but I'm still not sure of something I did in that year. I was reading JJ van Rensburg's autobiography, *Their Paths Crossed Mine: Memoirs of the Commandant-General of the* Ossewa–Brandwag. He had been feted in Germany before the war, and thought very highly of Dr Joseph Goebbels and especially of Mrs Magda Goebbels, 'a lady of charm and beauty and a gifted conversationalist and of extraordinary intelligence'. There staring at me, mid-book, was a full-page portrait of Julian Visser, convicted with Hendrik van Blerk of dynamiting the Benoni Post Office, causing a death, and sentenced to hang for their anti-war efforts. Obviously commuted and then pardoned by the Nationalists, there was Julian Visser, in the flesh, sitting opposite me in the staffroom, a newly recruited Afrikaans teacher. Is this you, I asked. *Ja*, but it was a long time ago, he said. What I did was inform Kriel who duly asked him to leave.

* * *

There was no shortage of spurs to get out of there. I have a rare blood group and was a regular donor at the Hillbrow Blood Bank. One evening, when the receptacle was full, I saw the nurse attach a label with a white circle on it. 'Is that what I think it is?' I asked. Yes, she said, the government is introducing a law to prohibit inter-racial blood transfusions and we're getting ready. A year later, in Canberra, I met Dr Maurice Shapiro, head of the Johannesburg Blood Bank, on his way to a haematology conference in Tokyo. There, God help him, he had to explain a law based on the premise that a Black infusion could turn you into one of them—lazy, stupid, promiscuous, cursed. I'm not entirely sure but I don't believe the Nazis ever went so far (formally, at least) in their pursuit of racial purity.

After Sharpeville we would look out our windows and see hundreds of Black Maria vehicles transporting thousands of men to the Johannesburg Fort, an imposing prison disguised as a hillock close to city centre. My neighbour said that when he looked out the window he only saw the pretty flowers in Clarendon Circle. One evening, at another friend's house in Benoni, a fair-sized mainly Afrikaner town—we joined the Obels for dinner and cards. We were proudly shown the new purchase, described as superbly designed, decorative, unobtrusive: it was a new gold-coloured, thin, electrified, platinum-wired burglar-proofing system on the windows, with 'a lovely diamond-shaped symmetry'. Similarly, I overheard an uncle telling a customer about his marvellous new silver-plated, streamlined, ebony-handled revolver. It was all too clear that only one of us was sane, or sane in my understanding of the word.

During 1960 I renewed a friendship with cousin Doreen (Shapiro) Nayman, and it turned out her family was serious about migrating to Australia. Derick Marsh was always at risk of being re-arrested in a crisis and there were no shortages of crises. His (then) wife Nicola wrote to various Australian universities telling them of Derick's history. Sydney University was the first of several to offer him an English Department position, sight unseen. Asher Israel from Damelin, with (then) wife Rene and three children, were also determined to migrate. The Israels went about six weeks before we did. The Nayman mother and daughters, the Marsh family and the three of us left together on the same South African Airways plane, a Douglas DC-6B turbo-prop that took 36 hours to get to Perth.

In essence, departing wasn't easy from a family viewpoint, but the societal framework was unbearable. Most Jews I knew went to Israel. Later I heard that thirteen Jewish families went to Australia in 1948, on the basis that life under the frightening Dr Malan wasn't liveable. When we left, the number of such families was 47.

In sum, why did we leave? In the late 1950s and amid the paranoia and horrors of life after Sharpeville it seemed to me that I had six choices. First, to identify with mainstream (racist) Afrikaner nationalism and ideology. Impossible for me, although tenable for some.

Second, to identify fully with someone else's (liberation) nationalism, in those days Black nationalism rather than specifically African National Congress or Coloured or Indian nationalism. Not possible. I wasn't a joiner and I didn't have the guts, if that's what it was, to be a Baruch Hirson or a Ben Turok, eminent (and imprisoned) White opponents of the *apartheid* regime, sacrificing marriage and children for a cause not fully my own. I had witnessed several instances of imprisoned or harassed White people being repudiated and scorned by Black activists for their 'uninvited' intrusion into their affairs. I was to see that phenomenon often enough in Australia, with Aborigines turning abusive towards 'do-gooders'.

Third, to join the Communist Party, one always more concerned with human rights and an economic place in the sun for Blacks rather than with the overthrow of colonial capitalism. It was a real challenge and a choice, but one I rejected for many reasons. One of them was joining simply because, historically, Jews found a sense of equality and social acceptance when for brief moments they became 'comrades' rather than Jews. I didn't want to be that kind of a comrade, tolerated in the name of a higher 'cause'. I felt there had to be more compelling reasons for joining.

Fourth, to put on blinkers and pretend that there was nothing amiss around me. That was quite out of the question. It was simply not possible not to see the blatant, visible, overt, obvious and outrageous discrimination surrounding one, suffusing one's daily life. One spent hours daily either confronted by 'the problem' or worrying about it. (On arrival in Australia people would ask what I liked best about the new life. My answer never varied: I had six to eight hours more per day to think about other things.)

Fifth, to write critiques of the system while still being, if not complicit in it, then at least a companion to it. That, of course, was what I was doing: attempting to teach the 'Native Question' as part of the school matriculation syllabus; writing my book-to-be while living in an apartment in an exclusively White suburb, serviced by Moses who lived in the servants' quarters on the roof minus wife and children. I couldn't continue living that kind of lie. It was that sort of rationalised complicity or collaboration, something I describe as 'companionship', that led me to the sixth and final alternative: to remove myself, my wife and infant son from that environment altogether.

Life there always made me feel encumbered, weighed down by the dissonances, the double meanings, the disregard for humanity, the deploring of humanism as communism or some more fearful form of treason (to 'our species'). I didn't flee, nor did any of the many thousands of South Africans who have come here. In 1985 an *Age* journalist in Melbourne asked for my help on a series of articles on 'South African refugees'. I told him acidly enough that there were only six real refugees from the system and named them. The rest, I said, were 'boat people'. Meaning?, he asked. Meaning that they arrived here and a week later they had a boat. That phrase made me semi-famous in the pantheon of original sayings—in the *Reader's Digest* of all places! In the letters following his headlined piece 'Professor Slams Boat People', one wrote that he didn't have a boat, only a dinghy; another said he had had to sell his boat so that he could send his son to Carey Grammar Baptist School.

I left in 1960 as I had promised. On 31 December to be exact. With a great deal of semi-bluff and surface bravado the family came to believe that

Scholarship winner and family face a new life in Australia

By a Staff Reporter

MRS. TATZ stood amid the jumble of upturned chairs and piled furniture in her flat in Clarendon Place, Johannesburg, and said: "It's a gamble—leaving the country and the people we know and moving to a strange, new land — but I will not stand in the academic path of my husband."

She was speaking of the new life she, 26-year-old Mr. Colin Tatz and their 15-month-old baby will lead after Saturday, when they fly to Canberra. There Mr. Tatz is to take up a three-year scholarship at the Australian National University, for a doctorate in political history.

Mr Tatz has been awarded the scholarship for his research for the M.A. degree which the University of Natal has just conferred on him. He is the first South African to have won the scholarship.

Life for the young couple has been difficult. While Mr. Tatz taught at a local college he was working on his M.A. — and supporting his family.

Colin Tatz

I asked Mrs. Tatz if her husband intended going into practical politics.

"Definitely not," she replied. "In this country he has been studying the political history of the Native, and in Australia he will study Aboriginal history and draw a parallel between the two."

And after that? "My husband would like to take up a post at a university, anywhere in the world." Mrs. Tatz told me.

"It wouldn't really matter where we went—as long as there was a typewriter to type his thesis!"

Jet arrives from New York

By the Air Correspondent

The Pan American DC8 jet clipper "Nightingale" arrived at Jan Smuts Airport at 1.35 a.m. today on a proving flight from New York.

The aircraft carried 10 senior officials of the American Federal Aviation Agency and a crew of 11.

The DC8 is due to take off from Jan Smuts this afternoon on its return to the United States.

Pan American will inaugurate its new jet service between New York and Johannesburg on January 3.

On the eve of departure, December 1960.

we were going to Australia for a three-year scholarship and the way was open to return. The university had given us three-fifths of the fares (after adjusting the assisted boat passages) and costs, keeping the remainder for a return, should we wish it. The whole family took to rationalising this as our coming back some time later and that helped ease tensions and grief. But we knew and deep down they knew that this was it. Sandy was seven months pregnant with Karen, Paul was fifteen months old and here we were taking away precious grandchildren. Perhaps all that family dysfunction had blunted my feelings about leaving them, but watching them see their grandchild disappearing was deeply painful. All the upper lips were kept stiff and the family talk was about 'Colin continuing his training' without any idea about the purpose thereof; there was no guilt-laden reproof, no questioning of why we were leaving and why we were so disenchanted with that way of life. Good for them because it made departure very much easier. Another piece of perversity: most migrating families are awash with guilt or castigation for 'leaving the sinking ship'. We left with blessings, a total of £400 and a quality Buhkara rug given to us by Bess.

Part III:
Post-Natal

Chapter 8

A PAIR OF HOLDENS

A nervous newcomer, I had a sense of adventure and a feeling of a clean start. The past wasn't quite unclean but it carried a heavy pall—deep shadows of a many-hued South Africa, shrouds of family history and a continuing sense of darkness within. I was more than ready to discard much of that baggage. Adventure, yes, but I was about to plunge into an unexpectedly depressing realm of Australia's race relations.

Despite the constant hullabaloo one hears (and has to endure), emigration wasn't all that difficult. But what of immigration? For over five decades I've listened to South African emigrés whinge about how much better things were back there (if it weren't for the Blacks); about how much nicer homes were there than those they now own in prized suburbs; and how irksome it is to have doctors who don't make house calls. And this, mind you, from many people who, in extraordinary numbers, had the means to come on look-see visits to check out the terrain, the schools, *shuls*, doctors, dentists, tax advisers and Mercedes mechanics.

For me at 26 it was a triple jump forward; for Sandra, 21, about to have a second child, it was often taxing and miserable. We had the Persian rug, the £400 and ourselves; we had to make it because there was never a question of going back. I needed a good degree to get a decent job and I was hell-bent on both.

* * *

Scene: over 37°C at Perth airport on New Year's Day 1961 after interminable flying time, flies massing, a wife heavily pregnant and apprehensive, a child fractious and people talking in drawly, twangy, sing-song cadences. First, 'Ow ye goin', mate?'—the phatic speech, the introductory non-speech form which I took literally. It came from the immigration official. 'Fine, and how about you?' I replied. Astonished, he sensed an impertinence. Second, I asked a cop where I could find a telegraph office; he walked me there, waited till I was done and bade me welcome to a new life. Back there, the mere sight of an eighteen-year-old uniformed Afrikaner youth (Black policemen were not armed) with a .45 Colt on his belt would have you pretending to window shop or suddenly decide to cross the road as cops were everybody's enemy, not people of whom you asked questions. This, I whispered to Sandra, is *the* place for us and henceforth I would twang, sing-song my sentences, *pak the kah* rather than *pork the core*. Even on this absurdly flimsy basis I felt that this was a place where I could belong.

We were met and taken home by Alec and Zelda Kowarsky, a caring pair of 1948 emigrés who were unwilling to live under that authoritarian regime. Alec took me to meet psychologist Ron Taft at the University of Western Australia, one of few Jewish academics there (or anywhere in Australia). Ron took me to his colleague Ronald Berndt, Reader in Anthropology: florid, fob-watched and an inveterate pipe smoker, he listened to my plans.

Earlier I had proposed a research topic to Leicester Webb on Australian 'Native Policy' but believed that the subject might already have been truly done over, a reasonable expectation about such a numerically small minority. No, he cabled, it hadn't been, so stay with that. Berndt—one of the few social anthropologists then remotely interested in current 'welfare matters'—was encouraging, giving me names and profiles of 'useful' anthropologists like WEH (Bill) Stanner. He dialled his wife Catherine to join us. Now puce rather than florid, he spluttered that Catherine (he called her Kaffwyn) wouldn't see me: 'Kaffwyn doesn't talk to Souf Africans on principle'. In later years we three were amicable colleagues.

The Perth stop was to be at Mike Hall's wedding, held over until we could be there. Mike and I were now on different tracks and the Damelin-duplicate dream was over. The stopover was pleasant, apart from massive mosquito bites and finding that even when plunging under waves 30 m out to sea, small, sticky flies congregated on forehead, eyebrows, eyelashes, lips and in nostrils. The next ten days were in Melbourne to see how the Israel and Nayman families were settling in and to get the feel of a city we might live in one day; we did, just over three years later. It seemed vibrant enough, Caulfield warm enough with its specialty bagel shops, a suburb that was always to be way out of our financial league.

For us, Canberra was at 10 Moorehouse Street, O'Connor, in one of the Australian National University's block of eight maisonettes for married students. Each dwelling had one downstairs area that comprised a living and eating-bar, kitchenette and adjacent laundry, two bedrooms and a bathroom upstairs, a wood-burner with metal chimney pipe that passed between the two single beds in the main bedroom, two square metres each of vegetable garden out the back, walls paper thin, ideal places for children to contract earache, croup and gastroenteritis. No phones or television or washing machines but a laundry with a copper tub the likes of which we had never seen and knew nothing of. Sandra could have been spared the handwashing of thousands of nappies. Taking the garbage out to the street was foreign. It still is. Neighbours came from Pakistan, Thailand, New Zealand, Kenya, Britain, Canada and one couple was Australian. Most were there for us when Karen was born shortly after we arrived; and still there when Simon was born in 1963.

On the first day I walked to the nearest pay phone, looked up J for Jewish, found a number and spoke to a public servant, David Smith, later the official secretary to five Governors-General and knighted. Stay where you are, he said, and 20 minutes later we were under his family's friendly wing. The very small Jewish community met for a few services at the Riverside Huts and for the High Holy Days in a hired trade union hall, and although we couldn't contribute financially we were accepted as fully-fledged members of that small society.

On day three I jammed Paul's finger in a flyscreen door. Two residents had cars and both were busy so we took a cab to the Canberra Community Hospital—whereafter I rushed to blow our entire capital on a 1954 FJ Holden sedan, described as 'crame with marone seats'. Our stake in Australia was now at a nerve-wracking low—the rug and a fortnightly stipend of £38 ($76), £10 of which went in rent.

Canberra was then a quaint country town of some 40,000 people, relatively lifeless and essentially soulless. On a Sunday the only cafe open was the Blue Moon in Civic Centre downtown, a place to buy a bottle of milk or a cup of coffee until four in the afternoon. Entertainment was largely what was on offer from the university. Life on a small stipend was tough rather than grim. Once a fortnight, two or three of us would journey to neighbouring Queanbeyan in New South Wales, pool money to buy a whole or half a sheep, have it butchered and distributed. Lamb lard lingered in our dwellings. Sandra and I clung to the tradition of having a fridge full of food on a Friday eve; some neighbours chose slabs of beer, stacks of sherry or cartons of claret, a predilection we found hard to comprehend but soon learned to accept. One or two bought rabbits, a dish I found difficult to handle. Rabbits weren't kosher in Lithuania, or anywhere else for that matter, and we had no experience of the creatures.

There was just enough money to buy a fortnightly tank of petrol, rationing weekend trips to nearby leisure places like Cotter Dam and little towns like Hall, even Bungendore. We bought an Australian Silky Terrier, a toy rather than a dog, small enough for the pockets of Sandra's maternity outfits. We named him Tickey after a South African threepenny coin. But we gave him to a neighbour when my fieldwork started and Sandra, regrettably, returned to Africa for the six months that I was to spend in the desert regions of the Territory.

There were no Australian-born kids in Moorhouse Street and all were too young to be in kindergarten. There was no television, only radio with impeccable announcers. Yet, astonishingly, when about 20 months, Karen would say that she wanted to go outside 'to royd me boyk'. Aussie strine accent notwithstanding, she and Paul were bright and I would bring them endless books from the library. One was on the fauna and flora of Australia and there, shamelessly, was a chapter on Aborigines.

***

Excited by this new life, but apprehensive, I attended the weekly ANU Politics seminars which included fellow doctoral students and about a dozen staff. After the first one I told Sandra I didn't understood a word and had perhaps chosen the wrong career. Ditto the next two. I then started asking questions, discovering that I had the ability to think critically and that my little red-brick provincial education in little colonial Natal could hold its own with the tuition and training offered by Oxford, London and Toronto. South African training was, in the main, of high quality—until the worst of the draconian years, the early 1970s to the mid-1990s, the period when cultural and academic boycotts became the norm and the country was cut off from the currents of world events, ideas and creativity.

The published material on Aboriginal policies and their administration took barely three days to read. The literature was almost entirely anthropological and redolent of quaint evolutionary relics—rich in details about dental plaque among Centralian tribes, their haemoglobins and haptoglobins, skull measurements, totemic hero cults, mortuary rites, bride promissory systems and their circumcision and sub-incision practices. Truly objects of scientific curiosity in such writings, with no indication of the laws and conditions under which they lived while they were studied in this way. The impression was always that the 'objects' under scrutiny were in some pristine state, unaltered by their enforced sedentary and confined lives on government settlements and church missions. It gave new meaning to the phrase 'to be taken out of context'. In neither Africa nor the Americas was there ever an ethnicity so dominated, so 'ruled', by the domain of anthropology.

At one point I drafted (with Ted Egan) a satirical dictionary of *Ab*(original) words—like *abscissa*, an instrument for cutting hair in a segregated barber shop. In the end we quit the project because it was too much of a swipe at anthropologists. The manuscript ('Poor Bugger Me') is in the library at what is now called the Australian Institute for Aboriginal and Torres Strait Islander Studies (AIATSIS) in Canberra.

I wanted to compare the way the Commonwealth did things in the Northern Territory (which it administered) with Queensland's care of Aborigines. Following genocidal massacres in the nineteenth century, colonial (and state) governments began protection by segregating the victims from people who, in no particular order, wanted to kill them, take their women or sell them opium. Protection by special statutes wasn't sufficient and so geographic isolation became an essential part of the system. Archibald Meston, appointed in 1896 to inquire into the Queensland slaughters, recommended 'absolute isolation' from the Whites who, 'coloured by prejudice, distorted by ignorance', committed 'shameful deeds'. The killings stopped (for the most part), as did the hunter-gatherer way of life, and sedentary institutional life began.

It was clear that this was quite different from the South African scenario: a small minority, (then) about 1.5 percent of the population (if that), as opposed to 80 percent; clans once hunter-gatherers and now confined as opposed to large tribes who were pastoralists and agriculturalists; an allegedly stateless people as opposed to fully-fledged tribal empires, complete with obvious chiefs, kings, courts and law-makers; a people perceived as fauna or curiosities as opposed to a people to be respected, albeit through real or imagined fear; a forgotten or disdained remnant of the Stone Age in contrast to a people who daily occupied one's space, mind and politics.

My supervisor was ex-New Zealander Robert Parker, a public administration expert who knew nothing of Aboriginal affairs but was brilliant at how a thesis should be constructed and presented. He had contacts within the (then) Department of Territories, organised regionally with units devoted to each of Papua–New Guinea, the Northern Territory, Antarctica and other possessions. Territories Minister Paul Hasluck insisted that every decision had to have his approval: he told me he'd been a public servant and he didn't trust the species. He liked the fact that I didn't belong to any of the denominations which ran missions, that I had a solid background in race relations from abroad. He declared me suited to assessing how his policies were faring; he approved of me, the project and the time frame. I was given the necessary permit to visit all Aboriginal centres of population. This permission included access to official current records without which this anthropology (or vivisection) of a White bureaucracy couldn't be done. A wily but doubting senior officer was appointed my watchdog and liaison man. It took him six months to 'clear' three files for me, a rate that would still have had me writing the thesis in 2015. Once in the Territory, the Director of Welfare Harry Giese said it was a matter of trust and good sense and he gave me access to all but one file. Parker approached Dr WS Noble, Minister for Native Affairs in Queensland. If the Commonwealth Government agreed to my proposal, he said, so would Queensland: in the end they said yes to fieldwork but there would be no access to records.

The eminent anthropologist Donald Thomson (with whom I worked later in Victoria) had done research on Queensland missions in the 1930s and then written some highly critical things about Presbyterian operations there for a Melbourne newspaper. Native Affairs was angry and ultra-wary, shutting off all further access to Aborigines. We ruled out what could have been a lopsided comparison and so the main focus was on the Territory.

Aboriginal administration had been sealed off from the start of the protection-segregation era in domains known as reserves. Christian missions and government-run settlements on such lands, secluded from the wider world, operating under special legislation that couldn't apply to other Australians. Permits to enter were rarely given, reasons had to be exceptional and one had to have a less-than-one-month-old chest x-ray for entry, ostensibly to prevent the spread of tuberculosis but in practice an effective way to keep people out. Journalists and curious others had no chance of observing anything in a world not only closed but close to the paranoid.

Despite the Minister's go-ahead I waited six months for a clearance from the Australian Security Intelligence Organisation (ASIO). It wasn't time lost. Our daughter Karen was born in March at the Community Hospital (now the site of the National Museum) with high drama. Sandra lost a lot of blood; the doctor attending refused to listen to explanations about Paul's problem birth. I learned what touch-and-go meant. Sandra deeply felt the absence of a mother or mother-in-law or aunt or cousin at that crucial time.

Eight days after Karen was born I was urged to fly to Brisbane to attend a meeting of the Federal Council for Aboriginal Advancement (FCAA), then three years young and the federal roof body of the many affiliated (private) organisations interested in Aboriginal welfare and progress. I made some lifelong friends but I didn't make a friend of Sandra, leaving her utterly alone in Canberra with two babies in nappies. My rationalisation then, and even now, is that I simply had to do the research that would help me get the degree that would help me get the job that would help me attain some safety for a migrant family.

I was accustomed to sophisticated Black politics. After all, the African National Congress was founded way back in 1912, and many of its leaders were doctors of philosophy or medicine, many with degrees from abroad. But even allowing for unfair contextual and historical comparisons, this conference was pathetic, the level of knowledge quite abysmal. A mature Perth lady, for example, presented her 'paper' on the state of affairs in the West. Ned, she said, had a clubfoot, the Department of Native Affairs had commissioned the appropriate boots but of the wrong size and refused to pay for another pair. Could she ask delegates for a donation? That was it. Other reports were better but not by much. Rhetoric, anger and breast-beating were evident but there was very little reliable information. The walls around the rural and remote peoples seemed impenetrable. In later years FCAA was to become more professional, the conferences better organised and held regularly in Canberra, the critiques better researched and presented. Joe McGinness, Kath Walker, Faith Bandler, Mick Miller and Charlie Perkins were forceful in presenting Aboriginal and Islander viewpoints; Gordon Bryant, Stan Davey, Barrie Pittock and Don Dunstan were significant non-Aboriginal voices. My role was always as a resource, an insider who could verify the constant maladministration.

I began rewarding meetings with different people at ANU. The much older Ian Turner and I had a common interest in sport and jazz. In the common room I had asked, perhaps too loudly, who on campus was interested in sport. Social philosopher Percy Partridge, then head of the Research School, peered over his glasses and murmured that if anyone present wanted to write about sport he should go study elsewhere. Some colleagues thought we were 'queer for sport'. Ian went to Monash University before I did and we both had to wait until we were well established in some other field before we could 'come out' and write about sport. Ian specialised in Australian Rules football and I covered sport in general.

I was befriended by Sir Keith Hancock, the doyen of Australia's historians, then writing a two-volume biography of General Jan Smuts. He asked to read my South African book-in-manuscript, particularly on the Natives' Representative Council created by Hertzog in 1936. In the Smuts volumes he acknowledged that chapter, saying he'd checked the sources, the work was 'sound' and he had used it. I was chuffed. The eminent Professor of Law Geoffrey Sawer was welcoming and most helpful on the legal aspects of my work. Sawer was then editing manuscripts of the late Justice Martin Kriewaldt, the Territory judge who was to declare that in all his years on the bench he was convinced that not a single Aboriginal accused understood the nature of the charges or the proceedings.

I had an especial friendship with John Playford, then studying the Communist Party in Australia. A member of the conservative dynastic Playford clan that ruled South Australia for so long, when John's first child was born I went with him to send a telegram to the family: 'Kliment Voroshilov born today, 8 pounds 6 ounces'. The squires squawked in Adelaide. John compromised on the name of this recently retired Soviet statesman and called him plain John! The older John introduced me to 'Boris', if that was indeed his name, a White Russian working for Immigration. Boris had copied endless telegrams from recruiting agents in Europe, many stating that applicants had Lithuanian, Latvian or other SS tattoos and asking for advice on what to do. The replies were uniform: as long as they are blond, blue-eyed, strong and not dark or swarthy 'Mediterranean types', take them. A profound shock to my newly arrived system and I suggested he pass this on to an appropriate Jewish organisation. He did just that—to the Jewish Council to Combat Fascism and Anti-Semitism, founded in 1942 in Melbourne. They passed the information to ASIO, which then investigated the 'Communist' Council rather than the Nazi war criminals listed in the dossier, the content of which came to the surface very much later, and loudly, in 1986.

There were many invitations to talk about South Africa and while this constant talking about that place and its problems was a way of maintaining links with a recent past, it wasn't nostalgia. The Committee for Human Rights in South Africa asked me to join. Instead I supplied them with accurate information and wrote some of their fact pamphlets. Two articles on South African themes were published in reputable journals, one on Christian National Education and its goal of brainwashing an entire nation and another on Dr Verwoerd's 'Bantustan' policies. These were my first journal articles.

The South African ambassador, Hamilton, a career diplomat, was then awaiting transfer to Sweden. We walked in parks because he feared (with good reason) surveillance by his embassy staff. A chance arose to meet Sir Robert Menzies, briefly, to inform him and Minister Paul Hasluck that a number of South Africans who had been 'deemed' Communists under the

1950 *Suppression of Communism Act* weren't Communists at all but often opponents of that ideology. This was the time of a very Cold War but they paid some heed about allowing some 'political' people to come in as migrants. In South Africa, men of Cabinet rank were remote, almost extra-terrestrial beings; here one could have access, discussion and civil argument. The contrast was breathtaking.

John Barnes, head of Anthropology, asked Parker for a meeting with him and his Reader, Bill Stanner. They proposed that I leave Politics to join Anthropology where I could undertake something neat and unmessy, like a 'nice' study of Aboriginal policy until 1900, supervised by Stanner. I was new, pretty insecure and at a loss: Parker said we'd talk further but quietly told me that this transfer wasn't going to happen.

Stanner was about to convene a major meeting at University House on the establishment of an Australian Institute of Aboriginal Studies (AIAS later AIATSIS), an independent body that would conduct research into the disappearing aspects of Aboriginal culture 'before it is too late'. The primary approach would be anthropological, defined and promoted as *the* 'science' needed for such work. Unstated but clearly understood was the injunction that the AIAS-to-be would *not* embrace 'current welfare problems'. Stanner's attempt to appropriate (and contain) me was as much to do with this mandate as it was about protecting the fieldwork preserves of ANU and the University of Sydney. Clearly he remembered Thomson and the aftermath in Queensland: he told me in so many words that he feared I would or could cruel the pitch for the future of this 'near-extinction-rescue' scholarship.

Stanner knew something of my ideas from Les Hiatt, then writing up his doctorate on kinship and conflict resolution at Maningrida in Arnhem Land (NT). Les and I golfed once or twice a week as student members of Federal Golf Club. He was pondering his ideas and I was waiting for ASIO. Although I was never a member of Stanner's adoration brigade, he was gracious about Parker's decision and resigned to my research. He suggested I attend the AIAS inaugural May meeting, on condition I said nothing about my intended work. I remained silent, with difficulty. Years later, in May 2011, I gave a speech at University House on the fiftieth anniversary of that meeting: I was one of only three surviving and still active members of the May 1961 group.

At one point, Sandra felt she couldn't cope with my intended fieldwork absence of at least fifteen months, so I asked for a change in topic, something sedentary (dull?) like the governance of the Australian Capital Territory. Unprompted, Robert Parker called to see Sandra, convincing her that this Aboriginal affairs exercise was crucial and a serious contribution to society. She listened and, as always, put my interests and ambitions ahead of hers.

***

I was grateful to Australia just for our being here. I looked to all the positives and was eager to see something different and something better in the treatment of native peoples. Exploratory field visits were essential. In May–June 1961, I headed for the Territory and Queensland. I met the energetic and always optimistic Harry Giese. He had been appointed Director of the Welfare Branch of the NT Administration a few years earlier, replacing Frank Moy in what had been the small Department of Native Affairs. In Alice Springs I was introduced all round, meeting a great deal of scepticism by the District Welfare Officer. Les Penhall, very senior in the Welfare Branch, drove me west, with much kindness and advice, to Jay Creek, Haasts Bluff, Hermannsburg Mission, Papunya, Yuendumu and Areyonga settlements and to Amoonguna, adjacent to Alice. During my long fieldwork days I lodged at Amoonguna, some seventeen kilometres southwest of Alice on some of the worst stretches of road imaginable.

At Yuendumu I met the initially suspicious superintendent Ted Egan, a man who told me he'd only ever read one book, the Bible. Much later, in one of the many books he wrote, he said something about his first meeting with

Ted Egan influenced my approach to Aboriginal affairs.

me and 'trusting my big brown eyes'. He tells me he still does (over 50 years on) and that pleases me greatly.

Les Penhall told me a Land Rover wasn't necessary—it seemed to be an essential for anthropologists who traversed the same areas of my study but who almost always managed to write off these vehicles—and that a manual gearbox Holden station wagon would do nicely. He taught me how to handle the soft sandy creeks, to organise jerrycans of water, extra spare tyres, rolls of mosquito netting (for flies more than mossies), a shovel and a an absolutely essential item—at least two six-foot strips of wire in case I got bogged. I typed a memo to Percy Partridge requesting an exchange of vehicles. He asked why. I answered briefly that a Land Rover cost four to fives times as much as a Holden. Don't be a smart-arse he replied, justify the change. Three pages of detail and drivel later he thanked me for the fine explanation and I was supplied with a Holden with sump and petrol tank guards welded underneath to prevent stones penetrating the machine's private parts. Later, two road kills secured the necessary kangaroo bars up front. (When I returned the intact and unscarred vehicle some sixteen months later, ANU was shocked: they'd written it off in their ledgers as per the anthropological tradition.)

In Brisbane I had a formal interview with the Director of Native Affairs Cornelius (Con) O'Leary, the most dinosaurian of the old-style, prehistoric administrators. In an ante-room I overheard him tell two complaining farmers that he'd rip their fucking heads off if they underpaid 'his' Blackfellas. His immediate opening to me was: 'Who are ya, where'd ya come from and whose paying ya?' I told him. Whereupon he said to meet him at a specific hotel round the corner at 4.30. Quaffing more than a few beers (as I matched him with brandies) he leaned over: 'I like the cut of your jib' he mumbled, 'you're on—go where you bloody well like but no records, mind you'. I blanched at the official letter he later wrote to all his staff: 'You are at all times to treat this man with dignity and respect.' Nobody had ever articulated admiration for my jib nor ordered such bureaucratic respect.

I had a brief meeting with O'Leary's deputy Pat Killoran, then based in the Torres Straits, who was to succeed him. Both men were the toughest of narrow Irish Catholics, both oblivious to an outside world, ill-educated, not well-schooled in that ubiquitous 'university of hard knocks', both imbued with implacable beliefs that they knew what was good for Blacks. They didn't.

The fieldwork preparations were successful but also painful. We had been advised (by Stanner mainly) that the Territory was no place for babies, no milk, few doctors and dreadful ailments. We had no relatives, no friends close enough to host Sandra and the children, and so with great reluctance I borrowed a large sum to send the family back to South Africa, ostensibly for about six to eight months, to stay alternately with her father Ben, an aunt of Sandra's and Bess. With great sadness and much trepidation we parted. My steps were hugely forward, hers backward. Ben and Elsa concluded that the marriage was finished, that I'd sent my wife and family packing while I cavorted with wild savages in the wilderness. I suspect that my family had the same feelings, though nothing was ever said or hinted.

Later we found that Alice had an adequate hospital, a few fine doctors and nurses—and a lot of milk, even if powdered. Back 'home' again, Sandra was shuffled and pushed around amidst much bickering. The only bonus was her work with Natal University Press, making suggestions, editing and proofing my MA thesis, resulting in the production of an excellent text with a remarkably good index, and graphic cover drawing by Jack Heath. Within a year a second run of another thousand copies of *Shadow and Substance* was needed.

Ben broke his promise to pay for Sandra's return to Australia with the children. She borrowed the return fare and the family joined me in Darwin after only six months of separation. In that interim period I wrote Sandra voluminous, lonely letters, forever trying to explain, perhaps justify, what must have seemed a very strange lifestyle, always eager (and anxious) for her exquisitely written accounts of life and lament back there.

For the long field research, the university supplied me with the armoured station wagon, safari paraphernalia, petrol and service vouchers and a field allowance greater than the travel expenses of the entire Politics Department for a year. I drove to Port Augusta, dropping off Marlene, the wife of one of my colleagues then in a temporary lectureship in Adelaide. En route we stopped in Gundagai and at a tearoom we bumped into a couple I'd met prior to migration, Rabbi Rudy and Mrs Brasch from Sydney.

The rabbi's nieces were at Damelin at the time and when they heard of our intended move, invited me to meet uncle Rudy for the lowdown on Australia. He asked me what I paid for the matches in my hand. A penny. Aha, he confided, you'll never make it in Australia where they cost fourpence. He elaborated: his Woollahra congregation in Sydney gave him free transport, accommodation and food in addition to his salary, leaving him 'just able to manage'. The rabbi made a mint and some kind of reputation out of books about the origins of everything, including sex and sport (separately). Meeting him again in Gundagai I introduced him and his wife Lee. They had not stopped staring at the long-legged, very tall, blonde *shikse*: meet Marlene, I said and walked away. About a year later we met again at a social event atop Mt Stromlo Observatory. Seeing me with Sandra, the couple exchanged relieved looks. No doubt they recited the prayer dedicated to those who were mistakenly thought to be adulterers.

On leaving Canberra, a visiting scholar, Michael Liffman, said I should look up his cousin in Port Augusta. Arriving there, and with a day or so to spare before boarding the 'Ghan train to Alice, I asked locals where I could find Leslie Lewis. They gave me a phone number. He answered, gave me directions and I duly arrived at Her Majesty's Penitentiary. He took me on a tour of 'his' Pen, the prisoners greeting him warmly, asking if son Gerald's cold was better. He offered me a drink from the biggest, finest liquor cabinet I'd ever seen: he didn't drink but one of his 'boys' was a carpenter and built it for him as a present. I drank and asked questions. What the hell was he doing here in one of the world's most misbegotten of places? Well, he explained, he came to Australia as a tailor, retiring from an East End of London *schmatte* (rag trade) business. In a recession here he couldn't make out. He was urged to apply for an entry to the state public service, which he did, whereupon he was invited by the Prison Service for an interview. The panel liked the look of him which was in fact unimpressive (he was the quintessential Jewish tailor in Wolf Mankowitz's movie, *A Kid for Two Farthings*), and they admired his values as they emerged from his entry tests. He became an apprentice warder in Adelaide, took and topped all the exams, was quickly promoted and now was in charge of South Australia's second largest of nine prisons. *L'chaim*, I toasted, to life and to his final destination, the big one in Adelaide, proof indeed of Jewish world domination even here at the head of Spencer Gulf. His son was taking drumming lessons by correspondence and from an inmate and I was asked to listen to this red-headed Gerald Krupa belting away, unaccompanied, in a room built into the colossal sandstone tower walls in relative coolth to the furnace outdoors. Mrs Lewis urged me to stay for dinner, which I did, and to eat more, which I did. The flavour of it all kept me going. But for many a year, that was my last encounter with anything remotely Jewish.

The 'Ghan, so named in honour of the original Afghan camel drivers who delivered the mail, travelled 1,200 km from Port August to Alice Springs, changing railway gauges en route. A stop at Oodnadatta, a landscape of gibber plains, loose rocks and stones for hundreds of miles—seemingly the very end of the earth, a place where tourists delighted at throwing pennies out the window for little piccaninnies to scoop up, not unlike feeding chips to gulls at Bondi Beach but less nutritious. It was half way to what I came to call 'the kingdom of the mad'.

Chapter 9

GULLIVER

The Territory was a place of inversion. It still is, even after the reconstruction and growth that followed the catastrophe of Darwin's Cyclone Tracy in 1974. Nothing was as it seemed, something I learned very quickly. Values weren't what you thought they were or should be, people weren't who they appeared to be, professionalism wasn't what that word means in a normal society. You learned not to ask (non-Aboriginal) people why they were there, or where their spouses were (the same applied to me, of course), or who or what they were evading in this outré outpost.

The place is bigger than Germany, France, Italy, Hungary, Luxembourg and Holland put together with 5,000 sq km to spare. In 1961, 18,400 Aborigines lived in the Territory, almost half the population of 44,704. The notion that such a Brobdingnagian landscape could be run, let alone tamed, by so Lilliputian a population was just one part of this often beautiful, sometimes dreary, but decidedly *dafke* domain.

I once drove 3,500 km from Darwin to Mount Allan Station and back for what satirist Jonathan Swift would have called a Yahoo Christmas party. It did last four days—appropriate, given the local folkways. Quadruple was the right description of everything: the quantity of flies, the size of the mosquitoes, the tall tales, the percentage of disordered personalities, the drinking appetites, diseased livers, broken marriages and the improbable dreams of statehood among other things. That particular party began with some men biting the heads off dead crows, ending with men 'bullfighting' by getting down on all fours and head-butting each other. I declined that one. I was now faced with two new states of being: cut off from what little I had come to know of 'normal' Australia and bereft of the relatively saner and certainly the softer, *shmaltzier* worlds of Mrs Slotkin and Mr Lewis.

* * *

The abiding issues discussed in my doctoral research (1961–1964) have, for the most part, remained abiding. Many of the disasters of today began earlier than the 1950s and 1960s, but their 'refinement', and several new ones, certainly emerged in the decades I studied. Here I traverse some of the realities I confronted because they help explain why there are so many disordered communities and hapless 'solutions' to this day.

For years now governments have clamoured about 'closing the gap' between White and Black Australians. I found gulfs rather than gaps between the two peoples, divides far greater than simply the statistics of social indicators like life expectancy and infant mortality. The work I began in 1961 is still my work in 2015: so much remains unfinished business for Aborigines, governments, the public and for Australia's record on human rights.

Who or what was the problem? Simply put, governments (and organisations) initiate a policy and expect it to work in practice. When it doesn't, they tend to see shortfalls in the policy which they either amend or repudiate. They rarely ask what causes the initial failure—commonly that the administrative machinery that exists to transport or translate policy into practice is either the wrong mechanism or it has serious engine trouble and simply can't deliver. Such was my case study.

To obviate international criticism and to provide equality for Aborigines in the 'land of the "fair go"', Paul Hasluck expounded his major policy in 1951. Assimilation would 'ensure that all Aborigines and part-Aborigines would attain the same manner of living as other Australians and live as members of a single Australian community, enjoy the same rights and privileges, accept the same responsibilities, observe the same customs and be influenced by the same beliefs, hopes and loyalties as other Australians'. Any special measures would be temporary, *not* based on colour, to protect the people from the ill effects of sudden change. There was to be no segregation, no assembly-line approach, only an individuated social rather than racial approach to a people 'whose only future lay in the White community'. 'Careful social engineering' would bridge the cultural and tribal divides, specifically through education and vocational training. Surprisingly, perhaps, he supported bilingual and bicultural education. Aborigines should enjoy 'full citizenship rights', disease had to be eradicated, trade union membership encouraged, equal wages paid; they should be housed 'after the normal Australian manner', recreational facilities had to be provided, and sporting and social contact encouraged. Nothing was said about political rights—and I was soon to find out why.

My introduction to Aboriginal sport, Areyonga Settlement, 1961.

Such general goals of non-discrimination and social justice befitted a proud democracy. But since White settlement in 1788, Aborigines have never been equals in anything and so the trick here was how to provide some correctional balance without creating further inequalities, how to provide 'primitives' (a Hasluck word) with new 'beliefs, hopes and loyalties' without further demeaning or further harming pretty damaged hunter-gatherers whose ancestors had spent 60,000 years in the landscape. How could one redress major imbalances and then provide 'citizenship plus', that is, some approximation of parity and then the additional pluses, the 'catch-up-close-the-gap' benefits?

How realistic were the policy ideals? Was there an appropriate context for these aspirations or a suitable administration structure to enable their achievement? If yes, how competent were the 'social engineers' involved? And if there was a gap between the government's aspirations and the realities on the ground, what were the obstacles and why were they present? The same questions beg for answers today.

* * *

One third of the Aboriginal population lived on thirteen government settlements, one third on fourteen church-run mission stations, and the remaining third lived or worked on cattle stations. Fourteen months were spent visiting 25 communities, measuring the policy *aims* against the realities on the ground and looking critically at the policy *claims* about achievements in light of the empirical evidence. How could 18,400 Aborigines, spread across these 1.34 million square kilometres, assimilate into 'European society' then comprising 4,648 citizens of Alice Springs, 12,326 in Darwin, 1,368 in Tennant Creek, 826 in Katherine and some 500 in each of Batchelor and Pine Creek? These urban residents were hardly members of a 'single Australian community' sharing the same hopes, loyalties, customs and beliefs.

Not all the Aboriginal communities were alike. Pintupi people at Papunya had emerged only in the 1950s from a desert nomadic life and the nearby Arrente people at Hermannsburg had been made sedentary and 'missionised' 70 years earlier. Many had different histories, languages, customs and, all too clearly, diverse legacies of contact with the outside world. They still do.

The context was improbable: six essentially White but very small urban settlements with dozens of geographically separated Aboriginal institutions and cattle stations with varying populations, cattle the only serious economic resource for some of them, and a bureaucratic structure centred in a Canberra largely ignorant, oblivious or not interested in the domain they were administering from afar. Apart from the Catholics, whose Bishop JP O'Loughlin lived and ruled from Darwin, the other three mission operations—Lutheran, Anglican and Methodist—were administered from Sydney and Adelaide by those also largely ignorant of or uninterested in the field. Classic colonialism where policies are devised in a metropolis and exported as universally applicable to outposts where they are inappropriate or incapable of implementation.

Certain terms now considered offensive were used officially. The *Aboriginals Ordinance* (1918–1953) defined 'full-blood' Aborigines and an array of people called 'half-castes'. The restyled Chief Protector, now the Director of Welfare, could 'undertake the care, custody and control' of any Aborigine if he felt it was in his or her best interests. Legal guardian of all Aborigines under eighteen, he could remove an Aborigine from one district to another and remove any groups camping near towns. Whites needed a permit to employ Aborigines and portions of wages had to be paid to the Director. A female Aborigine couldn't marry a non-Aborigine without the Director's consent and sex across the colour line was forbidden, as was drinking or having access to alcohol. Permits were needed to enter reserves and Aborigines couldn't leave them or be enticed from them.

The Ordinance's purpose was to protect all defined Aborigines 'against immorality, injustice, imposition and fraud'. But here was Archibald Meston's

1896 notion of protection turned into its value opposite: incarceration as virtual inmates of institutions, persons with no legal status or civic or civil rights as normally understood.

A masterpiece of sleight-of-hand, the new *Welfare Ordinance*, operational from 1957, allegedly replaced these earlier laws. Hasluck's injunction was that people be dealt with on an *individual* basis, a policy that appeared in the new statute. The Territory Administrator could now declare a person a ward—as if an at-risk minor or an incompetent person in need of state care—by reason of '(a) *his* manner of living; (b) *his* inability, without assistance, adequately to manage his own affairs; (c) *his* standard of social habit and behaviour; and (d) *his* personal associations.' So far so good. But when this Welfare bill came before the Legislative Council, members feared quite irrationally that Harry Giese could take control of non-Aborigines. To pass the law, an escape clause was needed. A bizarre 'preventive' device was found. Since Aborigines couldn't vote and were not expected to do so in the foreseeable future, the solution was that no existing voter, no potential voter (of the proper age) and no potential migrant voter (eligible to vote in time) could *ever* be declared a ward! Whereupon, *all* full-blood Aborigines who could be counted were placed on a Register of Wards and all, irrespective of need or ability to care for themselves, were declared wards, *en masse*.

The Register was a work of monumental contempt. Tribal names were rarely recorded, or recorded accurately, and wards were listed by their 'common' names: Paddy Number One, Paddy Number Two, Red-Ant Paddy, Green-Ant Paddy, Buggerlegs Henry, Hitler, Stalin, Mussolini, Nosepeg, One Pound Jimmy. The latter two elders were renowned: the Warlpiri man Gwoya Jungarai for his portrait on at least two postage stamps and surviving the 1928 Coniston Station massacre; Nosepeg Tjupurrula for his meeting with the Queen and his Pintupi paintings. Like their American slave-owning counterparts, cattlemen displayed their power over a class of serfs by saddling them with such contemptuous names.

Importantly, the 'half-castes', now called part-Aborigines, were no longer under the restrictive special laws, a forward step certainly. My task, Hasluck told me plainly, was 'to look at full-blood affairs, not at the *emancipated* community' (his adjective); hence I didn't delve into such matters as forcible child removals about which I heard a lot and saw a little. In four instances, including artist Albert Namatjira, a ward was exempted from that status and became a 'citizen', complete with a certificate saying as much.

The Ordinance of 84 clauses didn't mention the word Aborigines once yet could apply *only* to Aborigines. It re-inserted almost every clause, verbatim, of the *Aboriginals Ordinance*: no freedom of movement, no marriage or sex across the colour line, no alcohol, legal guardianship and custodianship of all children, no access to firearms. One difference was that all matters to do with employment, wages, training and rations were inserted in the *Wards' Employment Ordinance* (operational from 1959). It prescribed who could employ Aborigines and under what conditions; ration scales; wages in particular industries, pocket money portions to be paid from such wages, and the rest into a trust fund; and housing facilities.

***

Given the legal (and geographic) constraints, the policy aims were unachievable. 1 could well have stopped there. I didn't, but relentlessly explored all aspects of Aboriginal life under these impediments, an inquiry across the entire spectrum of Aboriginal life at that time, and always a lonely one. I began fieldwork in the Centre, moving slowly northwards to Darwin and beyond. I was in Darwin on 2 January 1962, a year and a day after our arrival in Australia and headed for the Immigration Department branch to ask for my citizenship papers, then available after one year for British subjects (which South Africans were then), and a passport. I couldn't wait to shuck off all that South Africa baggage. The political and racial aspects were easy enough to shed but the quintessentially funny-sad Jewish *shtetl* culture was a serious loss. Many friends down south couldn't comprehend this 'surrender of my birthright': I could and found it easy.

Several new friends were part of the group at Darwin airport in April—when Sandra and the children arrived—to see if they were for real. A joyous painful moment: exhilarated at embracing Sandra, but Paul asking 'are you my daddy' and Karen, aged one, not knowing who I was. Ted Egan had been shifted to Bagot Settlement where his active resistance to much of Welfare Branch policy could be kept under observation. Our families met often and Ted enrolled at Queensland University as an external student. I had the pleasure of tutoring him privately in English and Politics, in Shakespeare and Dickens—as a complement to the Bible.

Territorians always vied with Czechoslovakians as the world's number one drinkers. Yet just over 40 percent of the population couldn't drink. Aborigines peering into pub windows and courtyards was a grotesque display of the hapless envying the largely hopeless. I drank more in those two years than in all the years before or since. And without that boozy camaraderie no real information was forthcoming. Swilling with the Welfare Branch boys at 4.30 each day meant holding my own, rushing to the loo to scribble some notes, and swilling again. (Forcing oneself to stay sober while drinking was agony.) I was a brandy man, just short of being a metho drinker in their eyes. Finally I told the boys I'd been diagnosed with cirrhosis. Poor bugger, they chorused, and they gently nursed my remaining days with ginger ale.

Earlier, Ted had told me that one way of repaying hospitality (and information) was to carry a carton (two dozen cans of Victoria Bitter) in the wagon. Arriving at dusty, red and dismal Santa Teresa Mission, I found not only Father Summerhays and his Brothers but the Bishop himself. He'd come down from Darwin to check me out. At dinner he asked me if I'd like a drink. Not knowing (then) whether priests drank, I replied that lemonade was fine, My Lord. (That salutation stuck in the craw, but I got used to it.) Well, son, we're having a beer, he replied. Whereupon I rushed out, grabbed the carton, placed it on the presbytery table and became an instant friend of Rome. We lit cigarettes, listened to the racing results and starters, telegraphed bets, played cards, and made friends. I was baptised.

Things Jewish were at a great remove from this world, but not altogether. At Snake Bay (Milikipati) on Melville Island, I was to go on a day long fishing trip with an elder, Alfred Pickles, and his wives. He asked me to buy provisions at the store for 'our' trip, which I did, whereupon he left me with his half-brother Don to walk the mangroves to a catfish spot while he headed bush for a few weeks on my tab. Every sandfly attacked me, leading to aerial evacuation to Darwin Hospital at Fanny Bay. Placed on an unnetted verandah I was bitten by every mosquito in town. Evacuated by air to Bathurst Island (Nguiu), I was cared for by some marvellous nuns who applied the endless wet bandages to septic limbs. Sister Benedetta killed one of her precious chickens to make me 'medication' and was joyous when I told her that Catholics and Jews had something in common: a saying goes that when a Jewish farmer kills a chicken, one of them must be sick.

The other connection was when I showed my African slide collection—the inevitable giraffes, zebras, hyenas, rhinos, hippos and lions—to the Sunday night after-church mob. They asked me if I was a Jesus man. I explained. So you bin cuttim' cock?, they asked. Yes, and I explained the role of Reverend Glass. Let's see, they enthused. I showed them, they inspected closely and admired the knife work. One of the men explained to all present (women and children at a remove) that here, indeed, was a living Israelite. But they remain semi-converted.

At Snake Bay I was well tutored by the superintendent Brian Greenfield in the ins-and-outs of Aboriginal administration. At the end of my stay he told me the people wanted to say thank you (for what I'm not sure) and the women had been out for three days catching mud crabs for a (non-alcoholic) party on the broken-down jetty. I told Brian I didn't eat seafood but he insisted I be respectful. We conspired: I would wear shorts with four pockets, borrow his safari suit jacket with about six pockets, stuff each pocket with tissues, pretend to take in a mouthful and then spit it into the Kleenex and back into the pocket. Alfred Pickles, no less, took a giant crab, smashed a claw with a brick and handed me this white quivering slab. I bit—and was hooked for life. I'm still trying to catch up on all those missed years of oysters, mussels, prawns, crabs, cuttlefish and lobsters that the Old Testament so misunderstood.

My Catholic experiences were not at an end. I was told to talk to Miss Olive Pink, a knowledgeable, one-time research assistant to the godfather of Australian anthropology, Professor Adolphus Peter Elkin. Straight out of EM Forster's *A Passage to India*, she wore high button boots, ankle length skirt, long-sleeved shirt with ruffs buttoned to her larynx, white cotton gloves and, to top it, a pith helmet. We met at her private nature reserve, given to her by the much-harassed Paul Hasluck. Earlier she had lived alongside the

Miss Olive Pink, courtesy Northern Territory Library.

Alice Springs fire station and complained that the firemen were perving on her while she showered. She attacked Hasluck at all turns. At her new reserve she persuaded Civil Aviation to change the commercial flight paths because she claimed pilots were peeking at her in her outdoor shower hut. Over tea, sherry and madeira cake (bought for the occasion), she made me promise I'd give her 'the inside dope' on what those fiendish Catholics were doing at Santa Teresa mission. Some time later I saw her in Todd Street and ducked fearfully into the pharmacy. She followed and in a quavering, indignant, duchessy Maggie Smith kind of voice said: 'Young man, I had high hopes for you. I planted a tree in your name but since you have broken your promise I'm considering not watering you and letting you wither and die.' I learned nothing from her except venom for Rome.

* * *

My major interest was Aboriginal ill-health, an area that incensed me more than any other. Here I was seeing lack of care, attention, interest—suffused by what was often enough an unconscionable arrogance.

I met Father Frank Flynn, a former Macquarie Street ophthalmologist who was a senior man in the Darwin Catholic diocese. My research showed an incredible divergence in official trachoma statistics between 1954 and 1963. In 1954 there was one case, in 1957 the figure was 2,732, in 1962 only six. Father Flynn and Professor Ida Mann had found the disease called 'sandy blight' and had treated the cases with drops and sometimes by surgery (long before the hallowed Dr Fred Hollows came on the scene). The Commonwealth Health Department, responsible for Aboriginal health, claimed the good Father and the Professor had it wrong and amended the figures after Mann left the region; Flynn was too kind to fight the system.

I had seen appalling health among the Zulu and Pondo peoples in Natal and been encouraged by the integrated community health projects run by

Sidney Kark. I was keen, even desperate, to get some of this across to the Territory personnel, to make them see that what they were dealing with wasn't unique, that much of it was possible to alleviate, even resolve. They admitted to not knowing what they were up against or why Aboriginal health was so wretched and so they retreated into the safe zone of convincing themselves that all that was wrong was *normal for Aborigines*. Ten years later I would write one of my best critical essays, *The Politics of Aboriginal Health*—about the paradox of innovation without change. Little has changed in the main but nowadays there is more death from non-natural causes, more death from cancer, cardiac, renal and metabolic disease. I could simply have observed and recorded. But there was too much that was odious and dubious, not quite evil in intent but pretty close. Fiddling statistics was one spur to finding out what was really happening. Almost every statistic relating to health and infant death was fiddled and finagled to read—in official reports to Canberra—'health continues to be good'.

Disease data collection was a parody: patients were often assembled at airstrips with visiting doctors allowed an hour or two at most by the aerial medical pilots, doctors doing the most cursory of examinations, diagnosing on mere sight and making prisoner-like scratches against predetermined lists. I had a showdown with the chief pilot and with Harry Giese about these airstrip 'diagnoses', demanding to know if Mr Pilot would approve of his wife having her gynaecological problems assessed and discussed in a waiting room full of patients. 'How dare you!' yelled the fly man. I dared.

At Snake Bay a twelve-year-old was stung by a deadly box jellyfish. The sister did her best, the aerial medical base was closed for the weekend, the pilots wouldn't fly after 4 p.m. and there was no oxygen on the settlement. We were shown how to do mouth-to-mouth but the boy died at dawn. I later roared into Giese's office and demanded to know why there was no oxygen cylinder. I don't believe it's necessary said this Master of Physical Education. When I assailed the head of Health, he said his department wasn't responsible for settlement and mission health. And so it went, the division and deflection of responsibility between branches and departments, always to the point where the buck never stopped anywhere, and no one was responsible for anything, *und so weiter* to this day.

The original leprosarium was at Channel Island, run by the Little Sisters of Mercy. Aboriginal children born there were never returned to parents but taken to Bathurst Island as Catholics-in-waiting. Moved to East Arm Leprosarium on the mainland, the dedicated Dr John Hargrave tried to have the institution closed. (That only happened in 1964.) Both the Health Department and Welfare were adamant about maintaining the 1954 *Leprosy Ordinance* which, *inter alia*, mandated that a policeman could bring a suspected patient showing *any* skin lesion, in chains if necessary, to a police station, then to be placed in the lazaret for at least two years (where they sometimes contracted the disease).

Infant mortality was perhaps the saddest of sagas. My own figures, taken from deaths recorded on settlements and missions, showed a rate of 150 per 1,000 in Central Australia, figures seen only during earthquakes, exploding volcanoes, tsunamis and catastrophic floods. When nine babies under one died at Yuendumu in a matter of weeks, the Health Department didn't send in doctors—only health inspectors to condemn the Welfare Branch's hygiene and health practices. These figures began an outcry down south and the Welfare Branch reluctantly commissioned its own investigation. A zoologist heading the team had a mandate to look (only) for the *psychological causes* of infant mortality, seeking causality in some kind of infanticidal predilection in Aboriginal women. The short chapter on social and environmental causes of infant mortality (which are indeed the factors) was actually excised from departmental records, using razor blades. I never got to see it and remained incensed at the ignoring of social and environmental causes that underlie this massive death rate. (Infant mortality statistics have improved markedly in the past three decades.)

***

Health and well-being are not simply about the presence or absence of disease. The contexts of health are vital: access to qualified medical personnel, adequate nutrition, potable water, sanitation facilities, health education, general level of education, adequate housing and a modicum of income. Here is a short appraisal of some of these factors—then, and often enough, now.

The distribution of doctors and nurses was and is totally skewed: adequate or better for town dwellers, third and fourth world standards for the remote people. Personnel attending to the latter were either altruistic or inept, rarely lasting long enough to establish essential doctor-patient, nurse-patient relationships. There was widespread belief in Aborigines having 'an innate susceptibility to disease' and hence the almost dismissive shrugs that much of their ill-health was 'normal'. Better today, of course, but still nowhere near first world.

Environmental sanitation was often left to priests and holders of theology diplomas to organise and maintain. Water-borne diseases were rampant and no one connected the dots or acknowledged that there were dots to be connected.

The mandatory food scales were either never adhered to or over-adhered to on some items such as sugar and white flour. The two catering officers in charge of food allocation had no qualifications and no training in nutrition. There was no starvation but there was constant *mal*nutrition, a situation continued by today's junk food intake.

General education, let alone health education was and remains a problem—to the extent that today we have governments withholding income and welfare services unless children attend school.

The Welfare Branch took control of education from 1956. A specialised sub-unit, headed by the Superintendent of Special Schools (SSS) and two inspectors, it was responsible only to the Director. When the SSS went on six-months long leave Giese asked me to take his position on a temporary basis. We asked permission from Professor Partridge. Yes, he said, provided I didn't take legal responsibility for my actions and didn't accept payment. It was an unprecedented arrangement. Earlier I had taught, however briefly, in most of these schools but this was as inside as a researcher could ever get.

Educational failure was inevitable. Three senior education staff and 50 to 60 Branch teachers were located in a non-professional administrative unit attempting to operate programs across a colossal domain. They delegated education to missionaries who 'serviced' one-third of the Aboriginal population and exercised almost no supervision or control over such education as there was on cattle stations. Teachers on settlements and missions did not have their Territory experience acknowledged by state education authorities. Most teachers were one-year primary-certificated, and could (and did) rise to positions within the Branch that they could never hope to reach in a normal authority. There was no direct link between teachers and the head office trio with teachers having to submit to the whims of mostly untrained, under-educated and non-professional superintendents of missions and settlements. Vocational training was a cruel pretence. Hygiene, nursing and education 'aides' were sent for short courses, usually of between two weeks and six-months duration. The presumption, an old colonial one, was that they would work only among their own people—and hence a lowered standard would be acceptable as 'normal'. 'Butchers', 'bricklayers', 'carpenters' and 'bakers' were sent for two-week courses and given certificates of attainment, of no possible validity.

A wage scale was *prescribed*: usually £4 ($8) a week for males and £2 for females, well below the basic wage enshrined in Australian law in 1907. Wages came with a ration scale. Aborigines were given, at most, 10 shillings ($1) a week as pocket money and the remainder placed in a trust fund. In theory, anyone paying above these prescriptions was committing an offence. Here was another hallmark of Aboriginal policy and practice: *ascription*, imputing the characteristics and abilities or inabilities of a few to the entire population.

Social service benefits were said to be payable to Aborigines from 1959 onward. The guiding principle was that 'wherever possible, payment should be made to the individual concerned'. But there was also a 'benevolent home' model—where an inmate of an aged home couldn't manage his/her person, the home would be the recipient and would use the payment to maintain the patient. All wards were duly turned into benevolent home patients: every £5 ($10) weekly pension would go to the Welfare Branch, the mission societies and to cattlemen as a global sum from which 10 shillings ($1) would be given to the recipient as pocket money and the balance kept and used for their 'maintenance'.

Did anyone keep tabs on the remaining part of the benefit? No. Did anyone examine the expenditure of this 'maintenance' portion by missionaries and cattlemen? No. Was there any truth to the general rumour that it was 'cheaper to grow niggers than cattle' in the Territory? Yes.

Missions and cattle station managements were expected to maintain one adult worker, one wife and one child: all other dependants and family were supposedly cared for by a series of operational subsidies to these bodies (in addition to capital subsidies for housing and utilities). Did the missions and cattlemen provide balance sheets? Sometimes, but often in such a way that you couldn't tell whether the income from government was spent on staff holidays or long service leave or on their Aboriginal charges. The Catholics, of course, refused to keep or hand over balance sheets: the church, said the Bishop, is not an accountancy firm, we trust in God and so should you.

Housing was and remains a disaster—essentially because White society still insists on housing Aborigines 'after the normal Australian manner', insistent that we do the designing. Ted Egan's Aboriginal team quarried sandstone at Yuendumu and built a prototype one-roomed stone house with a spinifex thatch roof, a water tap and fireplace for £25 ($50). The Branch rejected his idea and insisted on 'transitional' housing—Kingstrands: a single-room aluminium hut erected on a concrete slab with open verandahs on three sides held together by nuts and bolts. Described as mobile Meccano sets, they were uninhabitable as the measured mean temperature at 11 p.m. was 18°F higher than the outdoor temperature and 23°F hotter than the adjacent spinifex-thatch humpy. No water, electricity or sewerage. The unit costs ranged from £600 to £800 for the base model and up to £1,170 for the 'deluxe', which meant that two of the verandah sides were built up, but again without water, electricity or sewerage. These units became the most expensive kennels in history with the people camped out on swags on the verandahs and their numerous dogs curled up inside. Nobody, but nobody, dwelt in them.

In criminal law courts the accused had no idea of the nature, let alone the language of the proceedings, something non-Aboriginal society insists on. There was no legal representation save for that by Welfare Branch officers who had no notion of the adversarial process. As often as not they would urge the magistrate to put the guy away because he was a 'bad man'. Most of the minor offences—88 percent of all Aboriginal offences—were drinking liquor, drinking metho, selling or possessing alcohol and being drunk. My work weighed heavily against prohibition. Apart from the civil rights aspect we all knew grog-running at outrageous prices was rife, but no joke when Aborigines were sold badly adulterated spirits or resorted to imbibing liquefied shoe polish, typewriter cleaning fluid, and in the end, the very real end, wood alcohol that caused blindness and sometimes death. Later, some Welfare Branch officers blamed me for the lifting of prohibition and the subsequent eras of chronic alcoholism but I was not the sole abolitionist. Even the police, who found (and still find) Aborigines a highly visible and easy mark and who notched up hundreds of impressive arrest records, became disabused and disgusted with the system. Judges and magistrates were fed up with the supplying laws, saying the sly-grog suppliers were prevalent, hard to detect and difficult to prove guilty.

From 1962 Aborigines were able to vote but were not compelled to register. The Methodist missionaries were in despair at some attempted recruitment of Aborigines to the Northern Territory Council for Aboriginal

Rights, one of whose leaders was a member of the Communist Party. The Council was urging Aborigines to learn to vote in preparation for the next election. The Methodist group in Darwin instructed Beulah Lowe, the local missionary and *Gupapyngu* linguist, to translate into the vernacular the pamphlets written by a loony Australian medico and Christian anti-Communist crusader (Dr Fred Schwarz), then living in America—of 'The Communist Menace' and 'Satan and the Communists' variety.

At Elcho Island I was asked by an elder to meet him at the beach after work. Are you an anthropologist, Sir, he asked in near Oxfordese. No, I explained. Pity, but do you know my friends the Berndts? Yes. I'm their informant, he told me. 'I have an Olivetti and get paid by the line.' Now I knew. He wanted to know what Communism was and I gave my first beach tutorial. Later I was told that he was the single source for the Berndts' book on *Sexual Behaviour in Western Arnhem Land*. Now I knew.

The Welfare Branch was not bound by its own legislation. Bureaucracies are not so bound unless a statute specifically states that they are. So Giese's men and minions had no duty to abide by *any* of the scales, standards and rules that were set for the mission and cattle station peoples. The latter were rarely inspected and if found in default were simply reminded of their duties. No prosecutions were ever undertaken. Missions complied to some degree but basically they took Welfare Branch heavy subsidies and did much of what they wanted to do.

Most serious was the constant assertion by the senior echelon of the very large (400-plus) Welfare Branch that they wouldn't dream of offering their services to the non-Aboriginal community because they had no qualifications—but were 'experts' on every facet of Aboriginal life. No more than two of them spoke a word of any Aboriginal language or dialect. The rest tried to get by with pantomime pidgin. With possibly three or four exceptions, none would have been able to hold a position in a normal welfare service organisation, yet they were escalated in seniority and salary way above their capacities.

HUMAN RIGHTS AND HUMAN WRONGS

* * *

Queensland's system, which I studied in less depth and over a much shorter time-span, was more draconian, more disciplined and consistent, less haphazard. Population centres were larger, often on better quality lands with more meaningful work available. Two even had resident doctors on a rotation system. But the incarceration flavour of it all was, nonetheless, as Meston averred to in his 1896 report, 'coloured by prejudice, distorted by ignorance'. The only man ever to have been de-licensed as an employer of Aborigines in the Territory, formerly at a Vestey's cattle station, became superintendent of Palm Island and was always accompanied by an armed bodyguard. Territory officials had no power to punish anyone other than by way of removal or exile to another reserve for a determined period. Territory missions would banish offenders to a nearby area or island for set periods.

Queensland officials and missionaries sent 'trouble-makers' to even more remote penal settlements like Palm Island and Woorabinda, most often without wives and children, with no rights of appeal and no time limits on their banishment. Exile, often to places more than a 1,000 km from home, was imposed for the flimsiest and most abbreviated of 'reasons', as these verbatim extracts from files indicate: 'unemployed, menace to young girls'; 'on discharge after serving a jail sentence'; 'absconder from Cherbourg'; 'refuses to work, addicted to drink'. The 'period of operation' on local settlements and mission lock-ups inevitably stated: 'During Director's pleasure'—for up to three weeks at a time. It was for 'crimes' such as playing cards, being cheeky, refusing to work, breaking out of a dormitory, calling the hygiene officer 'a big-eyed bastard', committing adultery, having a venereal disease, refusing to give faecal samples and furthermore, breaking the specimen bottle provided for that purpose, being untidy and being asleep in daylight hours.

The settlement superintendents voluntarily gave me access to these 'court' records. I wrote about this system in what I consider my most significant journal article, 'Queensland's Aborigines: Natural Justice and the Rule of Law', which appeared in 1963. Geoffrey Sawer insisted I send the article to the International Commission of Jurists (ICJ) in Geneva. I did. They sent it to the president of the Australian section of the ICJ, Edward St John, described as a zealous reformer. He replied that he was appalled but didn't want to embarrass Australia on a world stage.

However well intentioned they claimed to be, the bureaucrats and missionaries engaged in administering Aboriginal lives were out of time and out of touch with worldwide shifts in race politics, particularly changes wrought by World War II. They showed no inkling about decolonisation in Africa and the nearer Asia. They either knew nothing or didn't wish to know anything of the rules and standards of employment set down by the International Labour Organisation (ILO) to which Australia was a signatory. They were unaware of or ignored the United Nations' doctrines and declarations on human rights, the civil rights movements in the United States and England, the increasingly strident condemnations of racist laws and practices in South Africa, in the Southern Rhodesia that was to become Zimbabwe and in many American states.

We lived some months in Queensland in a cottage in Redcliffe where the family stayed while I spent solid time at Palm Island, Yarrabah, Woorabinda and Cherbourg settlements. But with Sandra pregnant with Simon, medical advice suggested we return to Canberra.

Chapter 10

CENTRE FORWARD

Simon was born in Canberra in 1963. There were, yet again, dramatic complications with the birth. His circumcision was rather unusual. The Jewish community offered to pay for a *mohel*, in this case a doctor, to fly up from Sydney, but they couldn't afford his day's loss of income. So the delivering GP performed it (against his will) with a prayer group (*minyan*) of ten, mostly non-Jews, one or two Muslims among them begging the doctor to let them have a go. Robert Parker was his godfather.

That was April. From January a jar of very sharp pencils and two reams of untouched paper sat on my desk. Four four-drawer filing cabinets were full of rich material, bundles of photographs and profound memories. I could write nothing, not a word. I sat like that for several months. My Masters set out to prove connections; here I was drowning in a welter of material with no hook to hang it on. Finally Robert Parker's advice worked; he gave me a piece of paper with potential chapters listed and deadline dates for drafts. I have been doing the same for graduate students (and several co-authors) ever since.

I began with a section I felt most confident about—on wages, employment and training—and had it written in two months. Two others followed at the same pace and thereafter it was a runaway train, almost on automatic. The 'hook' was plain. In administration there should always be a *continuum*, a mutual inter-connection between policy and practice: Ministers make policies and bureaucrats implement them, and bureaucrats in turn make policy when they see policy problems and flaws and when they provide feedback on progress. There shouldn't be a gap between the two.

CENTRE FORWARD

What I had confronted was a galactic gulf between policy aims and policy claims on one hand, and between aims and realities on the other, a chasm created by having to administer improbable policies and having administrators who weren't trained in how to accomplish even the barest of the achievable goals. What was being administered, in effect, was haphazard segregation, *apartheid* of a very similar kind to South Africa but without the vehemence, venom and violence. At times there was malice but more often the administrative practices were a mix of ignorance, arrogance and ineptitude amid improbable goals.

The chapters had to be sent to the Department of Territories for scrutiny and approval. An official in charge of the labour unit, but who had never been to the Territory, called round with the wages and employment chapter. There were some 200 little post-it type notes: you can't say this and you can't say that. When I remarked that the figures and facts came from his files, he was fazed but unmoved. After four chapters of the same treatment by other officials, Robert Parker and I asked to see Hasluck about ending this blatant censorship. He read every word, looked at every query and gave me a pass on all but one item, the names of the cattle stations cheating Aborigines in their local provision stores.

Just prior to submission, an ANU scholar had used, or rather misused, some file materials from the New Guinea unit of Territories, quoting personal stories that shouldn't have been on file. The permanent head reacted by closing all student access and forbade anyone to publish anything based on any of their files, me included. On appeal, he suggested with a straight face, that the examiners could assess my thesis but would have to sign statutory declarations to keep the contents secret! Hasluck's good sense prevailed.

Unbeknown to me, the Territories Department had never sent a single one of these vetted chapters to its Welfare Branch in Darwin and therein lay more than a hint of malice. What I didn't know was that Giese's old predecessor and nemesis, Frank Moy, was doing most of the Canberra vetting and that he and many of his Territories colleagues were secretly overjoyed at these independent critiques of the Welfare Branch. They had always been suspicious of cries for extra funding and were forever offended by the Branch's arrogance that it alone knew what to do and knew what it was doing.

The thesis was examined by an internationally renowned social science pioneer WJM Mackenzie at Manchester University and by Professor AP Elkin at Sydney University. Mackenzie knew nothing of Aborigines and Elkin knew nothing of administration theory. There were no middle-road examiners available in those days. Elkin conducted the oral exam in his Sydney office, tape-recording my answers for that 'silly Manchester man', a very perceptive and very unsilly man as it turned out. Elkin asked me to lunch with him in the University staff club. Friend Ken Buckley saw me and asked what I was doing there. When I told him, he asked who was paying. On hearing it was Elkin, he said I'd passed.

I was asked to produce 25 copies of the thesis, highly unusual in the days of typewriters and carbon paper and especially for a thesis that basically flayed the Department's efforts. So it was back to the wax stencils and the Roneo machines. Sandra and all three children had chickenpox at one point, yet she continued the laborious typing with pock-tipped fingers while caring for three infants. At the time Territories paid for these expensive reproductions. On completion they sent copies to the various churches involved in Aboriginal work and to Harry Giese. Predictably he launched into several orbits and ordered his staff heads to prepare an anti-thesis. The Branch's senior research officer Jeremy Long dissented, arguing that they didn't have the manpower to research and investigate my highly detailed findings, that they should accept the good, the bad and the ugly, make the best of it, change what could be changed and move on. Hasluck rejected all the drafted opposing views but accepted Long's advice. 'It seems we can do nothing right' Hasluck said to me but he accepted things with grace.

The work was always an analysis and exegesis of bureaucracy at work. It was never a personal attack on Giese, a man I liked, or any of his staff. Many were friends and this was not intended as personal criticism. Even so, it was often painful to be judgemental about their professional work after sharing so much with them socially and I recall the many hours of agonising about analyses that could or did cast them in a poor light.

I saw Harry Giese later in Darwin. He bore no malice but he still couldn't see how his enthusiasm, optimism and energy could be so unappreciated, so discredited. Somehow he had contrived to think of my work as a public relations promotion of his Branch. The noted filmmaker Cecil Holmes, editor of *The Territorian*, précised the thesis to 40,000 words and printed it under the heading 'What is the Tatz Report?' It was, I was told, read by the many hundreds of Territorians who disliked what they called 'Giese's Empire', who disliked all missionaries and who begrudged every penny spent on Aborigines. That wasn't ever my intention or my audience but I can say that the matter of Aboriginal affairs was never quite the same again.

That thesis had another legacy. It was what I call a 'hungry PhD', that is, the essential prerequisite for a first job rather than the more comfortable variety where one is in a job, married, settled and time isn't so precious. It left me forever guilty about 'not being at my desk, working', working towards the licence that would allow me a living and a way to provide for my family. I still look at my watch every few minutes, even in movies and eateries, reflexively anxious about not being 'at work'.

***

Within three-and-a-quarter years of arrival we were heading for a more permanent residence in Melbourne. From the outset we had a strong sense of belonging and blossoming, finding a new kind of freedom. Freedom wasn't simply feeling free from physical or political attack but the luxury of having people take you at face value—without nuances, inferences or raised eyebrows about your ethnicity, accent and place in the social hierarchy. No one asked me where I was from, my school, my ancestry... Not quite: my proudest moment was during question time at a public lecture I gave in Townsville in 1962. A woman asked 'Which part of South Australia d'ya come from, love?' All I was ever asked was what team I barracked for.

Freedom was also the ability to do things, to go places, to say, write, even to think in a way I had never known. Liberation—of the spirit, certainly. A great start and a growing sense that I had something to offer. Rufus Davis, Professor of Politics at Monash University in Melbourne, had heard my 1963 conference presentation on Queensland's Aborigines and the rule of law. He told Robert Parker he wanted me on his staff. 'So why doesn't he invite me?' I asked. Robert had to explain the correct appointment procedures. I wanted to know what kind of a man he was, as if there really was choice in the matter of my first job. Thoughtfully Robert replied: 'Rufe is addicted to good living.' I applied, was appointed a lecturer and was paid four rungs up the scale because of the doctorate and the book, a whole £2,200 (per annum), deedle deedle dum.

We lived in Mount Waverley—then a social and cultural disaster zone but reasonably close to Monash—and endured that suburban wasteland from 1964 to the end of 1970. The American Jewish comic Allan Sherman once said he lived in 10 Sparrowfart Lane; our house was definitely number 8.

Sandra landed a useful and attractive job at Jewish Welfare in South Yarra, as assistant to Walter Lippmann, an outstanding figure in Jewish, multicultural and migration affairs. Through her work there we discovered something we hadn't encountered in Africa—the Jewish poor. There was Jewish alcoholism, drug taking, prostitution, domestic violence. There were deserted children and those in dire need of financial help. In addition, Sandra had busy weekends and occasional nights typing correspondence and minutes for the Aborigines Advancement League (AAL)—at ten cents a page.

The only kindergarten was in a part of Mount Waverley heavily populated by a Christian Science congregation. The house we eventually bought in Ophir Road was the dead centre of the Scientists, a mere four-iron from their Huntingtower School. We were urged to approach Bialik College, a Zionist-oriented Jewish Day School in Hawthorn. Despite our inability to meet the fees, the Israeli principal wanted the three children. It was arranged that we could make desultory payments until our fortunes improved. The school was good for the children. They rode to school in a taxi subsidised by Bialik but even with that trip taken care of, Sandra drove something like 80 km daily.

The Monash Clayton campus was operational in 1961 but was very new and under the immense shadow of the University of Melbourne, founded in 1853. Economics and Politics made up the two-discipline faculty (ECOPS) with the likeable and dynamic economist Don Cochrane as dean. Rufus assigned me to teach Australian federalism to first year students. Appalled, I argued that in the reverse circumstances this was like my asking him to teach the unification of South Africa. 'Collie, my boy, it'll be good for you' he said. And it was.

Soon after arriving in Melbourne, I did it to Sandra again, flying off to Darwin (in a BOAC Comet, first class, free champagne, arriving a little worse for wear) to give evidence (on request) to a Legislative Council select committee on social welfare legislation. Pushed by the Department of Territories, Harry Giese introduced a Social Welfare Bill in February 1964: wardship would be abolished, Aborigines would be able to drink, own property, move freely, have sex with 'non-wards' and be paid their social welfare benefits directly. He contended that the 'new deal' wasn't because of the failure of his previous policies and practices but because they had been so successful! Wages and employment conditions wouldn't change—all those declared wards before the new statute came into being would remain wards for the foreseeable future (which was to be 1971). In short, civil rights (of sorts) minus the money.

The new Ordinance was broader than the previous one, giving the Director a mandate to provide social and economic assistance to 'certain persons' in a state of poverty or hunger or both. But despite the verbal fiddling and fudging, like inserting the word 'Social' in front of 'Welfare Branch', this remained essentially an Aboriginal law, vesting the Director with control over all Aboriginal reserves. The select committee had details of my thesis work (but not from me) and quizzed me with a strong sense of background (and foreground). The committee concluded that health and education within settlements should be controlled by the relevant specialist departments and not by the Director of Welfare, as I had so forcefully argued. It also saw 'some incongruity' in entrusting to a [new] Social Welfare Branch the administration of Aboriginal reserves 'with which administration of social welfare is ordinarily unconnected'.

My stance was unequivocal: if equality was to have any meaning then Aborigines should receive the services of specialist departments on the basis of the skills they were to provide and not on the basis of the colour or class of the people they were to serve. I argued that the Welfare Branch was an equivalent 'octopus' service, like that of nineteenth century Britain where a Board of Guardians administered all services to the poor. For me and for most Aboriginal leaders and locals, there was a sense of victory in witnessing the abolition of these chronic restrictions and encroachments on Aboriginal lives. I found that things could change, that I could help those changes and get through to people what they couldn't or wouldn't see. It wasn't all that different from opening minds in a classroom, but the going was tougher, the opposition very much fiercer, the politics of learning infinitely more bitchy. Ego, not blood, was spilled.

* * *

The May 1961 meeting to launch an Australian Institute of Aboriginal Studies (AIAS) had made its intentions pretty clear and they were confirmed by the parliamentary speeches introducing the AIAS statute in May 1964. The Institute 'would *not* concern itself with current problems as they affected Aboriginal people' but its work would be 'scientific and anthropological' (a conjunction which was particularly dismaying). WC (Bill) Wentworth

MP—the father and godfather of the Institute—insisted it was a matter of studying 'man and man's nature'. It certainly didn't include the study of bureaucracy and the White man's administrative nature. To me, the study of 'man and man's nature' through the Institute's lenses of the time seemed both prodigal and blinkered beyond belief given the reality of Aboriginal circumstances. All of this unproductive posturing was taking place in an international context suffused by racial issues. The years 1961 to 1964 witnessed the appalling consequences of rapid and ill-thought out decolonisation procedures, especially in Africa. Adolf Eichmann's trial and fresh evocations and exhumations of Auschwitz were in the headlines. The escalation of the Vietnam War and all its ugly undertones of 'zapping the gooks' generated fear and hatred. There were freedom rides and race riots in the United States, Mississippi was beginning to burn, Lyndon Johnson's Civil Rights Acts and Martin Luther King's 'I have a dream' speeches were resounding around the world. Papua New Guinea was seeking self-government, not ready to wait till their 'maturity' date, said to be somewhere around 2000. The Australian Liberal Coalition government was at first blocking a Gough Whitlam bill to give federal voting rights to Aborigines, then changing its mind after a 1962 enquiry; and Kath Walker (Oodgeroo Noonuccal) was declaring that 'Whites stick their heads in the sand and don't try to understand us'.

With much passion and fury at this constipated focus, I lobbied heavily to create a unit that would assess 'current problems'. I explained all this to a battery of powerful God professors, and with Don Cochrane's keen support proposed the establishment of what was to become, in December 1964, the Centre for Research into Aboriginal Affairs (CRAA). The essence was engaging the social, economic, legal and medical problems in an 'action-oriented' way. It still flourishes, much expanded, as the Monash Indigenous Centre. It has outstripped the Institute, not in resources but in teaching, action and outreach work.

Monash wanted confirmation that the Centre's work would not overlap in any way with the Institute's template of study. My address to the Institute's

Council produced affirmation of their narrow focus and our separate paths, and with a sense of relief AIAS quite sincerely wished the Monash project well. With some surprise I was appointed a member of AIAS in September 1964 but did not go near the place for almost a decade.

Named centres of excellence were then uncommon and there was a certain glamour about this one at Monash. The major supporters were the medical and science people, with a lukewarm response from the humanities cohort. Rufus was bitterly opposed to the idea—mostly out of concern for my academic future I think. Another slice of *dafke*, my patron lobbying to save me from myself. He had to succumb and did so with grace. Rufus was continually looking after me. He cautioned that my acceptance of an invitation to give a talk to the Jewish Council to Combat Fascism and Anti-Semitism would hurt my career. When I gave a second talk, I was advised by Rufe and Melbourne University's Law Dean Zelman Cowen not to go near these people because they were Communists. Several founders had been Communists but at that time only one office-bearer was an avowed CP member.

Apart from the size and resources of the Centre—namely me and secretary Sue McLean (then a fortnight shy of sixteen and now celebrating more than 50 years' service to Monash University as Sue Stevenson)—we were located in the Economics and Politics Faculty.

My operating philosophy as director was simple: join the administrators, church men, trade unionists and the employers rather than watch them dismiss, distrust and disdain each other; broker meetings between all those professing an interest in Aboriginal affairs but who never spoke or listened to each other; and co-opt the hitherto unco-optable. I contrived a Council of nine Monash academics to be joined by nine 'outsiders', persons of immense influence in Aboriginal and Australian affairs at the time. They included a pair of bishops, an Aboriginal trade unionist, a cattlemen's lobbyist, a few academics and some public servants.

My thinking was much influenced by the admirable South African Institute of Race Relations, an independent and overtly antiracist body dedicated to research and publication of the key issues of life in that racially divided country. Elizabeth Eggleston, a lawyer and historian, had seen an announcement of the Centre's birth in *The Age* and proposed some historical research. One look at her resumé and I persuaded her to undertake a doctorate on the application of criminal law to Aborigines in Victoria, South Australia and Western Australia. My work had dealt with that significant issue in the Northern Territory and Queensland and her study would make for an almost total national coverage. Law Dean David Derham and I supervised her work, later published as *Fear, Favour or Affection* and shown to her in the week that she died so young at 42. Elizabeth, then one of very few doctoral scholars in law in this country, succeeded me as director in 1971 and remained so until her death in March 1976. She made the Centre much more accessible to Aboriginal students and to the Aboriginal community.

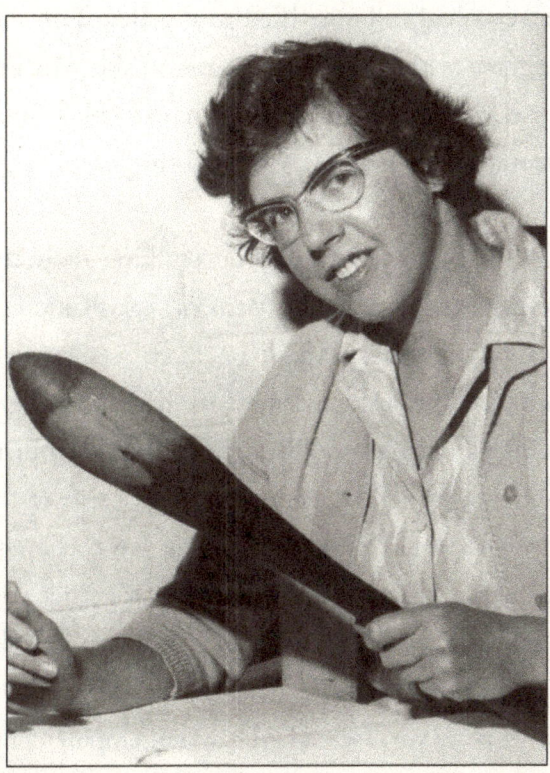

Dr Elizabeth Eggleston (1934–1976), courtesy Monash University Archive.

In 1967, Lorna Lippmann—a long-time member of the AAL and wife of Sandra's boss Walter—joined as my research assistant. A French major, she became a first-rate race relations scholar, publishing many essays, critical commentaries and two important books. Lorna was Elizabeth's deputy for a number of years. Between us—Lorna, Elizabeth, young Sue and me, some significant work was produced.

Worth noting is that Elizabeth, Professor Louis Waller (a criminal law specialist), barrister-solicitor Colin Campbell and I began the first informal legal aid service for Aborigines. Elizabeth typed up hundreds of slips on 'What to do when arrested' and distributed them within communities. These notices supplied our details and we were, of course, inundated with calls to meet arrested people, arrange their bail and representation. When I joined the statutory Aborigines Welfare Board (AWB) in July 1965, I was able to get to the Police Commissioner to secure a policy standing order that all Aboriginal arrests had to be notified to the Board or one of its staff. It became an ugly game with police ringing me in the witching hours to say that I needed to be in, say, Bairnsdale (290 km east) by 9 a.m. the next day if I wanted representation for x or y. We played this sleepless game as best we could.

Over the years I had listened to historians talking about the phases of the Aboriginal experience: exploration, settlement, pacification (genocide), segregation, assimilation, integration and so on. Such a sweeping typology across the continent could not be sustained until we had a definitive legal scaffold on which to build an accurate political history. An eminent retired constitutional law scholar from Perth, Frank Beasley, came to the Law School, joined our Centre and began a handbook of all laws relating to Aborigines from 1788. This idea of a major digest of laws, together with a compendium of court judgments, was eventually completed quite brilliantly by John McCorquodale as his doctoral work at the University of New England.

Among other projects we assessed Aboriginal employment in the mining industry, engaged in studies of Aboriginal health in Victoria as well as the

Aboriginal demography of that state. Ron Croxford was the head teacher at Yirrkala Mission when I spent time there, and while on leave in Melbourne in April 1966 he contacted me about legal advice on combating the imminent bauxite mining at the Mission. Elizabeth Eggleston, Louis Waller, Stan Davey and I met with the senior elder Daymbalipu Munungurr and Ron to discuss strategies to claim Aboriginal ownership of the land and/or to stop the mining operation. These meetings resulted in the ensuing *Mathaman* and *Milirrpum* Gove cases in 1969 and 1971 respectively. Aborigines lost these cases but they assuredly paved the way for a land rights inquiry and the subsequent *Aboriginal Land Rights (Northern Territory) Act* 1976.

Research began on wages and employment conditions on Northern Territory cattle stations preparatory to the 1966 Aboriginal wages case. The North Australian Workers' Union, once a staunch opponent of Aboriginal employment, now turned champion of their cause and brought a test case against the *Cattle Station Industry (Northern Territory) Award* of 1951 which excluded Aborigines from award payments. Regrettably, the price for access was that we wouldn't use the results in evidence against cattlemen before the Commonwealth Arbitration and Conciliation Commission which was to hear the case. Dilemma indeed, but I decided that knowing was better than not knowing.

I solicited Fred Gruen, perhaps Australia's foremost agricultural economist, to join me in this examination; Charles Rowley—then heading a project on Aborigines in Australian society, funded by the Social Science Research Council—asked if Frank Stevens, then enrolled for a doctorate on 'coloured labour' in North Australia, could tag along. Three very different musketeers: Fred, a *Dunera* boy from Austria who was once interned in Hay, Frank, a former national swimming champion and an ocker lad turned industrial advocate, and me, the Jo'burg boy. We did well, despite some heavy arguments, their lack of camping experience and bouts of sherry in the bush, the only drink on which we could compromise. We spent time at 26 cattle stations across the Territory.

Some of these cattlemen remembered me or had never forgotten or forgiven me. My crime? On a journey from Yuendumu to Papunya in my doctoral days I bogged in a sandy creek-bed. Unconcerned, I took my shovel, undid the six-foot wire strips and dug them under the back wheels. Heavy first gear and a thunderclap. When Les Penhall told me to carry wire he didn't say arc mesh wire used for concreting: I had bought six-foot strips of chicken wire—what else?—now bandaging my wheels like glad wrap. I lit a fire and waited for the rescue team from one of the settlements, a rule of the Territory being that if you didn't report in within a reasonable time, people would look for you. I didn't have a roger-over-and-out radio system. The fire was lifted by a strong wind against an adjacent quandong tree, a much-prized native fruit. The tree had a 'chimney', that is, it was half hollow but still alive. Two days later it was dead and so nearly was I, kept going only by hot beer and tins of Wing Lee bamboo shoots and water chestnuts. On the third day, 'fifth gear' arrived (about 20 Aboriginal men and a lot of tow rope) from Papunya, the excuse offered that each superintendent thought that the other should rescue me. I became a 'territorial dispute'. For a longish while I was known on outback radio schedules as 'the quandong killer', particularly after the manager of Napperby Station threatened (on radio) to kill the man who burned the only surviving quandong in Central Australia. I was now Dr Quandong.

A not untypical scenario was played out at Brunette Downs (12,000 sq km, larger than Lebanon) in the Barkly Tableland region. The manager was affable enough until approached by his Aboriginal foreman to take three days off to bury a 'big man', Uncle Toby, at Borroloola some 360 kms north. Charlie Weiss yelled that they were in a middle of mustering thousands of beasts and the answer was no. Whereupon everyone downed horses, sat under trees and rolled cigarettes. Charlie reached for his shotgun, whereupon the late Jack Jones from neighbouring Singleton Station called in, summed up the scenario, gave Roger the keys to his Land Rover and asked him to bury the elder as soon as possible. Charlie, like so many cattlemen, couldn't see the resistance in progress; he could only froth about Aboriginal stupidity, cussedness and worthlessness. He claimed bitterly that the expensive bore pumps regularly ran dry for lack of a simple, weekly oiling. I asked him if the Aboriginal camp bore ever blew up. No, he said, but he never saw the connection—which was usually tied to a refusal to increase the Aboriginal beef ration. There was Aboriginal resistance to many things, much of it seemingly passive but, realistically, very active.

At Newcastle Waters we spent time with Ted Egan, now graduated and with a teacher's diploma and head teacher at the station school. He showed us how a clever employer could get the best out of Aboriginal workers, for example, by giving innumerate Aborigines wooden pre-drilled templates for erecting fence posts instead of trying to get them to comprehend instructions about drilling three holes eighteen-inches apart. Several station managers were helpful, some surly and resentful, but we could see what was in the test case offing—that all Aboriginal labour (on which they were totally dependent) was 'costly and worthless'.

At Central Mt Wedge, the dead geographic centre of Australia, Bill Waudby—he of the enormous black beard and the most photographed man in the Territory—insisted we stay overnight and that I cook for him, something I had done often enough in my thesis days. A travelling food salesman found his freeze-trailer not working so he dumped his huge stash of prawns, bacon, eggs and Dutch strawberries on Waudby. Bill's homestead had burned down and he was living in the shell while two Alice Springs men were building a new home. Bill asked me to make my 'famous' cocktail: brandy, vodka, gin, orange- and grapefruit juice. He gave me a demijohn to fill. One of the builders, Dick Sweet, said he got cramps from spirits so I added a bottle of chlorydene (tincture of opium and chloroform) to the mix. His offsider said cocktails gave him headaches so Waudby added a dozen Bex (aspirin) powders as yet another preventive. There were six very sick men stretched out on wire camp beds next morning. Bill announced that all was well and that the after-effects were due either to the prawns being off or that he was allergic to seafood but he couldn't remember which. Outré indeed.

The Monash Aboriginal Centre held three national seminars, each three-day-three-night live-in affairs involving all the 'stakeholders': in 1966 on Aboriginal employment, wages and training; in 1969 on Aboriginal education; and in 1973 on Aboriginal health. All three resulted in books that remain basics in the literature. The employment workshop in May 1966 included a number of AIAS members or people strongly related to AIAS. It was absorbing to watch the cattlemen's representative Bill de Vos eating crayfish alongside wharfie Joe McGinness; Stan Davey (once a Churches of Christ minister) talking Christian matters with Bishop O'Loughlin; and Aboriginal leaders—Jacob Abednego, Joe McGinness, Kath Walker, Charlie Perkins, Bert Groves and John Moriarty—talking directly to people whom they had hitherto known as names on paper.

Significant papers were given and then published as *Aborigines in the Economy*. A great deal was achieved in a short time. It needed passion, energy and a sense of wiliness. When anger collided with uncertainty and a general sense that things had to change, opportunities arose for new approaches. There was no shortage of outrage on my part, and there were no shortages of outrageous laws and 'customs'.

What helped greatly was an emerging atmosphere of both guilt and shame, mostly from broadsheet papers like *The Age* and the newly born *Australian* and from the so-called 'left-wingers' said to be subverting the ABC, then and now. I did a great deal of radio and television work in those days, always able to produce irrefutable evidence of things that were awry. If you do your homework you can win nine times out of ten.

Chapter 11

THE REPRESENTATIVE

Amid persistent criticisms of Aboriginal conditions generally, Victoria's *Aborigines Act 1957* was amended in 1965 to reconstitute the Aborigines Welfare Board, the agency charged with their care and protection. The state Governor could now appoint an additional member from a panel of three names submitted by the Aborigines Advancement League (AAL). Hardly radical, it was a ploy to bring the League into the government's tent so that insistent criticisms would end or at least be a little muted. The League nominated Stan Davey, then AAL (and FCAATSI) secretary, Pastor Doug Nicholls, then chairman of the AAL, and me, never a member of that body. They wouldn't have a bar of either of those men and took the view that an academic would be less critical.

I wasn't paid sitting fees as were some Board members: as a university employee I was deemed a public servant and hence ineligible. This was to be my second stint as a 'public servant' in an unpaid position of authority—a remarkable situation for a migrant of five-year vintage. It also informs me about a lifelong unwillingness to accept payment for services of this kind, always rationalising that I work for 'good causes'. I have no resentment—only a lingering indignation at the huge fees often paid to others for doing seemingly or meaningfully nothing.

Between July 1965 and December 1967 I achieved one of my best efforts in Aboriginal matters by getting that abysmal form of administration abolished. Not that its successor—the Ministry for Aboriginal Affairs—was much better. At least it was a normal, daily-operational bureaucracy whereas

HUMAN RIGHTS AND HUMAN WRONGS

*Pastor Sir Douglas Nicholls KCMG OBE KStJ (1906–1988),
Governor of South Australia in 1976, friend and colleague.*

*Stan Davey (1922–2010):
devoted his life to Aboriginal advancement.*

the Board met once a month, delegated to the Board's superintendent something like $20 to disperse for emergency food or care for the destitute or homeless, while an unknown number of people waited for once-a-month decisions on welfare needs, employment, housing, education and places of domicile. The eleven-member Board didn't seem to know whether the Aboriginal population was 5,000, 10,000 or 20,000. It was probably 14,000 in Victoria at that time. No one seemed fussed about not knowing the number of people who had to be catered for, housed, fed, medicated, schooled or represented in the courts. Over many decades I found several 'native' administrations nationally engaging, budgeting, planning and programming without even an approximation of accurate population numbers.

The Act required the presence of an anthropologist. The well-known Donald Thomson was appointed and we formed a collegiality. Then only 64, he was already physically frail and often so ill as to be overwhelmed by the ugly politics of the Board trio—Harry Davey, Arthur Holden and Don Howe—who manipulated agendas and outcomes. The Board as a whole answered at first to an essentially good but busy man in Lindsay Thompson (Housing and Aboriginal Affairs), and later to an unsympathetic Minister for Housing (Edward) Ray Meagher. This was the era of the big bully-boy politicians, personified by Sir Henry Bolte and Arthur Rylah, his deputy Premier and Chief Secretary. Rylah was renowned for, among other things, his censorship, basing his benchmark on all filmic and written materials he believed unfit for his fourteen-year-old daughter. It all began in 1963 with Mary McCarthy's novel *The Group*. This was the era leading to the abortion inquiry by Justice William Kaye, the activities of pro-abortionist Dr Bertram Wainer, a man I knew and admired, the Melbourne vegetable market shot-gun murders and serious police corruption.

Board practice was sharply assimilationist in a peculiar way. It believed in 'pepper-potting', that is, scattering Aborigines in Board-owned houses across the state in some strange hope that since all roofs look the same from the air, all under them would become equal. After the Housing Commission, the Board was the largest owner of real estate. It took families from one geographic clan and kin region and dumped them in what amounted to alien clan areas. Even within such a small population, regional histories and legacies were very different and what was good for the populace at Lake Tyers Reserve in east Gippsland wasn't in the best interests of the clans of Framlingham Reserve in western Victoria. My good friend Diane Barwick, anthropologist turned historian, had documented these differences in her doctoral and subsequent work. To this day the failure to distinguish divergent communities in defined spaces (across the continent) has produced more problems than *any other* single factor.

Board meetings were concerned overwhelmingly with the allocation of houses, the building of houses, rent collecting and rent defaulting. The Board chairman, Harry Davey, was an ex-Housing Commissioner. His Board mates were Jack Gaskin, the Housing Commissioner; Arthur Holden, a Morwell accountant devoted to Apex work; and Don Howe, a Mooroopna tomato grower who employed Aborigines. Davey, Holden and Howe would hold private sessions before a meeting and star the items that suited them. They had an abiding belief that they *knew* what was best for Aborigines. They certainly spent more time on matters than other Board members. Four members were public servants representing health, education, housing and family welfare; two were Aboriginal pensioners, Con Edwards and Margaret Tucker. Staff consisted of the Superintendent Philip Felton, two trained social workers, two welfare officers, a housing officer and some ancillary staff. In short, more chiefs than Indians and a strange turn of events in that a very part-time Board was exercising more power and decision-making than the appointed full-time staff. The housing officer spent his time collecting or demanding rents, harassing tenants about their hygiene and nutrition and generally threatening evictions. My best source of help for the destitute and despairing between Board meetings was Peter Hollingsworth, then chaplain and youth worker with the Brotherhood of St Laurence. I misread him, never picking him for an archbishopric, let alone a Governor-Generalship.

THE REPRESENTATIVE

I didn't fight with these men at a personal level but certainly did so at the professional end. Amid much frustration and trench warfare some things were achieved. I had more Aboriginal questions asked in each Victorian parliamentary session than on all other topics put together, leading to staff and Board members not doing much else but answering them. Clyde Holding, then leader of the Labor Party in that parliament (and later a Commonwealth Cabinet Minister) was a constant help. I admit to relishing the moments when Harry Davey begged me to help him answer the questions I had posed.

Among other things we persuaded the Prothonotary's Office that it should provide legal aid to Aborigines without insisting on a means test and demonstrating that the cases had legal merit (their standard procedure for the general public). The Police Commissioner had agreed to notify the Board of every Aboriginal arrest. Soon after, I had a call from the welfare officer in Swan Hill to say that he'd been told that day of a young lad of 20 pleading guilty to a rape charge at a local preliminary hearing. He hadn't been notified as required and hence wasn't present to give advice or seek legal aid for the accused. Unrepresented and leaned on by the prosecuting sergeant to plead guilty, Darrell Charles, a cleanskin with no priors and literally, a choir boy, explained that at a party he had flirted with a 22-year-old White woman who was known to spend most of her time 'hanging out' with Aborigines. In the garden they had cuddled and she deposed that he had '*asked* me to take off my girdle'. The prosecuting sergeant said 'you mean he *told you* to take it off'. Yes, she said, and he was remanded for trial.

I phoned Legal Aid, had a barrister assigned, and asked him to get the trial listed at an appropriate venue. He could only secure a trial at the circuit court in Kerang before a judge reputedly savage on rape as a result of a family member having been sexually attacked. Try another venue I said, to which he replied that it would mean a delay of three months while Darrell remained inside. The lawyer insisted on taking pot luck in Kerang and I instructed him to plead not guilty. On the morning of the hearing this barrister didn't appear, claiming flu. His substitute that day pleaded guilty because, he explained to me on the phone, it would look bad to plead guilty at a preliminary hearing and change it to not guilty at trial. Bad for whom? The judge gave him twelve years with a minimum of eight.

Through the available Legal Aid service we appealed—a process which neither the prisoner nor his defence team were informed of or present at. It resulted in a reduced sentence of nine years with a minimum of seven. After much internal agitation and threats from me about going public here and abroad, the Prothonotary's Office of the Supreme Court finally suggested that I apply for a petition of mercy under the *Crimes Act* of 1958. Such a petition could be granted either by way of a full rehearing of the case by the Court of Appeal or by a pardon. The former was agreed to by Arthur Rylah with reluctance and much pressure from me about a possible article in *The Age* or a discussion on current affairs television.

I went through every rape sentence since 1957 and presented the Court of Appeal with an affidavit showing comparable rape sentences, listing ages of the accused and victims, circumstances of the crimes, previous convictions and maximum and minimum sentences. Darrell's original sentence was the most severe in recent Victorian history. The three Appeal judges thanked me for the interesting research but declared that debate about comparative sentencing was, though not improper, highly unusual and unacceptable. They then indulged in animated discussion about 'Brother x being a bit lenient there, don't you think, Brother y was too tough there' and so on. They had their day's entertainment and reduced the sentence to six and four, a half of Kerang. We had our day in court but Darrell should never have been there in the first place. It was a landmark case. It showed how exposed Aborigines were to the criminal justice system and to police pressure. It showed the gross disparities in Aboriginal and non-Aboriginal sentencing and it showed that one doesn't always have to succumb to 'the system'. Petitions of mercy are rare but they are there for the asking.

The Board was often asked to help place Aboriginal children, especially from Queensland, with White families, usually over Christmas holidays. All too often the middle- and upper-class families wanted to keep 'the cute kiddies' for longer and sometimes forever. There was a great deal of trafficking, fostering and adopting that left a bad and bitter taste. I once wrote that the Harold Blair holiday scheme was misused for this sort of unofficial 'fostering'. Harold was a noted Aboriginal opera singer, a man the arch Australian genocide denialist Keith Windschuttle claims I have defamed in this context but doesn't say how I did so. (Windschuttle was nowhere near these scenes, nor did he receive the phone calls asking for 'cute' holiday children or for their return.)

There was an evident looseness about the handling of Aboriginal children. We couldn't have known it at the time but the case of James Savage (born Russell Moore) was to have international repercussions. Taken from his teenage Aboriginal mother Beverly Whyman in Gippsland, under what may have been duress, he was adopted by a Salvation Army couple and taken to the United States. There he was later convicted of a drug-fuelled murder of a woman and sentenced to death in Florida in 1989. His sentence was changed to three terms of life without parole. His case sparked considerable public interest, especially in the manner of his removal and adoption. (The court was reluctant to listen to evidence about his Stolen Generation history.)

Another such case involved one (close) Monash University colleague who sought to adopt an Aboriginal child. I attended the application proceeding, objecting fiercely: the man had eight children of his own and I deemed this Samaritanism at its worst. My argument won the day and though I lost a friend, I have no regrets about my opposition to these kinds of adoptions.

* * *

In 1966 the Davey-Holden-Howe trio presented a three-line motion to the Board that Lake Tyers settlement, established as a mission in 1861 on some wooded and fertile 1,600 hectares, should be closed and residents scattered across the state. Rumours persisted that the Board wanted to sell the magnificently-sited property to Reg Ansett's airways empire as a tourist resort. They may only have been rumours but the trio had long had a dead-set against the place. Three years earlier their efforts had triggered a huge protest, led by Pastor Doug Nicholls. In February I urged Minister Lindsay Thompson to allow me to salvage the settlement by turning it into a rehabilitation and training centre. He agreed and the Board, with some hesitation, accepted a Lake Tyers Planning and Action Committee, operating from February 1966 under my convenorship. As with the CRAA model, I opted for several outsiders and key Board staff members. The report, completed in November, recommended Lake Tyers as a rehabilitation centre for those having difficulty living in the general community; those who were unemployed or unemployable; those who could be employed in forestry work, could run a cattle-fattening project, who could attend educational classes and enjoy social amenities. It was to be a five-year staged project with new staff, eight new houses, training programs (a minimum sixteen weeks), a vegetable-growing scheme, a play centre along the lines of Lex Gray's Maori model (where mothers were taught to become the instructors of their children), adult education classes and the restoration of the church. (In the 1930s Aborigines at Lake Tyers were the most successful pea-growers in Victoria but local farmers succeeded in stopping this activity on the ground that the Aborigines made the market competition unfair for them.) The report affirmed that physical placement in the White community didn't necessarily mean assimilation and that Aboriginal values and beliefs had to be given full recognition.

The AWB was due to meet on the report in December 1966. I provided copies of the 112-page document to the media with an embargo until the Board's date of meeting; I 'neglected' to put a time on the embargo. When the Board met that Friday it found itself looking at massive morning headlines and editorials commending the future of Lake Tyers and the general sanity of the government. It had taken all that effort to put a stop to such a unilateral, under-researched and unsubstantiated three-liner like the trio's 'close-Lake-Tyers' motion.

THE REPRESENTATIVE

Charlie Collins, a resident ally in the Lake Tyers battle, 1966.

These battles required friends in the media world. I never had to cultivate journalists with wine, food and gossip, but always delivered the goods for them: worthy stories, strong moral stories, lots of chapters and verses, ever ready to go on air to answer questions forthrightly.

As was common in Aboriginal affairs there was no articulation of policy—only a continually changing set of slogans and euphemisms. The absence of written policy allowed for the Ministry's defence of whatever was current practice—positive, negative or plain horrific. Policy was invisible yet forever invoked. It was time to nail something to the masthead as a yardstick against which to measure what was happening on the ground. In October 1965 I proposed to the Board that it appoint a sub-committee to define and enunciate its policies. Arthur Holden, Albert Booth, the Director of Family Welfare (who joined in July 1965) and I met regularly to formulate a policy document, a 'set of ideals by which we will be guided in our administration, and towards which we will strive in an attempt to overcome… the besetting social problem that has been with us for so long.' Albert (father of Douglas, in later years my finest student and firmest friend and colleague) was sympathetic and supportive while Arthur was bemused by it all.

We produced some grandiose statements: 'European insistence on Aborigines conforming to what Europeans deem is in their best interests is no longer acceptable'. While equality was an aim it is always subject to the principle that it 'is as unjust to treat unequals equally as it is to treat equals unequally'. Pure Aristotle. If the Board differentiated in treatment, it had to be justified on the basis of relevant differences in needs, capacities, interests, incentives and the weight of responsibility that could be borne—and never on the basis of race or colour. Straight Morris Ginsberg, a *Litvak* sociologist and philosopher at the London School of Economics, whose long essay on *Justice in Society* became a mainstay of my working life. We recommended the abolition of the Board and its replacement by a distinct Ministry and professional staff. Details followed on health, education, training, rehabilitation, housing, family welfare, reserves, legal questions and community participation. Lindsay Thompson wrote a foreword, I wrote Harry Davey's introduction and the *Aboriginal Policies of the Aborigines Welfare Board, Victoria* was published in December 1966. It was the first such public enunciation—and it remains the only one of its kind.

My time in that gloomy arena was both strident and sullen. There wasn't much that was funny or joyous but one episode is worth relating. Advised that the Bernard van Leer Foundation in The Netherlands was looking to fund projects to assist needy children, we invited an emissary, Pieter Kruithof, to visit 'Black Australia'. One of the Board's social workers was a pilot, so we hired a plane and flew Pieter back and forth across Victoria, visiting Lake Tyers, Framlingham, Robinvale, Swan Hill, Echuca and Shepparton. We at CRAA were very much taken with the Lex Gray play centre concept and persuaded the Foundation to give us $50,000 for a similar development in Victoria.

THE REPRESENTATIVE

I took Pieter to meet Lindsay Thompson, then also Housing Minister. Jack Gaskin was present. The Minister asked if Pieter would like to see anything else and he asked to see housing for the poor. Jack took us to Carlton to see the new high-rise Housing Commission flats. 'Good' said Pieter, 'but now where are the units for homosexuals?' Jack—an 'I-don't-have-any-bloody-letters-after-me-name-and-I-don't-fucken-well-need-'em' kind of guy—looked at me in horror and asked for clarification. 'He wants to know where we house the poofs' I replied (in Aussie). 'Bloody disgusting, that's what he is; dirty men these foreigners' he growled. Pieter explained that the Dutch government found so much molesting going on in public places that they built specific units so people could live as they wished. Jack walked off astonished at what his world had come to.

We got the $50,000 grant but the Monash educationists took it and ran standard, conservative kindergartens and missed the opportunity to innovate. The Carlton flats, incidentally, had no playgrounds for kids. I learned a lesson in political decision-making however, having been dragooned onto the committee of the Victorian Family Council, run by women like Senator Marie Breen, the Country Women's Association president and other powerful political wives. Over tea and scones one afternoon we mentioned that the Housing Ministry had given us a mere $500 for playground toys. Lady Bolte (wife of the then Premier) leaned across and said, 'Not to worry, dear, I'll have a word with Henry in the mornin'. We got $5,000 the next week.

Being a Board member representing the AAL often meant involvement in major political domains even though we were, largely, amateurs at the game. The League was never certain which of their roles was most pressing—that of service body or lobby group. It certainly worked better as a service organisation, giving succour, shelter and employment to scores of young men and women coming to Melbourne from rural domains. But what was certain was that lobby and pressure groups don't work well on a part-time basis. So the AAL, with much pushing from me, eventually came round to paying Stan Davey as their point man.

For all the important gains, and a number of losses, it was depressing stuff. Some Board staff bullied their clients, shuffling them to different domiciles regardless of roots and clan affiliations. Most Board members were well intentioned but paternalistic, unrealistic, out of their depths. And most were only involved for three or four hours a month. The controlling trio rarely left the staff alone to do their professional work. In short, they browbeat and created a pernicious little fiefdom.

* * *

In December 1966 I took the family back to South Africa for a two-month vacation. We wanted the grandparents to meet Simon who'd been born almost three years earlier. I was pretty sure that I'd lost all emotional ties; this visit would test our migration decision. We were adamant that we wouldn't visit unless Bess and Ben repaired their 'chasm' which had resulted from their one-time breathtaking clash (Armageddon shields clanging) on the subject of white or brown bread for breakfast for the children. They duly patched up, leased an eleventh floor apartment for us in Berea and paid Selina Mangope, niece of my mother's maid and companion Agnes Mkhambi, as our 'domestic'. It was a quiet two months, with many family get-togethers.

Visiting the Sunday African mine dances was a highlight for the children, especially the famous gum-boot dancing on corrugated iron sheets and the Zulu *impi* war dances complete with full head-dresses and leopard-skin cloaks. I also saw something of the abysmal mining compounds, some of them housing 10,000 male workers. What was impressive was to witness how miners from diverse origins—African, Afrikaner, Scottish, Swedish, German—had to learn to speak and write 500 key words of *fanagalo*, the mining *lingua franca*, before being allowed underground. The training lasted three weeks but most speakers graduated from that small vocabulary to full literacy in three months. At the same time I was being barraged in Australia with the message that it would take over a decade to get an Aboriginal child to junior school literacy levels. There is nothing worse than intransigence, truculence and arrogance among people who are capable of knowing better, trained and paid to do better.

Uncle Harry Isaacson walked the children two or three days a week to the fairly large public space near the city centre, known as Joubert Park. He would patiently explain to these inquisitive kids the meaning of *Blankes* and *nie-Blankes* painted on park benches and why they could sit on the *Blankes* ones and not on the others. This helped put an end to a piece of nasty socialisation that had begun to take hold two days after arrival. My mother, like most South African mothers, rang a bell for the servants to attend the table, serve the meals, remove the plates and bring the next course. Paul and Karen began to fight over control of the bell, Simon also demanding his turn at summoning the 50-year-old Agnes and echoing my mother's admonitions of why it took her so long to answer the bell.

One major change. I was no longer the nobody teaching in a nothing school, with Bess now the proud curator of a small coffee table sporting two nicely bound theses, and several of my books and journals on display. By now I'd lost my 'I'll show you' attitude and was immensely pleased for her.

The visit ended with drama. We left South Africa in February, the last date on which I could leave. We boarded the plane at about eight-thirty in the morning, taxied to the runway but suddenly came to a halt. A car drove up, steps were put in place and two men in safari suits boarded and came to my seat: 'Are you Dr Tatz? Please take your luggage and your family and accompany us off the plane.' Our first thought was that a family member had taken ill. We went back to the airport terminal, there to be met by a Qantas official who demanded to know what was going on with 'his' Australian citizens. By now I was convinced it was political. Prime Minister Dr Hendrik Verwoerd had been assassinated in Parliament a few months earlier and the country was still in turmoil. If it was political I had an idea of what to do. The officials urged us to return to my parents' apartment and await a phone call. What of our luggage? It hadn't been placed on board and that convinced me we were in some Kafka-like game run by the South African Bureau of State Security (BOSS). The extended family saying their farewells to us were now speechless. I have no doubt some were thinking: 'Indeed this is what happens when people get "liberal ideas"'.

I phoned Mike Schneider. He said to remain *shtum*, say nothing, do nothing, until the promised call came, which it did at about 3 p.m. A senior manager explained that because of the Qantas pilots' strike in late 1965, there was a huge backlog and wealthy Mauritian businessmen, he told me, had bribed an airport official to give them five seats from Mauritius to Australia, whereupon said official found our convenient five places and 'deleted us'.

The airways manager agreed that we would fly home via London that evening and he granted an extra night and day stopover in that city. We were met by Sandra's brother Eddie and his first wife Erica and son Gavin, then a few weeks old, and enjoyed the usual great London sights and the close family.

Back in Australia to pursue my work, some good and bad changes occurred in 1967. The good: the AWB and the Victorian Government agreed to the demise of the AWB by December and things worked toward that end. Donald Thomson resigned from the Board and I took his place in the 'anthropologist or sociologist' position. The bad: I buckled to Max Marwick's nagging and joined his Anthropology and Sociology Department, bringing the CRAA with me. Marwick was losing staff at a rate of knots and the explanation wasn't complicated. The only people he could trust, he said, were South Africans. In quick succession he appointed three South Africans, not one of whom had any university or teaching experience. All were given senior lectureships. The departmental secretary was a former British Special Branch policewoman in Kenya. Inside the cupboard in her room she would screw the name-plates of all staff who had left or were leaving: a horizontal plaque cemetery (in many of whose demises she had a hand). Not good.

THE REPRESENTATIVE

Soon after Sue, Lorna, Elizabeth and I made the transfer, we realised the error. Too late. Marwick stepped aside as head in favour of Michael Swift, a Malaysia specialist, a devout Islam convert and a man who had what we politely call 'a Jewish problem'. One of Marwick's appointees had one too, telling me that his greatest punishment at school in Windhoek was to be made to sit next to the only Jew in the school. Just prior to the move I had been promoted to senior lecturer in Politics and was then designated as senior lecturer in Sociology. I enjoyed the teaching enormously, developing courses on the concept of preparation for independence, comparative race politics and on applied sociology.

The Department then appointed a Jewish woman as an anthropologist. She was enormously talented but had some serious personality problems. She didn't get a fair deal from Swift but even so she began a series of allegations about antisemitism from colleagues she named. I had befriended her and several of us (including Rufus Davis and two Jewish academics in ECOPS) tried to inveigle her into therapy, which she acutely and smartly evaded. With some vengeful stupidity, Swift tried to 'get her' and finally found a trump when she refused to teach a particular class, one outside her ken and in a ridiculous time slot. He tried to have her fired for 'disobeying a lawful order'. She took her woes way up the line, finally to Dr Jim Cairns, then Deputy Prime Minister. Questions were hurled to and fro in both the Victorian and Commonwealth Parliaments and the Monash foundations began to rock. My advice was that she be given a cottage in the grounds, allocated a research fund to get on with her excellent work. Swift was adamant, stalemates were reached, lawyers enriched and Monash's Anthropology and Sociology unit was in total tatters. No sooner had I gone to New England in 1971 than I was asked to attend a tribunal to testify about her denouncing me as an antisemite. I refused. That she did so was of no great moment but it showed me that universities are capable of bad behaviour.

***

Sociological profiles of specific Jewish communities were common enough in the United States and came to Australia fairly rapidly after the arrival of European Jews post World War II. Walter Lippmann decided to conduct a major study of Victoria's Jewish community and assembled a team. Peter Medding, already established as a scholar of Melbourne Jewry, took on the bulk of the task together with a steering committee which included me among some prominent community members. The survey instrument—dull and boring—had questions like 'Do you describe yourself as very religious, moderately religious, somewhat religious, not religious at all, opposed to religion, or not sure.' As to fasting on the holiest of days, *Yom Kippur*, did you fast, didn't you fast, or fast partly? And so on. I have no time or patience for these kinds of sociological tools mainly because the questions don't search anywhere deeply enough and because you have to rely solely on what a respondent is prepared to tell you, to kid to you (or themselves) or plain lie to you; and for that dubious information you have to rely on the honesty, integrity and experience of the interviewers over whom you have little control and/or who know infinitely less about the intentions of the survey than the compilers of the research instrument. The book came out in 1973, mistitled *Jews in Australian Society*.

Another Jewish connection arose out of the voice and machinations of Norman Banks, a 3AW radio man and host of a Channel 9 television show, the Norman Banks Hour, with massive Saturday night ratings. Banks, a founder of Carols by Candlelight and a one-time novice Anglican priest, was a good radio commentator on Australian Rules football. He had been to South Africa in the early 60s and became a paid propagandist on the virtues of *apartheid* there and in Southern Rhodesia. This defender of 'Imperial virtue' could have shown today's right-wing shock jock Alan Jones a thing or two about bullying, outrageous comments, gross prejudice, defamation, dirty tricks and 'radio power'. Certainly he was more sophisticated, suave, velvety and unctuous than the generally ungracious Jones. Banks, forever asserting that 'some of his best friends were Jews', would invite Zelman and Anna

Cowen onto his program quite regularly—and for reasons unfathomable, they appeared arm-in-arm with him on several occasions. I understand Jews who want to belong, to be accepted as part of a mainstream, but for me this was a stretch too far.

I challenged Banks to debate South Africa on television under a mutually agreed chairman, preferably the competent Patrick Tennyson, his television program producer. He refused, saying publicly if he was forced to do so he'd resign from the Channel. (Surprising was that his major television sponsor was Gloweave, a Jewish-owned shirt manufacturer. They seemed not to notice or care about his 'Jewish problem'.) But he agreed to a radio debate with me about South Africa, Aborigines, racism, the Holocaust. He insisted, to our glee, that he be accompanied by two colleagues: Sir Raphael Cilento, an eminent tropical medicine specialist and rabid racist, and the notorious Eric Butler, head of the Australian League of Rights, an antisemitic, racist, 'White purity', 'Christian purity' outfit which sheltered behind his Anglican Synod membership and his Heritage Bookshop, peddlers of every racist tract on the planet. Butler's book, *The International Jew*, informed readers that Churchill, Roosevelt and John Curtin were Communists and that Russia was 'a slave Jewish state'. Isi Liebler, a prominent Jewish leader, refused to appear with me, rightly saying he wouldn't deign to discuss the statistics of the gas ovens with such men. I cajoled Dr Frank Knopfelmacher—the once red but now black sheep of academe, brilliant, erratic, coruscating, so very formidable—to join me. We won by several knockouts. More importantly, that radio debate forced Banks to concede what he'd always denied: his close associations with both Butler and the surprising politician Jim Killen, in ultra right-wing politics. This led Ken Gott, an excellent journalist, to put together *The Voices of Hate: A Study of the Australian League of Rights and its Director, Eric D Butler*. We tried about 30 publishers but no one would touch it for fear of church and Banks reprisals. Gordon Bryant MP, owner of a printing company and staunch AAL member, agreed to print the monograph in 1965. There was no response whatever from those whose voices were filled with hate. Butler did write one letter to *The Age*, pointing out a minor error in Gott's account of his short-lived military service.

***

I stayed on good terms with the AAL even as that body underwent its own paroxysms. In 1969 the AAL held its annual ball at the Northcote Town Hall, Sandra and I attending that Saturday night. The guest of honour—Papua New-Guinean politician Albert Maori Kiki—was one of the founders of the Pangu Party and later a Deputy Prime Minister. The Aborigines turned out in mothballed long gowns and too-tight tuxedos, engaging in barn and Morris dancing, quadrilles and other courtly gaieties. Maori Kiki stormed out, shouting that these people were puppets posturing and pretending to be White middle-class. On the Monday following, Doug Nicholls and his vigorous son-in-law Stuart Murray announced that the AAL would thereafter be run by an all-Aboriginal executive. Lorna Lippmann, Doris Blackburn, Barry Christophers and a few others couldn't quite grasp that a coup—negating their many years of endeavour on the Aboriginal behalf—had occurred. I could. It followed certain events and seemed, in medium hindsight, inevitable. The magnificent American singer-politician Paul Robeson had been there in 1960. Dr Roosevelt Brown, a Bermudan Black Power man, had visited and 'read the riot act' to polite Aboriginal leaders. The trends were clear and all it needed to push Aborigines beyond politeness and acquiescing to the claims from Whites that 'we'll hand over to you when you're ready' was this spur from Maori Kiki. (Historian Richard Broome has written a definitive account of the League and its struggles in his *Fighting Hard*, 2015.)

If there was one thing I learned at that time, it was to know when to get out of the way and let people do their own bidding. Doug Nicholls and I were always mates and I somehow found the strength to suffer Stuart Murray's spleen and frustration—to the point where we too became friends.

Chapter 12

RACE MATTERS

By now I was wearing a Sociology rather than a Political Science label. I was elected to the executive of what was then the Sociological Association of Australia and New Zealand (SAANZ) and in 1968 attended the annual conference in Wellington. I had been close to Whetu Tirikatene when she was a doctoral student at ANU; later she was the Member for Southern Maori for 29 years and a Cabinet Minister. With her help we established a number of key contacts in the country.

Sandra and I travelled with Walter and Lorna Lippmann for a few weeks to holiday at Mt Cook and other splendid spots and attend the conference. Lorna and I stayed on for six weeks looking at comparative Maori and Aboriginal health, education, land rights, juvenile justice mechanisms and political representation. The head of Maori Affairs, Jock McEwen, was a confident man and happy to have us shown around at every level. With Whetu's introductions and McEwen's generosity and expertise, we had an easier pathway through the long list of Maori grievances. Maori Affairs was a domain of so much less paranoia, secrecy and angst than Aboriginal administration.

McEwen offered us a quick tour and we were duly guided by a Maori staffer named George Simon. En route we asked him for his insights into the major problems facing his community. 'Marrying out' was his instant reply. Funny you should say that, we chorused, it's the same in our Jewish community, the religion with the highest propensity of all faiths to cross-marry. Shalom *chaverim* (friends, brothers) he replied, I'm also Jewish.

Googoo-eyed, we listened to him talk of his Maori father who had married Miss Rachael Isaacs from Golders Green in London. The children were raised to observe *Shabbat* on Friday nights and Maori stuff the rest of the week. He drove us past a *marae*, a communal or sacred place, where a 'watcher' was tending a corpse awaiting burial (also a very Jewish ritual) and so we went on a guided tour of Maori Jewishness. Later that night at a *hangi* (barbecue) we did explain that eating the semi-cooked, lukewarm, overly fat pork belly wasn't quite in the same rule book.

George reeled off Maori families who had been sired by the original Nathan and Davis emigrants, later the famous brewers, and how these men had left educational trusts for their unofficial progeny. (Some years later I befriended a Maori social worker who took her son to Jerusalem for his *bar mitzvah*, courtesy of one of these trust funds.) Informing the Wellington and Christchurch rabbis that they had much larger congregations than they thought didn't go down well. They had troubles enough, they replied, without additional Maori 'hordes'.

Rotorua taught me a great deal. We were invited to attend a community meeting of elders and government officials. One of the country's nastiest tabloids had published a headline on how American tourists were upset at the decrepit state of Maori housing in the village adjacent to the sulphur geysers. One after another the housing commissioner, tourism chief, and the heads of geology, lands and Maori Affairs stood up to show just where and how they intended relocating the whole *marae* and at what costs to the local population. After several hours of this, the Maori chief—collarless, jacketless and with vivid braces—was asked to respond. He stood up, only to murmur that his colleague next to him was a better speaker. Up stood a silk from Auckland who, unbeknownst to all present, was representing the community. We'll meet you in court on Monday said the barrister ever so briefly, and we can have a judge decide on the equity issues. End of story, end of relocation. So we learned something about corporate power and the effectiveness of civil suit (or a threat of it) when politics fails the powerless. From then onward I urged Aboriginal communities to engage in what Ivan Illich called 'convivial' civil law processes, almost always more successful in outcome and yet all too seldom resorted to.

We saw another strong and impressive side of law: community justice through show, tell and shame. We were invited to a temporary *marae* in Auckland, in this case a high school assembly hall used as a courtroom, with about 400 people present. The first case was a Maori couple openly exchanging severe marital disharmony. Much shame and shaming was abroad with me cringing and wondering why I was there listening to all this very personal stuff. At the end compromise came about, at least on the surface. The second case was a young man guilty of car thefts. Not before a magistrate but before his elders he confessed the offences, expressed some mortification (at being caught rather than having stolen) and was sentenced to pushing the disabled in wheel chairs for six months. What impressed me was that shame was still alive as a cultural norm and that here was a system that bypassed normal courts, criminal records and prison cells. Australia finally came to some of these ideas of community justice, shaming tribunals and diversionary programs 30 years later. But as of today, 34 percent of juveniles in detention in Australia are Aboriginal, yet they are 2.5 percent of the juvenile population. (The figures in the Northern Territory are almost beyond credulity: 97 percent of juveniles in detention are Aboriginal and in 2013 the figure for adults was 82 percent. This is but one of the legacies of the days when police were officially 'protectors of Aborigines' and when alcohol prohibition resulted in so much incarceration.) No lessons learned from across 'the ditch'.

We were very impressed by Lex Grey and his play-centre in which Maori mothers were taught how to recognise the motor development of their infants—it applied, in a sense, the ideas of Swiss developmental psychologist Jean Piaget on the ages at which young children learn to recognise, appreciate and conserve notions of height, weight, distance and volume. They nurtured their children through these stages. The mothers were urged to further their education and many did so. We learned about Maori generosity when some of these women, hardly-well-to-do, volunteered to go to Australia to help Aboriginal mothers. A few teams went but little came of it.

We returned to Australia having learned much in a short time. We had several positive discussions with Dr HC (Nugget) Coombs, still chairman of the Reserve Bank and about to become chairman of the Office of Aboriginal Affairs, located by Harold Holt in his Prime Minister's Department. The Office comprised the executive officer former diplomat Barrie Dexter, anthropologist Bill Stanner and Coombs and a small staff that later included Ted Egan. Coombs had seen him in action as a teacher at Yirrkala and insisted on seconding him to Canberra as his trouble-shooter.

By then Stanner had had an epiphany. He wrote a fine essay (in my view the best thing he ever did) entitled 'Industrial Justice in the Never-Never' on the 1966 Arbitration Commission's decision on the wages case—to wit, that Aborigines should be included in the cattle station award but not for another two years (until they learned to play with real rather than Monopoly money) and that thereafter cattlemen could deem Aborigines as 'slow workers' worth only a portion of a real wage. In normal society slow workers are always deemed as such only after the worker, his union representative and the employer appear before an industrial magistrate who then adjudicates on the degree of slowness and reduced productivity. Such a system was only right and proper. Contrary to fair practice, here it was simply a matter of wholesale 'deeming' by those in the box seat and with the most vested of interests.

As liberal, enthusiastic and determined as Coombs and his small team were, they managed to remain immured in the ideas, templates (and nightmares) that bedevilled Aboriginal affairs. They stayed with what they knew or knew of. Dexter, a career diplomat, at least had a fresher approach than the others. Stanner was still very much the 'full-blood' anthropologist from Daly River days and a man never comfortable with urban and mixed-descent communities. No public servant was sent to the United States, Canada or New Zealand or to learn about comparative ideas and practices.

The 'we'll-solve-our-own-problems-in-our-own-way' approach has always frustrated real progress.

*　*　*

The referendum of 1967 was a curious affair, suffused by mythology from the start. It was a miserable (and truly ambivalent) time for me. In 1944 the matter of the Commonwealth taking control of state Aboriginal affairs was a referendum question, together with thirteen other major issues like monopolies, freedom of speech, freedom of religion, national health and ex-servicemen's rehabilitation—all matters of weight. That referendum stood or fell on all fourteen points and was, of course, lost. The 1967 question arose from two sources: Harold Holt as Prime Minister wanted to increase the numbers in the House of Representatives without a corresponding ratio increase in the number of Senators [tied by a nexus in the constitution]. He knew it would be an unpopular question and so he looked for a 'nice' question to go along with it in the hope that there could be a positive 'donkey vote' response. Bill Wentworth had for years been lobbying Robert Menzies, who detested him, on a Bill of Rights and the two bones that were finally thrown to Bill were the creation of the AIAS and a referendum question in two parts: first, to count 'full-blood' Aborigines in the national census from which they had been excluded in 1901; second, to allow the Commonwealth not *sole* power but *concurrent* power with the states to make laws for Aborigines.

FCAATSI, especially when Stan Davey was secretary, wanted single control of Aborigines because with little financial resource it was easier to criticise and lobby one government rather than seven separate jurisdictions. He and his colleagues seemed to believe that if granted concurrent power, the Commonwealth would always override the nastier state laws of Western Australia and Queensland. And so the great Communist witch-hunter Wentworth joined hands, literally, with arch socialist Doris Blackburn in working towards a successful yes vote to the two Aboriginal questions. I once saw them actually holding hands while singing 'We Shall Overcome'. Amazing stuff from two ageing enemies. But the referendum—always represented as a 'new deal' involving voting rights, citizenship rights, drinking rights—was nothing of the sort. The Coombs Office rightly saw this 90 percent positive referendum response from the public as a mandate to do something very different. But as Charles Rowley pointed out, if radical changes were not made within five years of this powerful public sentiment, all would revert to the *status quo ante*. Sadly it did.

I was (inwardly) opposed to the referendum. By May 1967 Victoria was on the way to making some positive changes as was New South Wales, and Don Dunstan had shown what could be done in South Australia where he had passed a land rights act as well as an anti-discrimination statute. The notion that the whole of Australia's Aboriginal population could ever come to be guided and administered by the Department of Territories and a large Social Welfare Branch under men like Harry Giese was a night- and day-mare not to be contemplated. Administrations in the Territory and Victoria had shown no propensity to recognise local and regional differences that required differing approaches, so why and how one single, continental bureau would handle Australia's massive Aboriginal diversities was vexing. I would argue this with friend Stan but financial pragmatism came first for him and the prospect of a 'one enemy' target was his best hope. I didn't fight him publicly and appeared to be a supporter of the 'cause'. But I have felt undeserving of the accolade of one of the 'heroes of the referendum struggle'. It was always going to be a symbolic not a pragmatic 'struggle' and it has taken another 47 years for the next symbolic milestone to surface, namely, *mentioning* (but in no way empowering) Aborigines as 'first nation' people in the decorative preamble to the Australian constitution. (Canada formally got round to 'first nations' instead of 'Indians' 30 years ago.)

The referendum's success, with 90 percent of the electorate voting in favour of what they believed to be 'Aboriginal rights', was extraordinary and showed a marked psychological change in attitudes, in theory at least. It sounded good and it made most people feel that the country had come of age. As expected, the highest yes votes came from voters with least Aboriginal contact; the no votes emanated from people living in greatest proximity to Aboriginal communities. Eleven years after the referendum the Commonwealth tried to pass legislation to override a particularly discriminating Queensland law affecting the communities at Aurukun and Mornington Island. A political rather than a legal battle, Queensland won by a knockout. In sum, the referendum was a moral milestone, unaccompanied by any serious practical changes for decades to come.

* * *

By August 1968 I was entitled to a sabbatical, one I was eager to spend in Canada. Arthur Keppel-Jones, then Professor of History at Queen's University in Kingston, Ontario, secured the appointment for me. Queen's, one of Canada's leading universities, was situated in a beautiful city of 100,000 people, 240 km by road to Toronto, on the shores of Lake Ontario. I was to be an associate professor in the Political Studies Department comprising Politics and Sociology.

We flew via Johannesburg, a fortunate decision because Sandra was not well on the plane and on our first evening there she was in a state of collapse. Her brother Eddie, back in Johannesburg following the shocking death of his wife Erica in a car accident in Sweden, arranged Sandra's immediate admission to the Johannesburg General Hospital. Her physician diagnosed rheumatic myocarditis. Seriously ill for a couple of weeks, she was allowed to convalesce at aunt Babs's house, away from the children and general family issues. Queen's granted me an extra five weeks before I began teaching in the sociology program. The Johannesburg Jewish Day School, King David, took the children for that time.

Queen's housed us in one of those delightful four-storey, big-basement, huge-furnaced, old houses in the heart of the campus. My office was a block away, the kids at a provincial primary school of high quality. The smallish Jewish community was overwhelmingly kind and we were accepted as if we'd been there a lifetime. The rabbi and his wife were compassionate and sensitive: an example was the day our dog, Nipples—a five dollar deal from the pound, a cross between a dachshund and a weasel—was run over and killed. They made a grief house call bringing flowers and comfort to the children.

I taught comparative race relations and advanced sociological theory. This was the swinging sixties, the time of Trudeaumania, Leonard Cohen writing ballads and poems while high on LSD, an era in which most youth were less than serious and often bewildered about life and the future. Many Monash students would tell us that they were at university only because mum said they should go. Queen's students knew exactly what they wanted and where they were headed. When I asked students why they were there, there were answers like: 'I will be the chief justice one day', 'I'll be the chairman of Air Canada'. Their grades were remarkable and even the dimmer ones were good enough to pass. Most achieved what they aspired to.

I cared for them and they for us, visiting the house often, babysitting the children and the puppies, enjoying wine and coffee. One older student, Jim Kelly, called me aside soon after arrival and said in that soft, purry accent: 'Sir, the guys think you should take off the tie, wear a rolltop shirt, let the hair grow, wear a medallion round your neck, start using the word eraser instead of rubber and stop saying "bugger me"'. I've worn a tie perhaps five times since then but I baulked at the glittering medallion. [Though I do wear a necklace made of walrus ivory, an *inuk*, the shape or concept of man, acquired nearly 40 years later in the Inuit territory of Nunavut.] One fellow staff member was known to coerce students, male and female, into sex for good grades. The students consulted me and I prepared affidavits, then sworn by a notary, and placed them in a safety deposit box. They may still be there. Despite the evidence, Queen's, like Monash, fiddle-faddled as the offender threatened legal action. In the painful end they removed him.

Campus life was a joy. Sandra recovered her health and began her university English studies, enjoying every moment of great literature and equally good teaching. The children adored the bobsledding, the ice, shovelling snow from the footpaths and watching me plug in the car's engine heater every night. It was the smallest 'big' car I could find: an enormously long, two-door 1963 Pontiac Laurentian. I played a great deal of snooker with colleagues and the staff club was high quality; food included frogs' legs, a new item on my menu.

Hockey Night in Canada (HNIC) was an instant love affair. The telecasts of the National Hockey League games and the Stanley Cup playoffs were not to be missed. Canadian and American gridiron football paled by comparison with this exciting, passionate, violent and poetic ice ballet. Paul was old enough to savour the fortunes of the Montreal Canadiens, the team led by Henri Richard and the swarming, aggressive, tilting Jean Beliveau, Yvan Cournyer, Jacques Leperriere, Jacques Lamaire and Serge Savard, names to salivate over, to adore. (In Mordecai Richler's hilarious novel *Barney's Version* (1997), the dementing Barney Panofsky can barely remember his second wedding because he kept rushing to the television behind the bar every five minutes to see if Beliveau had scored.) Only one man couldn't evoke that exotic flavour, the goalkeeper. Be-masked like six phantoms of a dozen operas, he had a record of something like 300 stitches in his head. Names like Malcovich, Imlach, Lalonde and Gretzky are to be expected, but who else in life but a Canadian ice hockey goalie could have a name like Gump Worsley? Or play like he did?

***

Indian affairs were of obvious interest and an approach was made to the (then) Department of Indian Affairs and Northern Development. With the Indian Affairs Branch (IAB) officials in Ottawa I negotiated both a project and a very small grant of some $3,000 to add to the Queen's contribution of $2,500. The $500 difference was to be significant. In January 1968 the IAB instituted a series of seventeen regional meetings with Indian communities to discuss their responses to 34 questions posed by government on changes to Indian policy and legislation in a booklet called *Choosing a Path* (CAP). The summit meeting of the regional council chiefs, 'The Ottawa Conference', was held in April–May 1969. I was appointed 'a consultant on consultation' with the task of evaluating the regional and the Ottawa consultation process for the IAB. With an Honours student as my research assistant, we had to read the two or more million words in the transcripts of all the cross-country meetings.

Much of the Ottawa Conference was closed to non-Indians but I was allowed in to a few sessions and given access to the tapes of the conference. I interviewed, in depth, 22 of the 27 delegates to Ottawa and arranged for a welcome when I travelled to their home bases. The IAB wanted me to stay an extra six months on the project but the new Anthropology head insisted I return to Monash in August 1969 because of a 'staff emergency'—which turned out to be 'subbing' for one of his mates who had taken a fortnight's leave. As a compromise, I spent 80 days travelling the country from 13 May to 1 August.

We bought a foldaway campervan and set out on a trek that took us 8,000 km across Canada, ducking in and out of the United States, traversing 63° of longitude from Cheticamp on Cape Breton Island in Nova Scotia to Victoria on Vancouver Island in British Columbia. It was a breathtaking and breathless voyage given my time limits, all too rushed, too headlong (as always in my life). We spent between one and three days at some 26 reservations or Indian populations centres, half the time in motels, half in the campervan.

We drove east from Kingston though Quebec, New Brunswick, Nova Scotia, Prince Edward Island, then back to Kingston for a short break.

The trip east was wondrous, taking in the astonishing Percé Rock on the Gaspé Peninsula in Quebec. There we were taken to sea by French-speaking fishermen to catch cod, the easiest of catches as they don't bite the bait but simply allow themselves to be snagged. We visited the gannet breeding ground on Bonaventure Island opposite the Rock; Reversing Falls on the Saint John River; Magnetic Mountain at Moncton; a visit to Vermont and crossing Lake Champlain by ferry; unique small-scale models of castles at Woodleigh Gardens on Prince Edward Island; the quite marvellous mixed cultures on Cape Breton Island comprising Scottish fiddlers mixed with Acadian French and Mi'kmaq Indians. Son Simon adored the fiddlers who had to stop playing when they hit a certain pitch which attracted a zillion blackflies. Huron Village in Quebec is famous for its Indian canoe makers. We were treated royally by their chief, Max Gros-Louis, the most splendid human figure I'd ever seen. A professional wrestler, he wore an Armani suit and a magnificent plaited ponytail draped like a pet taipan on his immense shoulder. We learned just how deeply the Huron people hated the French Québécois, a reciprocated emotion.

My most memorable time was at Eel River Reserve in New Brunswick where Chief Wallace LaBilloise persuaded us of the sanity of the Indian lifestyle. Here we were dashing across that huge country and there he was thinking and fishing in contemplative style. On the first evening he asked if we wanted to meet 'grass-roots' Indians. Yes, but who would mind our kids? My thirteen can mange your three, he replied. We set off for a Restigouche County village on the Quebec side. The occasion was a wake for an Indian prince who had died in Detroit. I asked what was expected of us once in the home above an Indian convenience store. Follow the others was the laconic answer. We did, on bended knees before the embalmed one, muttering *Shema Yisrael* for want of Catholic phrasing. Normally olive-skinned, I was pretty tanned, wearing a lot of hair and a leather jacket. Word spread that I was an Indian prince of the Vancouver Haida mob. Explanations about Melbourne, let alone Johannesburg via Lithuania, were not accepted. So I was honoured.

But the real story was the arrival of the brown-cassocked priest. After about forty Hail Marys he left and we were ready to go home. Wait, said Wallace. A dozen church choirboys arrived at midnight, took off their surplices and proceeded to sing the deceased to a Mi'kmaq universe—in Mi'kmaq. These people had been nominally Catholics for over 300 years! One couldn't help thinking of the *conversos* or *marranos*, the Jews who were forced to convert at the time of the Inquisition and who remained as 'hidden' Jews.

The journey westwards from Kingston was long and enjoyable. I insisted on seeing deadly places like Sudbury, once a world producer of nickel, and Sault Sainte Marie, famous as the site of the great locks in the Great Lakes system—places I had taught about in my school geography classes. After a research visit to Fort Frances in Ontario, a diversion occurred when we visited International Falls on the border with Montana. At a motel run by an Israeli couple, by three in the morning the owner and I had consumed enough Israeli liqueur to decide to give up our occupations, form a partnership in a chicken restaurant where he'd raise them and kill them and I would cook them in my inimitable cacciatore style!

The Alberta's Calgary Stampede intrigued us and we bought tickets for the ten-day July event while in Kingston. Little did we know that for four consecutive days we would watch the same chuckwagon teams racing frenetically around a dirt track. Exciting once, twice, even thrice but by the fourth day we never wanted to see another race. Quite memorable was the friendliness of the locals, helping with directions, getting out of their cars to show us maps and the routes out of town.

The University of Calgary is a fine institution. I met some sociology colleagues there and had my long interview with Harold Cardinal, then 23, on the cusp of becoming one of the foremost Indian leaders in the country. He was then leader of the Indian Association of Alberta; he became head of the National Indian Brotherhood, the forerunner of the Assembly of First Nations. Even in 1969 he was arguing forcefully that Indians should be and would be 'the red tile in the Canadian mosaic'. In the south of that province we went to Cadston, then to Waterton National Park, inadvertently rowing a boat into Montana, with no border guards in sight.

A former doctoral colleague at ANU always insisted that British Columbia is 'Godzown country'. It possibly is. Samuel Coleridge must have seen the Jasper, Banff and Yoho National Parks when he wrote 'Kubla Khan' with its miracles of rare device. In Vancouver we spent time with several communities and learned more from Chief Joe Mathias Joe, head of the Nisga'a Council, than from most others.

What was this whole exercise about? Representatives of some 750,000 Aboriginal peoples (their phrase) were asked what changes they were prepared to accept in the *Indian Act* and in policy directions generally. Dozens of local meetings were held culminating in seventeen major regional consultations and climaxed by the Ottawa summit. Robert Andras, Minister without Portfolio, was a driving force and a man of immense integrity. In October 1968 he said of the consultation process:

> We are not going out of Ottawa with answers but with questions. We must, for the love of God, find a means of consultation with the Indians that is honest, open, complete, sincere and constructive. We must ensure that the choices dictated by their values are made available to them. The best thing the government can do is get the hell out of the way.

The Indians wanted to talk about their treaties and their treaty rights, particularly hunting and fishing rights, arising from cession of their lands. The British Columbia (BC) Indians were never defeated, no treaties ensued and they wanted a separate BC Act to fit their circumstances. At the consultations government officials were flanked by lawyers and the Indians had none. Indians talked of themselves as standing 'naked' before officialdom. I had always railed against the unequal contests between the corporate men of officialdom ranged against the 'naked' individuals whom they browbeat, cajoled, moved, removed, incarcerated, whatever. The most unequal of power struggles, I constantly urged Aboriginal legal incorporation, a device by which the corporate body could provide some kind of political and legal carapace that protected the individuals from so much open exposure. I did succeed to some extent: Aboriginal incorporations in Australia swelled to close on 8,000 in a very short time and, of course, that produced some nasty side effects. [It has led governments to ignore all individual approaches, to insist that any grievances or requests be addressed through 'their incorporated body'.]

Fear underscored many meetings. Indians insisted on a different sense of time, claiming that their way was to mull things over, not to make snap decisions; they counselled patience in the face of official impatience. They talked of five paths: the Ojibway one, the Cree one, and then the political, governmental and the official avenues to decisions. They liked the openness of Robert Andras but were exasperated by what they saw was the evasiveness of the Minister for Indian Affairs, Jean Chretien (later Prime Minister). They were right in their judgements.

On 25 June 1969, midway through the negotiations and discussions following the Ottawa meeting, Chretien produced a White Paper, *Statement of the Government of Canada on Indian Policy 1969*. It was as if not one of the consultations had taken place: it simply tore up the entire body of discussions to date. So much for honest, open, complete and constructive approach to Indian affairs. The hidden agenda was dishonest, closed and as unconstructive as possible: it advocated the elimination of the separate legal status of Indian people, transfer of the constitutional federal responsibility for Indian affairs to the [mainly unfriendly] provinces and basically terminated Indian treaties and the rights deriving therefrom. It was assimilation with a vengeance. Harold Cardinal immediately responded with a book, *The Unjust Society*, a flat contradiction of Pierre Trudeau's 'Just Society' proclamations. In the end the Act remained, with considerable strengthening from 1985.

What didn't remain was my report, entitled 'Consulting Indians'. Submitted to the Department of Indian Affairs in 1971, I asked if multiple copies could be made for distribution to my many hosts and to the key provincial bodies. The answer was a flat no, you can't show it to *anyone*. Stunned by this non-democratic Canadian response I appealed to Queen's University. The Dean of Arts was a constitutional lawyer I'd met earlier in Australia. The Political Studies departmental administrator was none other than Flora MacDonald, later a senior federal parliamentarian and the first woman to be appointed Minister for Foreign Affairs. I implored Flora, even then a powerful figure, to fight this censorship. She may have tried but Queen's buckled completely under an IAB dictate that since they had provided the larger share of the research grant, the material vested in them, not in Queen's and not in me.

I let it go—too difficult to fight from the University of New England where I went in early 1971—and eventually gave the material to Sally Weaver who published some of this in her 1981 book on Indian policy. Interestingly, she didn't make any use of the censorship story. A freedom of information request could locate the internal files on this matter but that would only show how nice Canadians can also be nasty Canadians.

A whale in Haida Nation art, British Columbia, painted by C. Greul.

***

Earlier, Queen's had asked me to stay on permanently. I said I'd like to feel the sun on my face once more before deciding. Two migrations in a decade seemed a bit much and we talked it over en route to delightful San Francisco and home to Melbourne. The Centre was doing well under Elizabeth and Lorna but the Anthropology and Sociology Department was lurching from one calamity to the next. While in Canada, secretary Sue sent me a telegram to say that Graham Duncan, a Politics colleague, had been appointed to the chair of Politics at Adelaide. Flabbergasted, it made me think something I'd never thought of—a professorship. Professors were stellar intellectuals to me, men of true distinction, at least in the forms of Brookes, Keppel-Jones, Durrant, Webb, Parker, Sawer, Hancock et al—not Duncan and not Tatz. But I also saw that professors were no longer simply majestic scholars: they were fund-raisers, administrators, managers, organisers, as well as academic leaders.

I renewed some tentative discussions I'd had with Waikato University in Hamilton in 1968. They asked me to come over and at interview I was invited to take a chair there in Sociology or Politics or Maori Studies. The latter made no sense and I said I'd take the Politics position. They insisted on a testimonial from my current head, Rufus Davis. When I approached Rufe for the letter, he looked over his reading glasses, sniffed disdain and said, 'Collie, New Zealand is strictly for holidays'. Whereupon he phoned Zelman Cowen, then finishing his stint as Vice-Chancellor at New England, and asked if the foundation chair there was still open. Zelman said I should put in a late application. That I did.

Top: Edgar Brookes.
Portrait by Tito Field.
Courtesy Joan Brookes.

Left: Yehuda Bauer.
Personal collection.

Top: Alec Cook (1928–1988), wise friend and golf mentor, Armidale, New South Wales.

Above: Our children, (left) Simon, Karen, Paul.
Both photos from author's personal collection.

Top: Pilsner and ale tree, Darwin Highway, NT, 1961.

Above: My Holden bogged at Mt Liebig Creek, NT, 1962.

Both photos from author's personal collection.

Top: Cover of my first book, drawing by Professor Jack Heath, 1962.

Left: Cover painting by Ainslie Roberts of a wedge-tailed eagle, meant to represent the tale told by One Pound Jimmy about Buk-Buk the Owl, Central Mt Wedge, NT, 1982.

Top: Deluxe Kingstrand hut—'of satisfactory standard for Aborigines in transition', NT, 1960s.
Personal collection.

Above: 'Averted eyes': Michael Mucci's cover painting for my book, *Aboriginal Suicide is Different*.
Courtesy of Michael Mucci.

Left: Pointing to a forest of murdered Jews buried north of Ponovez (Ponevezys), Lithuania.

Below: Suicide conference venue, the Middle School, Iqaluit, Inuit territory of Nunavut, 2003.

Both photos from author's personal collection.

Top: Mi'kmaq Nation portrayal of woman and man, hooked rugs, Eel River community, New Brunswick, Canada, 1969.

Above: Gift from the Yirrkala clan, NT: Miniature bone-post painted by Narritjin Maymuru (1916–1981).

Top: Officer of the Order of Australia ceremony: (left) Pam Tatz, Colin, Sandra Tatz, Gary Ella, 1997.

Above: Honorary Doctor of Laws, University of Kwa-Zulu Natal, Pietermaritzburg, 1997, with Vice-Chancellor Brenda Gourley.

Both photos from author's personal collection.

Part IV:
The Middle Ages

Chapter 13

RUSTIC AND HECTIC

The University of New England (UNE) is a reputable rural university in the northern New South Wales city of Armidale. Flown there in November 1970, I was taken to breakfast with two Queensland University professors, Colin Hughes and Ken Knight. I knew Colin from ANU days, Ken less well. 'Who else is on the selection committee for this foundation chair?' I asked. 'Oh, I'm not on the panel' said Ken, 'I'm a candidate.' Astonished that a full professor at a prestigious university should be an applicant, I was convinced, with reason, that Ken was the obvious choice and my interview was but window-dressing for 'transparency'.

We were met by the Registrar Ken Long at the gracious administration building, Booloominbah. He shook my hand but hugged his old mate Ken. Alphabetical said Long, so would Dr Tatz please wait on the chaise longue outside the Council room. Whispering staff came and went, eyeing and sniffing the potential newcomer. After an hour I was ready to leave with my bat, ball and crossword. As I stood up Ken emerged, hurriedly shared some of the questions before I faced a roomful of 23 men. Clearly they were satisfied with Ken and his 'safe' public administration background. One inquisitor asked if I wanted to come to Armidale to 'go to pasture'—given that some academics did just that, evading metropolitan life and stress, harvesting hectares, cuddling cows, sporting Akubra hats, moleskin strides and elastic-sided boots.

Midway, I found interest and zest enough to put some passion into this seeming charade. I distributed a one-page outline of what I thought a new

Politics Department ought to look like, which topics were essential, which elective, which new courses would complement existing social science and humanities offerings. We adjourned for lunch, whereafter Long asked us to sit in the rose garden while the committee was in session. We earnestly reassured each other who was the better candidate and who wanted or needed the job more. Long emerged a half-hour later—and with a startling disregard for niceties openly shook my hand and announced, rather loudly, that I had the job. I had the half-wit to say I'd have to discuss it with my wife before responding.

Later, when I was chairman of the Professorial Board, we shortlisted candidates for a chair in Asian history. I told Vice-Chancellor Alec Lazenby that it was open and shut and we needn't go through the hassle of interviews. My boy, he said, don't ever underestimate interviews: when you were a candidate the voting was 22–1 against you on a straw vote before the face-to-face meeting and 23–nil for you at the end of it. Lesson learned. But I also learned not to leave candidates stranded on a chaise longue or to wait with competitors in rose gardens.

Sensing they wouldn't share my pretty obvious enthusiasms and ambitions, I begged Sandra and the children to fly to this 'Athens of the North' for a look-see. Sandra declined, with her usual sense of putting my interests first. We drove from Melbourne via Canberra and reached Armidale on 22 December in my large Austin 1800 (two-tone green), towing the overloaded Canadian campervan, with three kids, one dedicated road-loving dog Lolita and her chronically carsick, dim-witted, doting son, Dimitri. We arrived at a house rented unseen from a fellow professor: outdoor dunny, giant cobwebs and rat traps that could encircle wombats. There were tears all round and a week of voluntary constipation. The shock of a lifetime.

Shock #2 was going to the Commonwealth Bank on Monday 4 January to open an account with a friendly deputy manager. I sauntered next door for a haircut at the bike and barbershop. 'So you're the new professor and you play off eleven' said the kindly Arthur Robins, 'and you're in Paul Barratt's house'.

No, not ASIO or any other surveillance agency, simply *Gemeinschaft*, village communalism where nothing can remain, let alone be, a secret. The banker was the golf club's handicapper and he'd phoned Arthur in the 30 seconds it took me to walk about 50 m for the trim.

Shock #3 was the discovery that I was reported—and perceived by some townsfolk—to be a radical, left-wing, black, South African Jew. How did *that* sit with the genteel, conservative, Christian squattocracy? My landlord, president of the Armidale Club, was overheard to have said, 'Of course we can't have him as a member', even as he took my rent. Zelman Cowen, later Governor-General, was Vice-Chancellor until I arrived and they wouldn't have him either. 'Big Zel' was much more establishment than I could ever be and much less outspoken, or much better spoken.

More shocks were in store for my children. From the warmth and comfort of the small Bialik College in Melbourne, Paul found himself at Armidale High School, and Karen and Simon at Ben Venue Primary. Paul was the only Jewish student in the school and endured teacher insistence that he was the one best placed to explain to the classes everything from Passover, the Crucifixion, the Crusades, to Fagin and Shylock. He didn't enjoy school life. Karen—always assured, confident and positive in her outlook—asked if she could sit the scholarship exam for entry into Presbyterian Ladies' College. She duly won a scholarship to that prestigious but toffy establishment, a place where she did well but didn't enjoy all that much. Simon eventually went to the new Duval High, graduated to driving his mother's orange Mini to school about 300 m away, and had fun despite a headmaster who was an ardent supporter of the League of Rights. He and Simon didn't click. A plus was that tough Aboriginal kids left him alone because he was 'Colin's son'. That 'protection' arose from many friendships in the rather divided Aboriginal community. The disparate trilogy of 'reserve', Housing Commission, and townspeople didn't see eye to eye but I straddled the factions by giving advice on strategies. I insisted on payment of ten cents, explaining that the fee bound me to a professional relationship with clients. They understood and I collected a few fistfuls of coins. Ex-Sydney barrister Neil Mackerras did the legal aid work while I assisted on a raft of political issues.

We built a fine Politics Department, men and women who liked each other, never fought, never split into factions and who spent a fair bit of social time together. Secretary Sylvia Morrow, who died prematurely in 1984, was a key to the pleasing atmosphere and harmonious workplace. I began teaching immediately: courses on racism and politics, key concepts in politics, and then racism and nationalism as an Honours course. The latter was the least amiable part of my teaching, sharing the course for two years with historian Russell Ward in a joint Politics–History offering. Russell had extraordinary ideas about racism, for example, insisting that colour alone was the distinguishing factor in prejudiced behaviour and that Jews could always evade discrimination by denying who they were. The students put paid to this venture, saying loudly enough that they liked the material but not the tension between the two professors. I maintained outwardly good relations because of his then wife's close friendship with Sandra.

Russell had some equally strange ideas about social justice. UNE didn't quite experience the 1960s and early 1970s student radicalism that pervaded Monash and other universities. It was a quiet place but startled by some student reactions, particularly from Melbourne rebel, Alan Oshlack. Alan failed a History exam, went to see Russell about a re-mark, which was refused, whereupon Alan snatched the handwritten script and fled to seek a second opinion. Commotion, lawyers abounding to determine who held copyright of an exam script—the marker, head of department or the student? UNE was about as inept as Monash and Queen's in dealing with such problems. Russell asked me, in furrowed earnestness, why Jews were always revolutionaries. My response was factually accurate but my tone was a tad unkind and perhaps impolitic.

UNE began life as a college of Sydney University in 1938 becoming independent in 1954. Always cringing a little about her 'little sister' status, UNE tended to raise the academic bars quite unduly. As much as I disdained external teaching on arrival, so much did I come to champion it. Correspondence students had to attend a residential school each semester, often involving at least 20 hours of face-to-face teaching. They were stimulating, mainly because the great majority of them were more mature, enjoying their first chance at higher education. The course notes were a marvel of good scholarship—putting one's expertise out there in print for all to see rather than relying on the often desultory, tired lecture notes in the live classroom. Depending on one's viewpoint, the mix of external students and staff resulted in some good/bad, marital/extra-marital arrangements. We also ran at least one weekend school in Sydney, always well attended. Ditto the inter-personal arrangements.

Sociologist John Nalson and I established a Master of Applied Social Science degree for which I developed a new course on political violence. The degree worked well, producing several students who went on to academic careers. Politics certainly became a notable department, contributing to the discipline by way of scholarly articles, conference presentations and books. Despite differing ideological outlooks, Graeme Starr and I worked well together in researching and publishing the Australian chapter on the state of the discipline in the significant American publication *International Handbook of Political Science* (1982). To be chosen for this task was an honour.

I was president of the Australian Political Science Association (1975–1977). For the latter's journal, *Politics*, I wrote a long essay in 1972 on 'The Politics of Aboriginal Health', referred to earlier. To date, progress has been more underwhelming than whelming; and the mantras and shibboleths about 'closing the gap' continue unabated and unachieved. Repeating the same mistakes is all too common among bureaucrats who either don't read or who won't read anything other than that which they deem 'current', an attitude that embitters me more than a little.

* * *

In the late 1960s and early 1970s movements began to allow teachers' colleges and similar institutions to grant degrees and upgrade to colleges of advanced education (CAEs). Such status was bestowed on, among others, Townsville, Armidale and Canberra. My association with Townsville CAE had begun before the Armidale days. At Eddie Mabo's suggestion, a tumultuous and heavily attended inter-racial conference was held there in December 1967 entitled 'We the Australian: What is to Follow the Referendum?' The speakers were Aboriginal and Islander leaders Joe McGinness and Faith Bandler, Charles Rowley and me. There was a heavy police presence. A friendship began with Margaret and husband and historian Henry Reynolds. Margaret was then a member of an appalling Queensland government front organisation called One People of Australia League (OPAL). She received a telegram from Director of Native Affairs Pat Killoran saying she'd be expelled if she appeared on a platform with these 'southern Commies and stirrers'. I urged her to ignore OPAL and resign from it. She did and went on to a strong and effective career as a Labor Senator. Townsville also generated the start of stronger connections on Aboriginal Studies with Henry Reynolds and Noel Loos, a fine historian and friend. Both kept me in the loop with Eddie Mabo's aspirations. Eddie was a gardener at the university.

Ted Egan was working for Dr Nugget Coombs in the Office of Aboriginal Affairs (OAA) in 1969. He and I suggested a nation-wide project for a subject called Aboriginal Studies to be taught in high schools, with follow-up courses at universities and CAEs. The premise was that 'one of the most effective ways to eliminate prejudice was to have Aborigines demonstrate the unreality of most beliefs and myths about them'. We proposed a two-year pilot costing $35,000. After much to-and-fro between Monash, the OAA, federal Treasury and UNISEARCH at the University of New South Wales (which received a grant but then quit on it), $1,750 for a two-year project was given to Armidale CAE, sited in a magnificent building said to have been the projected parliament house for a (stillborn) 'New England state'. The CAE leadership was enthusiastic and supportive.

Meantime, the Monash Centre's Lorna Lippmann had visited Britain and America to look at anti-prejudice projects. She reported that mere fact-teaching did nothing to stop prejudice, citing an anecdote from some English academics. Snipe, a London dockland kid, had written a one-line essay that alarmed the education authorities: 'Forriners is stoopid bastuds' he wrote. After two years of saturation materials about Christ, St Thomas Aquinas, Michaelangelo, Leonardo, Beethoven, Marx, Freud and Einstein, Snipe was asked by University of East Anglia researchers to write a fresh essay. 'Forriners is kunning bastuds' he wrote. We changed tack and based the courses more on attitude change than 'fact' correction.

Barbara Chambers, a final-year education student at UNE, agreed to do the evaluations of the final year teacher trainees who took the new course from 1971 onwards, about 250 in all. She used standard social psychology techniques for measurement of attitudes. Initially this compulsory Aboriginal Studies course comprised lectures from me, from anthropologists, public servants, educators and Aborigines. In 1975 I put together a book based on these lectures entitled *Black Viewpoints: The Aboriginal Experience*. Two years later Kevin Gilbert published *Living Black: Blacks Talk to Kevin Gilbert*, both books forming the platform for an Aboriginal literature where the people spoke on their own behalf. My family understood why I spent so much of my life trying to get a hearing for Black voices. The 'Armidale model' was successfully adopted by both Canberra and Townsville CAEs.

Teachers who were prejudiced before the courses remained prejudiced, those who were positive remained positive; importantly, the majority in the grey middle moved strongly to a positive position. Fortunately we were not entirely convinced and money was found for Barbara Chambers, then a postgraduate, to visit those teachers in their teaching placements. A minority had maintained their positive outlooks but most of the 'positives' had succumbed to the antithetical culture of their local environment and school staff—dismissive of Aboriginal ability in general, youngsters who were deemed unworthy of increased or special effort. We had made sufficient attitudinal impact for

Aboriginal Studies to become feature courses in CAEs and universities and eventually part of high school electives. No harm came from these courses and on balance there was enough good. Here indeed was a lesson—that education isn't always the magic panacea that cures such social ills.

Talks about amalgamation between the university and the teachers' college had begun early in 1971. But there were internal rumblings from a handful of dissenters at UNE about 'diluting the beer' which swelled to shouts. Some staff in Philosophy called me the 'horizontal professor', that is, one who couldn't or wouldn't see the virtues of 'vertical' or elite excellence. After some very messy politics the merger fell through.

Funding shortage meant that all of the Aboriginal guest lecturers stayed at our house in Campion Parade, a 'dress circle' street where we had bought a home newly designed and built. At $22,000, we mortgaged to the hilt, but it was a fun home, constantly inhabited by dozens of school-friends who didn't quite fathom the doorpost sign, 'Beware of the Dogmas'. Our children were enthralled by the visitors, especially the late Chicka Dixon who regaled them with stories of his life in prison, his literacy acquired there from an inmate called 'The Professor' and his subsequent reading of the entire *Encyclopaedia Britannica*.

The house was H-shaped with the kitchen and breakfast room in the crossbar area. Warm, friendly, it looked out onto a small glassed-in patio and the main sitting place was like a church pew. Sandra, who had started her tertiary studies at Queen's followed by a year at Monash, now enrolled in an Arts degree, gouging out a little time for study while mothering an eleven-, nine- and seven-year-old. She and her classmates held regular tutorials there, with canine approval. The children's friends were constant visitors to this very open home.

Midstream, Dimitri was run over outside our house. On the same day I sought a puppy to alleviate the general grief, including that of his mother Lolita and brought home what looked like a joey in a cardboard pouch— Jeremy the Labrador. He was hardly a dog, this gorgeous love of our lives (and of everyone else who got to know him). Self-taught, he collected the mail from the postie, brought in our newspaper (and those of the neighbours), picked up the washing in every room, item by item (because he could count, one sock equals one biscuit, two socks…) and placed each piece in the laundry basket. The tail of this literary hound responded in iambic pentameter as Sandra civilised him by reading aloud Milton's *Paradise Lost*. Never caged by kennel owners when we were away, he always wound up in the owner's lounge or master bedroom. When Lolita's eyesight diminished, he would take her head gently in his mouth, lead her to her food and then outside to do her business in the garden. Loved by all, he survived Armidale, then Lane Cove in Sydney, then Paul's home in Glebe, meeting the heavenly dog-taker at the end of 1985.

1972 was a big year. Paul was almost thirteen and the only realistic venue for a *bar mitzvah* was the Margaret Street Synagogue in Brisbane. His tutor Rabbi Engel was young and ultra-Orthodox, and later moved to Melbourne to sell cakes. Before that, he made a reel-to-reel tape of Paul's *haftorah* portion, set down for *Shabbat Shuva*, the most significant of Sabbaths, situated in the week between *Rosh Hashonah* and *Yom Kippur*. Paul's long portion was from Deuteronomy, chapter 31, the day Moses turned 120! Sandra would drive Paul in the Mini 850 to Brisbane and back, some 900 km, for lessons and a check on his progress.

Ben Melmed, our only parent ever to visit, came from Johannesburg for the occasion, and many of Brisbane's Jews attended for a somewhat unusual event. Friends from Melbourne and Armidale attended. Paul didn't miss a beat and his voice held firm. The Brisbane community put on the luncheon and blessings, and that evening about a dozen of us went to Mama Luigi's for a big Italian dinner. Sandra's father Ben was impressed: despite his Edinburgh medical training and extensive overseas travel, he needed reassurance that Australia had electric lights.

The rather quaint tradition of an inaugural professorial lecture took place some eighteen months after arrival and was well attended. I talked about comparative race relations in South Africa, Canada, Australia and New Zealand under the title *Four Kinds of Dominion*, published in booklet form by the university; it was also published in the British journal *Patterns of Prejudice* and, surprisingly, republished by the University of the Orange Free State in Bloemfontein, an Afrikaans institution with a good history archive. I suspect that they were happy to see three other countries receive strictures on race matters.

***

I had had almost no contact with the Australian Institute of Aboriginal Studies (AIAS) for about a decade. In May 1974 the Institute held its sixth biennial conference over sixteen days, at a remarkable cost (then) of $100,000. I was invited to chair a session on social and cultural change. At the grandiose buffet dinner at the Lakeside Hotel, Jacquie Lambert—the Institute's long-serving and marvellous administrator and later the Institute's insightful historian—asked me why I avoided the place. Memory says I was sounding off about betting that any grant application from me on current matters like health and education would be rejected. Someone behind me said 'you'd lose'. That was the voice of Peter Ucko, the new Principal, an impossible but brilliant London Jewish archaeologist. From that moment until his departure in 1981 and until his death in England in 2007, we enjoyed mutual respect, friendship, admiration and love. We smoked a few million cigarettes and drained vats of unremarkable red, sharing memorable times then as well as some serious diabetes and a little emphysema later. Sandra and the children adored him. Anger and disputation were rare and ended quickly, even if resolution was by way of his bizarre 3 a.m. phone calls.

Peter Ucko (1938–2007) brought the Australian Institute of Aboriginal Studies into contemporary events.

The May 1974 meeting was the forum for fights over a five-page open letter to Institute members signed by 'Eaglehawk and Crow'. All signatories bar Peter Thompson were Aboriginal. It attacked the Institute on several fronts and was the major catalyst in pressing the Institute to seriously reassess its relations with Aboriginal and Torres Strait Islander people. The letter attacked both the Institute and Peter Ucko for what he had been trying to achieve since taking office sixteen months earlier. The condemnation was fuelled by their decision to circulate replies to its open letter, several of which put a heavy boot into the Institute.

Criticism was rough and rife. The contention was that the conference would have no significance for Aborigines and their position in the world.

The conference cost was a 'worry' and so was the absence of Aborigines to speak on social and cultural change. The Institute was rebuked for its past and present policies, the authors deplored the partial breakdown of the Aboriginal oral intellectual tradition and the value given by society generally to the gospels of anthropologists. The Institute wasn't involved in land rights, it focused on 'tribal' Aborigines to the detriment of other Aboriginal people and it had no involvement in education and translation–literacy programs. Tokenism was deplored. Anthropologists should cease collecting and interpreting esoteric information but should act 'to help all people... understand the general and complex features of Australia's situation (unresolved colonialism, capitalism and privilege, and authority/power), and so work to change it in a more humanising, liberating direction'. Aboriginal communities should commission research and control funding which—together with a satisfactory land base with full land rights—was the only way of altering what was said to be the unsatisfactory relationship between anthropologists and Aborigines. Was any of this true? Yes, most if not all of it. I didn't exult but felt some pleasure at the discomfiture of some pompous scholars and much vindication of the paths I had chosen in 1964.

Council set aside a formal period to discuss the letter. No one present in the Coombs Theatre at the Australian National University on 25 May 1974 has forgotten the rage, outrage and passion engendered, the threats to ego, the strutting and posturing of some of the academics or the vigorous challenges to the status quo. *Götterdämmerung*, as in defeat or downfall in a field of battle! Not least was the tumultuous resistance to the Institute's proposed move from its cramped Lonsdale Street quarters into Mining Industry House, a time of an all-time low relationship between Aborigines and miners. (That move was stifled.)

The mood was set. At the request of two of the signatories present, the session was chaired by Ken Colbung, elected that morning as one of the thirteen new Aboriginal or Torres Strait Islander members. In that era, membership was seen as a special badge of honour with the statute fixing the total membership at 100 plus 20 members to be appointed by the AIAS Council. Following Colbung's departure mid-afternoon I was asked to take the chair. A satisfying honour in the circumstances and stirring stuff: *Sturm und Drang*, stress and dramatic storm, much fire and some brimstone from 'Eaglehawk and Crow' and their supporters. The politeness that had generally pervaded Institute gatherings was now out the doors and windows.

Earlier debate had opened up discussion about the possible restructuring of the Institute, leading to a resolution that a small committee, not necessarily comprising all Council members or a majority of Council members, should re-examine the nature, scope, function, academic jurisdiction, role, composition and membership of the Institute and report back to the membership. A postal ballot to elect five of 24 nominees was suggested and I was then elected as chairman together with Bob Edwards, Jack Golson, Dick Roughsey (the only Aboriginal member) and Bill Wentworth. We formed the steering committee on the 'The Institute's Philosophy and Function'. Several wheels had come full circle for me. In ten years I had moved from avoiding the Institute to presiding over its immediate future.

We presented the findings to Council in May 1976. In the sixteen months between 'Eaglehawk and Crow' and that date, much had changed. Peter Ucko led what could almost be called a charge and in this he had strong support. There were to be twelve advisory committees as opposed to the initial seven which basically ran the agendas. The newcomer committees included research and membership, Aboriginal advisory, publications, ecology, sites of significance and education. The latter—which I chaired from 1974 to 1978— showed how far the Institute had come from the earlier mandate. Change was occurring faster than we believed possible. AIAS responded to Aboriginal requests for materials, innovating and supporting 'action' programs that could improve the quality of people's thinking about Aborigines and their societies, publishing kit materials and bibliographies for secondary and tertiary teachers and disseminating work on race relations education in the United

Kingdom, the United States, Canada, South Africa and here (through the 'Armidale model').

This inquiry was able to conclude, with solid evidence, that 'the Institute is not in need of major revision of its nature, scope, charter, function, role or academic jurisdictions'. For me to preside over such a finding was an indicator of enormous change in Institute theory and practice given my hostility to the 'disappearing-aspects-only' charter of a decade earlier. I felt good rather than powerful as one of the instruments of change.

Years later, Jacquie and I wrote a chapter on 'Eaglehawk and Crow' for Peter Ucko's *Festschrift*. Jacquie's ANU doctoral thesis details these paroxysms, the Aboriginalisation of the Institute, relationships with Aboriginal administrations and community organisations, the internal and external reviews of the Institute, the incredibly quick developments of committees, and grants to encompass education, social issues, health, history (albeit only deemed worthy as late as 1982), and from my perspective, to take on board in 1978 the minefield that is the social impact of uranium mining on remote communities, discussed in the next chapter.

I was now glad I had become a member in 1964 and even more pleased that it took less than 20 years from inception for the Institute to shuck off the pretentious 'science of man' mantra, to see the currents of the contemporary contexts and to study and treat Aborigines not as man but as human.

In 1974 or 1975 a rather mysterious, heavily-bearded man arrived in Armidale, back in Australia he said, after a career as a science and maths teacher in Papua New Guinea. He was, he said, a former drover and horse-breaker in north Queensland where a horse accident had left him with a slightly crippled leg. I was charmed by him as were most people who came across him. He attended some of these teacher trainee sessions and asked me how he could best serve 'his people' and how he could be introduced to the Institute. I did just that, with my usual enthusiasm. I had established the Education Advisory Committee by then and so Eric Willmot took a place on that new unit and became my deputy. When I took a year's sabbatical in

1975 he took over that chairmanship. He soon became a Council member and from April 1981 he was Principal, for just over three years, to 1984. In these years there was to be some toxic atmosphere and much grief over this man and his administration.

* * *

Bess's heart problem dictated that we spend a half-sabbatical in South Africa in 1975. I contracted to teach a comparative race politics course at Witwatersrand University in Johannesburg. When South Africa became a republic in 1961, it withdrew from the British Commonwealth, resulting in both Australia and South Africa insisting on visas for each other's citizens. Applying to the embassy for a visa, a charming Ms Bastiaanse said she'd do what she could for me—which turned out to be a compassionate visa to visit a sick mother (true, but how did she know *that*?) and on condition that I gave no lectures (and how did she know about *that*?). We opted for a touristy visit, staying at a private hotel owned by Sandra's uncle. A cousin arranged a car and we set off on visits. One was to a Beatrix Mine near Welkom, a massive gold mine in the Orange Free State, some 2.2 km underground. Another was the nuclear facility at Pelindaba, about 35 km west of Pretoria, where Sandra's cousin was the senior nuclear chemist and where the country produced atomic weaponry in the 1970s. With Ben Melmed we spent several days at the 19,435 sq km Kruger National Park, a place I had never visited while a resident, always somewhat scornful of its iconic status. I was wrong as it is a quite spectacular and thrilling place. We all remember, vividly enough, an elephant charging at our car.

Friend Julius Horowitz loaned us his holiday palazzo in La Lucia, about sixteen kilometres north of Durban. Modelled on King David's palace, it was complete with harem baths, tiered courtyards, fountains, a dozen rooms, a janitor, two large black giant poodles and an Audi saloon. What was uplifting was a serendipitous meeting with members of the Durban Indian community, attending their markets and eating their special and different curry cuisine. We met with Durban cousins and with Professor and Mrs Brookes in Pietermaritzburg. Edgar was generous, proud of what I was doing.

We travelled the quite magnificent route down the east coast, through the Transkei, stopping over at Port St Johns and seeing something of traditional Pondo, Fingo and Xhosa life and culture. Then on to East London and Port Elizabeth (PE), after which we planned the famous Garden Route trip from PE to Cape Town. Sandra's cousins owned a hotel in PE where we indulged in all the niceties that white South Africa offered. An urgent call from Johannesburg informed us that Bess had fallen and broken an upper arm. My family, usually semi-paralysed at times like this, needed help. I recall the frantic drive of 900 km to my parents' apartment. There I arranged for Bess to be operated on and spent time with her in convalescence.

Meanwhile Maurice wasn't well and I took him to a thoracic surgeon who diagnosed a 'cannonball secondary' in his lung, biopsied it and pronounced it benign. It was a sad time for me: Bess and Maurice were deeply in debt and I arranged to pay some of their medical and pharmacy bills. This brought home the Jewish saying: when a father helps his son he does it with joy; when a son has to help his father, he does it with tears.

Despite the pretty sights, South Africa was more intense, more painful than anticipated. It was a time of relocating three million people from urban areas to the Black 'homelands'. It was a time of trade union resistance and the beginning of urban sabotage activities. A time when the Nationalist Government started on the quite disastrous path of trying to 'Afrikanerise' the African population, insisting on Afrikaans as the medium of school instruction. By 16 June 1976 that policy erupted in a 20,000-strong pupil revolt in Soweto resulting in 600 to 700 dead. Our visit reinforced earlier questions about how people could live alongside, or rather within, a racially violent vortex and not see it or feel it or query it. True, it was also the time when a fair number of Whites, who had the means and the will, started to leave, especially after the Soweto killings, and many came to Australasian shores.

We had a month in London at the end of that visit, in a rented apartment owned by New Scotland Yard, situated directly opposite their famous front entrance. A lot of sightseeing and enjoyment as we took in the usual cathedrals, statues, galleries, museums and theatres. I took Simon and Paul to a soccer match between Derby County and Queens Park Rangers at the Loftus ground in South Africa Road. It was, bar none, the coldest day in our collective experience and the price of the scalper tickets didn't help. It was a time of panic for Londoners: the Balcombe Street IRA bombing and siege occurred, streets were closed, bobbies were everywhere. It didn't deter us from eating in pubs in the neighbourhood of bombings, seemingly unconcerned about safety.

* * *

In 1976 I had the chance to visit Israel for the first time. A program called Academics for Peace in the Middle East sponsored a three-week visit. The aim was to recruit academics who would see the country, talk to the leaders and the people and come back motivated enough to spread the word that Israel was a legitimate state and deserving of a hearing (support?). To that point Israel had endured the 1948 War of Independence, the Suez war in 1956, the Six-Day War in 1967 and the Yom Kippur War in October 1973.

Arriving at Lod Airport was an emotional turmoil evoking pangs about why I wasn't there as a resident. Bob Hawke, later an Australian Prime Minister, was ahead of me in the customs line, there with his father to receive the Israeli government's honour of a forest planted in his name. We talked a little and he told me what had impressed him about Israel when he was there in 1971.

At the Banias, source of the River Jordan, Israel 1977.

For the most part the mission was brilliant. Accommodation was all too luxurious, travel a breeze, doors were opened wide and lectures and workshops were given by stellar figures like General Moshe Dayan, Prime Minister Yitzak Rabin, the Eichmann prosecutor Gideon Hausner, the ever-articulate former Foreign Minister Abba Eban. But for all of their insights, the mission provided little room to hear everyday people talk about Israeli–Arab relations, about local elections which were filled with turmoil, scandal and a new meaning to the term 'splinter parties': there were shards and bits of parties everywhere, making the Israeli proportional representation system almost unworkable. Tours were the inevitable tours but each so immensely rich: the Banias (a source of the River Jordan), Masada, the Dead Sea, the Qumran Caves where the Dead Sea scrolls were recovered, Lake Tiberias, the Golan Heights, the astonishing Mitspe Ramon Crater, Avdat (an impressive ruin of a second century BCE Nabatean city) and, of course, the wondrous archaeological sites around the Old City. The Golan Heights, captured from Syria in 1967, instantly turned our busload of doves into hawks. Sitting atop a ridge of gun emplacements with Damascus in distant view, one could see just how easily the Syrians came to rain shells down into the Israeli valley settlements below. One could visualise men dropping bombs by hand from those basalt ridges. Golan is breathtaking, with the very visible Mount Herman snow-capped all year.

I hardly needed such a visit to make me Israel-aware, but the visit made a profound impression and evoked an emotional reaction. I couldn't wait to go there again and again and again. It would be 1985 before the next visit.

Chapter 14

RADIO ACTIVITY

Life between my mid-forties and mid-fifties was particularly hectic, at times toxic, literally and figuratively. Uranium was a hot issue as was the sports boycott of South Africa. But there was time for some tranquillity in gentle Armidale, for a short sabbatical in Oxford, room for brief reflection on a major move and some new directions. The pain of losing my father made me realise just how much gulf there was between my life back in South Africa and what was happening in my life here.

Until the uranium project began to consume me, Armidale life was a little too tranquil. In 1975 a nonsense from nowhere popped into my head. I saw an advertisement for the governorship of Norfolk Island, a Commonwealth dependency in mid-Pacific Ocean, about 1,400 km from the mainland, a former convict colony and home to the Pitcairn Islanders. I applied and went to Canberra for an interview. My old friend Gordon Bryant, then Minister for the Australian Capital Territory, presided. 'What earthly reason can you have for wanting to go *there*?' he asked. Apart from a reasonable golf course and rumours of a good chef at Government House, I could only mutter that the Island was nearing the stage of self-government (achieved in 1979) and I believed I had the skills to help write the new constitution. Inwardly I grinned at the idea of this child of Lithuania taking royal salutes at this oh-so-colonial isle where God Save the Queen is still the anthem. 'It's not for the likes of you' intoned Bryant. And not too deep down I knew it wasn't.

From 1974 to 1976 I was deputy chairman of the Professorial Board at UNE and chairman in 1977. In 1978 I resigned one year into a two-year term, citing work pressure in order to obviate some 'interesting' interactions with a brace of academics who persisted in mounting a campaign to have me stand aside or be 'disciplined'. I said I had to meet a Sydney judge in chambers, thus indicating that I would take out an injunction against those two colleagues if they persisted. As chair of dozens of committees, including all the academic promotions, I had run into exquisitely honed bitchery from a pair of professors whose favoured sons didn't make promotion, and in one case, offended one of them who had opposed the promotion of a staffer he didn't like. Selection for promotion was tough—seven-person panels usually requiring at least a two-vote majority. But the offended professors didn't approve of what they saw as my refusal to get their boys through. My decision was to quit before all this could erupt; hot uranium ore was preferable to this lot.

My stint in university administration allowed me insight into just how bad academics can be as administrators and how bad professional managers were at understanding academic mores and values. I heard too often that universities could be great places to work—if it wasn't for the students. I also heard similar laments about '*having to teach*'. It made me realise, after four or five years of it, that I never wanted to be a high-ranking, highly paid executive officer. My medical friend George Tippett used to say how much he envied my life 'in a good, clean place with good, clean people'. Little did he know.

I chaired a new AIAS committee on education from 1974 to 1978 and served on the Institute's Council for a longer period (1974–1986). But my major interest was in a project that Peter Ucko was negotiating with Ian Viner, the (then) Minister of Aboriginal Affairs. In 1977 the second *Ranger Uranium Environmental Inquiry*, chaired by Justice RW Fox, recommended that Australia allow uranium mining and processing in the Kakadu region of Arnhem Land in the Northern Territory. Fox also acted as the first Land Rights Commissioner; he demarcated an area to be designated Kakadu National Park that would be 'owned' by the traditional Aboriginal clans he named. Here indeed was a confluence of three seemingly irreconcilable interests: Aborigines, a national park and uranium mining.

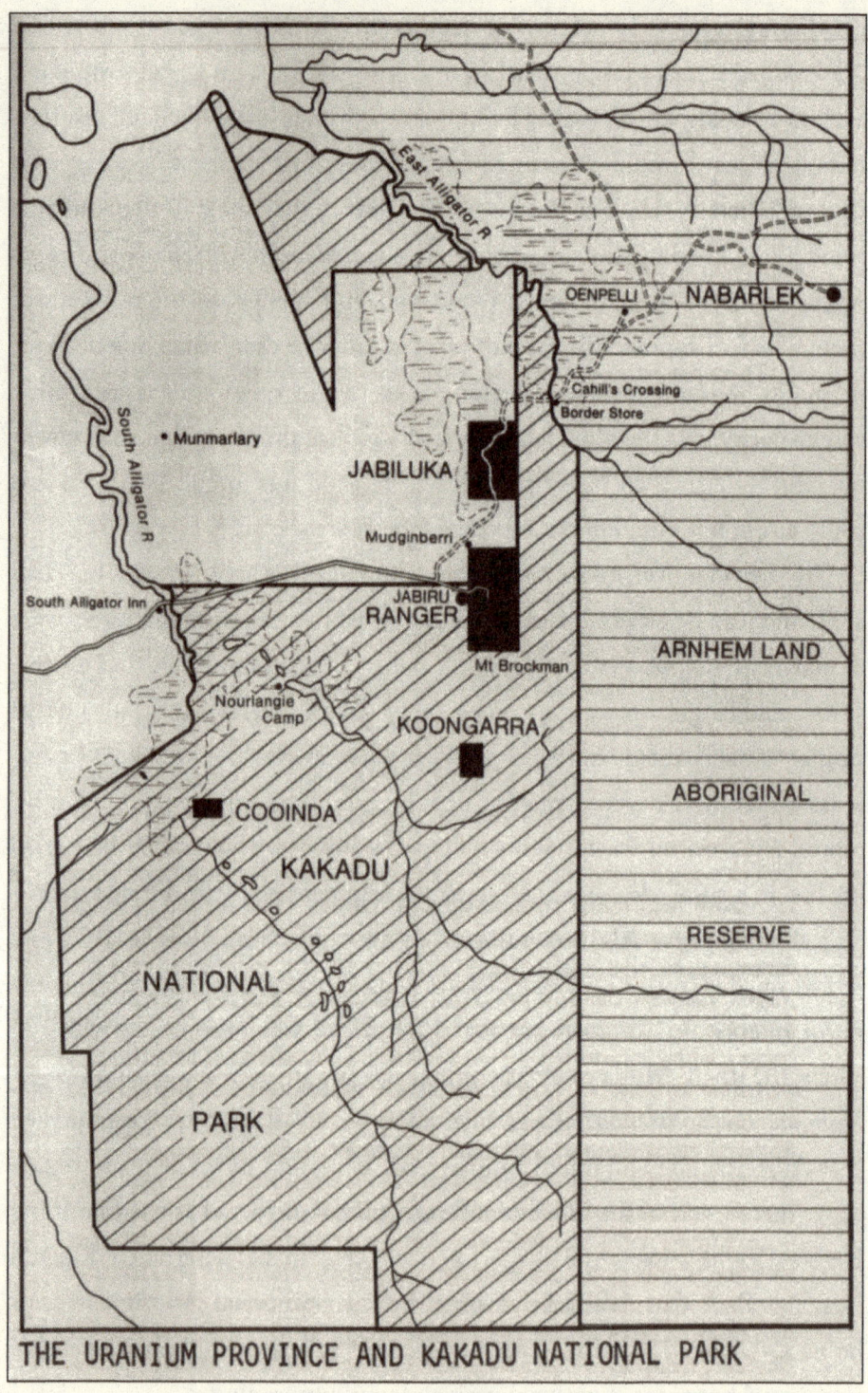

The uranium province and Kakadu National Park, 1982.

Aborigines had fought vehemently against any mining. They feared a shifting of their *djang* (the sites associated with spiritual meaning), the spread of White society and its influences, and pollution—'the leaves being unable to breathe'. They were greatly concerned 'by the grog thing' and expected that sexual predation, alcohol, drugs and other Western ills would produce 'kids who may not be true'. Justice Fox had said initially that there 'could be no compromise with the Aboriginal position: either it [their opposition] is treated as conclusive, or it is set aside'. In the end he concluded 'their opposition should not be allowed to prevail'. He did, however, record his many concerns about mining: the possible impacts of a new town near Aborigines, alcohol, venereal disease, an influx of single male workers, racial tensions and conflict.

In the event, the park's management plan barely considered Aborigines or any of Fox's concerns. An Office of Supervising Scientist was established to monitor the impact of this mining on the environment but that body had no interest (or expertise) in 'human' matters and essentially disavowed participation in any aspect of social impact. I found their values and attitudes woeful and said as much at every opportunity.

Ucko, who made a point of networking with parliamentarians, met with Viner to discuss a possible commission to the AIAS to undertake the monitoring of the social impact of uranium mining on the Aboriginal population. The matter came to Council and I openly said I wanted the job of chairing a steering committee that would run a six-year watch on the Alligator River exercise. Among ourselves we called it the *Wacht am Alligator*. Before the committee was established Ucko unilaterally appointed the two main staffing positions, the director John von Sturmer, a respected anthropologist and Sue Kesteven, a highly qualified linguist. I confess to irritation then and now: here again was the implacable belief that the only trustworthy 'keepers' of Aborigines and their interests were anthropologists. Nobody at that stage, certainly not Ucko, knew quite what was involved in an ongoing social impact study of an open-cut mining operation alongside large native populations living in a monsoon climate. Evidence of disaster at Shiprock, New Mexico was known but that was, typically, mining uranium in a desert region. The monsoon context was and remains unique.

Our project was truly pioneering, inventing aspects of monitoring as we went along. Our offices at Oenpelli comprised two demountables covered by steel canopies for heat protection. Between 1978 and 1984 I spent a considerable amount of time there, researching as much as steering the project. The requirement to present six-monthly reports to the Commonwealth Parliament was difficult and onerous. Meetings with Aborigines and with mining company people were frequent, usually awkward and often enough difficult. The one good thing was that mining people believed we had enormous power (we didn't) and had the clout to halt their activities (we certainly didn't). At the second international conference on hunting and gathering societies in Quebec City in September 1980, I gave a paper on this exercise. That conference was intended to shed light on the fates of indigenous hunter-gatherer minorities confronted by Western, capitalist, development-hungry societies. One colleague asked me how powerful our committee was. I modestly said I didn't know—at which point an eminent Canadian anthropologist interjected: 'Come, come, Colin, you are as powerful as you are perceived as being'. Right, of course, and thereafter I was to give a good imitation of a tough cookie in the politics of uranium.

The steering committee worked well, with few dissensions and usually antithetical ideologues (like Dr Nugget Coombs and Bill Wentworth) got along well. We established some new and important yardsticks for social impact monitoring, bearing in mind the lack of precedents or models. Innovative times. There were, of course, a few unpleasant moments. I engaged Carmel Schrire to provide an annotated bibliography on the health hazards of uranium mining worldwide. Some colleagues refused to accept her contribution because she wasn't a 'nuclear or medical scientist'. The several biological scientists we consulted all deemed uranium 'safe'—such were the times and the values. Dropping her from the team and the final report was painful; 24 years later I was able to vindicate her efforts when I returned to that field to look for the cancers that we predicted would surface. They did.

Sandra and Simon came on some field trips with me to the Northern Territory. They didn't much enjoy camping under nets and stars on the banks of the treacherous tidal East Alligator River, replete with water buffalo, large salty crocs, sharks and stingers. They did enjoy the wild barramundi scooped out daily from Oenpelli billabongs. Between mosquitoes and tents Sandra studied literature and Simon did a year's schooling by correspondence.

In 1982, before we had completed the uranium project, Heinemann published my book of essays on *Aborigines and Uranium*. There I was able to express more forthright views on uranium, the mining companies, the Aboriginal Northern Land Council and the personalities in the politics of all this. Clearly I wasn't a fan of the mining ethos nor of some of the representative Aboriginal bodies that should have been more supportive of Kakadu Aboriginal needs.

Early in 1982 we moved to Macquarie University in Sydney. Completion of the final report in 1984 was a difficult exercise, even more so than the hard work required to arrive at conclusions. Getting material from John von Sturmer was nightmarish (writing blocks and personal crises) and the deadlines could not be extended. In the end I wrote four chapters, and several of his chapters on the politics of residence and the politics of property were masterly. The conclusions were that Fox's fears were not realised. Mining didn't force any physical relocation or change in diet, didn't introduce venereal disease; Aborigines were not exploited by sly-grog or sly-sex merchants, mining didn't exploit Aboriginal labour (they were hardly employed), didn't increase racial tension and didn't invade Aboriginal privacy. But the food chain had been seriously contaminated by injurious spillages of chemicals and compounds. The allegedly safe tailings ponds were 'violated' by storms and high winds and streams and billabongs contained high doses of radiated material in frogs, prawns and fish. As a result the creatures that fed on them and which, in turn, were Aboriginal dietary items, were affected. (The mine is closed as this is written: man-made spillages have devastated the landscape.)

We concluded there should be a ten-year moratorium on new mining and similar developments to give Aborigines respite and breathing time; and there should be permanent monitoring teams to keep tabs on impacts. While uranium was not the sole or even the major cause, the civic culture of the Aboriginal people was fragile and constituted a society in crisis.

The report was delivered to the office of Aboriginal Affairs Minister Clyde Holding on Saturday 30 June 1984. That weekend a leaked set of the major recommendations appeared in the *National Times*. Much uproar and anguish within AIAS, including a request to the federal police to investigate the leakage. I emphatically denied my guilt. But in one sense, guilty I was. At that moment the Labor Party was talking about new uranium leases and not giving one moment's attention to our six-monthly reports which always highlighted the serious problems inherent in such mining. It was, so to speak, a one-morning stand. Holding, my 'friend' from Aborigines Welfare Board and Aborigines Advancement League days in Melbourne, tabled the report on the last sitting hour of Parliament that October and not a word was said or done until I raised the issues again in 2006. Incidentally, there was no real moratorium and no monitoring of anything to do with Aborigines and mining thereafter. This left me seething for a very long time. It wasn't the waste of our efforts but the reality that damage to both humans and environment was blithely continuing, unwatched. I was sufficiently incensed to return to that domain in 2006 to look for the health outcomes that Schrire's literature research had predicted were likely.

***

The Armidale phase of my life was a good one. Unlike most colleagues at UNE, I made a conscious decision to embrace the townspeople in our family lives. Playing golf at the one and only (good) course, serving on committee there for several years, playing in the A-grade pennants team, playing and captaining snooker pennants, having friends in the Aboriginal community—all helped. Playing golf pennants led to some passing friendships in places like Gunnedah, Werris Creek, Nundle and Tamworth.

In addition to friendships with colleagues at both tertiary institutions, we had close ties in the town with our medical practitioners, golfing mates, artisans, salesmen. Golf brought a friendship with Graham Cossey, well into wine selling—and consumption, which he and I turned into an unsophisticated art form, especially when we dined lavishly at each other's homes. We had a bizarre dream of opening a restaurant which served only one meal: a baron of spit-roasted rare beef, mustard, copious rounds of small potatoes roasted in goose fat, and fresh peas—cooked by me while he served three to four reds of his choice. Attached would be a three-hole golf course with six different tees, a layout we designed progressively more pretentiously on table napkins as the dessert wines got stickier and sweeter.

By now we felt a part of this town. An example of our acceptance was the townspeople's reaction to filmmaker Bob Connolly who came there to make a segment of an ABC series, 'A Big Country'. I was to be the subject of the story of a nice Jewish boy from Johannesburg in Australia's Presbyterian County. Bob wanted a warts and all profile and when he began asking people questions about us he was given very short shrift. Sandra, inundated with town and gown calls of indignation about the questioning, invited Bob and his team for a grand dinner and during dessert she told them ever so quietly to go home the next morning.

By 1980 Sandra had finished her BA, Paul was in Sydney, Karen had gained a place in the innovative medical school at Newcastle University and Simon was finishing school. Two things were still niggling. The uranium study meant that I needed to learn as much as possible about its effects. But with no one else at UNE interested in the subject I was forever travelling to cities where expertise was available or making costly long-distance calls for help. The other irritation was that I wasn't writing as much as I would have liked. So I sat down to write. In 1979 *Race Politics in Australia: Aborigines, Politics and Law* was published by the University of New England. The book dealt with the meaning of Aboriginality and identity politics in a racist society; the Liberal Party's attempt to frustrate Aboriginal voting in a Kimberley election in Western Australia; the civil law rather than the political avenue to Aboriginal progress; the abject surrender by federal Minister Ian Viner to the bullying tactics of Queensland's Johannes Bjelke-Petersen over the Commonwealth's attempts to legislate for Queensland's Mornington Island and Aurukun populations; and a lament about the way Aborigines had *not* sought to politicise their grievances abroad.

I learned what it was to be 'the senior Jew' in 'Goysville'. We celebrated Passover and other High Holy festivals for the sake of our children and the dozen or so Jewish students on campus. On a few occasions we had more non-Jews than 'real' ones at Passover services, the nuns always begging for a chance to see what kind of a last supper He had enjoyed. They loved it. We even convened the consecration of a small portion of the local cemetery as Jewish, particularly after my great friend Alec Cook had discovered a few Jewish tombstones in the graveyard near his home. Rabbi Raymond Apple flew up for the service, complete with old Hebrew texts that are traditionally buried when they are so tattered as to be unusable.

Our decade in Armidale was not Sandra's most joyous, despite some good education, friendships and voluntary work at the women's shelter. She always longed for her comfort zone in Melbourne. The children couldn't wait to leave the place but have never regretted the schooling and rural life there. It was a significant period of my life. I learned that I was a leader, could hold an audience's attention, could fight good fights (and bad ones), could innovate, make things happen and contribute to people's lives in quite significant ways. Perhaps the most significant lesson for me was that with much effort and without overdoing things I could get 'inside' an institution and a town, places that were not generally accustomed to or desirous of people like me. In the end, as I had come to learn, my ability to deliver put paid to reservations, doubts and deeply held prejudices. Besides which, I wouldn't have joined the exclusivist Armidale Club even if they'd invited me.

***

The year 1977 was a very mixed one. The uranium study still allowed time for other things, including a life-and-death visit to South Africa and a Michaelmas term sabbatical at Oxford University. In May came the news that Maurice had liver cancer that had spread to his lungs and brain. The university granted me a fortnight off my administration duties. I flew to Johannesburg and sat with Dad, in silence most of the time. On farewell, we embraced and I deeply lamented that we hadn't touched or spoken much in life and learned just how strong is the emotion called love. All too late, all too sad. He died in July aged a mere 72. There are times when I think that my emotional cylinders misfire, that there is a flaw in my emotional machinery. What I believe ought to be a case for grief or remorse or nostalgia is often not the case. I didn't and don't miss the land of my birth and early life. Some deaths, some disasters suffuse my being but they seem inappropriate, at least as compared to those which should be, objectively speaking, appropriate. Why did I not miss the family, the environs, why did I not return, however briefly, for funerals of my mother and father and similar occasions? I can rationalise the reasons but I feel I diverge too much from some imagined norm.

On that short visit I also talked with Rabbi BM Casper, then Chief Rabbi in Johannesburg, who lived in the same apartment building as my parents. I was concerned that Simon, who was turning thirteen, had no Hebrew skills and wouldn't be ready to be called to the Torah. Thirteen, he explained, was not the fixed date for eligibility for formal prayer services. Being called at any age to say a blessing is sufficient. Great comfort.

HUMAN RIGHTS AND HUMAN WRONGS

***

To that point I was one of Australia's foremost nicotinics, smoking 60 to 70 cigarettes a day, graduating to about fifteen cigarillos and then two to three tins of pipe tobacco a week. Sandra says I smoked the pipe in the shower and all furniture, carpets and curtains reeked of my trifold-mix of Dr Pat's Irish Mixture, Erinmore Flake and MacBaren's Burley, always rubbed for me by my sons. An irritating cough led my GP Arpad Got to send me to the newly arrived ENT man who said there was a serious vocal cord problem. It turned out to be a self-healing tumour caused not by the nicotine but by the heat of the tobacco. I had to quit, instanto. In trying to cope with the loss of a parent and a somewhat banal-by-comparison addiction, I was distraught, but succumbed to the suggestion of counselling, something I'd always abjured. My principle had been to solve my problems myself. Nevertheless I sought out the university counsellor and quickly recognised my intransigence. I owe him much and haven't stopped talking since. A few patchy marital moments led me to read Eric Fromm's *The Art of Loving*. It contains, among others, two indelible notions: forget about 'in' love and think about a relationship as being meaningful and cemented when a couple share 'with' love; and that that kind of love is much like playing the piano—you have to practise daily. I try to, with an occasional day off.

A pleasant Sydney encounter with John Stone, a visiting British sociologist from Oxford, led to my taking a sabbatical at St Antony's College, Oxford in 1979. The chairman, Kenneth Kirkwood, held what I thought was the perfect chair—Race Relations, from memory the only chair so named in the Western world. But he was less than energetic and networked rather than worked. No matter, we spent a quite outstanding Michaelmas term there, living in a quaint, sixteenth century house in Chipping Norton, a market town in the Cotswolds, about a 50-minute drive to Oxford city.

A cousin arranged for me to see his business partner in the car business. For a mere £100 we had the use of a Peugeot 401 for four months. Some Peugeot!

It was unregistered and had some irremovable water in the engine which meant erratic or non-starting, the need for engine blankets, old newspapers and sacking on cold nights. Apart from that albatross, Sandra and I revelled in the quaintness of the Cotswolds and the drives to villages and towns like Banbury, Bath, Boughton-on-the-Water and Cirencester.

I had always sniffed at the 'dreaming spires' and tradition surrounding Oxford but I really liked the place. I was expected to give two seminars in my term but elected to double that—to postgraduates, mainly a group of well-dressed and suave Sudanese leaders-to-be, some of whom later turned to genocide for a living. Most of all I delighted in the Bodleian Library, a place of tranquil astonishment. I found enough material there to begin a series of essays on the use of civil law as a weapon for achieving or recovering rights. Soon after I published four or five of them and included much of that work output in the *Aborigines and Uranium* volume.

My children were less enthused about the quaintness and the British traditions. Paul, just 20, had worked at AIAS for a while. He was studying photography at the Sydney College of the Arts and spent his time and money journeying to London to buy and listen to music. He played endless and fierce games of Scrabble with us. Karen (eighteen) knitted ferociously and impatiently, anxious to rejoin her boyfriend, Robert Westropp-Evans, whom she had met at UNE when he was a mature-age student and went on to marry in 1987. Simon (sixteen), who'd been a midnight disc jockey for Armidale's small FM radio station, was just restless, despite enjoying his grandfather Ben's visit and time spent at the last picture show in town. The wooden, two-storeyed, alcoved movie theatre held about 80 patrons, complete with a huge *ipussy* that wandered across the stage and cast his silhouette across the screen. At some point in Oxford I saw an ad for cheap flights to Israel and bought tickets for Karen and Simon. They happily flew off to our respective relatives and a lot more fun and sight-seeing for about four weeks. Paul was adamant that he would only consider going to Germany. The three of us had a wonderful time together.

While in Israel, Simon sought some rapid Hebrew lessons from my cousin Pauline Axelrod in Holon. He then took himself to Jerusalem. Alone, he went to the Western (Wailing) Wall, joined a prayer group, a *minyan*, explained his dilemma and unfamiliarity with such things. The quorum took him in, he said his blessings, read a small Torah portion and was duly deemed a man. Indeed, he had the plainest and most dignified of occasions in an era where *bar mitzvahs* have become an overblown, elaborate ritual often involving fanfare and grotesque gimmicks.

Chipping Norton had a huge knitting mill and we were charmed into buying suit lengths that were tailor made into coats and jackets. I became friendly with Richard Willey, then with the British Race Relations Board, and his partner the artist Celia Perceval, daughter of the renowned artists John Perceval and Margaret Boyd. They lived in Wales but commuted via our village. Later, we brought Richard and Celia to Armidale for a sabbatical and there she painted quite marvellous landscapes, of which we eventually owned four. Richard, regrettably, took his life some years later in London.

My greatest moment was an invitation to spend the day with John Arlott—the world's best cricket critic and commentator and a poet of note—in his home in New Arlesford, Hampshire. He had bought a pub and converted it into a book and wine repository. Almost on the eve of his last Test broadcast in 1980 he was willing to talk me through an idea about writing a book on the role of the umpire and referee in sport. My interest in umpiring was always stirred by the self-regulating sport of golf compared to the presence of about eight officials at a major tennis match. (Ron Luciano wrote *The Umpire Strikes Back* in 1982, a quite brilliant analysis of his life refereeing baseball. Reading that convinced me I could do no better and I left the topic.) Arlott was mesmerising, especially about his earlier days as a soccer commentator. He gave up commentating on that sport, he said, not because of the hooliganism of the louts and 'bovver boys' but as a result of the furious and vicious racial hatred that emanated from the members' stands.

RADIO ACTIVITY

I vividly recall a public pay phone call to Johannesburg after Arlott. Bess had congestive cardiac failure and her last years were wretched. She asked me when I would visit, and I couldn't answer. But Ben Melmed visited her many times a week and kept us in touch with her progress. Her twice-weekly aerograms, written in a neat, tiny hand, became less tidy and, as can happen with parent-child relationships, one realises many things too late. It was sad to see this dominant, dominating and feisty figure become so alone, so helpless. She died in 1980, aged 72.

* * *

In mid-decade, back in Armidale, I began writing a weekly golf column in the *Armidale Express*. Several friends thought it too good for the local press and urged me to write for a city broadsheet. In 1978 the *Australian* sponsored my attendance at the Australian Open at the Australian course in Sydney, newly designed by Jack Nicklaus as a likely permanent venue for an annual Open, akin to Augusta hosting the Masters (which failed to eventuate). I just loved having a press pass round my neck, free to wander in and out of players' tents chatting with the likes of Manuel Ballesteros, Seve's brother and the very successful American, Miller Barber. I recall my piece for the paper being placed on a non-sports page—which became the pattern for all my essays on sports criticism for that paper.

Early 1980 was a time of radio work and writing many long, critical essays for the *Australian* and *The Age*. I was determined to produce a genre I call sports criticism. Since there was a totally legitimate field called literary criticism, another called music criticism, why not sport? Why not, indeed? I didn't wanted to be a reporter but an analyst. I wrote on sport as war; sport and violence; unprofessional behaviour in sport; the sadness, shallowness and hypocrisy of the Olympic movement; sport as commodified and altered by television; international games amid the often gross circumstances of local inhabitants, and of particular interest, sport and the law. The notion that law in no way impinged on sport or that sport could breach law had to be demythologised.

That sport and politics don't mix is perhaps the most hackneyed and nonsensical catchcry of our times. The lamentable Springbok rugby tours to Australia and New Zealand in 1971 and 1981 respectively, demonstrated once and for all just how much politics was caused by those dreaming of a 'sport-and-politics-don't-mix' world. Between the 1980s and 1990, a series of so-called rebel cricket tours—by Sri Lanka, the West Indies, England and Australia—were held in South Africa. I spent time on radio and television deploring these 'bribery' tours, South Africa paying extraordinary sums to have the world believe they were still an acceptable nation. Some talks included confrontations with the dreadful Alan Jones. For many years he spruiked pro-South African views on his radio programs, eulogising the system and its 'virtues'. I once accused him of being a paid lackey; he denied being a lackey.

There were repercussions of course. First we had threatening phone calls and hate mail. Then Sandra's Mini was stolen from outside our Lane Cove house, the registration and other papers carefully deposited in the letter box. Third, bricks thrown onto the roof and against the French windows. Finally, shotgun pellets through the front door and shell casings on the verandah. John Avery, a Macquarie graduate, was then Commissioner of Police. I phoned him, he regarded it as serious and two Special Branch men arrived. They had a pretty fair idea of the culprits, some South African expats who had acquired addresses and numbers of people in the anti-apartheid movement in Sydney and who had firebombed the Greenwich home of critics John and Margaret Brink. Had they wanted to kill you, said the policemen, they would have. They just want to harass you and they have. Advice was to move to a security apartment and change our phone to a silent one, which we did in 1985. I didn't stop talking about the need for a sporting boycott.

In many ways sport is a vehicle for writing about many other things. I use sport as an avenue, a medium, even an instrument to attract the attention of those who are not serious readers but who will pay some attention to inequity, racism, economic enslavement and so on, when such themes are discussed in a sports package. In this sense of metaphor, sport is a way of conveying what may seem like non-sporting issues. In 1982 much of this culminated in a very long essay in what was then quintessential school, university and lay reading, the *Current Affairs Bulletin*. Entitled 'The Corruption of Sport' it said pretty much all I wanted to say about sport. In the mid-1980s the preposition 'of' in the title was to prove significant.

Radio commentary was a good way of communicating ideas to people. The ABC had a country station in those days and Margaret Throsby was heavily into current affairs work for that unit. She and I had many a conversation. That friendliness culminated in a one-hour Margaret Throsby in Conversation program on ABC FM many years later, together with five pieces of music of my choice.

* * *

It didn't take long to figure out that the trend in academia was to appoint younger and younger staff and that by 50 one was on the verge of being past it. At 47, what with the uranium project's needs, the last of the children readying to leave home and Armidale especially, I sensed the time was ready to move. In 1981 I was interviewed for the chair of Public Administration, vacated by Dick Spann's retirement at Sydney University and for the chair vacated by Don Aitkin at Macquarie University. Sydney's Department of Government with Henry Mayer still present, was fraught with factionalism, each group taking separate minutes at departmental meetings. Macquarie provided a strange challenge. Some Politics staff didn't want a professor, one wanted the abolition of seniority and a declaration that everyone was a professor, some wanted a 'shepherd', most just wanted to get on with their own thing. There was little interaction or collegial teaching with specialists teaching solo courses in political philosophy, Australian politics, Middle East politics, Pacific politics, public opinion polling, urban politics, Indian politics and later, international relations. Some staff would claim that they had been appointed to teach only their specialty and wouldn't co-operate on other, more general courses. Selfish stuff but seventeen people did their own thing, efficiently and effectively.

The Macquarie interview was chaired by the Chancellor Percy Partridge, former head of the Research School of Social Science at ANU (the man who wanted me to have a Land Rover for the doctoral research). He asked me quite pointedly whether, at 47, I had anything new to offer or anything at all to offer. I got the job—and if only to skewer this Partridge, started teaching two new courses on Aboriginal politics and the politics of racism from the moment of arrival early in 1982. When I phoned the Dean of Arts at Sydney to say I was taking the Macquarie post, he said he'd note on the file that I had withdrawn my application. I never inquired as to whether I passed muster at Sydney and nor did I much care. Frankly, it wouldn't have suited either party.

Chapter 15

OSCAR NOMINATION

Seventeen years is a large slice of one's working life. Such was my time at Macquarie University. I didn't quite dislike the place but I'm not sure I liked it. Akin to a liberal arts college, it didn't have any of the usual professional disciplines like medicine, dentistry, veterinary, architecture or engineering. It was an uneven institution with people, programs and patches of brilliance but much else that was peripheral and popular pap. When I went to Monash, then a mere six years old, it was certain about what it wanted to be. Macquarie was a relatively mature eighteen when I arrived there, yet it always struggled for an identity. Even so, I was given freedom to innovate courses and to establish a research centre that may never have been acceptable to Sydney University. For that I am appreciative.

UNE was almost all-residential, Macquarie more like a huge high school with few in residence and little or no nightlife. No attractive union building in which to congregate, mediocre Chinese cuisine, no serious coffee places. In my years there I couldn't find its soul. It might have had a jigsaw personality and one needed to find the bits and combine them to find the picture.

The academic legacies of the foundation professor, my former doctoral program mate Don Aitkin, needed to be confronted. He had introduced some strange practices and there was always the constant competition of sister departments. The School of History, Philosophy and Politics (HPP) was a battleground for resources and space, with Ancient History really a separate entity and calling most of the shots. In my time no Politics staffer was elected Head of School. We were a 'humanity' not a social science; we had no relationship to and with Anthropology, Psychology and Sociology, clustered together in another School. Of necessity my research interests had to be forged outside HPP; I enjoyed guest lecturing outside my School and found collegiality and work relationships in Law, the Urban Studies Centre, the Conflict Resolution unit, the Aboriginal unit and other disciplines.

Laissez faire is one thing in government; it was something else in the Politics Department at Macquarie. Staff and students enrolled in higher degrees seemed to have little discipline about giving seminar papers, providing work-in-progress reports, or knowing, let alone keeping, deadlines for candidature. Undergraduate students who failed assignments could re-submit, seemingly without due dates, even if only for a pass grade. I remembered precisely why UNE wouldn't accept some Macquarie undergraduate courses for cross-accreditation. Most universities had the standard fail, pass, credit, distinction and high distinction grades, but Macquarie had a bizarre A, B and C system of considerable width, and an even more bizarre rule that results had to conform to a bell curve of grades. If there were too many As, for example, one was called in for an explanation and justification. This edict extended to all courses, from Politics to Physics, Plant Pathology to Philosophy. My reply, always in writing, was that I was a bloody good teacher who attracted dedicated students and if they all deserved As, so be it. I was never 'over-ruled'.

Selection of examiners for Masters and doctoral theses too often looked for companionable outcomes. I once had to have a 'passed' doctorate re-examined and then failed by the post-graduate committee because the first set of examiners were clearly cohorts in cahoots. Over time, and with some strong pressures from me, these procedures were tightened and the (allegedly) Aitkin legacy of 'they'll-finish-when-they're-ready' came to an end. Macquarie had a deservedly high reputation for undergraduate work, but while the general Australian trend for higher degree completion rates in humanities and social sciences was poor, Macquarie's was close to abysmal.

Sandra landed a job in the student employment section of Macquarie, assisting in the placement of students in need of money. For the first time we worked in the same place, could travel and eat together. I joined Ryde-Parramatta Golf Club for a short while, realised that a good course could also have barren social relationships, and soon enough joined Monash Country Club (a course in Sydney).

We found a bizarre 1920 Federation home in Lane Cove. Great location, close enough to work, bought from an 'unchartered' architect whose wife seduced us with the best Armenian homemade biscuits in town. His refurbishing efforts meant there wasn't a straight line of wall or ceiling, the outside laundry had a toilet and taps with running water but no outlet pipes, the garden was grassless and flowerless and the driveway incomplete. Two enormous ballrooms inter-connected as if awaiting a congress of oil sheiks. Jeremy the Labrador had the biggest and best kennel in town. Sandra's justification for this homestead was that Simon might possibly want to come home, but our children were up and running elsewhere.

As with UNE, I began teaching at Macquarie on the day I arrived in 1982, starting new courses on Aboriginal politics and comparative race politics. Later I began a topic that was a delight for me and for students: race, politics and sport. It was an ideal way to talk about governmental attitudes to the UN, to the Commonwealth, to sanctions, boycotts and the propensity of nations to disregard both treaties and conventions. South Africa, of course, was the model of what not to do in terms of human rights, discrimination and the use of violence. The Mexico, Munich, Montreal and Moscow Olympics provided a superabundance of material for thought, and I was beginning to get a good handle on the place of Aborigines and Islanders in the sports arenas.

Macquarie had earlier established a Master in Migration Studies. It was intended as a professional qualification for Australian 'Anglos' who would work with ethnic migrants. I administered and taught in the program from the mid-1980s. All students were graduates and all were enthusiastic, diligent and produced excellent research deriving from their workplaces. Two studies remain in my mind. One was of migration archives showing how badly Australia reacted to contact between Japanese pearl fishermen in Broome and White sex workers. Despite vigorous immigration restrictions, government sanctioned the importation of a good number of Japanese 'comfort women', several of whom stayed after the pearling ended; a number became well-to-do businesswomen. The other was a study of curricula in medical schools to see what, if anything, was taught about Aboriginal health. The finding? Nothing of course. But that study did have some influence on some deans and slowly Aboriginal health informed several lectures and later, in some courses, a solid core of teaching. I made sure that Aboriginal movement to cities was an essential part of the migration degree. Some official documents actually listed Aborigines in migrant statistics tables, not in my sense of a people moving but as foreigners alongside the Greeks, Italians, Lebanese and Maltese. Sensibly, Macquarie abandoned the degree when it was plain that there were enough ethnic staff to work in agencies.

Postgraduate supervision was rewarding. Douglas Booth was my prize student, studying the effects of sports boycotts on South Africa and helping me teach the politics and sport courses. Doug, the son of my friend Albert Booth from AWB days in Melbourne, did very well; his examiners were the best we could muster—a policy point to be made but lost on all but a few of the staff. The thesis became *The Race Game: Sport and Politics in South Africa*. From then on Doug and I became fast friends and comfortable co-authors of a book on Australian sport, and many articles for a glossy sports magazine, *Inside Sport*. Other important doctoral work included a study of federal sports policies; another—on the origins and development of South Africa's *apartheid* laws going back to the eighteenth century—was outstanding.

The ABC and other media had a practice of ringing Macquarie (and other institutions less often) to get expert comment on current affairs for radio or television. Their phone rolodexes listed the Department and individual staff names for comments. The Politics secretary had Martin Indyk as the Middle East commentator. At that stage we offered two Middle East Politics courses, one by Indyk, later the United States ambassador to the UN, the other by the American Robert Springborg, a critic of *all* behaviour in that region but seen by most people as condemnatory only of Israel. When the Lebanese Christian Phalangist group under Elie Hobeikan massacred some two to three thousand Lebanese Shiites in the Sabra and Shatilla refugee camps in Beirut in September 1982, the ABC phoned for Indyk. He was on leave and the call was put through to Springborg—who thenceforth became the voice of protest against Israel. Official investigations showed that Israel didn't commit the atrocities but didn't stop them either, and was, therefore, indirectly responsible. Defence Minister Ariel Sharon had to resign.

Late 1982 was the time of bomb attacks on the Hakoah Club in Bondi and the Israeli consulate in Williams Street. At that time, the (NSW) Jewish Board of Deputies called a meeting of a few Jewish academics to discuss these issues and the bad press. Dr Zvi Gabay, then Israeli Consul-General, said he would debate with Springborg on ABC television. An esteemed Orientalist scholar and man of culture, his English was poor. We begged him not to go on television. They asked me to do it but I refused on the sensible ground that you don't go into debates like that unless you have the expertise and the conviction that you will win, perhaps draw at worst. Gabay did the debate and it was a disaster against such a highly skilled performer. Most often I didn't like what Springborg had to say, but he was professional. Indyk left Australia soon after and Springborg's voice became the most frequently heard from my department. I did most of the commentary on matters South African, Zimbabwean, and on sport.

My 'Corruption of Sport' essay in the popular *Current Affairs Bulletin* had dramatic consequences. Chris Masters and Peter Manning from the ABCs 'Four Corners' program arrived in my office to talk about sports corruption. They had misread or misinterpreted the title and the contents of the essay. The piece dealt with paradoxes and myths in sport, with politics and sport, violence in games, spectator violence, how sponsorship and television had altered the rules of several major sports and thereby corrupted them. That kind of material wasn't easily filmable and it was soon clear that they wanted a story of corruption *in* sport. As they trooped despondently to the door, I asked quite reflexively, why not look into rugby league? They did and the 'The Big League' program, subsequently very well known, went to air in 1983, alleging misappropriation by Kevin Humphreys at the helm of the game. Charged by police, his case was interfered with by Chief Magistrate Murray Farquhar who sought to have the charges dismissed. Almost immediately a royal commission was established to look into all of it. Premier Neville Wran had to step aside while the hearings took place. Farquhar got four years, Humphreys was convicted, fined and placed on a good behaviour bond; Wran was exonerated, later settling a defamation suit against the ABC. This big, big story arose out of a very small preposition.

***

From 1968 to 1987 Queensland was ruled by Johannes Bjelke-Petersen, of Danish, Lutheran and New Zealand descent. A draconian Country Party monarch, he trampled human rights, politicised the public service, created an almost McCarthyist political environment, elevated Queenslandership to an imaginary higher human plane, built good roads and dams, campaigned to become Australian Prime Minister and traduced Aboriginal aspirations at every opportunity. He wasn't responsible for Queensland's treatment of Aborigines and Islanders but he did reinforce the earlier legal restrictions with an *Aborigines Act 1971*, repealing the earlier controlled and assisted Aboriginal status to one where descendants of Aboriginal and Islander inhabitants were marginally freer but could still have their property and affairs 'managed' by officials. The abysmal 'private' court system on settlements and missions (discussed in chapter 9) was replaced by something approximating natural justice. I believe my 1960s exposure of this outrageous system contributed to the abolition of the system.

OSCAR NOMINATION

The populist Joh was some kind of a minor hero when he created an historic first: in 1971 he introduced martial law in peacetime—for several weeks—to enable the Springbok rugby team to play in the Sunshine State. Riot squads, tear gas, batons, attack dogs and barbed wire fences destroyed what little was left of a sporting contest that so divided the country. If you were pro-tour you were considered pro-Vietnam war; if anti-tour you were deemed an anti-war pacifist or a traitor. Joh enabled the rugby matches and for those who loved the game—the 'rugger-buggers'—that was all that mattered. New Zealanders, seemingly the world's slowest learners, put on an identical Springbok tour in 1981—but with almost ten times the ugly consequences, some of them lingering to this day.

The 1976 Montreal Olympics were boycotted by a third of the world's nations because of objections to New Zealand's presence because that nation had maintained sporting contacts with South Africa. After the massive boycott of the 1980 Moscow Games, something had to be done to maintain sporting continuity. In 1981 Commonwealth leaders Malcolm Fraser, Indira Gandhi and Pierre Trudeau produced the Gleneagles Agreement to combat *apartheid* by withholding support and discouraging any form of sporting contact with South Africa.

Against this background Brisbane was the site of the 1982 Commonwealth Games, dubbed the Friendly Games in contrast to the much fiercer and avowedly nationalistic Olympic variety. African and Caribbean nations were threatening boycott, not because of the treatment of Aborigines but because New Zealand would be present. Aboriginal interests were ignored but surfaced only when Bjelke-Petersen introduced a statute akin to Moscow's efforts to clear that city of dissidents (and Jews) in 1980. His *Commonwealth Games Act 1982* was meant to keep Brisbane clear of Aborigines. In force for two weeks, the Act allowed government to declare a state of emergency, to allow police and persons specially sworn in to seize persons and property, to take finger-, palm-, toe-, foot- and voice-prints of suspected persons. Designated areas were declared for designated people and any transgressions of the Act meant a $2,000 fine or two years' imprisonment. No criminal or civil action was allowed to ensue from any misdeeds by the police or sworn-in deputies. The statute would have made the Soviets and South Africans proud. This wasn't an era of terroristic attacks on iconic events and arenas. What was interesting was the silence of the various civil liberties agencies on this statute, mute testimony to the old-fashioned doctrine that, sometimes, sport does conquer all. Aborigines had been agitating to hold a land rights march, following Bjelke-Petersen's permission for a group to hold a pro-life, anti-abortion march. They were denied. Agitation grew and, grudgingly, Aborigines were allowed two marches. International journalists like the remarkable sports writer Ian Wooldridge, from Britain's *Daily Mail*, were more interested in the Aboriginal plight than in the running and jumping. I had been explaining these things to men like him.

The *Australian* newspaper paid my expenses to attend the Games and to report my observations for publication. For the first and only time in my life I marched in a demonstration. It was exhilarating walking Brisbane streets in concert with such people. People on trains and buses, little old ladies knitting, were talking loudly about the need for some change, and such talk became louder as the ABC broadcast a special land rights issue of 'Four Corners' on the first Saturday night of the Games. I wrote newspaper and other articles on how sport was as good a vehicle as any for the presentation of grievances, and that the Australian catchcry of 'sport-and-politics-don't-mix' was not just a shallow shibboleth but a furphy and an utter nonsense. In all, a fruitful interlude.

One seemingly small but in fact quite significant point emerged on sports mythology. I talked with the Canadian women's track relay team, all of them Black. How come? I asked. It turned out that each had a mother or aunt from Jamaica who had emigrated and immediately joined an athletics club as a place of warmth and camaraderie. So, too, their offspring. This affirmed my conclusion that cultural environments always did more for their speed and fervour than genes or the presence of Type I or Type II slow or fast twitch fibres in calf muscles.

OSCAR NOMINATION

* * *

Some time in 1983 Carmel Schrire invited me to attend the third international conference on hunters and gatherers, only this time it was to be held in Bad Homburg vor der Höhe, a wealthy spa town of some 50,000 people near Frankfurt. Les Hiatt and Diane Barwick would be participating. I said I had no wish to visit Germany. A second, insistent invitation followed, adding that all expenses would be paid. No. The third solicitation explained that the exclusive 25-strong conference of experts was being paid for by the Werner von Reimers-Stiftung, a foundation deriving from a chemical company that operated during World War II. No, I said, never. The final epistle conveyed the Stiftung's message that those giving papers were asked not to stray into areas of moral and ethical concern. At which point, my outrage was uncontainable. I'm going, I yelled.

Lester (Les) Hiatt (1931–2008), a major figure in Aboriginal Studies, a fine colleague, good friend and golfing mate, courtesy AIATSIS.

Bad Homburg was pretty, forested, with lovely parklands, the conference luxuriously ensconced in a medium-sized *Schloss*. A Saturday afternoon walk led to a pavilion *mitten im Wald* with late middle-aged couples waltzing away to incessant Strauss, complete with white cotton gloves and bow ties. A remarkable sight as one tried to balance historical times and memories of what once happened with Germans and Jews *im Wald*.

A week is a long workshop but we learned so much from each other. My paper entitled 'Aborigines and the Age of Atonement'—what else on German soil?—was well received. The vehement argument was against the prevailing trend, a 1977 Nugget Coombs vogue, to have Australia sign a treaty with Aborigines. Diane Barwick was much in favour, not surprising given her background in Canada where treaty rights were perhaps the major issue in Indian and Inuit lives. I pointed out that Canadian treaties dated back centuries and it was their abnegation or their non-fulfilment that gave them an upper hand politically and morally. In 1983 you couldn't post-date a treaty that never was and then demand that its non-compliance could give Aborigines valid claims and special rights. Nor could one treaty embrace the diverse histories of some diverse communities. Apart from which, no generally phrased treaty would possibly embody the detail and specificity of granting rights that a long statute could achieve.

An Aboriginal group, ill-advised I believe, proposed a *Makaratta*, a traditional way of settling tribal disputes. The treaty proposal was bedevilled by the constant use and misuse of the word 'sovereignty', something not defined as legislative sovereignty or international relations sovereignty or as a supreme coercive power or as the strongest political influence. There was the inherent problem that the powerful and the powerless can't really negotiate: as George Peabody wrote, 'If both should come to the same bargaining table, the latter is simply a beggar'.

A treaty wouldn't make Aborigines any more powerful. Apart from which, the treaty memorandum that was presented stated that Aborigines should be sovereign over territorial waters, air space above their designated lands, and timber and mineral resources on such lands; that Aborigines should be granted a percentage of the gross national product for 195 years thenceforth, and a seat in Parliament. Some items in this 'invoice to the nation' made sense, and several were so improbable as to create derision. Several colleagues were upset at my paper's publication, but they got over it and so did the treaty protagonists. Later, one of my doctoral students, Stuart Bradfield, produced an excellent thesis that dissected and analysed the whole treaty saga.

Something in me baulks at group enthusiasm or group antagonism. It is not that I don't want to be part of the common denominator or that I want to be different. Rather it is a reluctance to go with the herd view. When I see a group view forming and then cementing, I stand back a little, aware of being engulfed by group excitement and hesitant about the certitude of conformity. The Aboriginal Treaty case is a good example. The advocates, including fine-minded people, latched on to an idea but seemed never to analyse the ingredients let alone the mechanics needed for the concept. It foundered because it had no historical basis and because the diversity of Aboriginal communities made a 'one-treaty solution' inappropriate. Like my opposition to the 1967 referendum I seemed to them to be perversely critical.

On a free afternoon we journeyed to Frankfurt where I sought out what was said to be the famous historical museum. At the entrance there was a large glass case containing the wax figure of a German child in Hitler Youth uniform. Bad start. I asked for the Jewish section and was sent to the appropriate room, relatively small, with a series of framed pictures on the walls. Left to right, woodcuts and lithographs of thirteenth and fourteenth century depictions of satanic Jews complete with horns, hooves and tails, eating pig excreta, suckling or penetrating sows, trampling the poor—Jews beyond the pale of humankind. After another few centuries' worth of these drawings, one arrived at the modern era, represented by a crayon drawing of Nazi concentration and death camps, a photo of Heinrich Himmler visiting the IG Farben chemical works, another picture of the British ramming and boarding the *Exodus* ship of some 4,000 Holocaust camp survivors in 1947, and a colour shot of a 'triumphant' Israeli flag. Jews in German history, the nutshell version. For a country that has almost daily harangued its populace never to forget, this portrayal of history was a disgrace and left me aghast. Though it was a late entrant, Frankfurt's Jüdisches Museum was opened on 9 November 1988, the fiftieth anniversary of *Kristallnacht*.

From Germany via Brussels to Paris for three days, sightseeing, eating superb food, overwhelmed by Ms Lisa, the Louvre, the Tower... And time made for a nosh at the famous Jo Goldenberg's kosher restaurant in the Rue des Rosieres ('The Pletzl') in the Marais district, now gone. The best rye bread, *matzo* balls, and chopped liver in the business. I made time for a visit to Glasgow and to the small spa town of Moffat where I stayed with my friend Alec Cook's two sisters, played a round of golf on a poor course abutting a gem of a castle, and took in some local sights.

In London I gave a seminar to the Institute of Commonwealth Studies presided over by South Africa's esteemed Shula Marks and Australian historian Geoffrey Bolton. Again many visits to the Tate and other galleries. This was a much quieter political time than 1979. Somewhere along the way I contracted a form of Legionnaire's pneumonia and returned to Sydney a very sick boy. My lungs had been savaged by the decades of smoking but this episode set off a more acute emphysema—a condition I attribute, in part, to the Germans. Did I have to go there? Good or bad decision? I'm not sure even now.

***

In 1997 Michael Kirby wrote a tribute to the late Oscar Schmalzbach OBE. It was with a tinge of dismay that I read the eulogy from a man for whom I have the deepest respect and affection, a friendship which began when he chaired the Australian Law Reform Commission between 1975 and 1984. There is no doubt that the Australian Academy of Forensic Sciences was

OSCAR NOMINATION

Schmalzbach's creation but I have some trouble with Kirby's description of him as 'extraordinary' while concurring with the 'unforgettable' comment. True, Oscar did possess a unique mixture of middle-European charm, Jewish *chutzpah* and persistence that sometimes bordered on frenzy. My negative reaction has a history.

Some time in 1982 a *mittel*-European voice—like Peter Sellers doing the Dr Strangelove film character—called. 'Schmalzbach here from ze Academy...' he began. A conference was to be held at ze Opera Houze on 'Evil in Man' and he had heard that I was someone who might be of value. He regaled me with the Academy's stellar office-holders: Patron-in-Chief the Right Hon. Sir Ninian Stephens, the Governor-General; patron Air Marshal Sir James Rowland; past president, the Right Hon. Sir Harry Gibbs, and such Council members as Justice Roden, Professor RJ Walsh (who was to do an external review of AIAS), Justice Kirby, et al. Oscar himself was Secretary-General (with capitals) and editor of the *Australian Journal of Forensic Sciences*.

Oscar's paper was a delicious shocker, entitled 'Evil in Women—"Delilah Syndrome"—New Psychiatric Syndrome'. It was Polish-born Oscar, the eccentric psychiatrist, at his best. My paper was on 'The Evil of Racism'. Next to me was another presenter, Irenäus Eibl-Eibesfeldt, a zoologist/biologist and a dedicated eugenicist and biological determinist from the same mould as his fellow German hero Konrad Lorenz. He spoke on 'Biological Aspects of Evil'. We made a very odd bunch. My paper was loudly applauded, whereupon Oscar—very short, very fat, morning-suited, monocled, long-haired, massively dandruffed—jumped up from the back of the room and shouted 'Dolink ve publish you!' And duly, in December that year, my copy of the journal arrived, described on the heavily embossed cover as the 'Official Journal of the Australian Academy of Forensic Sciences'. Great stuff, until I listed this publication for the University's annual report to state and Commonwealth governments. Back came a polite comment: we can't find the Academy or the Official Journal. Together we searched, in vain, for an official accreditation, an authoritative licence, an imprimatur or charter, a university or institutional affiliation or a registered constitution. The whole apparatus was a flummery, the Walter Mitty dream of unforgettable Oscar, a man of genuine *chutzpah*. He fooled everyone. I keep the item on my CV: it looks good and I had a few pleasant moments believing I was once part of a formidable forensic fraternity.

***

By 1984 the uranium saga was over, with the presentation of a six-years-in-the-making report to the national Parliament. It was time to move to something different. By the mid-1980s I realised I had spent almost 20 years talking about race politics in many societies, including the politics of antisemitism. It struck me that I had been omitting the consequences of a simple-sounding prejudice; that since my working definition of prejudice—borrowed from St Thomas Aquinas—is '*thinking* ill of others without sufficient warrant', then racism is *acting* upon those thoughts. So what actions result from antisemitism? Antiochus IV trying to eliminate Judaism (and Jews) in 167 BCE, Christian Crusaders killing Jews *en masse* from the eleventh century, pogroms throughout the Middle Ages and modern Europe, the rise of antisemitic political parties in nineteenth century Europe and their effects on Jewish life, and then, of course, the Hitlerian 'dream' of making Europe *judenfrei*? All that, yes, but I always stopped short of dealing with the essence of the Holocaust cataclysm. I feared to go there. I would teach students about the events leading up to 1933, the era of un-citizening Jews in 1935, the pogrom of *Kristallnacht* in 1938, the forced emigration practices of 1938–1940. But once the round-ups and street killings by the *Wehrmacht* began in Poland in 1939, and the *Einsatzgruppen* began their mass shootings, I had to stop. I couldn't look down that tunnel, at those ever-disturbing black and white pictures of naked women trying to hold onto their pathetic dignity at the edge of pits and mass graves.

I explored this blockage in 'Breaking the Membrane', an essay published in 2002 in *Pioneers of Genocide Studies*. The editors wanted very personal accounts of how 24 pioneering scholars came to their interest in the subject. My explanation is there, but the critical moment is summed up in lines from English novelist Alexander Baron, talking about his 'Jewish preoccupations'. A personal incident, he wrote,

> broke through whatever membrane of resistance had formed in my mind, and I was completely invaded by the knowledge of what had happened, by horror at it, and by horror at my own previous superficial reaction to it all. Since then it has been the master obsession of my life. It is a literal truth that at the present time not a single day passes without some thought or picture of the *Churban* [another word for *Shoah*] assailing me.

The tough, fibrous, selective membrane that separated my thinking, feeling, teaching and writing about those appalling years of 1941 to 1945 wasn't broken by a single incident. It was there, beginning with the *Pears' Gazetteer*, the BBC News, Belsen footage, teacher Phil Green, the Watchers of the Ox Wagon, Christian A *versus* Jewish A school games, Edgar Brookes, Oswald Black, racism in Australia, Canada, New Zealand merging into a stream of consciousness—and preoccupation. But it still needed to reach its own boiling or breaking point, and when I studied at Yad Vashem in Jerusalem in 1986, two conferences helped reach the final breakthrough.

The first significant venture was when I gave a paper at the Goethe Institute in Sydney in July 1984. Konrad Kwiet and John Moses organised a conference 'On Being a German–Jewish Refugee in Australia'. I compared state responsibility and the matter of reparations across Germany, South Africa and Australia. But it wasn't so much immersion in Nazi–Jewish relationships that started breaking my separating tissue as the contentious presentation from La Trobe University historian Tony Barta. His 'After the Holocaust: Consciousness of Genocide in Australia' raised, for the first time in such language, the probability that genocide had indeed occurred here.

Outrage followed and I recall the editors—who presented these papers in a special edition of the *Australian Journal of Politics and History*—asking me if I thought the paper should be excluded. I may have hesitated for about three seconds but I urged its inclusion. Barta set my wheels going about seeing not parallels or analogies but echoes of the Holocaust here—at the very least making me realise that genocide doesn't have to be a sharp, annihilatory episode confined to 1939 to 1945 or, as in the Armenian case, 1915 to 1923. A new field of interest began for me but I still couldn't get to the black pinheads of malignancy of the destruction years. Another conference would get me there.

In May 1985, the recently formed Australian Association of Jewish Holocaust Survivors held a three-day conference at the University of New South Wales. On the fortieth anniversary of war's end the audience listened to a range of expositions. My paper was on a subject that still troubles me and about which I have written a great deal: 'Racism: the Role and Responsibility of Intellectuals'. Later I was to write about such men as 'the doctorhood of genocide'. The intellectual genesis of genocide is still the least researched, the least talked about item on a large agenda list. It really isn't that difficult to find minds that justify the resort to biological solutions to social and political problems. The intellectual aspects of racism are a much more compelling domain of study than the thuggery and violence of those deemed to be 'the rabble'.

Chapter 16

ROMANS AND JEWS

In July 1985 Sandra and I travelled to Israel, this time on a sabbatical leave and in time for me to participate in the Maccabi Games. A Russian teenager (Yosef Yekutieli) was so taken with the 1912 Stockholm Olympics that he proposed a world-wide Jewish games to be held in Palestine, an idea that came to fruition in Tel Aviv in 1932, a date coinciding with the 1800th anniversary of the Bar Kochba Revolt against the Romans. Run by the Maccabiah World Union, it is sanctioned by the International Olympic Committee. The 1985 Games, the XIIth, were contested by 40 countries with 4,000 athletes competing in 28 sports. While most competitors were not of Olympic standard generally, the Games have boasted a few acclaimed sportspeople over the years.

Australia had an open men's, women's and masters golf team. At 51, I captained the oldies, but there was a hitch: the team was to comprise four players with the best three scores counting over each of the four rounds. Our fourth dropped out, meaning that all our scores had to count. Two Melbourne men and I played well enough to finish with a bronze medal behind the United States and Israel on the very difficult Caesarea golf course, then the only layout in Israel. Caesarea, built by Herod the Great shortly before the Christian era was, by turns, Roman, Christian, Arabic, Mamaluk, Ottoman, Muslim and finally a Jewish town of some 4,000 people. Midway between Tel Aviv and Haifa, it boasts some major buildings, a Roman amphitheatre, a fine museum and the somewhat over-the-top (for the time) Dan Hotel.

The course is a par 72 with a rating of 75 off the black (back) tees. What is so remarkable is the presence of dozens of Roman relics, steles, broken columns and headstones that are deemed 'immovable obstacles' and you can't get relief if you land behind one. Another feature is the rough which consists of ti-tree bushes that dwell in sandy dunes. Don't get into Israel's rough! Following the stroke rounds there was a 36-hole stableford event for the masters players: I won and had to pose with my certificate, complete with already greying goatee beard. Beating the fancied lower-handicapped and ever-so-serious and competitive Americans was a rewarding experience.

The most wonderful feeling was marching in the opening ceremony, identical to Olympic tradition. During a clothing swap, I collected a Canadian Mountie-coloured scarlet jacket. In 1987 I took the badge off and proudly wore it to daughter Karen's wedding—except that the garish garment, which I believed was my best outfit, didn't go down all that well. A vivid family memory more than a quarter-of-a-century later and a good example of my daughter's tolerance towards me.

Inevitably there was a glitch. Before the Games, Canada and Mexico announced that they wouldn't take part if South Africa participated. The Maccabiah Union and the Israeli Olympic Committee devised a plan. Israeli law allowed a special 'about-to-be-resident' status to persons who were likely to *make aliyah* (literally a 'going up' or return to the land of Israel). They called such people *modi'im* (immigrants in transit). Sure enough, some 220 South Africans, one Lebanese and one Russian marched into the Ramat Gan stadium wearing a specially-badged uniform of *Maccabi Modi'im*. An unhappy bunch but it was either that or no play.

I took offence at this boycott. How, I demanded, could Jews be refused participation in a Jewish event in the Holy Land? And what's more, Jews with such a long history of support for Israel? The Israeli Olympic Committee agreed that I should draft a proposal that might be acceptable. I recommended that future Games be held on a club basis. In short, 'de-nationise' the event and let all Jews assemble in one place, which was the

*Medal winners, Maccabi Games golf Masters, Caesarea, Israel, 1985:
(left) George Oshlack, Les Kausman, Colin.*

founding intention. Not acceptable said the Americans and Canadians: their athletes gained brownie points for achievements at the Maccabiah and this helped their world rankings—and that weighed more than the South African Jewish participation. It seemed to me a *dafke* set of values, but you win some, lose some.

We stayed on in Israel for several months. On a tour to Haifa we were befriended by our guide. He offered us shared accommodation in the Giloh apartment he shared with another guide, high on a hill in the now very contested terrain near Bethlehem. During the three months there we revelled in their tours and knowledge of ancient and modern Israel. Yaakov Shoshan was a great healer and we learned several eye-of-newt and frogs-balls remedies for a range of ailments; strangely, they all worked.

Bombings were not uncommon, including one at our bus stop at Giloh one morning shortly before we were to travel into Jerusalem. Israelis accepted these attacks on life, limb and property with *sangfroid*, never complaining and ever quick to clean up body parts and debris. In the end, we took the shoving, shouting, undisciplined behaviour of people alighting and boarding buses much more seriously than possible shrapnel.

Much more significant in life was our visit to Yad Vashem, a name stemming from the Book of Isaiah meaning 'a name and a place'. This Holocaust site is in Beit HaKerem, a beautiful suburb of Jerusalem. The idea of a Holocaust memorial began as early as September 1942, became much more tangible in the post-war era, put on hold because of the 1948 war, and finally became enshrined in law in 1953 as the Martyr's and Heroes' Remembrance Authority. Situated on the western slopes of Mount Herzl and adjacent to the Jerusalem Forest, it lies in an exquisite valley. Driving down the winding road through magnificent trees one hardly expects to find the unveiling of manufactured death in so wondrous a landscape. It is a place of inspiration, of intense learning, revelation, explanation and enduring sadness.

When I visited there after the golf, the annual (English-language) Holocaust educators' course was halfway through—too late to join. I befriended the Director of Education, Polish-born Shalmi Barmore, and his chief offsider, big and loveable Canadian Elly Dlin. We talked a great deal and they insisted I attend the 1986 course, which I did. Thirty people participated in that July program, all but three of us Americans. The latter dominated the only course then taught in English, and they were a distracting mob for the most part: noisy, brash, show-offy, at times belligerent about their knowledge (which was often off-centre) and given to *kvetching* about the quality of the hotel, the toilets, toilet paper, soap, soup, Arab waiters and the air-conditioning.

The three-week seminar was another membrane-breaker. Most of the key lectures were given by Yehuda Bauer in his fullest flow, the best flow I have ever heard. Truly the doyen of Holocaust scholars, this Czech savant is steeped in history, in historical facts, in historical cycles, in historical shapes and forces. He is a man of immense breadth and Olympian overviews. He uses history as a weapon of appreciation and understanding. To be taught by him is to be educated in every sense and he remains my mentor and inspiration.

Other scholars of renown talked to us, worked with us, answered questions long pent up. I had never given much thought to the matter of 'God in His wisdom' but the discourses by rabbi and philosopher Emil Fackenheim and Protestant theologian Franklin Littell were an almost magical tapestry of history, geography, sociology, philosophy and theology. The general level of scholarship was inspirational. It didn't take long to figure out the focus on minutiae, specifics which were to be available for both war crimes trials and to thwart the denialists' assertions that these things never happened. No other genocide in history has seen this level of 'excavation' of detail by scholars of all faiths and viewpoints, and that, as we came to know, produced some problematic fractures in genocide studies.

Here I was, some 30 years in the teaching business, now a student, a learner, being given to by others. It was to be one of my life's most excellent moments. We plunged into my nightmare tunnels, tracing the history of antisemitism and its role in the building blocks leading towards the 'final solution', the 'solution' in operation, the differing camps and their methods, the medical experiments, attempts at rescue and resistance, the behaviour of the righteous among Gentiles, the post-Holocaust analyses, memorialisation and commemoration, the search for some kind of justice, the battle for restoration and reparations. For three weeks—daily and in group tutorials at our hotel till late at night—we saturated but never sated ourselves on burning questions.

The most significant moment for me was Bauer explaining that the Holocaust was not some meta-historical or metaphysical event, some inexplicable *tremendum* that had to be met with nothing but silence and then sacralised. It was, he said plainly, a human event perpetrated by humans upon humans in mid-twentieth century in 'civilised' Europe and was therefore explicable. He made the significant point, still lost by so many, that the Holocaust was genocide, an age-old phenomenon and it had to be viewed (however comparatively) through that lens. It was startling coming from the doyen of Holocaust history, particularly since almost all other Holocaust scholars stayed wholly within the bounds of the *Shoah* (or *Churban*).

Aware of my own discomfort among the Americans, I suggested to Yad Vashem that they run a winter course in December–January for Australians and South Africans (few of whom were ever to attend). Every year from 1987 until 1993 I took groups of educators and others for the end of year course. The 1991 mission was remarkable. Knowing a Gulf war was likely in Iraq, we ventured to Jerusalem, staying in the seventeen-storey Knesset Tower Hotel. Early in the course the war broke out, with Scud missiles flying every which way. Yad Vashem closed. The authorities believed that Saddam Hussein might use chemical weapons and so we held lectures on the hotel's eighth floor which was too high for heavy gas to penetrate. Gas masks were issued to everybody and were worn or ready to hand. Lecturers snuck in and out with their masks. Families in Australia were aghast and in panic but as head of the group I assured them that Jerusalem was a highly unlikely target because of the holy Islamic places. The Australian Ambassador concurred but Australians were locked into an hysterical CNN coverage. We managed to get two young adults out via Haifa. We also had two who quit for other reasons: an Afghan student from Macquarie was always fretful about Israeli security questioning him; and an unmissed and unlamented Anglican priest, James Murray, whose 'Jewish problem' grew to palpable anguish as he confronted an entirely different version of Jewish history from the one he believed in. The Jewish dead didn't trouble him at all, only the living. Apart from those four, the rest completed the course.

The year 1991 was significant in another way. Operation Moses and then Operation Solomon involved the dramatic air rescues of Ethiopian Jews. We assembled at a midnight landing at Lod Airport to see these astonishingly beautiful people descending the flight stairs, dressed traditionally, eager to begin life anew. They had been promised recognition of their faith and customs. Soon after, Orthodoxy withdrew its 'recognition' of the disparagingly named *falashas*, now known as *Beta Israel*, and they were deemed unkosher. Some 6,500 arrived in 1984–1985 and the largest wave came in 1991. On later visits I assisted some of the *Beta Israel* elders with political strategies, particularly the use of the media to draw attention to their plight. The politest people I have ever known, they were good pupils.

* * *

After Israel we decided on a three-week excursion to Italy. We went on week-long visits to each of Rome, Florence and Venice, with fruitful hours on the long and tiring visits to countless galleries, churches, forums, ruins, sculpture sites, gardens and markets. We discovered a temporary gallery near our hotel that housed several Titians and El Grecos. I visited there every day while in Rome. On *Yom Kippur* we attended the weird (to us) service at the magnificent Great Synagogue in Florence, built in the 1880s and modelled on Moroccan–Islamic and Italian architectural styles. Nazis tried to destroy it during the war but the Italian resistance defused the explosives. The service seemed to be conducted in Ladino, a Sephardic blend of Spanish and Hebrew. Rome was full of Romans. Venice is special for everyone and we lingered long and emotionally in the original Venetian Ghetto area dating to about 1516. One can still see the wooden door jamb where the gates locked Jews in after trading hours. We delighted in the shops, kosher restaurant, the *yeshiva* (seminary), upstairs synagogues, and the bakery. Some 500 Jews live there. I bought Sandra a quite beautiful blue Murano glass pendant with an inlaid golden *Magen David*, which she treasures.

From Rome to London and some research in the British Museum Reading Room. When I held my reader's card I felt as if I had entered the gates of some celestial palace. To work there is a special privilege. One Saturday we went to visit my old friend Val from 'Maritzburg and her husband in Finchley. You look awful she said, as the door opened. I felt awful. She took me to a physician friend who examined me and sent me for tests at Westminster Hospital. Late that afternoon she announced that I had lymphoma, evidenced by low white cell counts. Return to Sydney immediately for treatment, she concluded. We had a ticket home via Rome and decided to fly there for me to think about mortality at 51. Dying early I thought I could cope with, but not this way. One really understands the physical absurdity of having one's stomach heave up into one's throat, and there it resided for four sleepless nights and days while we paced the streets of Rome drinking double shots of espresso. I phoned Sandra's surgeon brother and told him of the situation. Nonsense, he said, by diagnostic phone from Dallas. So get me the best oncologist you can find, I asked, and we flew to Texas. Two days later I was told I had been misdiagnosed and had shingles, very painful but not lethal. Lesson: listen to the neurotics who say one should always get a second opinion.

Worried in mid-life.

ROMANS AND JEWS

* * *

On return my immediate priority was to initiate and begin teaching a final year undergraduate course offering a conspectus on genocide from antiquity through the Middle Ages to the modern eras. 'Genocide Studies' was essentially a comparative analysis concentrating on the twentieth century: the Herero and Nama peoples of German South West Africa 1904–1906, the onslaught on Armenians from 1915 to 1923, the Nazi era and all its victims, the post-war era of Burundi, Bangladesh, Rwanda, Congo, Nigeria, the fate of Kurds in the Near East, Bosnia, Sudan, native tribes in South America and Asia. The Aboriginal case was included, despite student discomfort. The essence was always to get 'inside' the behaviour described often as 'the crime of crimes'. Who were the ideologues, who the field 'mechanics', who the compliant bureaucrats, who the consciously or unconsciously assisting bystanders, who the rescuers, the resisters, the righteous who saved lives, who were tried in court and who weren't?

My quest was to help students and me locate responsibility. The Holocaust was of course the paradigm case, the one more analysed, studied, dissected, filmed, dramatised than all other cases put together. But it is the yardstick by which we measure many things and it forms the highest point in what has been my research agenda these past 25 years, to devise a 'Richter-Scale' that can help us locate the intensity, immensity and severity of a case so that we don't equate all genocides. They are not equal in intention, scale, method, outcome, legacy and so on, and some assessment of their levels or grades is sorely needed so that the My Lai massacres in Vietnam and Israeli responses to *intifadas* are not remotely equated with what happened to Armenians and Jews in the last century.

The course began in 1987, taught at Macquarie until 1999, then at University of Technology Sydney from 2000 to the present, and at ANU from 2004 to the present. When the *Australian* newspaper carried an article in early 1987 that this course, the first in Australia, was to be taught, a call came to me within 24 hours from the Turkish Ambassador wanting an immediate interview. The next day two federal cops arrived 'to case the joint' and to see to the diplomat's safety. True, there had been attacks on Turkish officials at that time. He sat down with my rather ironic tray of Greek coffee and said he wanted to know why he shouldn't tell the world that Macquarie wasn't a university but a propaganda machine. At the end of an hour I asked him what he wanted from me. A Turkish viewpoint he said, and we agreed that he would provide an English-speaking scholar who had seen the post–1894 Ottoman archives, to give a two-hour presentation to the students. When do you want him to come? I asked. This week, he replied.

I received the Turkish visitor ten days later. Nice guy. We lunched, talked food and recipes because he owned two restaurants in San Diego, and discussed his doctorate which was on Turkish foreign policy since 1945. His presentation was a disaster, at least from a Turkish viewpoint: under-informed, no evidence of any archival material to assist the Turkish denialist case, and a lame defence that what happened to Armenians, Pontian Greeks and Assyrians couldn't have happened because the word genocide was only 'invented' in 1944! This wasn't to be the only Turkish diplomatic attempt to stifle any open discussion about the events of 1894 through to 1923. Among other things, Turkish diplomacy has no regard whatsoever for international rules and protocols about non-interference in domestic matters. Together with local 'Mutual Alliance' allies, they are still frenetically badgering, harassing, intimidating, arguing, 'debating', threatening law suits about events almost a century old as I write this.

***

The biennial Australian Society for Sports History (ASSH) conference was held this time at the Melbourne Cricket Ground (MCG) in 1987. On the day of the event my long piece on Aboriginal sporting inequality was published in the *Australian*. While at the MCG a call came from Frank Seres, a somewhat mysterious man who was then in his Sydney dentist's waiting-room reading the article. He traced me to the hallowed ground and wanted to know if I would write a television treatment for a sports series scheduled for Channel 7 television. To be called 'Blood, Sweat and Tears', it would be an eight-part documentary on sport in Australia. I told him I'd think about it but would need helpers as I simply didn't know enough to do it alone.

I gathered a few sports historians to discuss the proposal. We agreed to the treatment, provided Seres put us in a good hotel (the Manly-Pacific) for three days, and paid us what we thought was a great fee: a total of $6,500. Crazy—and stupid. For three days of wine and lobster we sold our souls, producing first-rate scenarios on nationalism, imperialism, militarism, anti-feminism, feminism, racism, triumphalism in sport—all on a mini Apple Classic computer, then considered a quite wondrous thing. My share bought us a Parker rosewood six-chair dining room suite, a daily reminder of a missed opportunity: one senior research officer would have cost Seres about $50,000 for a year's work!

The television program went to air, successfully, paid for by a merchant bank (Tricontinental) that went belly up soon after. Seres wanted us to write chapters on each episode for a book of the television title. We declined but accepted a small fee to vet the chapters written by reporters and hack journos he hired. It was awful stuff and Seres naughtily made sure readers were 'informed' that the book had our imprimatur—which it assuredly didn't. By then our sextet decided that there was some money to be earned and we duly formed the Australian Sports Consultancy.

Before all of this, in April 1984, an article appeared in the anthropology journal *Mankind*. Written by Steve Thiele, a young UNE sociologist who had done some work for me on the uranium study, it was a savage attack on the way I had become 'a persuasive proselytiser' who had 'imprisoned the Aboriginal question in moral and political shrouds or shields so as to constrain, stultify, even nullify true inquiry thereof'. It was quite something to find myself, at 50, being 'done over' by an academic journal—not because of what I was now writing but because my earlier writing had somehow stopped others from writing about a subject that I, single-handedly, had somehow placed off-limits. Thiele based his entire analysis on one 30-page essay, 'Aboriginality as Civilisation', which had appeared in various places. It remains an important piece as it tries to get readers to take a larger view of the totality of Aboriginality and not to see them as simply a race, class, caste or minority.

I'd heard something like this in my Monash University days: a student riding on an escalator said to a mate that he wasn't going to one of my lectures because he didn't feel like 'being emotionally persuaded'. Is that what I did? Perhaps. To be persuasive is one thing, to stultify and nullify is quite different. Have I been guilty of placing the Aboriginal experience in some kind of sacralised glass case, elevating their plight to some meta-historical plane that demands only guilt, apology, reparation and reverence for what once was? Have I foot-faulted those who want to study that experience but have shied off because they're not Aboriginal? Am I responsible for stopping social science inquiry into the good, the bad and the ugly, places those disciplines should be able to probe? I hope not. My writings on Aboriginal violence, for example, have led extreme right-wingers like the late Liberal Minister Peter Howson and others like him to gleefully quote me as 'proof' that 'even the good professor' thinks there are faults and flaws in those societies. In my *Mankind* reply I did make a somewhat pointed reference to the fact that Thiele is a WASP and wrote from that stance; that I was a WASH (a White Anglo-Saxon Hebrew) in whose work a 'degree of empathetic experience intrudes'.

Much of the 1980 decade was spent teaching and writing about politics and sport as well as legal issues. My 1983 inaugural professorial lecture at Macquarie was on the trilogy of 'Race, Politics and Sport'. ASSH began its journal, *Sporting Traditions*, in 1984 and it was agreed that my lecture would be the first article in the first volume. Academic sports historians and sports culture people were indeed suffering at the hands of academic snobbery as second-class citizenship for indulging in 'an irrelevant topic'. Many were denied promotion because of their involvement in this field. To have a 'professorial' piece lead off the journal was considered good strategy. It didn't work, as much of what followed in the journal and at conferences was relatively poor stuff. Very few *compadres* saw sport as a medium or forum for social and political commentary. I think the secret of good sports writing lies in *not* being a 'jock', a locker-room addict who wants to smell the wintergreen, dine on torn cruciates and regale us with what 'Gaz' (that is, Gary aka Sir Garfield Sobers) told someone in a Trinidad bar about bowling off-cutters.

Aboriginal friends talked of boycotting the 1988 Bicentennial celebrations. We have nothing to celebrate, they claimed, no reason to participate in the Tall Ships and all the other hoopla of colonial 'arrival'. I said they did: that there was some incredible and indelible sporting achievement despite huge obstacles. I hastily produced a small, 150-page book, *Aborigines in Sport*, published by ASSH in 1987 and dedicated to Pastor Sir Douglas Nicholls, one of my first Aboriginal mentors. It is not a great book—perhaps goodish as an innovation—with research assistance from son Simon and great photographs by son Paul. It was, I was to say later, but a sketch, very much a work-in-progress. ASSH did a fairly shoddy job of presentation and over-printed for the available market. Years later they were put to positive use as I handed them out to Aboriginal prison inmates who treasured the publication, while ASSH still tried to flog $10 copies.

***

Energy and time went into trying to reform things. In 1983 the Australian Law Reform Commission was investigating the recognition of Aboriginal customary law and I contributed analogous material on the recognition of what was called Native Law in South Africa. The House of Representatives standing committee on Aboriginal Affairs received from me carefully prepared, formal submissions on both education and access to legal aid. Much of my research and writing was on the lamentable non-use of civil law remedies by Aborigines and legal aid lawyers. The latter shied away from such litigation and said their precious resources had to be used for criminal matters. My retort was that one didn't have to spend all those years at law school and a year of articles to stand up in court, plead guilty in almost every instance, and beg for mercy or leniency and a bond for a lad whose mother was sick and needed him.

I dug up just about every civil law suit that had been conducted on the Aboriginal behalf, and initiated some of them. The evidence was clear: given the lower level of standards of proof required—the balance of probability as opposed to beyond reasonable doubt—and the fact that defendants were exposable on the witness stand, made for a better outcome for 'justice'. Ivan Illich, a priest, philosopher and social critic, once used the phrase 'convivial' about civil suits, about 'recovering legal procedure'. In common law actions for damages there is the uncomfortable glare of publicity in open court, the compulsion to obey a summons, to produce documents and papers on subpoena, the suffering of cross-examination on oath, the spectre of losing, of orders for damages and costs. It is an ultra-democratic way for the beggar to pit himself against corporate man. The early civil suits about land rights are a good example, as were efforts to stop some unscrupulous writers and photographers who used private, unacknowledged, unsanctioned material for crass gain.

The Lake Nash case in the Territory was another example. I helped the local Alyawarra residents with their case against King Ranch of Texas, the property owners, who were trying to force the locally-born population to move, by among other things, refusing to cash their welfare cheques and then closing the store that did so, and that, of course, was their only source of food. Those Aborigines were forced to travel to Camooweal in Queensland for money, food and fuel. With some help and encouragement from then visiting American Ambassador to the UN Andrew Young, we obtained a permanent court injunction to stop these abysmal practices.

Several legal cases resulted in the righting of fostering and adoption malpractices. Many people claim only the rich can afford this luxury procedure. Not so, at least since the advent of legal aid in the 1970s. If nothing else, these suits resulted in bringing to light that which would otherwise have been hidden. The heroic figures in all this were Illich and the American Ralph Nader, who took on the corporations who believe themselves inviolate and invulnerable within the company cocoons. One other case is revelatory. While at Monash, I had a call from solicitor Dick Ward (later Justice Ward) in Darwin. An Aboriginal couple had wandered into his office and wanted his help in retrieving their children from Bathurst Island Mission. Frank Gannangu and Elsie Darbuma were Oenpelli people who suffered leprosy. Taken from Arnhem Land to Channel Island and then to East Arm Leprosarium, they were released to be treated at home after Dr John Hargrave introduced that sensible regimen (see chapter 9).

The couple asked for the return of three of their children—taken by Catholic nuns to Bathurst and raised there as Catholics, a very usual practice. Bathurst replied that they were happy Romans. I instructed Dick to prosecute the case in civil court. He did so, and in the Darwin Supreme Court in 1965 Justice Bridge rejected their application, declaring that these children were never legally or physically in Arnhem Land. That day, the only two people in the court who were not Catholic were Frank and Elsie, the parents: the judge, the defence team, Bishop O'Loughlin, the senior Welfare Branch officers were all of the faith. I urged Dick to raise this seeming religious bias, but he declined, thinking it unfruitful. Leave to appeal to the High Court was denied. The trials cost the church much in energy and money. In 1966 Bishop O'Loughlin was at one of my live-in Monash seminars; over dinner he lambasted me for these costs and upsets but never again did the church 'confiscate' children in quite this way.

An irony followed. In 1981 Justice John Toohey, in an Alligator Rivers land rights claim, ruled that Frank and Elsie's three 'Bathurst' children—Elizabeth, Marie-Carmel, and Marina—were traditional owners of that Oenpelli domain. Sometimes, a few times, the meek and the weak do inherit the earth.

My colleague Eric Willmot, discussed earlier, comes in for more mention here because I was the one who introduced this man into the AIAS fold and vouched for him. When Peter Ucko resigned as Principal of AIAS in 1981, Council advertised the position, hopeful of an Aboriginal candidate. An executive committee selection panel comprised Les Hiatt, two other non-Aboriginal men and three Aboriginal members—Ken Colbung, Jack Davis and Willmot. I well recall Les Hiatt phoning me on a Sunday eve about a 'problem'. Before the panel was to meet, he received a telegram stating that Aboriginal John Moriarty, a senior public servant and a kinsman of Charlie Perkins from St Francis' House in Adelaide, was applying. Charlie believed the Institute was an expensive 'wank' and often, in my presence, talked of incorporating it into his Department of Aboriginal Affairs (DAA), thus divesting it of its independence. Les feared that Moriarty was the messenger of destruction. The panel met on the Monday after the Friday 'telegram' arrived and agreed to appoint an Aboriginal person and an ally, immediately. No such candidate was visible and Willmot was suggested. After protestations (to me and to others) that he wasn't 'ready' for such a post, he 'succumbed'. Apart from conflict of interest concerns, and despite lack of referees' reports, the panel recommended him to Council. Nothing was trumpeted about his Aboriginality. Referees reports were read to Council at its meeting, following which it endorsed the panel's recommendation. Willmot told Council that his descent, culture and life experience made him a complete human being and he wouldn't be 'a Black figurehead'.

Chairman Les Hiatt was misled. The 'telegram' was a piece of trumpery as Moriarty was never a candidate. Willmot served for three years, won an international inventors' award and several gold medals for engineering

Charles Perkins (1936–2000), always a friend, always a fighter.

innovations, and pushed strongly on health and education matters. But, as AIATSIS historian Jacquie Lambert says, he had few managerial skills, and he and I clashed about an internal secretarial position which had arisen long before Willmot appeared. I suggested strongly that he butt out of this festering matter, one in which the disputant had asked me to represent her interests before Council or any other likely tribunal hearing. He chose not to and the Institute came perilously close to paralysis over this industrial case.

Charm notwithstanding, Willmot created a great deal of discontent within the Institute. Perhaps his best or worst contribution was his insistence that only Aborigines could be 'guardians of their own culture'—which is no bad thing in a general sense, but when it became a weapon of censorship, favouritism and bordered on cultural fascism, it became serious. I always argued for a distinction between Aboriginality and Aboriginal Studies: I couldn't ever know what life on a riverbank must be or how one responds to the removal of one's child, but I am expert enough on the laws about Aborigines and the way they were administered and can 'profess' the subject. The distinction between 'inside' history and 'outside' history is not too difficult to draw, but Willmot would have none of this.

When seeking membership of AIAS in 1978, Willmot claimed 'Aboriginal descent', born at Cherbourg and listing his father as from that Aboriginal community and his mother from Augathella. To reporters he mentioned his birthplace as Cribb Island, now the site of the Brisbane airport; and his honorary Doctor of Letters citation lists that as his birthplace. The only problem is that there is no outward, inward or even sideways evidence that Eric is Aboriginal save his own declarations on the matter. Birth certificates attest that he was born at Laurels Nursing Home in Brunswick Street, New Farm, Brisbane, to Eric Charles Willmot born in Brisbane and Mary Pauline (Bell) born in Roma. In 1987 his sister Mary (Appeldorff) and mother Pauline Willmot wrote a letter to the *Brisbane Sunday-Mail* (1 November 1987): 'If we were of Aboriginal blood we would be proud of it… The fact is we are not, and neither is Eric, and he has no right to claim their heritage.' Sister Christine wrote a letter in similar terms (*Brisbane Sunday-Mail*, 18 October 1987). Notarised statements to the curator of the Museum of Australia in Sydney and other bodies by brother Jim, sister Christine Davis, sister Mary and mother Pauline affirm Eric's early life and fortunes.

On the publication of the *Sunday-Mail* letter and before any further publicity, Willmot told the *Sunday-Mail* that he was 'puzzled' by his family claims, that he had 'a vague idea' who was behind the assertions and his solicitors were 'looking at it'. The rest has been silence, apart from at least two people who have told me that Eric confessed to them that he wasn't Aboriginal. Willmot went on to become, among other things, a Professor of Education at James Cook University, the head of the Education Authority in the Australian Capital Territory, the Head of Education in the South

Australian public service, to achieve an AM award for work in Aboriginal affairs and an honorary doctorate from Newcastle University. He authored a book on Aboriginal warrior and raider Pemulwuy. Most of us in this domain have always insisted that an Aboriginal person is one who says he or she is one, that self-identity is the only sane and moral way to approach these matters. This case, of course, has many more dimensions to it. Willmot had another kind of *chutzpah*, leading Les Hiatt to proclaim him 'the inventor of the twentieth century'.

Fast forward a little. When I retired from Macquarie in 1999 I spent a year helping teach politics courses at the University of Western Sydney, Campbelltown campus. I taught a student from the Philippines who asked me one day if I knew anything of a fraternal organisation created to honour and uphold the ideals of Philippine national hero Dr José Protacio Rizal Mercado y Alonso Realonda, known as José Rizal. Established in 1911, it was founded by Colonel Antonio Torres who later served as the first Chief of Police of Manila. It is a civic and patriotic body, cultural, non-sectarian, non-partisan and non-racial. It has grown to over 10,000 members belonging to chapters located in about a dozen countries. I was formally invited to become a member and the ceremony was duly held at a drab community hall in Minto, a dreary suburb some 50 km southwest of Sydney. Time of the event: six on a Sunday evening.

Sandra and I arrived at the hall about ten to the hour and found everything locked. Eventually we saw a man carrying cold drinks emerging from a nearby but closed bottle shop. Is there to be a ceremony, we asked. Yes, yes, he said, about 6.30. By 8 p.m. there were four people present, swelling to about a dozen, with platters of cake, Coke, cookies and chicken ferried hither and thither. By nine we were introduced to a one-time jockey and a local maths teacher who were also to be honoured, and by 9.30 about six guys in puffy and frilly white shirts conducted me, the jockey and the algebra man to the bare floor of the hall. Blindfolded, we were ordered to kneel, whereupon someone touched us on each shoulder with a toy wooden sword and chanted,

'Arise, Sir Knight'. The blindfolds were removed so that we could let in 'The Light'. Amid some great chicken and Fanta, I was presented with my box of ribbons, chains and a huge, shiny medallion that could have sat proudly on the outsize chests of Idi Amin and Augusto Pinochet. I think Oscar and Eric would have given their eye teeth to be recipients.

Chapter 17

OBSTACLE RACES

The Yad Vashem course during the 'Scud' or 'Desert Storm' war in December 1991 was memorable. So too was my participation in an Israeli workshop on teaching about antisemitism in university courses. It was run by Gideon (Gidi) Shimoni, author of significant works on Zionist ideology and an informed analysis of Jews and apartheid that I referred to in chapter 7. Besides seeing Gidi, I met and made friends with some stellar figures in this universe.

Leonard Dinnerstein was a particular joy. I talked to this key historian of American antisemitism about his renowned book *The Leo Frank Case*. Frank was a New Yorker who became superintendent of a pencil factory in Marietta, Georgia. In 1913 he was convicted of killing 13-year-old Mary Phagan, a factory hand—solely on the ground that he was the last person to see her alive. Although sentenced to death, the state Governor commuted the penalty to life imprisonment. But this was a time of American class and race hatred at its worst. Mary was the pure, virginal Protestant, 'our little girl', Frank the satanic northern Jewish economic and sexual predator. Frank was abducted from his cell in Atlanta, dragged off and lynched by the 'Knights of Mary Phagan'. Frank was pardoned posthumously in 1986 and the names of his (prominent and respectable) murderers were published in 2000.

My contribution to the teaching seminar was a model syllabus on 'Racism and Antisemitism' in which I argued that most Western universities would not offer a course on antisemitism alone, but would perforce do so if that topic formed part of a wider perspective on racism, assuredly in vogue. This was what I was doing at Macquarie—teaching a course on the politics of genocide, locating the centrality of the Holocaust in that conspectus and explaining the antisemitism that is contextually central to that event. There is academic validity to my approach, but it is sad that no Australian university sees any intrinsic value in courses on antisemitism and Holocaust alone—unless the private Jewish Higher Education Committee in Sydney subsidises or pays for them. Macquarie's HPP School was well sprinkled with dedicated 'Festival of Light' Christians, and a course solely on antisemitism (or Holocaust) across the ages would have been unthinkable.

Sandra was with me for the 1992 Yad Vashem course—fortunately, because I developed a serious bronchial infection and needed help. Aid also came in the shape of my cousin Rabbi Dr Akiva (Kevin) Tatz, the son of my father's half-brother Koppel. Akiva is a medical doctor who turned to Torah and became renowned in South Africa, Britain and Israel as an almost messianic figure much beloved of youth. Akiva works for *Ohr Somayach*, a Jewish outreach organisation that talks to young persons interested in Judaism. It also helps find place for lapsed Jews, forgotten Jews, estranged ones, perhaps even never-were Jews who want to be. I have watched him at work, quite outstanding as a humanist, teacher and preacher. He found some antibiotics, cured me for the moment, and then attended one of my Yad Vashem lectures on Nazi biology and medicine. In return I went to hear him at his organisation's *yeshiva* where he talked for nearly two hours on the philosopher Spinoza. I understood much of what he said but I don't think the backpackers and nomads did. No matter as they were mesmerised by the emotion and the feeling, by his quite tangible emanation and aura.

I went alone to the 1993 winter course and took a weekend off to rest at what is my most beloved place in Israel, the holy northern city of Safed. Built high on a ridge, it has many buildings bullet- and shell-marked from the 1948 war. I always stayed at the Rimonim Hotel, once a *caravanserai*, and noted for both the remarkable view of the valley below and its art gallery, the ultimate place of peace for me. On Friday eve I decided to go to *shul*, of which there are about a dozen, mostly small, one-roomed affairs for diverse groups like the

Tunisian emigrés, the *Kabbalah* people and those who venerate Yosef Karo. I was heading for the last, walking down a flight of beautiful stone steps, when I experienced what felt like a hand-grenade exploding in my right clavicle area. I know what that is, I thought, wrong side but something very cardiac, something I never fretted about but had been expecting for a long time, given the genes and generational diet. I rested, went to *shul*, walked there and back ultra-slowly because normal steps hurt. Back in Jerusalem I talked to two doctors on the study mission: they said to go home and be investigated. I saw through the course and returned safely.

In Sydney, my doctor and close friend Con Phillips wasn't overly concerned but told me to watch what happened when I exerted myself. Clever boy, I had a book and a research project I wanted to finish and so for nearly half a year I didn't play golf or exert myself. I finished a detailed report on the relationship between sport and delinquency in Aboriginal communities in April. By June, the pain on walking quickly was acute and I saw a cardiologist. An angiogram determined that four bypasses were needed. The surgeon and I agreed that since we were both busy men I would have the operation three weeks thence. Did he have a video of the procedure? No, said Peter Brady.

A day before the operation I lay in bed feeling as if someone was using a brace and bit to drill through my sternum. Next day I was sent directly into Royal North Shore Hospital, a heart attack diagnosed, emergency ward, but fortunately not severe enough to postpone the operation. Only three bypasses could be achieved. The post-operative pain was something else, especially during the compulsory aerobics classes at the hospital. The cardiologist suggested I remain off work for at least six months (to avoid 'bypass blues'), a period about which Macquarie was gracious and generous. Two senior genocide studies students took over my course, admirably.

I had met Ernest Hunter, a psychiatrist, when he lived, briefly, across the road in Wollstonecraft. I spent tutorial time with him on Aboriginal affairs and health especially, an area in which he was to do outstanding work. He had come with me to Yad Vashem in 1991. By surgery time, Ernest and partner Patricia Fagan were ensconced in Cairns doing work in Aboriginal and Torres Strait Island communities. They were in the Torres Straits for several weeks and lent Sandra and me their house and car in Clifton Beach, a quite remarkable venue for recuperation. We swam daily, collected vongole, rested, walked, and put the finishing touches to *Obstacle Race: Aborigines in Sport*.

On return, Peter Brady called to ask whether, in the absence of that video, I would like to watch him at work. Begowned and scrubbed, I was introduced as 'the professor' and the theatre thought me some eminent specialist. The operation was brilliant and absorbing, a cross between mediaeval butchery and Belgian tapestry-making. The public patient was a large 40-year-old male and my contribution was to remind Peter that he hadn't pressed down the knots of the titanium wires that restitched the rib cage. (Despite my swearing that day to never again cheat on healthy eating, I do.) Whatever it was that Peter did, he re-energised me and gave me the zest to do more, and better, since the operation in mid-1994 than I had done in the previous 20 years or so.

***

The genocide course was always a third-year offering usually taken by students in the last semester of their degree program. By and large enthusiastic, they knew how to write long essays and coped well with assignments that posed questions to which there were no ready answers in textbooks (or the looming internet). 'Genocide groupies' sounds odd but we had a coterie of such young people wanting to join this morbid search for meaning and understanding. One student nagged me about starting a genocide studies centre, to which I replied that one centre was enough in my life (the Monash one) and that I didn't have the energy (on the eve of the cardiac episode) to lobby for such a body. She said she'd do it. And she did. Lara Esam talked with academics and with Michael Kirby, then Macquarie's Chancellor. I found myself having to take an elaborate proposal through the academic Senate and from there through to Council, and to find an enthusiasm I didn't really feel. It wasn't the subject matter but the hassle of administration, fundraising, acquiring accommodation and finding national and international support that was daunting.

Things went well until we reached the Council hearing. I wanted the simple title 'Genocide Studies Centre', but Edwin Judge, the Ancient History professor, said, ever so softly, that he was worried—worried that the centre might be too, too, you know, too... I ended the sentence for him—'too Jewish'. He mumbled something about wanting 'balance' and objectivity. My sharp rebuke was that there could be no such thing as a pro-genocide viewpoint and that if he expected me to have an ex-Nazi camp *Kommandant* give his point of view, the answer was no. Laughter—for which this good Christian never forgave me. We compromised by calling it the Centre for Comparative Genocide Studies (CCGS), to be located in HPP with me as director. An advisory board comprised a good mix of Macquarie academics and representatives of the Aboriginal, Jewish, Armenian, Cambodian, Guatemalan and Romani communities.

The Centre's aims were wide ranging. We set out to establish the meaning of the term 'genocide' and to inform people about what events were and weren't in that legal category. From the outset my personal and abiding research concentrated on measuring the magnitude of genocide, seeking a kind of 'Richter-Scale' which could establish dimensions and scales of the crime. One starting point for all of us was that there is an almost inevitable relationship between racism and genocide. Another agenda item was to locate the legal and moral responsibility for genocide policy and practice. Other priorities included 'colonial genocide', a phenomenon too often consigned to the too-hard basket, and addressing the assumption that there are 'worthy' and 'unworthy' victims.

The Centre was abuzz with young scholars, establishing resources for students, producing a quality journal, a newsletter, running adult education courses in several suburbs, writing theses, and preparing for a volume series entitled *Genocide Perspectives*. Amid this reflection on death it was a place of warmth, camaraderie, even excitement. It was also a place of seemingly misplaced humour, insider jokes that put all that suffering and death at a little remove, enabling a little laughter amid the ever-present tears.

There was no shortage of resident visitors. Archaeologist Richard Wright and his wife Sonya wrote up their notes on their excursion to Serniki in Ukraine to excavate a mass grave in the local forest. That 'field' research was a prelude to the war crimes trial in Adelaide of forester Ivan Polyukovich. Sybil Milton, senior historian at the US Holocaust Memorial Museum (USHMM) and her husband Henry Friedlander, author of an outstanding book on the origins of Nazi genocide, spent six months with us.

The late Ruth Wajnryb sponsored an annual lecture in memory of her father Dr Abraham Wajnryb, a survivor of the Lodz ghetto in Poland. There he had to practise medicine and to choose between those who would get insulin or sulphonamides and those who wouldn't, a choice he agonised over in later years. I gave the first Abraham Wajnryb Memorial Lecture in December 1994 on *the Politics of Remembering and Forgetting*. We had an audience of three hundred. Purdue University's Robert Melson followed. Robert is one of very few scholars to write a comparative text on the Armenian and Jewish genocides. Konrad Kwiet was next on the Holocaust in Lithuania, a place of rehearsal for mass murder. Two of the world's foremost Armenian scholars lectured in this annual commemoration: Richard Hovannisian on denial of the Armenian genocide and Vahakn Dadrian on German involvement and responsibility in that event. Richard Breitman gave the last of this series on *The Secrecy of the Final Solution*. Senior American, Canadian and South African scholars spent time with us and with students.

In 1995 I was invited to attend the first meeting of the association of genocide scholars held at the College of William and Mary in Williamsburg,

Virginia. Founded in 1693, the second oldest university in America, it was Thomas Jefferson's place of study. Quaint, beautiful, serene, with an old model town where people dressed in seventeenth and eighteenth century costume served you meals, coffee and doughnuts; our host was the delightful and erudite Roger Smith. Most of the academic 'heavies' or 'about-to-be-heavies' were there. One vivid memory is of an independent London scholar imploring study of the fate of Romani people and traducing Holocaust scholarship to bolster his case. I was appalled then, and remain so, with those who seek to magnify their case study interests by denigrating or eschewing the Holocaust and its overwhelming and detailed literature. It was occurring to me even then that there was a fracture on the horizon, that Holocaust scholars avoided this group and that this group hardly ever attended Holocaust conferences. I was and still am one of the few who work in both 'camps'.

In December the same year I was fortunate to visit the US Holocaust Memorial Museum, courtesy of a ticket from Sybil Milton, and also attended the conference on the fiftieth anniversary of the Nuremberg Trials, run jointly by the Museum and the Library of Congress. Sybil organised this array of historians, legal scholars and former prosecutors. I met some remarkable people, including the fierce bantam Benjamin Ferencz, chief prosecutor at the *Einsatzgruppen* Trial. He gave astonishing insights into the criminals and their attitudes. Robert Jackson's son William talked (somewhat disappointingly) about his father's role as the chief prosecutor of the Nazi elite. A Rwandan prosecutor explained the urgent need for the tribal justice system known as *gacaca*, given that there were some 80,000 people in prison awaiting trial. A Tokyo professor made a poor case about victor's justice at the Tokyo trials. I met and talked with Holocaust historians and German prosecutors.

I learned much about the vast number of 'smaller' trials in West Germany, East Germany and Austria where there were well over 100,000 such trials, yet the conviction rate was only about ten percent. Time lapses, confused memories, illnesses, bewildered witnesses, led to so many acquittals. No matter: as I always argued with Konrad Kwiet, there were trials, under spotlight, there was concrete evidence that something specific had happened, there were atrocities, and there were dead victims—even if the perpetrators escaped punishment. Konrad has always been bitter about the three Australian acquittals for war crimes, even in the face of the evidence he helped assemble as senior historian to the Australian War Crimes Investigation Unit. I can see his point of view but I confess to placing much more value on the evidence that emerges from trials than on convictions and punishments.

I attended the third Association of Genocide Scholars in Madison, Wisconsin in 1999. There I was elected vice-president in an executive of four and my job was to enlist members in Oceania and Asia. Madison is everything a university town should be, with the local authorities totally dedicated to university and student interests.

In 1996, I gave a paper at the fourth Lessons and Legacies of the Holocaust forums, this time at the University of Notre Dame in South Bend, Indiana. My panel comprised Helen Fein, the doyenne of genocide studies, and Richard Hovannisian. Many of the world's great Holocaust scholars were there and I revelled in meeting with them. They were, I must say, a league above the genocide scholars I had heard to date. I visited Purdue University at that time, staying with the Melsons, and marvelled at the architecture, the size, and particularly the football, baseball and athletic arena under a closed roof. I gave some lectures there and enjoyed the student enthusiasm.

A close neighbour of the Melsons was an American-born Turkish medical specialist, a man who shared camping trips, basketball games, barbecues, babysitting, food and wine with them for about twelve years. When Robert returned from a trip to Yerevan with Helen Fein and Roger Smith to help set up university courses in Armenia, he brought back a large coffee-table book of Armenian genocide photographs from old newspapers and English magazines. The neighbour called in to borrow milk, saw the book and never spoke to the Melson family ever again.

*Robert Melson,
Purdue University, Indiana.*

*Konrad Kwiet,
Macquarie and Sydney universities.*

*Henry Friedlander, Auschwitz survivor, City College of New York, with Colin,
at CCGS, Macquarie University.*

We published the first of the *Genocide Perspectives* volumes in 1997. This was to be a vehicle for a younger set of scholars, hopefully some of them Australian. Volume I was a success, quickly out of print.

Though we passed some 1,200 students through the genocide courses over the years, built up an enormous library of books and films, and established contacts with over a hundred international Holocaust and genocide scholars who became associates of CCGS, one failure perhaps was to interest many Macquarie staff in our endeavours. Winton Higgins, a Politics colleague, agreed to examine several theses, became a devotee, a fine colleague, and spent time thereafter studying at Yad Vashem, visiting death centres in Poland and Germany, writing *Journey into Darkness*, an excellent and insightful memoir of his travels, constantly alluding to Australian social and political issues. He became a member of our group.

Panayiotis Diamadis, a Greek scholar, joined us and helped form an Armenian/Greek unit of the Centre, attracting both money and community interest. In 1999 he organised a two-day Centre conference: 'Portraits of Christian Asia Minor'. The acting Turkish Consul in Sydney, Cenk Karadum, approached Vice-Chancellor Di Yerbury demanding she cancel the conference on the ground that it was 'educationally unsound and politically motivated'. To her credit she sternly told him to go away after giving him a lecture on academic freedom. The keynote speaker was the Columbia University Literature Professor Marjorie Housepian Dobkin, a long-time scholar and writer on the Armenian genocide. She died in 2013, lauded throughout the academic world.

Before the conference, consul Karadum prevailed on Panayiotis to include a Turkish speaker should the conference go ahead. I was in America when he agreed (to my chagrin) and the consul offered us the services of Dr Salahi Sonyel, a known denialist then at Belfast University in Northern Ireland. My bias led me to place his talk under a session called 'Denialism'. He complained but ploughed on. He and Dr Abdul Maasih Saadi had a quite savage verbal clash about events in World War I Turkey, with Dr Sonyel much encouraged by a number of 'Grey Wolves'—an ultra-nationalistic and neo-fascistic Turkish group of Kemalist supporters—in the audience of 150 people. In the end, the University's 'grey men', the security people, escorted some shouters and wreckers from the assembly. I wrote a letter of protest to the Australian Government protocol office providing written evidence of diplomatic interference in domestic matters. The official agreed that it had occurred but he wouldn't take it further for fear of damaging Australia's romance—fast becoming a full-blown love affair—with Turkey and Turkish–Australian history.

In 1998, the university acted on its policy of reviewing centres after five years of operation. An impressive panel prepared a longish report which gave us glowing ticks on all fronts but fundraising. In the years we averaged about $90,000 annually in donations, most of it going in book and film acquisition. Salaries were not an issue: my professorial salary was outside of these funds, and we had no paid staff. Sandra joined with students and community volunteers in working, helping and seeing to the running of the Centre. As we told the panel, few people wish to invest in death and funds were always likely to be a problem. But the serious problem was the Macquarie executive. Some creative accounting in HPP led to some of our funds being used to shore up deficits in the School and clarity was always troublesome. The University, in its corporate mania, wanted a profit from the Centre. It had already lost a brilliant Climatology Centre to another university, and then it lost its innovative HIV Studies Centre as well.

A showdown on money was inevitable. The Centre was squeezed out of its space, people had nowhere else to work in tandem and concert, and in a sure sign of academic miserliness, photocopying was severely rationed. The knockout came when the Head of School stated, quite openly, that the solution was to change the name of the Centre to one with an overtly Holocaust title 'so that the Jews can pay for it'. Whereupon, in 1999, with the backing of all our colleagues and associates in the enterprise, I wrote Di Yerbury and her minions a divorce letter, telling them we were out of there.

Astonishment! Universities fire staff or close centres, not the other way round. We duly re-formed as the Australian Institute for Holocaust and Genocide Studies (AIHGS) and located ourselves, for several years, within the Shalom Institute at the University of New South Wales. Macquarie refused to hand over the several hundred books and films we had acquired and placed in the main library, claiming that one day they could be of use to genocide students—which was never to be.

I was 65 in 1999, and the place was culling and carving frantically to meet a 'corporate budget'. Good people left, some good people stayed and were grossly overworked, little fresh blood came in, casual staff proliferated, named degrees of dubious title and content spawned, bums-on-seats-never-mind-the-quality-or-content was the prevailing ethos. One Pro-Vice-Chancellor was heard to say that if only Macquarie could be the School of Financial Management it would be a world-beater! Several key politics staff considered taking the redundancy packages on offer and my accountant advised to take the money and run. I did, without the slightest regret, but with a sweet and sour taste.

Across some 60 years of university life I found the Macquarie experience the least professional and collegial, yet it was the place where I discovered my preferred roles as a 'contextual historian' and an action-oriented fieldworker of an anthropological and sociological bent. There I was able to mature and achieve most of my goals in comparative race politics, Holocaust and genocide studies, youth suicide studies, migration studies and sports history.

***

My somewhat frenetic efforts on the sports history front were a way of deflecting the horrors of the genocide lectures, talks, conferences. My doctor once insisted I was depressed. No, I replied, gloomy, not depressed. Gloomy indeed, as I worked for years in the fields of violent race relations, death and destruction by others, and death by people at their own hands. Sport, as I saw it, was hardly funny, or even fun, but it was relatively light relief and it allowed for critical observation in a much freer and easier way than is required by heavy academe.

The eighteenth century English poet William Cowper once wrote of 'Detested sport,/ that owes its pleasure to another's pain'. I don't detest sport, only some aspects of it: the hype, hyperbole, hypocrisy, for a start; the nationalism and chauvinism for another; the commercialisation of the 'product' and the a-historical mentality of players, administrators, commentators and spectators. Above all other aversions, perhaps my pet is the shibboleth about the separation of sport and politics. A more inane and unreal belief is difficult to find. Max Weber once defined power (and politics) as the ability of an actor or actors to realise his or her will in a social action even against the will of other actors. Any under-11 soccer match, with actor–parents on the touchlines, will tell you just that.

The decade was replete with sports writing. I did long pieces for *The Age*, *Australian* and *Sydney Morning Herald*. Doug Booth and I began a long series of monthly opinion pieces for the glossy magazine *Inside Sport*. Suffused by over-the-top sports pictures of guys mid-surf or mid-mark or mid-scrum, it was decorated with the coyest soft porn pictures possible, young ladies showing just enough but not enough to qualify as porn, art, aesthetics or anything else other than tiny bikinis surrounded by flesh. Doug and I suggested 'The Serious Page' as a title for these essays, usually of a thousand words. At first the editor liked it, realised the inference and changed it.

Our first piece was on the need to legitimise the use of drugs in sports and have a panel of doctors supervise their use. We argued that drug cheats almost always won out, that the allegedly licit substance regimens of most sports people constitute enhancement, that far too many athletes are harmed permanently or die from their drug diets. (Belatedly, in 2013, the Australian Crime Commission released its findings on 'the blackest day in Australian sport', with damning evidence of all of the above.) The ensuing letters to the editor were what we expected: egg-heads, boof-heads, ivory-tower poofs, how dare they!

From there we tackled the ugly side of sport: racism and sexism, the nature of sport heroism and villainy, pink dollars from gays in sport, the Australian inability to lose and to win gracefully, to be competitive without snarling, the role and problems of umpires, sledging on the field (an Australian 'tradition' unknown to Don Bradman), greed in sport, South Africa's alleged rebirth and abolition of inequality in sports selections, the super-abundant myths about the Olympic Games and the realities of the untouchability and unaccountability of their executives, including their often ultra right-wing political affiliations. Our scalpel on sacred 'Olympism' was anathema to readers.

One essay was on the use of Asian child slave labour by companies like Nike and Adidas. Of all the running-shoe manufacturers, only one, Reebok, declared its opposition to 'social injustice'. The essay was prepared and accepted, then withdrawn by the editor on the day before printing because, he said, there was pressure from their advertising department fearful of losing revenue. I immediately sent the essay to the *Sydney Morning Herald* which promptly published the article under the banner: 'This article has been banned by an unnamed sports magazine and appears here as written.' The *Inside Sport* editor went ballistic, claiming that everyone, but everyone, would know which magazine had defaulted. I was duly 'fired' and Doug continued the column alone for a while.

I did write one solo essay for that glossy on 'The Dark Side of Australian Sport'. Well received, it was subsequently reproduced in David Headon's *The Best Ever Australian Sports Writing*, and observations on that theme appeared in several other international publications. My thoughts and feelings about inequality on the playing field culminated in the *Obstacle Race* book, which was a vehicle for analysing the Aboriginal experience from about 1850 to 1995. The frontispiece was a short poem from actor Ernie Dingo:

> Aboriginal achievement
> is like the dark side
> of the moon,
> For it is there
> But so little is known.

The work posed questions of identity, the stolen generations, the matter of intent and malevolence in the era of 'pacification' (genocide), the purposes and practices of segregatory statutes, the miracle of Aborigines (and Islanders) playing any sport given the conditions under which they lived. Of particular importance was the notion of inside and outside history. I quoted Charmaine Papertalk-Green's little poem:

> I come from another world
> One you will never know
> You may try to understand
> But you never will.

The book constantly referred to inside history as Charmaine's world, that personal and internal ingredient that is the essence of Aboriginality, and the outside history, the narrative and chronicle of what has befallen Aboriginal people, with good and mostly bad faith, over time. I accepted my inability to fully understand her other world but found I was good at the latter.

There are individual chapters on cricket, professional athletics, boxing, Australian football, ruby league, rugby union, and 'singular' sports like squash, wrestling, tennis, rodeo and the like. In the end it was not a sports book but a serious volume about not just overcoming opponents but also history, geography, isolation, incarceration, prejudice, racism, alienation, exclusion, children stolen and a myriad other obstacles. It has enough photographs to be enjoyed by the non-literate, enough statistics to keep the neurotics and fanatics happy and more than enough context and chronicle to satisfy historians. The last chapter was a true innovation: the original

Aboriginal and Islander Sports Hall of Fame. I put forward that notion to several people and the first 'Hall', comprising 129 men and women from 1868 to 1995 was elected by four Aboriginal selectors—Mark Ella, Syd Jackson, Faith Thomas and Charlie Perkins—and three non-Aborigines—Ted Egan, Alick Jackomos and me. By 2008 the members numbered 224. Unbeknown to me, Macquarie University Vice-Chancellor Di Yerbury entered the book for a competition that turned out to be the Australian Human Rights Awards. *Obstacle Race* won the Non-Fiction Award for 1995 and immediately another thousand copies were printed with a tagline about the prize overprinted on the cover. A nice kindness from Di Yerbury. This was one of the sweet parts of an otherwise fairly sour sojourn at that university.

Ted Egan was adamant that we had to get this work to remote communities and we embarked on an ambitious project to have the first group of 129 photographs enlarged, captioned, multiple-copied and distributed. It proved too costly and I hit on the idea that Paul and I should reproduce photographs of the Hall members in an inexpensive format, a daughter book. John Iremonger at Allen & Unwin was eager and in 1996 we produced 17,000 copies of *Black Diamonds* (selling for $20). Another rare book nowadays, but its virtue was that communities could cut the full page (A4 size) pages, laminate them and produce their own exhibitions. Marcelle Jacobs, a senior museum curator, ran a *Black Diamonds* exhibition at the Homebush sports centre for four months. Successful, other exhibitions of this kind were held in Adelaide, Darwin, Ipswich, Brisbane and at Sydney's Museum of Contemporary Art for the months preceding and during the Sydney Olympics in 2000.

Paul and I published a much fuller digest of Aboriginal and Islander sport in 2000, entitled *Black Gold*, which updated both the *Obstacle Race* book and the Hall of Fame. A much better and fuller book than *Black Diamonds*, it was a lavish, glossy-paper production with more recent photos and profiles of the (then) 172 Hall of Fame members, informative chapters on national representatives and on women, plus chapters on individual sports. Pat Dodson and Mick Dodson wrote forewords. Publication coincided with the exhibition of the Hall members at the Museum of Contemporary Art, opened and launched by Ted Egan. About eight years later when a third daughter of *Obstacle Race* titled *Black Pearls* was set to follow, we faced an insurmountable obstacle in the form of a request from the book publishers, Aboriginal Studies Press, for a $36,000 subsidy. Money was tight, sponsors short and it proved impossible. I withdrew what would have been the best of this series.

Part V:
Pre-Mortem

Chapter 18

GROUCHO

The Royal Sydney Golf Club advertised in 1990 for an historian to write their centenary history, to be ready for their celebrations in 1993. I wasn't enamoured of the kind of people who wouldn't have me (or the eldest Marx brother) as a member. My Sports Consultancy colleagues argued strongly for a bid, which I opposed, but they sent me a draft for vetting. Invariably, my editing pen (brown, not red) flew over the words. The consultancy was summoned to an interview, which I wouldn't attend. Next came a call from the club asking me to appear before their centenary committee. I quickly checked out the members and reluctantly met them. In the elegant boardroom some deviltry in me kept asking, 'Why is a nice Johannesburg Jewish boy sitting in a place like this?' 'And why not?' If ever there was a chance for an outsider to look inside, this was it.

I wasn't aware that my partners had radically reduced the internally agreed fees in order to get the nod. The meeting agreed to the tender and so it was that Brian Stoddart and I were slated to write six chapters apiece, with milestone dates for chapters and payments. Chapters submitted had to be read and returned to us within 30 days and if not amended the texts would stand.

I was given a suitable office for three years, a temporary membership card giving me both clubhouse and playing rights. This club was the most generous, respectful and professional outfit I have *ever* encountered. Some staff were members of the Hakoah Club in Bondi and whenever I gave public lectures there I had my small band of Royal Sydney groupies. One January, during this writing commitment, when Sandra and I returned from a trip to Israel, we found Paul in hospital following knee repair surgery. We nursed him at home, but the deputy-secretary Alan Wilson expressed a sincere offer that the club would have nursed him in residence, if necessary, because he was the son of a member! Amazing stuff.

I played many rounds on the exclusive turf, and interviewed dozens of gracious and helpful members. The staff—about whom I wrote a chapter entitled 'Above and Below'—suggested by the then popular television series 'Upstairs, Downstairs'—were a testament to skill and service. All minutes were available to me including the 1908 decision that 'with the exception of the one candidate [Septimus Levy] before it, no further members of the Jewish faith would be admitted'. This, the committee said, was due to 'the pressure of general social opinion', which of course was not explained. I consulted Suzanne Rutland, historian of the Australian Jewish community, and others, but we could find no such social or political issues at that time. In 1905 there was some hysteria about the 'Russians [Jews] are coming', but such emigrés, had they arrived, would assuredly not have played golf, bridge, squash, lawn tennis, bowls or croquet. There were some Jewish members before 1908 and there have been a few since, but the 1908 minuted decision has not been formally rescinded.

Things began smoothly enough but went awry fairly early on when Brian Stoddart, after writing short first drafts of a few chapters, decided he wouldn't continue. There had been no arguments or disagreements to that point, yet he gave no reasons. The centenary committee chairman threatened a law suit if the book wasn't finished on time—a warning some members thought distinctly un-Royal Sydneyish. Royal Melbourne's 1891–1991 centenary history loomed large: their book wasn't ready when the celebrations took place, with much egg-on-face all round. The Sports Consultancy urged me to complete the book, which I did under pressure of other work. It wasn't an easy exercise.

The club's committee wanted Stoddart's name deleted from the cover page of the handsome Allen & Unwin production. He pointed to the contract and insisted not only on his name being there but taking his half share of the fees. The only way out of an acute embarrassment was to place my name as first author and for me to write a barely disguised preface which explained that for the drafts of chapters two and three, and initial very brief sketches of chapters four, ten and eleven, Dr Stoddart used the following sources…; for all the remaining chapters and final versions, Professor Tatz used such and such resources. The extent of his contribution will not be lost on anyone reading that preface carefully.

There was much excitement when the book appeared. It isn't just a golf biography but a social (and political) commentary on values, class, elitism, about inclusion and exclusion, insideness and outsideness. Common enough member statements were that the club was 'a home away from home' and 'we wouldn't have as members people we wouldn't invite home for dinner'. On publication, the committee invited me in for a drink and presented me with a silver centenary medal, but no badge for Brian. After several drinks I asked whether they knew who I was when we were given the commission. Yes, they said, it took as long to check you out as it took you to check on us. How come you let me write so much about your anti-Catholicism, antisemitism and so on? Professor, at our first meeting you said one cannot tamper with history. Did I really say that? Yes, and we heard you, and we didn't. Remarkable questions and answers.

I will pass this earth wondering whether they decided that a Jewish author would be a good way to de-claw their reputation as an antisemitic club or whether they really wanted an honest history, warts, prejudices and all. The latter is my guess. The last paragraphs of the book were about the new era of political and legal equal opportunity and changing community values. The concluding sentence was that 'no doubt Royal Sydney will respond as it always has done to pressures of this kind—with professional good sense'. Soon after, women not only got the vote in their club affairs but Royal Sydney became one of the first Sydney golf clubs to allow women to become board directors.

The Jewish question is their problem, not mine. But there is certainly what I call 'a politics of writing Jewish'. There was criticism from the Jewish community for doing this history. 'How could you?' they asked about this 'font' of antisemitism. Quite easily, I replied, their exclusionary attitude is not of any real moment. 'Yes it is', was their chorus, 'it all has to start somewhere'. I tired of explaining that Haman, Herod, Hitler and Hamas had no need of golf clubs as a training ground, that the Holocaust rested on no such origins, and that no Jew ever suffered harm by exclusion from such social organisations. Most Jews I know still can't accept *that*. Next question: would I join? No, not then, not now.

This kind of challenge reminded me of Yehuda Bauer's view that Jews have little or no understanding of the nature of antisemitism, and if they do, few have the skills to combat it. True in this context. While people in 1993 were bemoaning a golf club's anti-Jewish attitudes, arsonists lit fires in at least five synagogues and memorial sites in Sydney and Melbourne; Ali Kazak launched virulent daily attacks on behalf of the Palestinians; the League of Rights was very active; blood libels were being bandied about in the media; Australians in Nazi uniforms appeared on some television shows; the Commonwealth Government said it was cutting the funds of the War Crimes Special Investigation Unit; Germaine Greer was campaigning against male circumcision; and the United Nations resolved that 'Zionism equals racism'. I said much about this and about the equating of the unequatable in the 1991 ABC television's 'Thinking Jewish' series referred to earlier.

An ugly aftermath did ensue. When I asked my consultancy colleagues for recompense for completing the project on my own, the reply was 'we thought you were a team player'. Never a fan of that puerile sporting 'ethic', I insisted. The matter went to mediation and compensation was ordered. We agreed on a smallish sum and a new computer, but my connections with what I had started came to an end. I had always advocated that money lay in providing town and shire councils with models for community leisure, sport and recreation facilities, not in writing unsellable books about women in cricket, pony racecourses and immigrants in sport. All worthy in their way but hardly gold nuggets. My colleagues seemed to think that designing programs of the kind I had in mind was either too difficult or too time-consuming.

* * *

Two separate grants from the Criminology Research Council in Canberra allowed me to travel extensively across Black Australia. In 1989 a small-scale study began into whether or not sport reduced the growing adult and juvenile delinquency rates in Aboriginal communities. Sandra and I envisaged six months of fieldwork in 45 communities: it turned into a massive project involving 80 communities over five years.

Armed with a Toyota Hiace, a lot of notebooks and music tapes, we interviewed 520 persons: Aboriginal men and women, government officers of various specialisations, sports officials, police and corrective service staff. The fieldwork area was vast, truly vast, from as far afield as Moree and Condobolin in New South Wales, to Doomadgee and Mornington Island in north Queensland, to Lombadina and Mowanjum in remote Western Australia, to Kintore and Santa Teresa in the Northern Territory, to Port Lincoln and Ceduna in South Australia, and to Swan Hill and Lake Tyers in Victoria's Gippsland, and all the centres in between. The mileage was huge.

People were ever helpful, most warming to anything to do with sport— and some officials were only too willing to denigrate Aboriginal people and to legitimise their stereotyping. Whatever the motives, co-operation was universal, complete with recorded views (in and out of pubs) and statistics from local police stations. Some findings were startling, many predictable. New was the quite overt evidence that sport plays a more significant role in the lives of Aborigines than in any other sector of Australian society. Sport provides a centrality, a sense of loyalty and cohesion that has replaced some of the 'lost' structures in communities that so recently operated as church missions and government settlements. Sport is one of the few activities that helps communities survive the imminent danger of social disintegration. And sport had significantly reduced the considerable amount of internal violence—homicide, suicide, attempted suicide, rape, self-mutilation, serious assault—prevalent in some, but not all, disordered communities.

Plainly, sport is effective in keeping youth out of serious (as well as mischievous) trouble during football and basketball seasons. Involvement in sport—both playing and its associated activities—has allowed some groups to exercise some autonomy and sovereignty where they run sport and cultural festivals, as at Yuendumu and Barunga in the Territory, and in New South Wales with the annual Rugby League Knockout tournament. One conclusion upset many who read it: 'that sport takes place in circumstances and environments that resemble Afghanistan in war time and Somalia in drought time'. A common question in this land of 'the level playing field' was, 'How can that be?' Easily, as one saw (and photographed) the gorse bushes on the so-called footy field at Gingie Reserve near Walgett, the salt pans with tree sapling goalposts at Lombadina, the red dirt 'oval' at Yuendumu, the spinifex clusters on the 'pitch' at Doomadgee, the rats feeding on veritable mountains of cricket gear sent to Mornington Island and so on. A few bright spots were at Woorabinda, Bathurst Island and Moree, with pools, grass pitches and lights, albeit that these facilities were enabled only by the local Aboriginal canteens pushing more and more grog to pay for them. It was heartbreaking to see multiple cases of trachoma at Doomadgee—because the chlorinated swimming pool that helps eradicate the disease had been empty for several years by the time we got there.

My major conclusion was that while sport is not and cannot be the sole solution to the multitude of problems in Aboriginal and Islander society—because it cannot be played or practised 365 days in the year—it can be a 30 to 40 percent solution to those communities now literally in peril. Despite the

The salt-pan and sapling 'oval' at Lombadina community, Kimberley region, Western Australia, 1992.

ballyhoo generated by Australian football and rugby league administrations about how much they now put into Aboriginal sport and how much they are doing by way of community assistance, much of what I wrote in April 1994 about the poverty of Aboriginal access to sport pertains 20 years later.

One aspect of this research threw me. At Murray Bridge in South Australia we called into the local Aboriginal council office, and *en passant* a male elder mentioned that young girls were 'playing silly buggers'—but it was nothing to worry about. A female voice out back cried out, 'How can you call it that?' *That* turned out to be daughters and their friends swallowing liquid paper correcting fluid, thumb tacks and every pill available from a mother's bedside. Towards the end of 1989 I gave a public lecture at Flinders University with a large *Nunga* attendance. Women raised the suicide issue. At that time, the Royal Commission into Aboriginal Deaths in Custody was in session and several of its fieldworkers coincided with our visits. Not new, but new to me was a seeming epidemic of parasuicide, the name for attempted suicide, often of a repeated nature. Even newer was the reality, once I started looking, that there were far more Aboriginal deaths by suicide outside of custody than in custody. The ruling thesis that people were committing suicide because they couldn't handle incarceration was about to be discarded.

In 1996, Criminology Research Council funding allowed me to continue with an investigation of Aboriginal suicide *in situ* rather than engage in the usual collection and analyses of statistics held by state coroners. There is a galactic difference between the local and the city-held data. Sandra assisted me greatly in our interviews—396 persons over a total of 27 months across 55 communities in New South Wales, the Australian Capital Territory and New Zealand. My approach to this study was 'towards an anthropology of suicide', largely ignoring the grossly under-reported official statistics. We talked, ate and drank with deceased people's siblings, parents and relatives; we talked to police, ambulance men, doctors, psychiatrists, psychologists, priests, social workers, prison officers, local assistant coroners and youth who had survived their attempts. I am not saying that suicidologists are lazy; simply that if you want a profile of a deceased you have to go to the local coroner's office and read all the witness depositions there—from family, relatives, police, medical and other related personnel. These files are not available in the State Coroner's Office as the sources there are short summary sheets and autopsy reports. Playing pool with teenagers (inevitably losing) was an extraordinarily fruitful interview venue. There was (and is) an urgent need to get away from stolid suicidology and its gross obsession with statistics and rates and long lists of at-risk factors—as if those figures, decimal points and catalogues could or would prevent further suicides.

The essence of this study is that there was almost no suicide in the various and different Aboriginal societies before the 1960s. I scoured every record—from police, missionaries, linguists, anthropologists, government reports and psychiatrists' articles—and found nothing to report. From virtually nil rates, the Aboriginal figures leapt to among the highest on the planet. Something was terribly awry and it wasn't custody. My conclusion was spelled out in two books, one published in 2001 and the expanded edition in 2005, entitled *Aboriginal Suicide is Different: A Portrait of Life and Self-Destruction*. My findings were heard politely enough at Suicide Prevention Australia, psychiatrists' and coroners' conferences. I soon realised that there was an industry here gathering momentum, funds and public support—essentially for the prevention of White, middle-class youth seeking self-destruction. My work didn't conform to these patterns, predispositions and prejudices, and most practitioners were unwilling to see any differentiation between mainstream suicide and these 'unfortunate clusters and contagions'.

A few critics—notably psychologist Joseph Reser at James Cook University, Professor of Psychiatry Robert Goldney in Adelaide and friend Ernest Hunter to a much lesser extent—were somewhat disturbed. Reser demanded, in print, an explanation of the concept of 'different' and Goldney lacerated me for not looking at biochemical and genetic factors in young suicides, especially in Taiwanese youth. Reser couldn't or wouldn't see that the major places of suicide were remote or rural contexts like no others in Australia, that they had histories and legacies like no other groups, that they had been forced from incarceration and segregation and protection into 'freedom' without preparation or aid, as no others. They were societies that knew no suicidal behaviour, no concept of self-death—in ritual beliefs, language and in art—as very few others. They were places of sudden epidemics of younger and younger self death, of family and friendship clusters, of deaths mainly by the confrontational method of hanging (asphyxiation in reality), as no others. There was no evidence of 'mental issues', of warning signs. If all that didn't make Aboriginal suicide different, then he had a problem. From time to time Reser has insisted the evidence of Aboriginal suicide before 1960 must be somewhere. Nobody has yet found that 'somewhere'. My stoush with Goldney was printed in journals. I was troubled by the question of genetics: since most suicides were in mixed-Aboriginal persons, exactly whose genes and whose 'biochemical imbalances' were we talking about? He couldn't answer.

The 2005 edition flayed the medicalisation of the subject and the overwhelming emphasis on depression, mental ill-health, genetic tendency, chemical imbalance causation that is trumpeted everywhere—in courts, inquests, movies, television, newspapers and conferences. The very sad point to be made is that no one understands why people commit suicide (apart, perhaps, from the terminally ill patient who doesn't want to suffer and says so). James Hillman, a noted American psychoanalyst, writes about trying to find the 'soul of the suicide'. We have yet to find it. Holocaust survivor Jean Améry wrote a brilliant book on the subject: suicide is, he wrote, not an exit from life but an entrance into death. That takes some digestion, but so many Aboriginal suicide survivors have told me over the years that life is so appalling down here that they want to see what it's like in another place, up there. 'Is there an up there?' I ask; 'Professor, do you know?' I retreat and take Améry's word for the idea of an entrance to somewhere else. (Améry suicided.)

Slowly, more and more of the medicalisers and practitioners have conceded they have to look at causality in socio-political and environmental factors. They are not going to find an 'evil' or 'rogue' gene, let alone a prototype model of a chemically balanced mind. They are not going to stop suicide rates, which increase as I write, with anti-depressants, talk therapies, telephone hot lines, life-be-in-it and similar programs and slogans. They will find more suicides as police and coronial reporting practices improve—and they have, markedly, since men like Michael Barnes, the former Queensland State Coroner, began investigating the need for improved reporting.

My findings on sport and delinquency have relevance in this suicide arena. In the past decade, in formal submissions to a Senate, Northern Territory and House of Representatives inquiries, I have argued that sport is as relevant to suicide as it is to delinquency rates. I have never claimed that sport prevents suicide. Suicide isn't measles or smallpox—there are no vaccinations and no serious preventatives. But there are strategies for deflection, deferral, diversion—and sport is the very best of them because it has several attributes: it provides a sense of belonging, loyalty, inclusion, the opposite of what sociologist Durkheim called social isolation. It provides a chance to play, and if one's musculature is not good enough, there is enough room and space to be a scorer, touch judge, referee, rosette-maker, fund-raiser, organiser, newsletter-writer. If nothing else, simply a fan. But more than anything else, sport is both a present- and future-tense activity—today's game, tomorrow's, next season's. Most would-be suicides I know are only past- and present-tense oriented. I take some satisfaction in having helped things move forward from the days of the thumbtacks and liquid paper girls who were merely 'playing silly buggers'.

* * *

Edward Idris Cardinal Cassidy came to his homeland, Australia, from the Vatican in July 1999. At a public gathering he presented a noticeably short (eleven-page) document that had taken the Vatican twelve years to prepare: *We Remember—A Reflection on the Holocaust (The Shoah)*. The enlightened Governor-General Sir William Deane was the chair, and the Cardinal was followed by long, formal responses from the Chief Rabbi Raymond Apple and from me. The organisers published the speeches that year. Cassidy talked of 'the sons and daughters of the Church… who fostered long-standing sentiments of mistrust and hostility that the Vatican documents refer to as anti-Judaism'. If only that Church's attitudes and behaviours had been merely mistrust and hostility—*that* the Jews could have lived with as they have done for two millennia and longer. But Jews have had to live with and die from things infinitely greater than those ignominies. Jews have also had to live with the reality, expressed by Christian philosopher Marcel Dubois, that 'the centuries-old Christian anti-Judaism prepared the soil for modern antisemitism and the Holocaust'.

The Cardinal conceded that 'many Christians did, in fact, fail to give every possible assistance to those being persecuted'; he talked of people who 'failed to give the witness that might have been expected of them as Christ's followers'. The tenor of this is that at worst the Catholic Church was merely one third of the Holocaust triangle; the other two—the perpetrators and victims—as well as the bystanders, those who by their indifference, or even their hostile indifference allowed it to happen. Many churches and churchmen were more than bystanders: they were accessories, accomplices, collaborators, certainly companions to both ideas and actions—and murderers. The Vatican document has several references to the church or its adherents as co-equal victims. There is a blasphemy in equating the fate of the Jews of Europe with the fate of the Catholic Church or even several hundred of its servants. And there are also curious omissions of the dead in *We Remember*, notably the 22 million targeted non-Jewish victims of the Nazis.

Some aspects of the Church's involvement need brief discussion. The essential thrust of *We Remember* is the 'we' and 'they' dichotomy: 'we' were the anti-Jewish church leaders and ideology makers who taught and preached a doctrine of contempt, which they admitted and now regarded as morally and ethically wrong; 'they' were an aberrant group of pagan Nazis whose roots lay outside Catholic Christianity and who murdered in the name of blood and race. This kind of rationalisation does not become the Vatican. It echoes the German historian Ernst Nolte who talked about the 'us' Germans, the good people, the anti-Nazis, and the 'them' Germans, Nazis who seemingly descended from some alien spaceship in 1933 and who were vanquished by the forces of good in 1945.

That night with the Cardinal led me to a decade-long study of Catholic and Protestant behaviour during that period; it led to my writing 'Noughts and Crosses: The Silence of the Churches in the Holocaust Years', published in *Genocide Perspectives IV* in 2012. It details Catholic, Protestant and even Jewish abnegation of moral stances and responses even in the face of catastrophe unfolding before them, a lot of noughts amid the crosses. This exercise nicely complements the work of two of my brilliant students: Paul O'Shea, author of *A Cross Too Heavy: Eugenio Pacelli*, which delves into politics and the Jews of Europe from 1917 to 1943; and Darren O'Brien whose monumental *The Pinnacle of Hatred* catalogues the inventory of blood libels against the Jews from the eleventh century to the present.

Yehuda Bauer once said that if the death of 50 million people worldwide because of Hitler's war against the Jews doesn't deter people from hating, baiting and harming Jews, then nothing will. A sobering thought as I have come to accept his dictum that antisemitism is part of the Western world's intellectual and populist baggage. It has always been there and always will be despite some valiant efforts by Jewish organisations to combat it. Antisemitism exists where there are no longer Jews, and it exists where there have scarcely been Jews as in Senegal, Malaysia and Japan. If one believes that antisemitism is a 'disease', a 'mental disorder', one can understand the efforts at therapy. If one accepts it as 'normal', one can stop chasing down badly or insultingly worded crossword clues, offbeat comments on talkback radio, criticism of Israel and its military and Royal Sydney's membership policy. I believe that sanction is the only plausible remedy, one that can halt overt action against people and property; some Australian jurisdictions are halfway there with the criminalisation of hate speech and incitement to racial hatred. Although you can do something to stop antisemitic *behaviour*, you can't stop the mindsets.

In 1999 AIATSIS published 1,500 hard copies of my long essay 'Genocide in Australia' as a research discussion paper. Well received, it went online and became a 'bestseller', if there can be such a thing in this domain. The template was a legal one, showing in what ways Australian killings, creation of living conditions calculated to destroy a people and to cause them serious physical and mental harm, and the forcible removal of children, conformed to the acts of genocide defined in the 1948 Genocide Convention. A good number of people were duly shocked, upset and bewildered by this portrait of Australia as a genocidal society, one always held sacred as a land of good and decent colonists and good and decent democrats. Some conceded atrocities and mistreatment but pleaded that it was arrogant ignorance, ignorant arrogance, or misplaced benevolence, with no intent on the horizon.

Perhaps the real significance of the paper was the absence of response from the small coterie of denialists who surfaced loudly at the time of the inquiry into the stolen generations conducted by Sir Ronald Wilson. They attacked all and sundry, especially Wilson and academic Robert Manne but limited their comments on my essay to a statement that I had applied the Genocide Convention template to the Australian case. Only Ron Brunton, a former Monash Honours student of mine and an arch-denier of this vision of Australian history, contended in print that had there been a 'genocide' (by child removal) in the Northern Territory, I (Colin) would have 'seen it and stopped it' (single-handedly, it seems). My Macquarie colleague, anthropologist Ken Maddock, said that even though I and two other of his Jewish acquaintances 'with interests in Zionism' had worked in Aboriginal communities, we hadn't 'caught a whiff of genocide'. Ken, like so many, could only visualise genocide as Auschwitz.

My paper was much expanded in 2011. By then the word genocide had become part of the Australian political vocabulary, discussed in chapter 21. Only Keith Windschuttle continues his stream of denialism, citing me as Australia's 'most-fixated' of writers in this field. If I am, I'm only a tenth as vociferous, verbose and voluble as Mr Windschuttle, author of dozens of papers and two books on *The Fabrication of Aboriginal History*.

Our collective interest in sport and in writing about genocide came to a head when Douglas Booth and I co-wrote *One-Eyed: A View of Australian Sport*. The book is a strong and provocative piece of social and political criticism—of militarism, Empire-ism, Britain's motherhood, sport and war, sport as moral education, anti-femininity, racism, playing styles, audience attitudes, national sports policies, commercialisation, and the extraordinary pursuit of gold, gold, gold. The late cricket writer Peter Roebuck said it taught him a lot about Australia. Author Peter FitzSimons said the book was wider than a tennis court and bigger than a football field. That elegant journalist Martin Flanagan thought it 'an argument waiting to happen', one that 'invites the reader to argue back'. Our colleagues in ASSH seemed uncertain about whether to laugh, cry or cringe. We did take some heavy swipes at the hagiographic, the iconic and the moronic in the received wisdom about Australian-style sport, at the lack of insight and the unwillingness to seek any insight. For them, sport was beyond question, whatever its shape and form. Only a suspicion, but I think that sports history colleagues were a little intimidated, wary of tackling two of the 'big boys' in this society of historians. But it didn't take us long to find an immovable reality, that critical books of this kind will never sell more than a few thousand copies while so-called autobiographies of the as-told-to variety, detailing which jockstraps were the most suitable for which weather conditions, will attract 50,000 buyers. For the serious sports historians this book was like a big pothole: either you straddled it or you swerved sharply to avoid it.

Two events of recognition came about in 1997. First, an Officer of the Order of Australia (AO) 'for service to the community through research into social and legal justice for people disadvantaged by their race, particularly the Aboriginal community, and to promote the equal participation in community life of all Australians'. If I had had any doubts about belonging, this little badge of recognition assuaged it. My sister Pam was the initiator of this exercise; Aboriginal friends and sportsmen Gary Ella and barrister Lloyd McDermott were my chief referees, which pleased me greatly. Recently an old friend asked me whether I was pleased to have such nominals after my name. I paused a little while, but only a little while, and said, yes, I was chuffed at the prize. And I do wear my lapel button on many occasions.

The second was a letter from Natal University inviting me to receive an award of Doctor of Laws *honoris causa*. An interesting tale. I said thanks but no thanks, giving all manner of excuses like not flying without Sandra; when they offered to pay her fare I again declined because Sandra would want to go to Cape Town to see her 91-year-old father. We'll pay for that too, they said. I wasn't looking for gifts of this kind but rather trying to wriggle out of attending. Agreement reached, they phoned me a few days before departure to say that while they had intended no speeches at the graduation ceremony, and because neither of the other recipients (anti-apartheid activists Peter Brown and Albertina Sisulu) wanted to speak, would I please now speak on behalf of the degree recipients. Peter was one of the founders of the Liberal Party (see chapter 5); Albertina was the wife of Walter, Mandela's compatriot in the ANC and at the dreaded Robben Island.

Before we left I contracted with the *Sydney Morning Herald* to write a feature essay on 'the return of the native son' or some such. The ceremony was a real occasion—held in the Pietermaritzburg YMCA gymnasium/hangar with over 2,000 people in the audience, this being the first cohort of undergraduates under Black rule. Parents, most of them still in menial jobs, were exhilarated at seeing their sons and daughters on the first pathway to a new rainbow society. I made a good speech—a former insider's view from the outside, outside but with enough experience and insights to look inward as if one of them.

The previous day I had met Christopher Merrett, then the university's chief librarian. He gave us a tour of the premises and pointed to places where students had taken their grievances to a dramatic level—burned and trashed buildings or objects. One grievance related to high failure rates and an impossible demand that 'one passes, we all pass'. We became friends then and have remained steadfastly so since. I took Sandra on a tour of where I had worked, eaten and played as a student, and was devastated to see the number of guards with assault weapons outside shops and banks, and banks with three or four 'airlock' chambers where one was scrutinised before being able to cash a traveller's cheque. My Sleepy Hollow was now a centre of massive political (and criminal) violence. I put my head around the door of the *Natal Witness*, talked with a delighted editor about my days working there. He asked if I intended writing something and I told him of the *SMH* contract. Could he reproduce it in the *Witness*? Of course.

Back home, the article appeared and was duly sent to the 'Maritzburg paper. Within a week a letter arrived, signed by David Maugham-Brown, Principal of the 'Maritzburg campus, on behalf of the university executive and especially of Vice-Chancellor, Brenda Gourley. 'Is this how you repay our gift to you?' he asked. 'We believe we may have erred in awarding you this degree because you have now betrayed our trust in you, you have slandered the university by talking about trashing that never occurred, and it is people like you who caused disinvestment in a struggling South Africa.'

Quite the most astonishing letter I have ever received.

My reply was in two parts. First, could they please tell me if they were withdrawing the Doctor of Laws because I was having new letterhead stationery printed and needed to know which nominals to include. Second, not only Merrett but also senior economist Yusuf Bhamjee, who sat on a university inquiry into some of these events, had corroborated the trashing events, mentioned by me in but one short line in the feature article. Accordingly I asked what was the difference between the old Nationalist authorities censoring some of my work and the new regime that seemed to be doing the same thing. Maugham-Brown closed the correspondence by saying 'the degree is safe' because Dr Colin Gardiner's laudation said the award was based more on work done in Australia on the Aboriginal behalf than work done for the African cause, something like ten pages for the former and only eight for the latter! Good old Natal U—but better behaviour by far than the catastrophes of corruption, exclusion of White academics, censorship and intimidation that have occurred there in the past decade.

Chapter 19

BREATHLESS

Limited lung capacity should have kept me talking less at this time. But there was too much to say and seemingly little enough time left. I wasn't sure how long the repairs from the triple bypasses would last, and with the onset of adult diabetes as an added spur, I began a near-frenzy of talking and writing. Life after official retirement has been a breathless rush to get it all done, with little time for reflection.

A Charles Sturt University graduation ceremony was a prickly and appropriate occasion to address those about to become Bachelors of Police Studies. Assuming that Australia's history of whistle-blowing would be of professional interest, I suggested, among other things, that for $25 a year they could join a whistle-blowers' union as the best option in town. Those graduating liked what they heard but the bemedalled brass didn't even try to hide their chagrin over a cup of tea. I once addressed *HMAS Penguin* on the need for critical thinking. With a touch of barb I referred them to the anti-intellectual messages in two best-selling naval novels, *The Cruel Sea* by Nicholas Monsarrat and *The Caine Mutiny* by Herman Wouk. That, too, was frowned on heavily, with barely a word of thanks from the admiral on duty.

Addresses to the Armenian, Hellenic Greek and Jewish genocide commemoration ceremonies were appreciated. Only the Canberra Jews were less than happy when I condemned infatuation with 'shrinology' rather than immersion in Holocaust history. There is still a widespread attitude of sacralising the Holocaust, enveloping events in don't-touch glass cases as if amulets to ward off evil. Astonishing, too, that any audience would expect to hear 'nice things' about the *Shoah*.

I taught Politics courses for a year at Western Sydney (2000) and supervised good Honours students from that cohort. In the same year I initiated a genocide studies course at the University of Technology Sydney (UTS), and in 2003 I asked ANU if they'd be interested in a similar course. They were and from 2004 to mid-2009 I taught a semester course of that name to third-year students, introducing a second course on 'Genocide Post-1945' from 2006.

Doctoral students emerged as a result of the ANU and UTS teaching. There were nine ANU Honours students working on genocide topics in one particular year—an unusually high number. The ANU courses, now taught by a staff member I mentored, continues to attract over 150 students in each course, and the UTS course continues to fill a ceiling of 65 students each year.

Writing has helped defeat time, ageing and illness. Son Paul and I published *Black Gold* in 2000 with Aboriginal Studies Press. Earlier, the Tatz family had given the initial 129 Hall of Fame photos, each blown up to an enormous 76 x 114 cm, to the National Museum in Canberra; 72 were already mounted. Finding out that the museum (then in a crisis of directorship) was not displaying them, we withdrew the gift by mutual consent and donated the whole collection to AIATSIS for permanent safekeeping, display, and in turn on loan to communities.

Aboriginal Studies Press published *Aboriginal Suicide is Different* in 2001 and produced a second edition in 2005 in a more reader-friendly format with a new introductory chapter. The cover by Michael Mucci—originally drawn for my opinion piece in the *Sydney Morning Herald*—shows a White face, eyes averted from the problem.

The year 2000 was ostensibly the fiftieth anniversary of Monash Country Club at Ingleside, but their history goes back to 1931 when a Jewish club of that name was literally begging and scrounging for games at public and a few private courses in Sydney. These young men—an early sub-unit of the Young Men's Hebrew Association (YMHA) formed in 1929—were not admitted

Hall of Fame members:

Cheryl Mullett (Drayton), born at Jackson's Track, Victoria, winner of fifteen Australian badminton titles in the 1960s, courtesy Dorothy Proctor.

Jack Marsh, from the Clarence River district, was a champion sprinter and played six first-class cricket matches for New South Wales, 1901–1903, courtesy NSW Cricket Association.

to membership of any of the championship-quality courses in Sydney. Royal Sydney was hardly alone. The Monash men played at venues like Eastlakes and Moore Park. Their first break came from a Catholic group—the Niblicks—who also suffered exclusion and who built their own course, St Michael's, near La Perouse, in the late 1930s. They allowed the Jewish men to play at allotted times but wouldn't let them into their clubhouse, providing them with a prefabricated steel Nissen hut as a separate social facility. By war's end the Jewish golfers had had enough of discrimination, borrowed $7,700 to buy the land at Ingleside and by 1950 had built a quite excellent course from scratch.

Towards the end of the century I told the Monash committee that I would do the history, from beginnings in 1931 (not 1950), for no payment. But if they wanted the standard model of sweeping vistas of green, groves of trees, gardens of pretty flowers, locker-room jokes, bad caricatures of esteemed members and endless lists of trophy winners, they had the wrong bloke. If they wanted a full-scale social and sporting history about the politics of inclusion and exclusion, they had the right one. They agreed.

Monash was the antithesis of Royal Sydney in every way. Not only no archivist but no archives, and most of the minute books, records and photographs had been lost in a 1957 fire. This biography was done backwards, with the history first and the archives following. The difficulty was tracing all the shareholders. On establishment, the land owners, Monash Holdings, had to borrow money and debentures were issued to those who bought them for a nominal £50 each. One had to affirm membership of 'the Jewish faith' to have a share in Holdings.

There wasn't a hint of censorship. The book, *A Course of History: Monash Country Club, 1931–2001*, was much less restrained than the Royal Sydney biography. It tells the tale of a club born out of discrimination, which built club membership on a policy of openness to all. It was never a club exclusively for Jews but a Jewish club open to all. That was realistic as there would never be enough Jewish golfers to sustain a championship course, but there was generosity in a totally open membership—or persons other than Asians, that is. Several of the founders had bad World War II experiences and the first Asian member was admitted as late as 1976. Non-Jews don't have a monopoly on exclusion.

That policy wasn't of much moment to members, but women were. In 1984 three professional women applied to Monash to become full-playing members, able to golf on a Saturday rather than on Tuesday, the traditional ladies' day. Till then, all women were called 'associates' (of their menfolk) and entitled to play croquet, going back to the first Royal Sydney days. Australia was the last Western country to abandon that denigratory category. I was on committee at the time and my pleas for the admission of women members were howled down: 'end of the world', 'thin edge of the wedge', 'slippery slope', and 'we'll fight them on the beachheads'. I told my colleagues that I had some input into the 1977 NSW *Anti-Discrimination Act* and they couldn't possibly win.

Nonetheless the matter went to the Anti-Discrimination Board for a first conciliation hearing. Commissioner Graeme Innes told the women they could have a representative, preferably not a lawyer. They chose me, thus providing a nice conflict of interest. At the December 1985 full hearing I sat with my 'clients' on one side of the table with the club president and his mates on the other. For openers Innes tabled a judgement in an earlier Human Rights Commission case, heard by Justice Dame Roma Mitchell, on women applying (successfully) for equal playing rights at the Keperra Country Club in Brisbane. He asked us to read it. We did, whereupon the president raced across and whispered: 'Col, what does this mean?' 'You're f****d was the reply. Never has such a six-letter word sounded so good or more appropriate. They were, and women (albeit few in number) were able to enter the Wednesday and Saturday playing ranks.

Another key issue was (and is) the machinery for ensuring continued Jewish membership. The articles of association and the Holdings lease to the country club stipulate that the golf club's committee would always have a majority of at least one Monash Holdings (Jewish) member. Today the board comprises nine of whom at least five must be Monash Holdings members. In 2005 a member challenged this as discrimination, claiming that as an aspiring office-holder he had only one chance in four of being elected a director rather than one in nine. Nothing in the rules says that a non-Jew can't be elected president, vice-president, treasurer or captain, the four most senior portfolios. The club was in disarray and I was able (with great difficulty) to persuade the president to hire a lawyer versed in complex human rights law. On the eve of the tribunal hearing the complainant withdrew his case—whereupon the Monash directors claimed victory. They didn't seem to grasp that there was never a trial of the issue and the victory remains hollow and untested. Discussing this one day with Justice Michael Kirby, he told me he'd love to have adjudicated on this matter. My reply was a simple question: in terms of human rights, which is the greater discrimination—one member's arithmetical opportunity or the greater discrimination arising if one dark day Jews find themselves disbarred from the club they built initially as a response to discrimination?

* * *

The *Genocide Perspectives* series continued with volume II in 2003 and volume III in 2006. Some 60 percent of the chapters came from young Australians and significant original material was published. Brandl & Schlesinger produced handsome paperbacks in conjunction with our Australian Institute for Holocaust and Genocide Studies (AIHGS). Sandra, as ever, did the hard yards and the leg work.

At some point in 1998 I was approached by journalist and filmmaker John Pilger who had read *Obstacle Race* and wanted to make a documentary on the sporting (and social) conditions of Aborigines before the Sydney 2000 Olympics. He had my enthusiastic support and help in producing 'Welcome to Australia', shown across the country in 1999. Chagrin, outrage and indignation, some malevolent responses and some approving ones, followed. A comment from journalist and public affairs man Gerard Henderson was that he couldn't understand how I could bring myself to associate in this way with that outrageous left-winger. Gerard is much consumed by 'left-wingism'; he hates or pretends to hate several people in public life and Pilger is in his top five. I have viewed the video since and it is as reasonable a portrait of Aboriginal 'sporting life' as we will ever get. I write for Gerard's journals from time to time so I'm no longer sure what wing I am.

Over dinner Pilger suggested I write my own Holocaust and genocide book and as his publisher was then Verso in London, he would suggest me to them. *With Intent to Destroy: Reflecting on Genocide* was published in small and elegant hardback in 2003. I'll never know whether this 'left-wing' press took it on as an antidote to or leavening of a contentious book they published by Norman Finkelstein in 2000, *The Holocaust Industry: Reflections on the Experience of Jewish Suffering*. Finkelstein, an *enfant terrible* by all accounts, had troubles at his university, was later sacked and was savaged by, among many, Harvard lawyer Alan Dershowitz. Like so many of his ilk, he claims that his credentials are those of a child of survivors and that entitles him to instant expertise and the right to comment on the Holocaust without question.

With Intent was launched in Melbourne and well received. Chapters included my journey into genocide, the membrane metaphor used earlier, an examination of the differing approaches to genocide, a deep look into the German genocidal engine, the matter of genocide in Australia, the denialist phenomenon in various genocide cases, teaching about genocide and, for me, an important chapter on whether or not South Africa fits the label. The short answer is no: South Africa warranted every conceivable appellation—totalitarian, repressive, neo-fascist, brutal, often homicidal, but never genocidal. White society always wanted more Blacks, not fewer.

In 2004 I was given an honorary fellowship by AIATSIS. To reciprocate, I suggested a project that had been in cold storage for 20 years. The 1984

Aborigines and Uranium report predicted that within two decades of open-cut mining alongside indigenous communities (as happened in Canada and the United States) there would be outbreaks of lung, cervical and possibly oesophageal cancer. AIATSIS provided a small grant for me to do some more fieldwork and as this wasn't a solo task I invited three colleagues—Drs George Tippett, Alan Cass and John Condon—to join me. We spent time in the field, not looking at patients but scouring all the local and head office records, visiting the Ranger (ERA) mine to investigate how wonderfully 'safe' this yellowcake substance was, and interviewing several medical specialists and nurses. As with the 1978–1984 study, the mines claimed they had no records, nor had they ever kept records of any non-Aboriginal employee who may have contracted illnesses, and so no comparative study has ever been possible. On return I began the first drafts of a paper, later published by AIATSIS as a research discussion paper entitled *Aborigines and Uranium: Monitoring the Health Hazards* (2006). We found that at least 120 'incidents' or 'mishaps' had occurred in the mining region, mostly spillages of toxic materials into the landscape. And there was a significant overall increase of cancer among the Aboriginal people in the Kakadu region.

There is a Keystone Kops story here but with some nasty connotations. By this time AIATSIS was presenting the research discussion papers (RDPs) online, and Graeme Ward, my friend who instigated this present book, was editor of the Institute's research program publications. The essay was to be posted online at 4 p.m. one Friday in December 2006. At that time, Prime Minister John Howard had appointed Dr Ziggy Switkowski, a nuclear scientist and businessman, to head a team to assess the processing of nuclear energy as 'an opportunity for Australia', all in a very gung-ho, let's-do-it tone. At about noon that Friday, Graeme phoned to say that the Principal had pulled the publication, with no real explanation apart from the comment that the paper needed to be read by all Council members before publication, a procedure unheard of to that point. AIATSIS publications always carried the usual disclaimer that the editorial board did not necessarily share an author's views, so there was, as I saw it, no reason to suggest such a process unless, as I suspected rightly, this was the usual paranoia about being closed down if the Institute annoyed Government. Chairman Mick Dodson was overseas. I insisted that all Council members be emailed a copy for a reading, forthwith, and that Dodson be given a copy at the airport on his arrival home.

An ABC radio journalist in Darwin picked up on the embargo, rang the Institute and was told both directly and then by a press release, believe it or not, that I had no association with that body and AIATSIS was not behind any report *purporting* to emanate from me. I went on Darwin radio that day and told a little story about the findings and about what looked like crass censorship. I told Mick Dodson that if he didn't respond to my threat within five days I would make the research paper, the shameful press release, and the embargo public. Meanwhile Switkowski, with breathtaking *chutzpah*, released his report, which was prepared without any consultation with the public, stating that there was only a ten-day opportunity (just before Christmas) to respond, failing which it would be published as a 'unanimous' verdict on the nuclear question.

Mick solved his problem in a good way and in a way that put the Institute fully behind the publication. He suggested the uranium paper be submitted formally by AIATSIS, not the authors, to Switkowski and incorporated in the latter's final report. The RDP was published on 14 December 2006 together with Mick's formal letter of submission and an extract from Switkowski's response: that 'it can be concluded that the reported increase in cancer incidence in Aboriginal people of the Kakadu region, if it were to be verified, cannot be attributed to radiation exposure arising from the mining of uranium'. However, a social monitoring program 'would be an important step in resolving past difficulties in this area'. Nice work from a team that had no medical expertise, no epidemiological training, no access to cancer registries and hospital records—and of course gave no evidence of having read the 1978–1984 monitoring study. Dr Switowski and his team, together with the Ranger mining company, insisted to the media that such cancers (which they now seemed to concede—verified by the NT Health Department in 2014) were due to alcohol, smoking and lifestyle, to which we could only point out that such factors were prevalent in every Territory Aboriginal community and this was the only one that mined a particular mineral. As far as I know there is still no social impact monitoring program anywhere in Australia, but as discussed in the last chapter, there is some chance of that earlier model regaining a life.

Fast forward. In 2010 I revised the 1999 RDP on genocide in Australia and discussed it with the new publications editor of AIATSIS. In 2008 we had enjoyed a most successful partnership when the Institute's journal, *Australian Aboriginal Studies*, produced a special edition entitled 'Unlevel Playing Fields: "Race" and Sport in Australia'. The revised genocide essay is twice the length of the original and not only updates but contains a great number of eye-witness accounts of both the killing and the stolen generations eras. Between February and October 2011 there was no response from external readers and no effort by the new editor to encourage deadlines for their reviews. I confess to being miffed that the successful original needed an external assessment, believing the Institute was well qualified to examine it in-house.

Yet again, and quite reasonably in the circumstances, I took my bat and ball elsewhere and hit upon the notion of sending it to the Monash Indigenous Centre (MIC), my original 'baby'. The Director Lynette Russell and Melissa Castan at the Castan Human Rights Law Centre there had it reviewed in two weeks and it was online and in hard copy by early December 2011. Lynette wrote a lengthy foreword about me—interesting because several readers who knew me well knew nothing about my earlier life and work in South Africa and in my Monash days. The joint MIC–Castan publication is called *Genocide in Australia: By Accident or Design?*

***

I still had an abiding interest in Jews and social action. I began writing articles on Jewish activism in South Africa and the United States, at times questioning whether there really was an over-representation of Jews in the civil rights movement and in the anti-*apartheid* struggle. Clearly there was a notable presence, but what were the attitudes, values and actions of those who were not visible activists? Were they silent but disapproving witnesses or did they go along with the mainstream? I can only speak with authority about the wider South African population, most of whom went along with and often endorsed the repressive system and certainly profited and benefited from it. What was pushing this interest was a niggling, irritating question: I had little involvement in Judaic ritual, prayer and observance but I have always had an unshakeable admiration, even a veneration, for what I call Jewishness (discussed earlier). But here was a thorn of some kind, a question perhaps of too much veneration and too little questioning. Historian Cecil Roth's dictum about Jews being the eternal protestants loomed large: could I reasonably protest at some Jewish behaviours? I remember my mother's catchcry that 'our crowd' didn't ever commit murder or rape but only white-collar crime that didn't really hurt people. Quaint, but unrealistic. She had no answers to my questions about who occupied the cells in Tel Aviv and for what crimes.

Dr Saul Issroff produced a massive four-volume work on *The Holocaust in Lithuania, 1941–1945*. He and Professor Milton Shain at Cape Town University were working on Lithuania Jewish emigrants to that country. Would I like to add an Australian segment? There are no archives here, I replied, and the best I could do was write an addendum chapter which looked at those *shtetl* descendants who had moved on to Australia and New Zealand. A grant from the Isaac and Jessie Kaplan Centre in Cape Town started what became a 360-page book. As it began, the philanthropist Mendel Kaplan came to Sydney. We met, liked each other, talked for hours, and he financed the study.

I needed partners and from 2003 Peter Arnold and Macquarie statistician Gillian Heller joined me. They confessed to not being writers and so the task of putting it all together fell to me. Peter designed an elaborate and careful e-mail questionnaire which was sent to some 1,800 addressees; when we had 608 valid responses—a remarkably high figure—we stopped looking for respondents. The book, *Worlds Apart: The Re-Migration of South African Jews*, was published in 2007. Peter did prodigious work to produce a massive appendix containing the names of every Lithuanian town and *shtetl*, each with its Lithuanian, Russian, German, Polish and Yiddish spellings. It is an amazing gazetteer for scholars of this lost world. Gillian's statistics and graphics were attractive and crystal clear.

The survey elicited some interesting and significant material. But the book is essentially a contextual history of political and social issues, of values and behaviour both there and here, as an essay in *verstehen*—German for intuitive understanding, a technique of anthropology—by a once patriot of sorts and an expatriate who had enough *verstehen* of life there and here to publish analytical and critical comments. Even though I had participated in survey research I find it constricting because results (findings) are based solely on what respondents are willing (or not willing) to tell you. The book is a good volume, rich in context, detail and enriched throughout by personal reminiscences, memories and stories from respondents. It was launched at the Sydney Jewish Museum in August 2007 by the inimitable Joanna Kalowski and Malcolm Turnbull, then campaigning to keep his federal seat of Wentworth. I admired the way he put aside his notes after hearing Joanna's detailed analysis and winged it with rich and Yiddish-spiced anecdotes. His Jewish audience bathed in his *goyish* sunshine—he won his seat.

Our AIHGS has worked well with the Sydney Jewish Museum on several projects, especially the annual professional development courses for New South Wales teachers. We also cooperated on an exhibition, wanted by the local South Africans, on South Africans in Australia—their stories, achievements and so on. I wasn't an enthusiast but did help in portraying this rather bizarre group of emigrés. The *Worlds Apart* book explained their uniqueness—their high rate of tertiary education and their ability to come on what we impolitely called the 'LSD trip'—the majority came, they looked, they *shlept* (carried, hauled) and deposited assets to start or extend businesses here; they often pre-bought houses, enrolled kids in Jewish schools, arranged to buy cars, selected their professional advisers and attendants. Remarkably, some thought of themselves as refugees or people who had fled! My passion about this is not bitterness at how we came and what we didn't have but at the posturing, drama and histrionics about how difficult it is to migrate in circumstances such as theirs.

The social action thing still niggled and in 2004 and 2005 I wrote a piece on the Jewish–Aboriginal relationship. A later version expressed not just my hunches but my intense research, expressed as 'An Essay in Disappointment: the Aboriginal–Jewish relationship'. I looked in vain for a reasonable history of social action by Jews on the Aboriginal behalf and could find only two or three before the 1980s and 1990s when several Jewish lawyers engaged in land rights cases. Apart from that of short-term emigré painter Yosel Bergner in the 1930s and 1940s, only Lorna Lippmann and I were really active.

Since then there has been a flurry of activity by formal bodies like the NSW Jewish Board of Deputies, scholarship programs at the Shalom Institute and College, student action at Toomelah, literacy programs with Israelis and the like. My gripe is not that there is an absence of such action as there is; it rests on false claims of a *tradition* of such interest and activity and that the action is so simply because we are Jews. The tradition is hardly that and the *ergo* arguments don't hold water—hence my disappointment.

One more essay on a Jewish theme is worth mentioning, a chapter in James Jupp's *Encyclopedia of Religion in Australia* entitled 'Diversity in Jewishness'. I dissect the strains and strands of Jewishness, the clashes of history, historical narratives and their meaning, belief, ideology, practices and non-practices, values, between ideals and behaviour. My text tries to demonstrate the non-monolithic nature of an historical people, an ethnicity, a persecuted minority, who are almost always seen as 'one', as indivisible, inseparable and hence indelible. I don't expect it will stop antisemites from viewing Jews as a kind of awkward, evil, world-controlling problem, but I hope it helps Jewish students and readers come to terms with what kind of Jews they are and want to be.

Genocide Perspectives IV took a long time coming, partly through lack of sponsorship. In the end we discovered the twenty-first century and its high tech. In May 2012 we met with UTSePress, took less than 20 minutes to agree on a publication, and have the Sydney University Press facilitate print-on-demand hard copies. By July the book was done, placed on the internet for free with hard copies available by August. Despite the volume owing so much to Sandra, my name is listed as the editor-in-chief. Fourteen chapters, all by Australians, amounted to a 495-page book. Michael Kirby launched the book at the University of Sydney in an auditorium with some 200 people attending. As always, he had read the book in its entirety, and was able to comment on each of the chapters.

A few more of the book chapters and articles written in this past decade warrant some commentary. One of the more trenchant and critical essays was on 'reconciliation', a new approach to Aboriginal affairs much vaunted since the mid–1990s. Reconciliation, as defined in a good dictionary, means restoring friendship or compatibility or harmony, a rectification, settling, remedying. It is never defined in the Aboriginal context: it is a word simply parroted, leaving one to struggle for meaning and purpose amid assumptions about what it means. Like all new visions it began as a non-Aboriginal concept, the invention of Robert Tickner, then Labor's Aboriginal Affairs Minister (1990–1996). It was to be a program lasting ten years, aimed at improving race relations, increasing understanding of Aboriginal and Islander culture, history, and the causes of their continued disadvantage in health, housing, education and employment. It came to mean very different things. For Prime Minister John Howard and Aboriginal Affairs Minister John Herron it meant 'practical reconciliation', that is, more money for better health, education, housing and employment (while providing less). The 'gift' was not by way of what should be a normal government duty of care and financial provision of such services, but a bonus, a special new largesse.

For many it signals a moratorium—each party desisting from causing injury to the other without specifying what injuries Aborigines cause to the mainstream. For some it is 'a walking together', a talking together, towards *anything* that simply has to be better than the past or present. For others, reconciliation meant the national Australian Government bringing itself to say 'sorry' for the forcible removal of children, to talk of atonement and make restitution or reparations for these practices. For the majority, reconciliation signifies a new deal, a fresh start, a 'moving on'; it is a synonym for 'forgiving and forgetting'.

Reconciliation has become a shibboleth that is unconvincing, piecemeal and erratic. This new vision comes at a great cost to the victims. It is *they* who must forgo the desire or need for retributive justice; *they* who must eschew notions of guilt and atonement, and all too often they who receive no compensation for the harms done. It is they who must agree to the diminution or even abolition of that shared historical memory that holds victim groups together. It is they who must concur in the substitution of their memory with our memory and their history with our history. It is they who must connive at ignoring the importance of accountability for the criminal acts against them and agree to the blurring of responsibility for who did what to whom. It is they who must cease being so hysterical about denialism—that major tributary of forgetting which claims (all too often) that there was nothing to remember in the first place or at least nothing all that serious.

One fight has been a loss: the nomenclature by which Aborigines, Torres Strait Islanders and South Sea Islanders are known. The only conquered peoples in Western society who have never been allowed the names of their choice, they were Aborigines from day one. By the 1970s and 1980s a strong identity movement led to the appearance of self-chosen terms: *Koori* or *Koorie* in Victoria and New South Wales, *Murri* in Queensland, *Nyoongah* or *Nyungar* in Western Australia, *Nunga* in South Australia and *Yolgnu* in the Northern Territory. The Torres Strait people were given official, separate, legal recognition in 1994 and the Queensland Government similarly recognised the South Sea Islanders in 2002 by name and their own flag. Too much of a mouthful for many, some academics began the practice of calling everyone 'Indigenous', believing it cute and nicely correct. This has led to some quite absurd usages, such as 'Indigenist' points of view, 'Indigenous' genocide and 'Indigineity' and so on. The reality is that no census can (sensibly, logically, linguistically) ask whether a person is 'indigenous'. In some 54 years here I have yet to hear an Aboriginal person say 'I'm an Indigine'. But the battle is lost and 'indigineity', with or without the capital letter, rules.

My interest in sport has flagged, except in the domain of its use as an essential tool for deflecting suicide and as a regimen for a people suffused by the kind of ill-health that requires some physical regimen. I suspect that my essay, 'Who Won and Who Cares?', is my last word on the subject. Sport is a cultural and social institution and sometimes a political one. It has always been there and probably always will be. Sport is solid, an essential institution at the centre of societal coherence and coalescence. But the very games that make up the institution are transient, ephemeral, like each day's weather. In terms of memory and classicism there is an inherent weakness in each sport: their very nature is present and future oriented—this afternoon's match, next week's, next season's.

The nature of the sports beast makes the academic impact on the public nigh impossible: it is here today, maybe even yesterday, and it will be there tomorrow—but last week is already swamped and overtaken by concerns about events in waiting. We can and do, of course, make an impact upon ourselves, our collegiality, our disciplines, our students (for the time being); we enhance our CVs, gain brownie points for work in refereed journals (now the high bar in most universities for appointment and promotion), and get to conferences here and abroad. But can we find any comfort in this paradox: that just as sport expands exponentially, and as more universities recognise sports studies, create positions and promote people of quality, so our academic endeavours figure less and less in the day-to-day or even the long-term making of sports policies, sports planning, programs, events, contests, social awareness. Even if we venture into the public policy arena as I have with sport as an alleviator or deflector of youth suicide, the time lag in the social sciences between publication of an idea and its acknowledgement and acceptance is between five and fifteen years. For example, the knowledge that sport of any kind is a key factor in the treatment of a number of diseases, especially of the metabolic and cardiac kind, has been around for a long time now. Yet Australia remains wedded to sport at the elite level and hardly ever recognises sport as an essential element in public health. Perhaps another lost battle?

Throughout my writings and teachings, I try to deal with the vexed hypotheses of responsibility for genocide: one-man theory, the small coterie of true-believer theory, the ideologically-brainwashed theory, the evil-in-man viewpoint, and least discussed, the notion that a whole nation, a whole people can be complicit. With my South African background, and after reading works on *what* the German public knew and *when* they knew, I conclude that there is much of national complicity—not necessarily as perpetrators but as companions to these events, complicit by silence or silence indicating acquiescence and hence providing legitimacy for a murderous regime.

Since 2004 both AIATSIS and the ANU have given me Visiting Fellow status. I enjoy that and always remember a fine think piece from one-time journalist Anne Susskind. It was simply called 'From'. Her message was plain: if you want to get somewhere, get anything, do anything, you really have to be 'from' somewhere. It helps if you have two things: a prefix of some gravitas, like doctor or professor, and a kind of suffix which says that you belong, somewhere.

Somewhere at this time, my one-time colleague John O'Hara and I were given life membership of the Australian Society for Sports History, for services rendered to that area of study. Doug Booth made the speech and there was great joy in listening to my star pupil.

Chapter 20

SELDOM SOFTLY

My activism is motivated by both personal and societal alienation. But another spur comes from heeding Daniel Levinson's *The Seasons of a Man's Life*, a book of profound influence on me because I used to believe, seriously, that I wouldn't make it to 20 or 30, let alone beyond. We misconceive ageing, Levinson wrote, because we think only of four crass divisions like childhood, adulthood, middle and then old age. There are many more seasons, more even than the seven in *As You Like It*.

Levinson helped me envision the later stages, and the decade plus from 2000 to the present has been one of growth and productivity—based on the reality of time running out and a concerted attempt to stave off ageing of the mind. The body is something else, a let-down, angry-making, ailing, failing, unbending (literally), high maintenance, and kept upright only by the good graces of the best companion and carer in the world—and my sense of unfinished business.

Good teaching and good writing come from regular researching and that requires travelling, meeting, networking, attending conferences and seminars. I have managed a fair few voyages, sometimes rushed voyages, in my so-called retirement period.

One such was to Aotearoa—always the easiest and most pleasant of places. Sandra and I visited Doug and Gaye Booth on more than a couple of occasions when I gave lectures and seminars to both history and sports students and staff at the University of Otago and Waikato University. Otago is solid, venerable and innovative in its way. The Medical School is an eye-opener in that it insists on teaching (examinable) aspects of Maori health in every sub-discipline in the curriculum—to the point where no graduate can emerge without knowing a great deal about what ails that fifteen percent of the 4.4 million population; a far cry from mature big brother Australia. The University of Waikato in Hamilton, the place that once offered me a job, is now an acceptable institution—which it wasn't in the eyes of sister universities in its formative years. It still has problems as we will see.

Time was spent considering Maori youth suicide, increasing at an alarming rate, especially among young girls. I had some profound disagreements with the approach of the Canterbury Suicide Project but tuned in well with two Maori psychiatrists on cultural, ethnic and minority group history. Much of what I saw and heard there is reported in my suicide book. In 2013, Tangi Hepi, a Queenstown-based Maori elder and therapist, sought my review of his life's work on Maori self-destruction. Age, it seems, brings a certain 'guru' status—it sits well with me. It allows me to pontificate more broadly after all those decades of frantic researching and detailed reporting.

Travels in what Maori sometimes call 'the land of the wrong White crowd' found place in the *Worlds Apart* book. The chapter there on New Zealand migration, a place regarded as the ultimate democracy, begins with the striking view of historian James Belich. He described New Zealand's 'racial template as Aryanism' and its immigration policies as 'not White, but Aryan'. My chapter illustrates a chronic anti-Jewish theme, never violent or physical, just plain discriminatory. I do not share the judgement that these attitudes are merely 'misguided' or 'the mistakes of ignorance'. Otago Medical School, for example, actually petitioned the authorities, pre-World War II, to prevent European Jewish refugee doctors from landing, for fear of 'overcrowding' the profession, and the Auckland branch of the British Medical Association was even more concerned (and active) about 'preventing the crush'.

The actions of two universities don't make a country an antisemitic society but two case studies—Waikato and Canterbury, which I examined at both first- and second-hand—are a litmus of many things. In 1993 Joel

Stuart Hayward submitted his MA thesis to the University of Canterbury in Christchurch on 'The Fate of Jews in German Hands: An Historical Inquiry into the Development and Significance of Historical Revisionism'. In our field important questions are asked about 'historical revisionism' and whether it is the same as Holocaust denialism, and so Hayward's thesis had a potential value. Awarded first-class honours in History, Hayward completed a doctorate in 1996 and was appointed lecturer in History at Massey University. In 1999 the NZ Jewish Council denounced his Holocaust thesis and called on Canterbury to revoke the MA degree, clearly a pretty drastic step.

The Hayward case wasn't about conservative versus radical views, freedom of speech or the free marketplace of ideas. Rather it was about outright denialism, about a defence of denialism by Hayward's supporters and about a stand made by the Jewish leadership that led to extravagant claims of a (Jewish) McCarthyism at work. A Canterbury lecturer and warm supporter of Hayward summed up this latter perspective: 'The Jewish Holocaust is one of those delicate topics about which certain beliefs have become so fashionable as to be unassailable regardless of intellectual considerations'. The question then was just how much intellectual consideration did Hayward engage in? Canterbury appointed a working party—a retired High Court judge and two senior professors of History—to investigate claims against the thesis. They deemed the work 'seriously flawed', not deserving of the high marks awarded, but they found no racist malice and did not recommend the withdrawal of the degree. The president of the NZ Jewish Council then asked Richard Evans, Professor of Modern History at Cambridge and recognised as one of the world's foremost experts on Nazi Germany (and the final authority on the veracity of David Irving's genre of Holocaust denialism) to assess the work. He did so at length.

The thesis, he wrote, 'lacked scholarly rigour and thoroughness'; Hayward's account of the work of other denialists was 'extremely superficial'; his endorsement of American denialist Arthur Butz's claim that the SS spent enormous sums trying to save Jewish lives at Auschwitz was 'a breathtakingly outrageous statement'; and Hayward's assertion that he couldn't say whether or not the 'Protocols of the Elders of Zion' was antisemitic 'beggars belief'. The whole, he concluded, was a work of Holocaust denial—to wit, arguing that there was no systematic extermination of Europe's Jews by the Nazis, that gas chambers were not used to kill Jews in significant numbers, that the total killed was 'far less' than the accepted figure, and that most of the evidence for the Holocaust comes from 'post-war fabrications notably by self-proclaimed survivors'. Taken as historical writing, Evans concluded, 'this is a thoroughly tendentious, biased and dishonest piece of work'. The University placed an embargo on library access to the thesis until 1999. I have no idea why the ban was so short or why it was lifted.

The second postgraduate, Hans-Joachim Kupka, disappeared from Germany in 1988 having withdrawn from neo-Nazi Republican Party activities and allegedly fleeing a debt of one million marks. He arrived in New Zealand as a wealthy immigrant and soon began an internet 'newsgroup discussion' promoting Holocaust denial materials, contending that the existence of the concentration camps was as mythological as UFOs, the 'fact' that only 340,000 Jews died, mostly of natural causes, and that Elie Wiesel was 'a revenge-seeker of the sickest sort… the rabble-rouser who wants to persecute the Germans and hold them responsible unto the tenth generation'.

Kupka had attempted an MA enrolment at Massey University but was rejected. He then enrolled for an MA in the German Department at Waikato, insisting that his thesis be written in German. His grade for the MA coursework was insufficient for entry into a doctoral program. His work was neither internally nor externally moderated, as required. His doctoral application was to conduct research on 'Germans in New Zealand' and academic rigour required that he interview, among others, Holocaust survivors.

A messy and murky business began. A Jewish professor, Dov Bing, and a non-Jewish academic, Norman Franke, wanted Waikato's ethics committee to look into what is now called 'the cultural safety' of this project, especially in the light of Kupka's well-established 'Jewish problem' and his intended interviews with survivors. The buck passed between 'accountants, quondam politicians, amateur lawyers and titular professors' as the Waikato philosopher Professor Benjamin Gibbs called them. Disdainful or unsympathetic, each protagonist said there was no reason for any concern about 'ethnic sensitivities'. The most defensive position was taken by Vice-Chancellor Bryan Gould, a former British Labour MP. He accepted internal advice from unqualified staff over and above a panel of eminent historians (including Konrad Kwiet) who were asked to pronounce on Kupka's Holocaust denialism. He constantly referred to his opponents in the matter [the Jews for the most part] as 'spreading false information' and 'staging a witch-hunt'.

'Messy' well describes the protests, demonstrations, university Council motions, back pedalling, death threats, and [an admitted] false accusation by a Gould staff supporter that 'someone' (the Jews in all likelihood) had intimidated her and her property. Material on the matter was leaked to a student newspaper, with strong inference that the leak came from Bing and 'the Jews'. It came, in fact, from the Vice-Chancellor's main advisor throughout the whole affair. The Council demanded an enquiry with the Vice-Chancellor stonewalling and eventually acceding to 'a review'. By now Kupka had withdrawn his candidature and his German mentor and supervisor had left—with all of Kupka's Master's and doctoral files, an unusual procedure indeed.

A former Director-General of Education conducted the review. The university, he concluded, should make a public apology to the Jewish community for its lack of sensitivity to their 'legitimate cultural concerns'. It 'did not live up to its obligations under the university charter in the way it dealt with Jewish cultural concerns'. The Vice-Chancellor made the required public apology but his internet apology insisted that 'much of the concern expressed on the issue of cultural safety has been based on misinformation'. Gould left in 2004 and several of the reviewer's recommendations have yet to be implemented. My part in it was confined to a few newspaper articles and interviews about this brand of anti-Jewish values in democratic New Zealand.

***

In 2002 and again in 2005 I participated in the 'Play-the-Game' sports conferences in Copenhagen. These events were essentially designed by Danes to provide travel and networking for sports reporters and journalists from Asia and Africa. Travelling alone in 2002, I showed slides of Aboriginal and Islander Hall of Fame members and explained the historical and political context of each athlete. I met up again with John Hoberman from the University of Texas in Austin and we delighted each other with stories. He taught me much about the role of the 'Jewish posture' in antisemitic literature. I became a friend of Andrew Jennings, an engaging and 'notorious' vivisector of both the international soccer body FIFA and the International Olympic Committee. I got to know and admire Laura Robinson, a one-time sportswoman and journalist who braved the rampant lions and tigers of Canadian ice hockey when she went public with information about hideous sexual initiation rituals organised for junior players. I learned much from British Dr Ivor Waddington, once a club doctor, about the way soccer club doctors dope players to keep them in a game. He had excellent credentials to pontificate on coaching, management and player involvement in 'supplement regimens'. Strange indeed that Australia should only become aware of peptides, anti-obesity drugs and about 10,000 other substances a full decade later.

These conferences were supportive and comfortable affairs but I ran into trouble with a sports sociologist and gender specialist, Professor Gertrud Pfister. She gave a 'eureka' paper on 'The Kournikova Effect'. Anna Kournikova was a very attractive Russian tennis player; the 'effect' under the microscope was that spectators were more interested in Miss K's attractions than her racquet skill. I had to inform Gertrud that France's Suzanne Lenglen had shown an outrageous pretty ankle or two in the 1920s and that in 1950 'Gorgeous' Gussie Moran, an American with not that much talent but great frilly underwear, created near-riots at Wimbledon. Within hours the showdown was on emails or internet blogs around the sports historians' world. Academics have some strange topics and agendas, and at full time yielded a scoreline of Colin–1, Gertrud–0.

Sandra was with me on the 2005 trip where I talked about sport as a survival mechanism for racial minorities. We visited the Dansk Jødisk Museum. Designed by Daniel Liebeskind with uneven walls, tilted floors, irregular-shaped display cases, ungeometric ceilings, it is a small work of genius. The whole, in my view, is to make the viewer feel off-balance, out of kilter with a set of dioramas that are, by their nature, out of kilter with a normal world. Of course there is emphasis on the Danish rescue of its 8,000 Jews and the powerful story of how Danes, unlike the Dutch, refused to make distinctions between Jews and Danes when the Nazis demanded lists. However, nothing was visible or displayed about the rescued Jews returning after the war to find that Danes had occupied Jewish apartments and refused to return them or the contents. Nevertheless, the museum was a highlight of the visit.

At an earlier conference of the Canadian Association for Suicide Prevention (CASP) in Toronto, Inuit delegates from the autonomous territory of Nunavut 'hijacked' the chosen 2003 venue and insisted that it be held in their capital Iqaluit, population then about 5,000. Iqaluit is on Baffin Island, high above the tree-line in the Arctic archipelago and the whole territory has a land mass of 1.87 million sq km, which (with its water regions) makes it just about one fifth of Canada and the fifth-largest subdivision country in the world. This gigantic place has a tiny population and a huge problem with youth suicide.

I was invited to give the keynote speech to an audience of about 600 people from the continent's circumpolar regions. The event took place in the

Middle School, sitting in the permafrost and brightly painted like all Arctic community places. To my amazement (and approval) the school walls and noticeboards were filled with scraps of paper mourning dead schoolmates, giving emergency phone numbers and counsellor names, or were pleas for help with suicidal feelings. Everything was out in the open. This was in strong contrast to most Australian schools which, until very recently, wouldn't entertain any guest speakers (let alone open discussion) on the subject of self-harm—in case the kids got ideas!

My talk, presented as informally as I could, was appreciated. Delightful people, they were grateful that someone should travel the earth to take an interest in them. As had happened in such talks to Canadian Indians in 1968–1969, every sentence about Australian Aborigines was interpreted as their quintessential and very own experience. Like Maori, they showed an enormous sense of empathy and goodwill towards Australia's Aboriginal people.

We were showered with gifts including magnificent black, grey, sometimes greenish soapstone carvings of walruses, seals, bears, and importantly *inuksuit*. An *inuksuk* is a stone man (*inuk*), a representation of man in nature. *Inuksuit* are used as travel markers, danger signs and to indicate places of respect and celebration (and to be seen on the Nunuvat flag). Since then I wear a walrus ivory *inuk* round my neck, convinced of its magical charm. Inuit art, including its many hunting and survival themes, has an exquisite line and beauty.

We lodged in a fine, private, bed-and-breakfast home owned by John and Charlotte vander Velde, both public servants. The house opposite had a polar bear skin stretched out across the whole frontage, displaying that family's one-a-year hunt catch. John's house was on the banks of Frobisher Bay and it was amazing to watch the seven-metre ice tides rise and fall each day. The hundreds of dogsleds and snowmobiles had to time their runs to avoid being unable to land on level ground. Disconcerting of course was the 22 hours of sunshine, even in spring, and sleep was a problem. So was the cold: minus

Inuit stone-marker, an inuksuk, *a representation of man.*

17°C one day, plus 4°C the next. There were only five or six kilometres of road, all taxis charged a standard single fare and carried as many passengers as the car could hold, and roads were simply frost with soil covering. Some wag had planted a road sign in the permafrost: 'Beware of the Kangaroos'.

The women were particularly willing to talk because Sandra was alongside me: we were solid elders, complete with pictures of children and grandchildren. The women were especially comfortable with Sandra and were grateful for a non-official or non-therapist listener. The men proudly took us to the quite beautiful but small (19-member) legislature building with its igloo-like construction, outstanding carvings and well designed seating which suited the building.

On First Air—the Inuit-owned airline—the large stewardesses provided the best breakfasts of any airline we've flown with: ham omelettes to remember, and as many helpings as one liked. We flew back to the takeoff point, Ottawa, spent a few days there and went on to visit Jim and Bev Kelly from Queen's University days in Kingston. The campus looked, as always, gracious, conservative but with a warmth unexpected of greyish stone. Some buildings and venues had changed but Kingston was still a place of fond memory.

From there we flew to England, visiting cousins in London. One of the world's great Holocaust museums, funded by Elizabeth Maxwell in the Imperial War Museum, was where we spent an entire day. It has several floors of first-rate exhibits with particularly good captioning. But when we reached the top floor the tone changed. Indeed, it became callous. Dedicated to 'other genocides', it had rows of plain stone benches, no exhibits, and continuous footage screening fragments, potted history, and bits and pieces (literally) of Rwanda, Darfur, Bosnia, and the fate of Romani people. I thought it not only undignified but unbecoming for a museum of such grandeur and fame to skew history in quite this way.

For two weeks in Scotland we went sightseeing, gallery-watching, whisky-sampling, bed-and-breakfasting, Loch-Nessing and so forth. It was a great moment of respite from work and gloom. From there by ferry to Ireland, to Belfast and Queen's University before travelling south to Dublin. We saw Trinity College, the Guinness beer factory which dominates that city's life, some amazing property developments, and experienced a new-found sense of Irish identity, one located in Europe rather than with 'Mother Britain'. The wealth and well-being, so apparent when we were there, wasn't to last. We were met by London friends Val and Stan Clingman, and the four of us travelled by road, enjoying each other's company, much Irish scenery in the south west and outstanding food.

A visit to the famine museum at Skibbereen in West Cork was sobering. The specially designed building portrays many aspects of the years 1845 to 1847, with exhibits of cooking implements and pots for a special British-designed medical 'diet' that turned out to be as deleterious as the starvation.

What was so alarming is that while there is much signage about *Phytopthora infestans*—the potato blight—there is not a single word suggesting British 'omissionary' behaviour at that time. It makes one think that no human agency was ever involved in that human disaster. Historians still debate whether this event qualifies as genocide but there can be no doubt about the mass death, the privation and the level of 'contributory negligence' involved.

At Galway I presented a paper at the National University's International Association of Genocide Scholars (IAGS) conference. Galway was a delight, especially the sight of salmon fisherman chained, literally, to the banks of the frenzied rapids in the Corrib River which runs through the city.

* * *

The visit to Lithuania and Poland was timely, albeit late in my life. Amidst its sadness Vilnius (Vilna) was a special joy. Jewry is kept alive by some 5,000 souls in this gracious but very Russian–European city of 700,000. We saw three worlds: one from before the war, one that was annihilated and the world that is. The Jewish communal centre teaches in Yiddish and Hebrew, runs a nursery school, a 200-strong day school and all social welfare services. Jewish poverty is rife. Several meetings of the World *Litvak* Congress are still held there. Jewish theatre is alive, artists flourish and the English-language *Jerusalem of Lithuania* newspaper appears quarterly. Community chairman, barrister Dr Simon Alperovitch, deplored current media anti-semitism but conceded there was no impediment to his or any Jew's professional work. Yet schism prevailed even in this minute community. The *shul*, which normally sustains two *minyans* (quorums) a day, was closed so as to block the allegedly 'imperialistic' *Chabad* rabbi, a man unacceptable to the *misnagdim*, the traditional non-*Chassidic* Lithuanian Jews. An unpaid Russian rabbi provided services while the battles raged.

Old streets had been renamed. In the areas known as Ghetto 1 and Ghetto 2 under the Nazis we saw Jew Street and Gaon Street. The monument to Elijah ben Solomon Zalman, the Vilna Gaon (sage) is there. Plaques abound—maps of the ghettos, the numbers of Jews deported and killed, where Talmud Torahs (Hebrew schools, *cheders*) once stood. One of the latter is now, by some bitter irony, the German Embassy. Despite government initiatives in commemorating lost Jewry, the remnant community has to pay for the upkeep of the monuments and plaques. It was pleasing to hear that several former Jewish villages were erecting monuments to their former residents even amid growing antisemitism and a conflating and equating of Nazi and Communist brutalities. All synagogues, apart from the 110-year-old Choral Synagogue in Pylimo Street, had been destroyed. The Nazis needed the Choral to store medical supplies. Close by is the site of the first Jewish round-ups in Novogorod Street, the Jewish quarter where some Jews were killed by Germans and Lithuanians, some hid and some smuggled guns. It is also where the first shots of resistance were fired. One is almost disbelieving at the startling mix of musty, stale, decrepit tenements and newly restored apartments sharing the same foundations.

The Vilna Gaon Jewish State Museum is an outstanding representation of *Litvishe* life and its destruction. Rachel Konstanian-Danzig, Deputy-Director, was our guide. She apologised for the lack of artefacts and memorabilia. No need—this is where it happened and Vilna doesn't need artificial and transplanted recreations, the virtual reality of Yad Vashem, the US Holocaust Memorial Museum and the Imperial War Museum. Vilna has the essential documents, the *Einsatzkommando 3* killing reports, the lists and maps of deceased communities, dozens of pre-1941 photographs, familiar and familial faces and enough horror sculpts to convey the messages.

The third cemetery of Vilna is in a forest, strange to those of us accustomed to neat, treeless burial places. The Vilna Gaon lies here as do many notables, many Russian Jews who wanted no Hebrew lettering, many Lithuanians with ceramic photographs adorning their stones. Family graves and vaults abound. There was once some wealth there but nothing to match that of the Warsaw and Lodz cemeteries.

German nationalism, Aryan ideology and Nazi anthropology began, so it is said, in the primeval forests. Ponary forest is the most poignant and painful place of all, more so perhaps than Auschwitz–Birkenau. While a few hundred Jews hid and survived or were assisted in forests, over 100,000 were killed and buried in such places of intense beauty. Here Jewish dead numbered 70,000; non-Jewish victims 30,000. Five burial sites are known: petrol-storage pits considered suitable for mass graves. 'Tasteful' monuments attest to the mass murder of Jews, Russians and Lithuanians. We wanted this place to be bleak, bare-leaved, ugly, raw. But the trees shone, there was greenery, inviting picnic grass—until we realised that this ground shouldn't be trodden on, until we remembered who we were treading on.

Kaunus (Kovno) was yet another killing spree, only this time much of the killing was done by Lithuanians even before the Nazis sought their help. In the grisly IXth Fort, 30,000 Lithuanian and other Jews were killed between 1941 and 1944. Only 400 of Kovno's 40,000 Jews survived.

Our guide Chaim Bargmann recognised my name tag and said he knew a Yoseph Tatz, surely my cousin, a dairy-milk engineer in Kaunus. We arranged to meet and as the bus drew near the appointed place, my tour group exclaimed how much we resembled each other. An hour later Yoseph and I agreed we weren't related. As the bus departed, the bus chorused, 'Nah! He looks nothing like you!' Two *shuls* operated and Yoseph wouldn't go to the main one! We did also hear he was banned by the *shul* chairman from going there. Such is life amid the death.

On a day of *shtetl*-seeking, we went first to Panevezys (Poinevez), population 120,000, with innumerable plaques and a public park that was once a very large Jewish cemetery. It had the merit of saying, in stone, what was once there. Some eight kilometers south, a sign on the highway reads *Zydu genocido*. Pajousté, like Ponary, was forest beauty: tall trees in just less than a hectare, dignified stone markers indicating that below lay the Jews of

Panevezys, perhaps 8,000, murdered by Germans and, if I read correctly, by 'German–Lithuanian fascists'.

We found Pumpenai (Pompian) and the town's historian found us. She remembered families by name—familiar South African names like Sachs, the once rich innkeepers, and Abel, Abrams, Kaplan, Margolis, Nathan, Shapiro. She knew the names and houses of Isaacson and Levine, my grandparents' names. She showed me a house lived in by Levines. 'He was a doctor' she said. No relation, I murmured, if there had been a doctor we'd have known about it. Yet, whether relatives or not, I was walking where my family once walked, in streets and alongside houses that had remained frozen in time. Jews occupy seventeen lines in the 220-page Pumpenai history book. Yet before the War there were 500 Jews in a population of 1000. Today there are none—only a building that may have been a *mikveh* (ritual bath), a grass patch that was the *shul*, and a few illegible gravestones that were probably transplanted.

Poland's elegant Cracow, established in the thirteenth century, once had 60,000 Jews in a city of 250,000. Today Cracow has 800,000 people, Warsaw two million and Poland's 'registered' Jews number a total of 7,000 (out of a pre-war total of 3.25 million). There could be as many as 20,000, with many assimilated, aloof, not identifying—until funeral time. We visited all the *shuls*. A whole Jewish world of learning, of ethical and moral values is to be found in the old cemetery at Remu. Somewhat less authentic were the numerous Jewish-style restaurants in the Jewish area, the Kazimierz. We ate at the Klezmer Hois (House). Good (*goyish*) *klezmer* music and a cosmic Jewish menu, incuding 'five kinds herring'.

Then, a mere two hours by bus from Cracow, came Auschwitz I and Auschwitz-Birkenau. There is no description that can convey this other planet. My message is to go and see it, feel it, cry, gasp, take very deep breaths, and then recognise, in this very place, the stark reality that Jews will never be liked, let alone loved; that despite European Jewry enriching the world, much of the European world wanted to be rid of Jews and assisted the Nazis in their mission. In these areas there is Jewish life, but Eastern Europe is for the most part *judenfrei*. More than a sobering thought is that Europe now has fewer than two million Jews as opposed to the ten million there in 1939.

The Cracow market square is a place to behold—huge, with colonnades, arches and beautiful little stores and stalls with breathtaking and irresistible amber on show. The throngs, especially of young people, are delightful, as are the busking musicians, and the flower markets. What little else we saw of Poland was depressing. Kielce, en route to Warsaw, was where, in July 1946 (that is after war's end), the residents murdered 42 Jews as a reprisal for *Ritualmord*, the alleged kidnapping and killing of a Christian child. The child had gone walkabout and he came home three days later. The plaques commemorating this post-Holocaust pogrom are poignant and include a plaque of acknowledgment from the residents. It was both depressing and revelatory.

In the main cemetery in Warsaw, with 250,000 mainly pre-war graves, there were many great Holocaust figures in big edifices: a statue in honour of the heroic Janusz Korczak (Henryk Goldszmit—a Polish physician who was the director of a Jewish orphanage in Warsaw), Mordecai Anielewicz and Adam Czerniakow. Korczak moved to the Ghetto in 1942 and was offered a chance to escape but chose to accompany his 200 children to the extermination camp at Treblinka. Anielewicz was the leader of the Jewish Combat Organisation (ZOB) that led the uprising in the Warsaw Ghetto. Czerniakow was the leader of the Jewish Council (*Judenrat*) in the Warsaw Ghetto, a man revered by many and scorned by others for committing suicide the day after the Nazis ordered the deportation to death camps of 6,000 inmates a day. His note said: 'They demand me to kill children of my nation with my own hands. I have nothing to do but to die,' and to one of his fellow members of the *Judenrat*, he explained: 'I can no longer bear all this. My act will prove to everyone what is the right thing to do.'

At the *Umschlagplatz*, the transfer point from where hundreds of thousands of Jews were deported to camps, stands a monument. Dignified stone markers in honour of heroic and notable figures lead to the site of the last stand of the Warsaw Ghetto uprising, Mila 18, and to various monuments, including one to *Zegota*, the clandestine Polish underground movement that rescued Jews. We saw what little was left of the Warsaw Ghetto, fragments and a few brick walls. It is now the site of a new Museum of the History of Polish Jews, funded by Polish taxpayers. The promise is that it will tell the Poles something of their history and reveal the horrors not only of the Ghetto but of towns like Jedwabne where 40 Poles burned 300 Jews alive in a barn. The remnants of contemporary Jewry in Poland and Lithuania need visitors, praise, encouragement, moral support. Their museums and archives need friends and even time and skills from Australians prepared to spare them a month or two.

Throughout these visits I would brief the group at breakfast and de-brief them late at night. Nobody was in party mood and no one sought late or fun nights. They learned, as I did. My role as guide ended at Warsaw airport en route to Israel.

Israel was light, light relief and there was a kind of vengeful pleasure in being there, even amid the *intifadas* and rocket attacks. We saw much, ate much, saw relatives, visited Yad Vashem where we were able to see, at least from the outside, the spectacular new history museum building designed by Canadian Moishe Safdie. We held a ceremony in honour of one of our group Harry van As, honoured in the avenue of Righteous of the Nations. The Yad Vashem teaching staff greeted us with fanfare and warmth and Sandra and I were delighted at being together again in this place which has been so significant in my life.

The Australian-funded water projects, dam-building, bridge-building, anti-evaporation system, were a marvel, as were the Negev desert fish farms where barramundi (our very own Australian species) is regarded as the best species to grow. We visited the Rimon crater, my second-best favourite to Safed and the cave city of Avdat. At Mitzpe Ramon we saw some spectacular ibex goats tip-toeing on precipices. We also observed and talked to a few

Russian immigrants trying to tip-toe into life in a new and very different place and culture.

While I have visited many places, there are always regrets about where I have not been. I have not seen Prague or St Petersburg, two places of obvious historical, cultural and aesthetic importance. I didn't make it to China or to India, except to the latter en route to other places. I rationalise that I wouldn't have gone there: the prospect of seeing human degradation is too daunting. Having seen human despair in Africa, I don't want or need to see any more.

Chapter 21

FOURSCORE

Most of the main characters in the Jewish novels I admire (and often envy) are 'f****d up', to use their language. They can't make sense of their origins, surrounds, parents, their parents' bowel movements, parenting, marriage, divorce, fidelity, yearnings to sleep with *shikses*, belonging, food, ethics, morality, health or the absence of it, Israel, where they stand and where they don't. At the start of this chronicle I said that these novels are as much about the authors trying to explain themselves and their Jewishness to themselves and to others as they are about telling a tale. They would have done better with an historical rather than a psychiatric (and very locale-oriented) approach to their Jewish identity. Historian Simon Schama has defined our complex being in a succinct way: the story of the Jews, world-wide, is one of suffering and resilience, endurance and creativity, by a people who are fiercely argumentative.

I cannot offer a model that explains me, but I have followed some dotted lines, some set down by others, some self-created and, food legacies apart, I think I have found some contentment or at least a zone of comfort. That it has taken me nearly eight decades to get there is by the by. One step in getting there (or here) came from Rabbi Mordecai Kaplan (1881–1983), a *Litvak* who co-founded Reconstruction Judaism in the United States. In his *Judaism as a Civilization* he contended that apart from the life that a Jew shares with the non-Jew, there are, for a Jew, certain social relationships to maintain, certain cultural interests to foster, activities to engage in, organisations to belong to, amenities to conform to, and moral and social standards to live up to. Judaism for him and for me is far more comprehensive than difference in religion: 'It includes that nexus of a history, literature, language, social organization, folk sanctions, standards of conduct, social and spiritual ideals, and aesthetic values, which in their totality form a civilization.' And, of course, the suffering, endurance and resilience.

The Kenyan academic Ali Mazrui also helped. He sees the essence of Jewishness—what he calls 'the Talmudic tradition'—as three essential elements *in fusion*: religion, ethnicity and intellectualism. Jews (he argues) have both sacralised and intellectualised their national consciousness. Jewishness is most often centred on a particular aspect of what I call '*Judaicness*', where the emphasis is on the Covenant with God. But for him and for me the *broader* senses of Jewishness—the ethnicity and intellectual ingredients—embrace a code of ethics and conduct in human relationships, a concern about the role of Jews in human affairs generally, the role and place of Jews as a people in and of history, and a land-based nationalism. Mazrui would concur with historian Cecil Roth that this intellectualism is also about protesting at the insufficiency of any status quo. There is indeed a Jewish existential value which asserts that history has taught us that whatever is, no matter what it is, it is not good enough—hence the moral dictate of *tikkun olam*, that one is compelled to try to repair a flawed world. Mazrui made the crucial point that one can belong to this group even as one retreats or sheds one, two or even three of these characteristics.

Herein lies the great quality of diversity in Jewishness: the debates, even schisms, about which elements are mandatory; which, if any, are elective; what allows an outsider to still remain within. I remain within even while lacking faith, ritual, observance or any sense of Covenant. Assuredly I am not an apostate or heretic. And that, by the way, is what makes being Jewish so democratic, so freeing—as opposed to the conventional view of it as a religion of constriction, conformity and 'punishment'.

'As it is written' is the foundation of the Talmudic tradition—an abiding reverence for the written word, as in the Torah and the *Mishnah*, which is the written version of the Oral Law. But Jewishness is as much made up of sounds and shapes: the tones and intonations, the rhythms and cadences, the sounds of the liturgical music, the body mannerisms, the shrugs, disdains, the ever-present deprecatory and interrogative tenses of body and voice. A line I heard in a documentary about film is a good definition of what makes me run: *to be funny, you first have to think sad*. And seeing how much of my life has been about things that are sad, I do see the funny side—or at least part of it, part of the time.

A driving force isn't enough: one has to assemble an 'engine' that can run, and I had some guidance with that from Harold Lasswell, a colossus in American scholarship. In his *Politics: Who Gets What, When, How*, he named three key values that a person wants and pursues in life: deference, income and safety. Deference can mean status, standing, rank, esteem or respect; income is income and doesn't need explaining; and safety means being free of war, assassination, terrorism, expulsion, discrimination, poverty, volcanoes, tsunamis. One can achieve both deference and income in politics and in life through a variety of skills: military, oratorical, literary, scientific, professional or vocational. Lasswell also listed 'personality' as a skill or a value. In the context of politics (and in life I believe) he described two possible approaches: the contemplative and the manipulative, that is, knowing how to use the skills one has to achieve an aim. I understand him to mean how one garners or marshals one's skills to *fashion* a weapon for challenge or change rather than the ugly sense of manipulation.

Above all, Lasswell argued that social science should try to solve the problems of society and to promote human dignity. In early life I didn't know I had any values and certainly didn't know I had any skills or personality or even the potential to acquire them. Certainly my mother, family and schoolteachers, with about five exceptions among all of them, didn't think so. One thing led to another—sometimes by happenstance as with Phil Green, sometimes by luck as with Edgar Brookes and Yehuda Bauer, sometimes (as I discovered) by my own design. I don't believe in the commonly held view that one has an eternal 'lot' in life—as in the cards that destiny, God or the gods deal to one. True enough I got *Bobbe* Isaacson and her daughter Bess but I learned to fight that experience and overcame the adversity they presented.

A few inklings and propensities emerged from fairly early on. For me, promoting human dignity counts above all other considerations. I didn't consciously follow Lasswell but seemed to do so more subconsciously. I found the way to promote human dignity is by using one's acquired skills consciously to observe, inquire, write, talk, teach, preach if necessary—to change the order of things. Whatever else, I am a 'product' of Lasswell, of Cecil Roth and his notion that Jews (or some Jews) are the eternal *protestants*, of the doctrine of the Jewish Sages about *tikkun olam*. It is a synonym for social action, a conscious manipulating of skills to be proactive rather than reflective or contemplative.

***

In my early days in my new country I wouldn't allow myself to be critical of anything Australian. My gratefulness put asunder any doubts. It had so much more to like than my part of Africa. But while one can like the whole, there are warts, some of which I have watched grow into malignant lumps. Ambiguities and stark contradictions aren't difficult to find: the way Australia allows one to accommodate so readily; the way it accepts most people at face value; the way it recognises and appreciates merit (some of the time); the way it allows class interaction while pretending it has no classes; the way it preaches and promotes fairness even while engaging in gross inequities; the way it venerates and practices the arts, music and literature while so often disdaining *kulcha*; the way it regards wisdom and intellect as disabilities yet dines out on the achievements of those who have those qualities; the way it plays sport so successfully while displaying the worst possible grace in both winning and losing; the way it loves the beauty of the mostly empty landscape yet presents some of the ugliest urban streetscapes on the planet; the way it intermixes sensitivity with boorishness; in short, the way it copes with the many swings and the same number of roundabouts. If this sounds cynical it isn't meant to be: there is delight in much of the dissonance—the treatment of Aborigines, refugees and asylum seekers apart.

Governments at all levels love ambiguity; while it means a lack of clarity in lines of communication, it allows a diffused sense of who is responsible for decisions and actions, an uncertainty about outcomes of conflicts and often an absence of or abdication from accountability. In my sense, Australian ambiguities also provide choices, alternatives, new chances, escape routes from the uncomfortable. For example, federalism in itself is an ambiguity. If you don't like the education system in Victoria, go to the Australian Capital Territory; if you don't like living under a despotic Joh Bjelke-Petersen in Queensland, try enlightened Don Dunstan's South Australia. Yet, once you have lived under an authoritarian, all-powerful central government as in South Africa, a federal system is a sometimes chaotic, often an expensive and inefficient *mitzveh*, a blessing. To *that* I can belong, owe a sense of loyalty, have a degree of pride—and enjoy the freedom to express rage and outrage at many of the things that aren't at all ambiguous.

South African society has obviously been a major factor in how I have learned, behaved and lived. Do I owe it a debt? Yes, of course. While it taught me many positive things, it also taught me how *not* to live, think and behave. Whether the names were Green at Yeoville Boys' School or Black at Natal University, both men showed me an antithetical scale of things. In the middle, so to speak, there were the teaching, training and inspiration of Isaac Kriel at Damelin College, Edgar Brookes, Arthur Keppel-Jones and Geoffrey Durrant in Pietermaritzburg.

In South Africa I learned to live in a Lithuanian *communitas*, a transposed *shtetl* world of like-minded, like-speaking, like-behaving people. It was a society in transition from Tsarist oppression to a semi-welcomed ethnic minority moving into modernity. Like so many of my second generation,

I hankered to know more, even to be more of that first generation, back *there*. Unlike so many modern-day people I didn't see that 'old world' as unproductive, stifling or dead. A romantic view maybe, but mine. I needed to know what made the transplants run, what made my parents' generation tick, where I fitted.

I found what drove them, a simple enough truism that was nonetheless most difficult to articulate: when you are a minority, especially a despised minority like ours, to make any grade, to gain any level of acceptance, let alone recognition, you had to show yourself doubly good in order to rate as either human or, better still, as an equal human. The way you did that was by excelling in business or in professional or artistic life, by achieving income and thereby some deference and hence acceptance. With no interest in money I pursued knowledge and passed it on to others. Oswald Black said I needed a fifteen percent margin to rate some kind of parity for a chance at a scholarship; I'd say that for most Jews in South Africa, it was closer to 50 percent.

In Australia the margin isn't important, certainly nowhere near as important. I arrived in Australia on 1 January 1961 as a doctoral student. Exactly ten years later, to the very day, I was appointed a foundation professor at a quality university. In between, no one asked me for personal details about my origins, schooling, affiliations, beliefs. In my case, no ambiguity. I can't think of another society that would allow such a pathway.

I have taught many courses on South African racial history and still find the energy to read of events in the 'rainbow country'—even with a doom-laden sense of watching a failed state or one looking perilously like one. To a limited extent South African society impinges on my life as a writer and commentator on South African migration to Australia, especially the 15,000 Jews among them. The *Worlds Apart* book said what had to be said. The first few families arrived in Australia in 1948, the next 'wave' came after the Sharpeville massacre in 1961, the next after the Soweto killings in 1976, and the bulk came for essentially economic or 'fear of crime' or 'fear of Black government' reasons from the 1990s. My problem with them, or their problem with me, is the way they have huddled in their new-found relocation spots. They do business with the mainstream but socially, spatially, culturally, religiously, they huddle in enclaves of their creation. No real estate seems out of their bounds and in no suburb do they 'devalue' property or sully the neighbourhood. There were, at last count, 38 synagogues in Melbourne, but the South Africans have built a $5 million *shul* for themselves. That is pure huddle.

Why? One understands Lebanese Christians and Muslims, for example, moving to a suburb of fellow linguists, co-religionists, mosques and churches, eating and meeting places. Their *communitas* is not mainstream and they have yet to find the vehicles, vowels, skills and styles to venture into an Anglo-Australian world. But these South Africans are the world's most educated emigrés, 70.8 per cent at tertiary level, the most well-heeled, the most cosmopolitan in the way they travel, the only migrant group capable of spending time and money coming on visits before selecting their relocation spots. They are Anglo, Anglo enough to *walk right in*. From both long personal experience, and evidence provided in our survey, most have chosen to remain *out*.

Again, why? I can offer two possible reasons. One is that the *shtetl* remains engraved in their immigrant souls. They huddled (perforce by the politics of oppression) in *Lita*, they huddled (by some social and by some personal forces and choices) in Johannesburg, and they huddle here. The other is another legacy of life in *Lita*: the spectre of antisemitism, the dark shadow of rejection by an antisemitic and intolerant world next door. Remaining *in* means you can relax, at least for a while—laugh, cry, be brash, busy, creative, funny and not worry about what the *goyim* think. I watch them, endlessly hospitable, vociferous, efficient, vibrant, argumentative, ambitious, successful in their own company but like a turn of turtles or a bale of tortoises, the collective necks withdraw into their carapaces when 'outsiders' appear. A closed-circuit television camera in my golf club lounge would neatly capture that phenomenon at work.

I don't feel any sense of superiority about any of this. Their non-movement into the Australian world that I find so attractive is a loss for both sides. One or two people have whispered confidentially to me 'have I missed something?' Hell, yes. Their children will move, cross the borders of the mind and suburbs and truly immigrate. They will 'marry out', that is, marry non-South African spouses, even non-Jews. To be fair or at least fairer, I have to concede that they didn't travel my chosen paths (and apprenticeship in moving *in*): they didn't live at Oribi, work for the *Natal Witness*, live in Alice or Darwin or Kakadu or Armidale, make friends in Werris Creek or write about Royal Sydney.

There is a paradox here. So much of this earlier life, exactly one-third of my life, was indelible and formative, yet I have a sense of wonderment about everything to do with that domain, that one third. In one breath it is sometimes distantly present in my memory, but omnipresent in the sound of my speech.

* * *

People often ask whether my work in Aboriginal affairs has achieved anything. Every situation is altered by one's participation and more so by one's active intervention. I did intervene, throw pebbles, sometimes boulders, into the pond and often enough waves ensued. For me the obvious change needed was to get researchers, bureaucrats, politicians and journalists away from a singular focus on 'noble man', 'man in nature', the quaint anthropological curiosities and the hapless urban fringe-dwellers. I managed to instil in a few bureaucrats the recognition that Aboriginal communities vary widely despite a common history of oppression and discrimination, and that universalistic approaches always fail. Unlike the earlier historians who wrote Aborigines out of the public record, from the early 1960s onward I made sure they were written in, listened to, heard through voices like mine or the increasingly strident voices on their own behalf. In place of early spokesmanship on their behalf I turned to matters that didn't have Aboriginal expertise or voice, to fields of endeavour where I wasn't trampling on toes or terrains which are now distinctively Aboriginal. All of that gives me a feeling of fulfilment.

What is now the Monash Indigenous Centre gave legitimacy to Aboriginal Studies at the tertiary level. My role at the AIATSIS was also of practical use. The partnership with Peter Ucko produced some significant changes for a while, but only a limited while. Revisiting the uranium and health hazard problem was my last such venture, and that issue may yet resurface as corporations seek to re-open old uranium mines and open new ones.

But AIATSIS is now a shell, a matter of lament after some heady and significant days. It is an organisation with too many chiefs, not enough Indians and almost no audience. It no longer has an audible voice, offering little apart from being a great repository for scholars. Once it was at the centre of events, now it is arcane and archival. If it contributes to public knowledge or debate, the members don't see it; if it provides government with advice, we don't know about it. In fact, the members hear nothing about the Institute's work apart from glossy brochures, new book titles and fancier websites. There is a truism in administration theory, once articulated by the famous Chester Barnard (the New Jersey Bell Telephone man): for any organisation to flourish, it has to embrace its clientele as partners or at least as a significant part of the executive's enterprise.

Much of my activity was in the health field and I regard 'The Politics of Aboriginal Health' monograph, written in 1972 as my best contribution. It was a powerful indictment of the allocation of functions to government departments, about whether Aborigines (and their wellbeing) were better off attended to by a 'client-based' department like the Welfare Branch or by a professional Health Department which applied its skills for the whole population. Therein lay (and lies) a major dilemma. The Northern Territory showed that an octopus-like department devoted entirely to Aborigines was unprofessional, largely unskilled and cut off from mainstream techniques and applications. The reverse was true of my experiences in the Aborigines Welfare Board in Victoria: Aborigines received services from mainstream departments with the AWB acting as some kind of watchdog, but one without enough teeth, time or full-time staff to keep an eye on most things. The answer must be a skill-based service but with special Aboriginal units that are taken seriously. That model has been tried in several domains, like the prisons, but it needs a very powerful head of such a separate section to get a voice heard above the concerns and currents of the mainstream.

Ours is an essentially assimilationist society and deviations from universal practices come hard. There are some aspects of Aboriginal and Islander life that must have separation for historical, geographic, cultural and social reasons. Always, according to the moral philosopher Morris Ginsberg, such divisions require explicit justifications, not just generalised 'race' or 'colour' reasons. Australians are still beset by South African notions of *apartheid*, that any form of separatism now is somehow discriminatory. Some of the hysteria generated by my 'Aboriginal suicide is different' work stems from rejection of any separatist notions. There are, indeed, times and places that require an especial and differential treatment, justifiable on grounds that stand up to scrutiny.

I marvel at developments since the early 1960s. My early work on Aboriginal health revealed a literature, then, of six articles on Aboriginal health and three on Aborigines and the criminal law. Today each of those sub-disciplines has a literature of thousands of items. I make no claim for that other than that I helped expose the gaps, the chasms and the sometimes terrible secrets of what was happening in that dark world of Aboriginal administration.

What of the present? In 2001 I gave a paper to an AIATSIS conference called 'From Welfare to Treaty: Reviewing Fifty Years of Policy and Practice'. I looked at what had happened to Aborigines over half a century across some ten agendas. My final paragraphs were:

Aborigines and Islanders are part of the national scene, whatever the scene. They demand a place, but more importantly, they command a place. The time span from *Nicht-Menschen* to *Menschen* [non-persons, non-humans to humans] has been relatively short—within my working lifespan and, therefore, within the lifespans of many Aborigines who began as 'wards' and ended up, if not Cabinet Ministers, then as leaders, speakers, policy makers, filmmakers, writers, broadcasters.

One could end this review with a long inventory of minuses, of rampant ill-health, unacceptable rates (and causes) of suicide, breakdown of family life, continuing poverty and absence of all manner of facilities. For someone who has always been regarded, and seen, as a pessimist about Aboriginal affairs, what I see now is painful optimism for all, but still some optimism.

That was written before the Howard Government's 'emergency intervention' in 2007 which involved sending in civilian task forces (largely untrained in this work) and the military (even less qualified) 'to save the children' from reported child abuse, sexual molestation and neglect. It also involved the suspension of the Commonwealth's *Racial Discrimination Act* (and therefore the protections it offered) and the Northern Territory's anti-discrimination legislation. That harshly condemned suspension was revoked and the Act restored on 31 December 2010. The intervention remains, and still involves the suspension of the permit system which allows Aborigines to decide who can enter their domains; the search for sexual predators continues but with glaringly few charges or arrests in the past seven years of operation; the quarantining of all social welfare payments is in place; there is still physical medical examination of children; and the banning of alcohol obtains. Legislation in 2011 ensured that social service payments would be tied to school attendance. We appear to have returned to the (then necessary) thinking of Archibald Meston in 1896, of having to 'segregate' Aborigines as much as possible from the mainstream'. Only this time the enemy is not White predatory society but the Aboriginal population itself. We are now back to the old world of ascription, that is, the blanket characterisation of all people as 'wards' in need of special care and protection—as defined by us. The past is omnipresent but we don't see it. As mining magnate Andrew Forrest produces yet another 'vision' of 'welfare distribution and income management' in 2014, so we need to look long and hard at the history of failure all about us, the history we don't see or don't want to see.

Allied to this 'intervention' is the new policy of 'closing the gap', that is, reducing the stark differences between Aborigines and non-Aborigines on a wide range of social indicators. Aborigines have (again) become the targets of statistical portraiture. Some researchers have pointed out that this approach reduces Aboriginal Australians 'to a range of indicators of deficit, to be monitored and rectified towards Government-set targets'. As each set of statistics on key social indicators like life expectancy and infant mortality appears to improve, so other indicators like deaths from non-natural causes worsen. As more and more babies survive their first five years, so more and more young adults develop diabetes, heart, lung and kidney disease. As more education, training and intervention programs are established, so more and more youth are imprisoned. Some 28 percent of *all* prisoners in custody are Aboriginal, a figure that brands them as the world's foremost criminals.

The point is that yet again we have a universal approach to what are assumed to be universalist problems, common to all those diverse persons now lumped together—irrespective of domain, culture, language, history—and dubbed 'Indigenous' people. The human face of all this is not apparent. The statistical pictures are pre-eminent and a pertinent question remains: is all this activity to relieve Aboriginal distress in many domains or is it to make the 'rescuers' look better, more like decent and democratic colonisers? And if it is both, which weighs the more?

Cartoonist Alan Moir's view of 'closing-the-gap', 2013, courtesy of the artist.

Several things I still don't understand. One is the reluctance of Aborigines to go international with their grievances. There is some external activity but not nearly enough when compared to the strategies of other minority groups. One explanation is Aboriginal politeness, yes politeness, an unwillingness to 'dob in' because 'it isn't cricket'. I could never convince Doug Nicholls to discard this 'cricket ethos'. (Besides which, Australians play that game in an essentially nasty way.) Another conundrum (for me) is their inexplicable loyalty, even to regimes that brutalised them. I recall a young Aboriginal man arriving at our Armidale home seeking refuge from a police hunt. He had bashed two Queensland policemen. He received haven, and several weeks later he and I sat down to watch a State of Origin rugby league game. He was screaming for Queensland. How can you barrack for them, I asked, especially after your life and times at their hands over two-and-a-half decades? 'I'm a Queenslander' he replied, astounded at my question. I remain confounded by his answer.

I have looked at many things that others have ignored or overlooked or found less attractive. I have been, perhaps, almost alone as the anthropologist of the White tribes of policy makers and bureaucrats. I am possibly the most published of those who have excavated the Aboriginal involvement in sport and the conditions under which they lived and played or couldn't play with any ease. The uranium work is a first and the social impact monitoring model may one day be implemented as a standard of how some things can be done. Institutional memory looms large for me. Much of my activity, and that of colleagues of various disciplines, is past tense. 'Ours', we assert, 'is a new world'. 'That was then and this is now' was the condemnatory point made by the political analyst, the late Tony Judt. It is a nice phrasing of the reality that we live in an a-historical era where memory is last year and the present is all that matters. I look at institutions, at most of my universities, at places like AIATSIS, even my golf club, and find little or no memory, no understanding of the accretion processes that made up their organisations, leaving the participants with little comprehension of how they got where they are or of where they are heading.

Genocide absorbs, fascinates and bewilders. The case studies are enervating enough but even more draining are the darkest questions that have no clear cut answers. How is genocide *humanly* possible? We have a pretty fair idea of why it happens, who decides on such a 'solution', who are perpetrators, victims, bystanders, beneficiaries and who the denialists. But how does the physician who once attended and befriended a member of a victim group become the patient's experimenter, torturer, executioner, the man who decides who goes left and who goes right in the Auschwitz queue? How does the unindoctrinated, unschooled nurseryman from Hamburg's Police Reserve Battalion become an arch killer in Poland's Lublin district—and then bring his wife over for the weekend to see the fruits of his week's work? Conformity, at least male conformity, seems to be the likeliest explanation. Even so, what kind of conformity is involved in decapitating your lifelong neighbour, your one-time friend and babysitter?

At the other end of the scale, who survives and why? Luck, Yehuda Bauer taught me, is the only common factor in surviving an apparatus that seeks the death of all who are so defined. Primo Levi and Viktor Frankl talked about the 'drowned and the saved', those whose personalities determined their survival instincts (assuming they weren't selected for death in one or other of the exterminatory processes). One can readily believe in the phenomenon called 'luck' as opposed to 'destiny'. But in all that cauldron of calamity, I am always nagged by the thought: what if it had been me? Could I, would I have cracked, tried to escape, resisted, become a partisan, killed a guard at least? While I was eight, nine or ten and nowhere near those scenes, in the safety and (White) deference zones of Johannesburg, the questions interjected as one read—and never really went away.

Suicide is a much easier subject for the soul. It is more tangible, acceptable, understandable. Not fully so by any means but more so than the human factors involved in genocide. I don't view suicide as the calamity that society says it is. I don't see it as more disastrous than the greater legions of young who die daily by drugs, alcohol and road accidents. Much of society sees suicide as the ultimate rejection—as rejection of us, our love, family, achievements, our entire civilisation. Secretly, I believe, most people are more affronted than confronted by such acts, often enough castigating the young suicide while bemoaning 'the waste', the loss and the (all too real) devastating effects on the family.

The suicide work may have increasing value because I have been able to point to factors that almost no medical men and women have been trained to consider. Suicide is about men and women in society, about why, when and how some persons want to opt out of society. Modern medicine is so preoccupied with 'evidence-based' medicine, so obsessed with locating and treating the illness within the body, that it doesn't see the societal contexts of so many illnesses. Once upon a time universities ran courses on the social history of medicine. No more.

* * *

FOURSCORE

There is a framework I use for intellectual and academic qualities. It comes from my admiration of the English soccer's system of league tables where teams aspire to be promoted from fourth division to third to second to first. I use it because it makes sense to locate oneself in one or other of these divisions, to know where one stands, to know one's limitations, one's realistic ambitions. Division one players are quite visible: innovators, inventors, creators, inspirers, men and women of stature in their fields, and who are usually conscious contributors to the society of which they are members. Many years ago I settled for a place somewhere near the top of the next division. That may sound pretentious but it has the virtue (for me) of some honesty about my professional life and it keeps me within realistic boundaries.

I would have liked to have discovered the virtues of critical and analytical history earlier in life. I would have liked to have undertaken some original research in Holocaust studies. That would have been a truly tough test of my being. I didn't. Rather I became a voracious reader, analyser, synthesiser and disseminator. I am certainly a wide-ranging, competent comparativist. Nor, apart from the Aboriginal case, have I done 'fieldwork' in other genocidal cases. I still look in awe at the inspirational writings of the great Holocaust scholars, always deeply admiring of their intensity, passion and dedication to both detail and to the broader sweeps of that history. I know the top premiership players when I see them. And when I hear and read Yehuda Bauer I acknowledge and revere that great mix of intellect and humanism.

When my colleague Winton Higgins read the first drafts of this manuscript, he commented that it sounded as if it was written in 'the locker room after the game'. Jolted, I asked myself whether I am done with the game, if the fuel tank has run dry? No. I find myself involved in a daunting 'Richter-Scale' book (with Winton) on the magnitude of genocide across the centuries; in a major research project on coronial determinations of suicide; and participating in conferences a few years ahead. That brings a smile at the recollection of a wonderful piece of *chutzpah*: at close on 95, famed conductor Leopold Stokowski was asked by RCA Records to enter into a recording contract; yes said the maestro, but only if it's for 25 years. They agreed. I'm looking for that kind of contract.

Fourscore.

Appendix

AUTHOR'S PUBLISHED BOOKS

1. *Shadow and Substance in South Africa: A Study in Land and Franchise Policies Affecting Africans, 1910–1960*, Pietermaritzburg, University of Natal Press, 1962, pp. 238.
2. *Aborigines in the Economy*, eds. IG Sharp and CM Tatz, Brisbane, Jacaranda Press, 1966, pp. 382.
3. *Aborigines and Education*, eds. SS Dunn and CM Tatz, Melbourne, Sun Books, 1969, pp. 362.
4. *Black Viewpoints: The Aboriginal Experience*, ed. CM Tatz, Sydney, Australia and New Zealand Book Company, 1975, pp. 124.
5. *Race Politics in Australia: Aborigines, Politics and Law*, Armidale, University of New England Publishing Unit, 1979, pp. 118.
6. *Aborigines and Uranium and Other Essays*, Melbourne, Heinemann Educational Australia, 1982, pp. 190.
7. *Aborigines in Sport*, Adelaide, Australian Society for Sports History, 1987, pp. 151.
8. *The Royal Sydney Golf Club: The First Hundred Years*, with Brian Stoddart, Sydney, Allen & Unwin, 1993, pp. 284.
9. *Obstacle Race: Aborigines in Sport*, Sydney, University of NSW Press, 1995, pp. 408. (Winner of the Australian Human Rights Award for Non-Fiction, 1995.)
10. *Black Diamonds: The Aboriginal and Islander Sports Hall of Fame*, with Paul Tatz, Sydney, Allen & Unwin, 1996, pp. 150.

11. *Genocide Perspectives I*, ed.-in-chief Colin Tatz, Sydney, Centre for Comparative Genocide Studies, 1997, pp. 375.
12. *One-Eyed: A View of Australian Sport*, with Douglas Booth, Sydney, Allen & Unwin, 2000, pp. 262.
13. *Black Gold: The Aboriginal and Islander Sports Hall of Fame*, with Paul Tatz, Canberra, Aboriginal Studies Press, 2000, pp. 280.
14. *Aboriginal Suicide is Different: A Portrait of Life and Self-Destruction*, Canberra, Aboriginal Studies Press, 2001, second edition 2005, reprinted 2007, pp. 249.
15. *A Course of History: Monash Country Club, 1931–2001*, Sydney, Allen & Unwin, 2002, pp. 340.
16. *Genocide Perspectives II: Essays in Holocaust and Genocide*, eds. Colin Tatz, Peter Arnold, Sandra Tatz, Blackheath, Brandl & Schlesinger with the Australian Institute for Holocaust & Genocide Studies, Sydney, 2003, pp. 351.
17. *With Intent to Destroy: Reflecting on Genocide*, London, Verso, 2003, pp. 222.
18. *Genocide Perspectives III: Essays in Holocaust and Genocide*, eds. Colin Tatz, Peter Arnold, Sandra Tatz, Blackheath, Brandl & Schlesinger with the Australian Institute for Holocaust and Genocide Studies, Sydney 2006, pp. 262.
19. *Worlds Apart: The Re-Migration of South African Jews*, with Peter Arnold and Gillian Heller, Sydney, Rosenberg Publishing, 2007, pp. 360.
20. *Genocide in Australia: By Accident or Design?*, Indigenous Human Rights and History: Occasional Papers, Monash Indigenous Centre and Castan Centre for Human Rights Law, Monash University, Melbourne, 2011, pp. 100.
21. *Genocide Perspectives IV: Essays on Holocaust and Genocide*, ed. Colin Tatz, Sydney: Australian Institute for Holocaust and Genocide Studies and UTSePress, 2012 (ebook).

INDEX

Black and white images are indicated by page numbers in **Bold**. Full-colour images located in the image section are indicated by **[CP]**. References to Colin Tatz are indicated by (CT).

Abednego, Jacob, 164
'A Big Country' (TV series), 227
Aboriginal and Islander Sports Hall of Fame, 288, 311, **312**, 332
Aboriginal and Torres Strait Islanders, 276, 298–9, 323, 353–4
Aboriginal art, **[CP]**
   see also specific artists, e.g. Jungarai, Gwoya.
Aboriginal Australians
   administration of, 117, 119–20, 121, 124, 131, 138, 151, 152, 156, 165, 183, 188, 214, 275, 353
     see also Centre for Research into Aboriginal Affairs (CRAA)
   citizenship rights, 132, 188
     see also referendum of 1967 (Australia)
   courses/studies on, 206–8, 239, 352
   'first nation people', 188–9
   infant mortality, 355
   inter-racial marriage, 136
   inter-racial sex, 136
   intervention in affairs of, 354, 355
   opposition to mining, 212, 221–3, 361
   protection-segregation, 119–120
   race relations, 131, 132, 133, 137, 114, 143
   rations for, 136, 163
   reconciliation, 323–4
   social service benefits, 145, 354
   standard of living, 131
   treatment of, NT, 119, 130
     see also Welfare Branch, NT
   treatment of, Qld, 118, 242
   treatment of, Vic *see* Aborigines Welfare Board, Vic
   violence, 264, 298
   vocational training, 132, 144
   wages and employment, 132, 134, 136, 144, 150, 151, 155, 160, 161, 163, 164, 186
     see also Aboriginals Ordinance; Aborigines and the law; cattle stations; *Wards' Employment Ordinance*; *Welfare Ordinance*
Aboriginal Australians and education, 144, 150, 164, 177, 207, 355, 361
Aboriginal Australians and sport 3, 6, 131–2, 265, 297–9, 316, 357, 361
   see also Aborigines in Sport; Australian

Society for Sports History (ASSH); Australian Sports Consultancy; *Black Diamonds: The Aboriginal and Islander Sports Hall of Fame*; *Obstacle Race: Aborigines in Sport*; *One-Eyed: A View of Australian Sport*; specific sports, e.g. boxing

Aboriginal health, 140–3, 144, 160, 164, 183, 205, 240, 252, 253, 275, 323, 353, 355

see also 'Politics of Aboriginal Health, The' (essay)

Aboriginal history, teaching of, 5–6, 70

see also specific educational institutions, e.g. Monash University

Aboriginal housing, 136, 143, 145, 167–8, 174, 175, 323

Aboriginal identity, 324–5

Aboriginal land rights, 161, 188–9, 242, 244, 268

Aboriginal life expectancy, 131, 355

Aboriginal nutrition, 143, 168, 226

Aboriginal Policies of the Aborigines Welfare Board, Victoria, 174

Aboriginal population, 133, 136, 181, 188

Aboriginal Studies courses, 206, 207, 208, 270, 352

Aboriginal suicide, 353

see also youth suicide

Aboriginal Suicide is Different: A Portrait of Life and Self-Destruction, [CP], 301, 311, 362

Aboriginality, 228, 264, 268, 270, 287, 324

Aboriginals Ordinance, 111, 112, 134, 136, 155

Aborigines Advancement League (AAL, Vic), 154, 165, 175, 182, 226

Aborigines and alcohol, 134, 136, 137, 146, 155, 185, 223, 319, 354

see also Aboriginals Ordinance

Aborigines and the law, 6, 135, 146–7, 148–9, 154, 159, 160, 169, 170, 185, 187, 196, 242, 265–6, 297, 300, 301, 353, 355

civil law suits, 185, 266

community justice programs, 185

customary law, 265–6

deaths in custody, 300

incarceration rates, 135, 148, 185, 287, 300, 301

legal aid, 159, 160, 353

Aborigines and the vote, 135, 146–7, 157

see also assimilation, of Aboriginal Australians

Aborigines and Uranium (report), 3117

Aborigines and Uranium and Other Essays, [CP], 225, 231, 317, 361

see also Aboriginal Australians, opposition to mining; mining, uranium

Aborigines and Uranium: Monitoring the Health Hazards (report), 317

Aborigines in Sport, 265, 361

Aborigines in the Economy, 361

Aborigines Welfare Board, Vic, 160, 165, 167, 168, 170–1, 172, 173–4, 176, 178, 226, 240, 353

see also Welfare Branch, NT

African franchise, 93, 95, 96, 97, 98, 361

see also *Shadow and Substance in South*

INDEX

Africa: A Study in Land and Franchise Policies Affecting Africans, 1910–1960
African National Congress (ANC), 102, 107, 120
African night classes, 53, 57
Africans, Indigenous (Bantu-speaking), 51
Afrikaans language, 52, 53, 59, 72, 86, 216
Afrikaners, 79
Aitkin, Don, 235, 237, 238
Alice Springs, NT, 124, 127, 133, 351
alienation, 8, 54, 72, 77, 287, 327
Alligator River, NT, 223, 225
  land rights claim ('Bathurst children'), 268
Alperovitch, Simon, 337
Alyawarra, NT, 266
Améry, Jean, 302
Amos (father's delivery man), 58–9
Andras, Robert, 195, 196
Anielewicz, Mordecai, 341
anthropology, 118, 119, 125, 321, 339
anti-apartheid movement, 56, 59, 103, 234, 308, 320
antisemitism, 15, 43, 44, 52, 64, 67, 70, 179, 181, 203, 241, 250, 257, 295–6, 303, 305, 311, 322, 337, 338, 350
  courses on, 273–4
  see also Hakoah Club (Bondi), bomb attack on; Israeli consulate (Sydney), bomb attack on
apartheid, 51, 94, 95, 102, 104, 107, 151, 180, 240, 243, 273, 353
  see also Jews and *apartheid*; segregation; sports boycotts

Apple, Chief Rabbi Raymond, 228, 303
Areyonga Settlement, NT, 124, **132**
Arlott, John, 232, 233
Armidale, 201–3, 226–9, 235, 351
Armidale Club, 203, 229
Armidale College of of Advanced Education (CAE), 206
'Armidale model', 207
Arnhem Land, NT, 267
Arnold, Peter, 320–2
Arrente people, NT, 134
assimilation
  of Aboriginal Australians, 131–3, 160, 167–8, 172, 353
  of Canadian Indians, 196–7
assimilationists, 6
Association of Genocide Scholars (IAGS), conference, 337
Aurukun, Qld, 189, 228, 266
Auschwitz, 157, 306, 330, 340, 357
Auschwitz-Birkenau, 339, 340
Australia
  life in, 113–360
Australia, views on, 347–8
Australian Academy of Forensic Sciences, 248
Australian Association of Jewish Holocaust Survivors, 252
Australian Institute for Aboriginal and Torres State Studies (AIATSIS) 118, 269, 305, 311, 316, 317, 318, 326, 352, 353, 357
Australian Institute for Aboriginal Studies (AIAS)
  establishment of, 123–4, 156, 157, 158, 164, 187

history, 1974–, 210–15, 221, 223, 226, 231, 249, 268, 270
Australian Institute for Holocaust and Genocide Studies (AIHGS), 224, 315, 321
Australian Jews, 6
Australian Law Reform Commission, 248, 265
Australian League of Rights, 181, 203
Australian National University (ANU), 101–2, 110, 121, 123, 126, 151, 183, 195, 201, 214, 261, 311, 326
political studies seminars, 117
Australian Political Science Association, 205
Australian Society for Sports History (ASSH), 262, 264, 265, 307, 326
Australian Sports Consultancy, 263
Australian War Crimes Investigation Unit, 280, 296
Avery, John, 234
Axelrod, Pauline, 232

Bad Homburg vor der Höhe, conference in, 245–8
Bagot Settlement, NT, 137
Baker, Herbie, 38
Bandler, Faith, 121, 206
Banks, Norman, 180–1
Bantu Homelands/Bantustans, 95, 96, 98, 122
Bargmann, Chaim, 339
bar mitzvah (CT), 44, 45–6, 89, 209
Barker, Ray, 53
Barkly Tableland region, NT, 162
Barmore, Shalmi, 256
Barnes, Michael, 302

Barnes, John, 123
Barta, Tony, 251, 252
Barunga, 298
Barwick, Diane, 168, 245
'Bathurst' children, *see* Alligator River, NT, land rights claim ('Bathurst' children)
Bathurst Island Mission (Nguiu), NT, 138, 142, 267, 268, 298
Bauer, Yehuda, 3, 46, **[CP]**, 256–7, 296, 305, 346, 357–8, 359
bauxite mining *see* mining, bauxite
Beasley, Frank, 160
Belich, James, 328
Bell, Drummond, 40
Belnick, Maurice, 37, 38
belonging, sense of, 54, 55, 75, 99, 153, 302, 307, 344
Berea, 10, 14, 19, 27, 37, 85
Berea *cheder* (Hebrew school), 19–20
Berea *Shul* (synagogue), 19, 38, 83
Bernard van Leer Foundation (The Netherlands), 174
Berndt, Ronald, 114, 147
Bialik College, 154–5, 203
bilingual education, 123
Bing, Dov, 330, 331
birthplace (CT), 10
Bjelke-Petersen, Johannes (Joh), 228, 242, 243, 244, 348
Black, Oswald, 64, 65, 67, 73, 251, 348, 349
Black Africans
attitudes to, 17, 42, 51, 58, 75, 76, 85, 176
housing, 85, 176
parliamentary representation, 95–6

INDEX

wages and employment 97, 102
Black Diamonds: The Aboriginal and Islander Sports Hall of Fame, 288, 361
 exhibition, 288
Black Gold: The Aboriginal and Islander Sports Hall of Fame, 288, 311, 362
Black Viewpoints: The Aboriginal Experience, 207, 361
Blackburn, Doris, 182, 187
Blair, Harold, 171
'Blood, Sweat and Tears' (TV series), 263
Bolte, Lady, 175
Bolte, Sir Henry, 167
Bolton, Geoffrey, 248
Boon, Eric, 49, 50
Booth, Albert, 173, 240
Booth, Douglas, 173, 240, 285–6, 306, 326
Booth, Gaye, 327
Booysen, Peter de Villiers, 67
Borroloola, NT, 162
Botha, General Louis, 96
boxing, 38–9, 49, 56
Braamfontein, 14
Bradfield, Stuart, 247
Brady, Peter, 275, 276
Brasch, Rabbi Rudy and Mrs, 127–8
Breitman, Richard, 278
Bridge, Justice, 267
Brink, John and Margaret, 234
 see also anti-apartheid movement
Brisbane, trips to, 209
Broederbond, 86
Brookes, Edgar, 69, 72–3, 74, 76, 93, 97, 99, 101, 198, **[CP]**, 251, 346, 348
Brookes, Mrs Edgar, 216

Broome, Richard, 182
Broome, WA, 240
Brown, Peter, 74, 308
Brunette Downs, 162
Brunton, Ron, 306
Bryant, Gordon, 121, 181, 220
Buckley, Ken, 152
Butler, Eric, 181, 182

Cairns, Dr Jim, 179
Campbell, Colin, 160
Canada
 sabbatical in, 189–97
 travels in, 192–4
Canadian Association for Suicide Prevention (CASP) conference, **[CP]**, 333
Canberra, life in, 106, 115, 116, 117, 118, 120, 124, 126, 149, 150–3
Canberra College of Advanced Education (CAE), 207
Canterbury Suicide Project, NZ, 328
Canterbury University, NZ, 328–9
Cape African vote and politics, 95–6
Cape Blacks (Africans), 94
Cape Coloured franchise, 51, 54, 56, 80, 94
Cape Coloureds, 51, 54, 56, 80, 94
Cape Town, visits to, 28, 49, 53, 85
Cardinal, Harold, 194, 196
Casper, Rabbi BM, 229
Cass, Alan, 317
Cassidy, Cardinal Edward Idris, 303–4, 305
Castan, Melissa, 319
Castan Human Rights Law Centre, 319

Cattle Station Industry Award (Northern Territory Award 1951), 161, 186
cattle stations 151, 161, 186
   see also Aboriginal Australians, wages and employment; North Australian Workers' Union
Central Africa Federation, 75
Central Mt Wedge, NT, 163
Centre for Comparative Genocide Studies (CCGS), 277, 278, 282, 283–4
   see also Australian Institute for Holocaust and Genocide Studies (AIHGS)
Centre for Research into Aboriginal Affairs (CRAA), 157, 172, 174, 178
   see also Monash Indigenous Centre (MIC)
chabad, 337
chassid(im), 6, 7, 8, 337
Chambers, Barbara, 207
Charles, Darrell, 169–70
Charles Sturt University, 310
Cherbourg Settlement, Qld, 148, 149, 270
child removals, Australia, 136, 267, 306
child trafficking, Australia, 171
Chinese in South Africa, 79
Chretien, Jean, 196
Christophers, Barry, 182
chutzpah, 46, 249, 250, 271, 318, 359
   see also *dafke* (perverse)
Cilento, Sir Ralph, 181
circumcision (CT), 10–11
Clingman, Stan and Val, 336
'closing the gap' (between Aborigines and Non-Aborigines), 131, 133, 205, 353, 355, 356, **356**

Cochrane, Don, 155, 157
Colbung, Ken, 212, 213, 268
College of William and Mary (Williamsburg), 278–9
Collins, Charlie, **173**
Committee for Human Rights in South Africa, 122
communism (Australia), 158, 181
Communist Party (Australia), 122, 147
Communist Party (South Africa), 91, 105, 107
Condon, John, 317
Coniston Station, NT, 135
Connolly, Bob, 227
Cook, Alec, **[CP]**, 228, 248
Coombs, HC (Nugget), 186, 188, 206, 224, 246
Corbett, Roy, 52
Cossey, Graham, 227
Course of History: Monash Country Club, 1931–2001, A, 313, 362
   see also Monash Country Club
Courtenay, Bryce, 54
Cowen, Anna, 180–1
Cowen, Zelman, 158, 180–1, 198, 203
Cracow, Poland, 340
criminal law, 68, 146, 146, 159, 160, 353
Criminology Research Council (Canberra), 297, 300
Croxford, Ron, 161
Crystal Deli, 23, 47
Curtin, John, 181
Czerniakow, Adam, 341

Dadrian, Vahakn, 278
dafke (perverse), 14, 46–7, 48, 82–3, 158, 255

INDEX

Daisy (nanny), 12
Damelin, Dr Benjamin, 59
Damelin College, 59, 77, 78, 79, 80, 82, 83, 101, 348
Darbuma, Elsie, 267
Darwin, NT, 130, 133, 134, 136, 351
Davey, Harry, 167, 168, 169, 171, 174
Davey, Stan, 121, 161, 164, 165, **166**, 175, 187, 188
Davis, Jack, 268
Davis, Rufus, 154, 155, 158, 179, 198
de Klerk, FW, 86
de Lemos, Carlos Pereira, 88
de Villiers, Beulah, 64
de Vos, Bill, 164
Deane, Governor-General Sir William, 303
denialism, 316, 324, 329–31
   Armenian genocide, 262, 280
   see also Windshuttle, Keith
Department of Aboriginal Affairs (DAA), 268
Derham, David 159
Dexter, Barrie, 186
Diamadis, Panayiotis, 282
Dinah (cook), 66
Dingo, Ernie, 286
Dinnerstein, Leonard, 273
discrimination, 346
   against Aboriginal Australians, 133, 134, 188, 313, 314, 351–2, 351, 354
   against Jews, 204, 313–4, 315
   in South Africa, 23, 108, 239
Dixon, Chicka, 208
Dlin, Elly, 256
Dobkin, Marjorie Housepian, 282

doctoral research (CT), 119–20, 131, 150–3, 236
   see also masters research (CT)
Dodson, Mick, 288, 318
Dodson, Pat, 288
Doomadgee, Nth Qld, 297, 298
Doornfontein, 14
Dubois, Marcel, 303
Duncan, Graham, 198
Dunstan, Don 121, 188, 348
Durban, South Africa, 67–8
Durrant, Geoffrey, 69, 70, 198, 348

'Eaglehawk and Crow' (letter to AIAS), 211, 213
East Arm Leprosarium, 267
Echuca, Vic, 174
education (CT)
   BA (Law), 65
   LLB, 73
   matriculation, 63
   see also doctoral research (CT); masters research (CT); political science studies (CT)
Edwardians (KES, old boys' club), 46, 52
Edwards, Bob, 213
Edwards, Con, 168
Eel River Reserve, Canada, 193
Egan, Ted, 118, 124, **125**, 137, 145, 163, 186, 206, 288–9
Eggleston, Elizabeth, **159**, 160, 161, 179, 198
Eibl-Eibesfeldt, Irenäus, 249
Elcho Island, NT, 147
Elkin, Adolphus Peter, 139, 152
Ella, Gary, 307

Ella, Mark, 288
elocution lessons, 39
Engel, Rabbi, 209
Esam, Lara, 277
'Essay in Disappointment: the Aboriginal–Jewish relationship, An', (essay), 322
Ethiopian Jews (*Beta Israel*), 258–9
European Jews 6, 180, 328–42, 337–42
  see also German Jews; *Litvak/s*, *Ostjuden*
Evans, Glynn, 53
Evans, Richard, 329

Fackenheim, Emil, 257
Fagan, Patricia, 276
family health and old-fashioned remedies, 15, 24, 25–6
  see also shtetl food
Farquhar, Chief Magistrate Murray, 242
fascist organisations, 41, 52
  see also *Ossewa Brandwag*
Federal Council for Aboriginal Advancement (FCAA), 120–1, 187
Fein, Helen, 280
Felton, Philip, 168
Ferencz, Benjamin, 279
fieldwork (CT), 116, 119, 123, 124, 136, 284, 297–9, 317, 359
  see also doctoral research (CT)
FitzSimons, Peter, 306
Flanagan, Martin, 307
Flynn, Father Frank, 140
Forrest, Andrew, 355
Fox, Justice RW, 221, 223, 225

Framlingham Reserve, Vic, 168, 174
Franke, Norman, 330
Fraser, Malcom, 243
Freedom Party see Inkatha Freedom Party
Friedlander, Henry, 278, **281**
'From Welfare to Treaty: Reviewing Fifty Years of Policy and Practice' (conference paper), 353–4.

Gabay, Zvi, 241
Gannangu, Frank, 267
Gaskin, Jack, 168, 175
genocide, 5, 42, 251–2, 306, 316, 319, 326, 339–40, 357
  Armenian, 252, 261, 262, 278, 280, 282, 310
  courses/studies, 70, 251, 257, 261–2, 273–5, 276–7, 280, 282, 284, 311, 319, 363
  Jewish see Holocaust
  see also Australian Institute for Holocaust and Genocide Studies (AIHGS; denialism; Lithuania, genocide; *With Intent to Destroy: Reflecting on Genocide*
Genocide Convention, 305–6
'Genocide in Australia' (research paper), 305–6, 319
Genocide in Australia: By Accident or Design?, 319, 362
Genocide Perspectives I: 278, 282, 292, 362
Genocide Perspectives II: Essays in Holocaust and Genocide, 315, 362
Genocide Perspectives III: Essays in Holocaust and Genocide, 315, 362

INDEX

Genocide Perspectives IV: Essays on Holocaust and Genocide, 304, 323, 362
Gentiles *see goy, goyim,* Gentile(s)
German Jews, 6, 248
Ghandi, Indira, 243
ghettos, 278, 338, 351
  see also shtetl(s); Warsaw Ghetto
Gibbs, Benjamin, 331
Gibbs, Sir Harry, 249
Gibson, Gay, 50
Giese, Harry, 119, 124, 135, 141, 144, 147, 151, 152, 153, 155, 188
Gingie Reserve, Walgett, NSW, 298
Ginsberg, Morris, 174, 353
Glass, Reverend (*mohel*, 'Rev Cut Glass'), 10, 91, 138, 150
Goldney, Robert, 301
Goldstein, Gerald, **13**
Goldszmit, Henryk, 341
golf, 32, 57, 70, 227, 232, 233, 239, 253, **255**
  see also Course of History: Monash Country Club, 1931–2001, A; Monash Country Club, NSW; Royal Sydney Golf Club
Golson, Jack, 213
Gordon, Teddy, 53, 54–5
Gott, Ken, 180–1, 182
Gould, Bryan, 331
Gourley, Brenda, **[CP]**
Government Settlements *see* specific settlements, e.g. Areyonga Settlement, NT
goy, goyim, Gentile(s), 16–17, 41, 71, 228, 257, 321, 350
grandparents *see* Isaacson, Faiga-Ita (née Levine, *Bobbe*); Isaacson, Morris-Behr (*Zeide*); Tatz, Annie (grandmother); Tatz, Kivel (grandfather)
Gray, Lex, 172, 174, 185
Grobberbond, 86
Green, Major Phil, 41–2, 251, 346, 348
Greenfield, Brian, 138
Gros-Louis, Max, 193
Groves, Bert, 164
Gruen, Fred, 161

Hakoah Club (Bondi), 293
  bomb attack on, 241
  see also antisemitism
Hall, Mike, 80, 81, 83, 86, 101, 115
Hancock, Sir Keith, 121, 198
Hargrave, John, 142, 267
Harwood, Sir Ronald (Ronnie Horwitz), 53
Hasluck, Paul, 122, 131, 133, 135, 136, 139–40, 151, 152
Hawke, Bob, 217
Hayward, Stuart, 329
Heath, Jack and Jane, 71
Hebrew language, 7, 17, 19, 45, 229, 232, 337
Heller, Gillian, 320–2
Henderson, Gerard, 316
Hepi, Tangi, 328
Hermannsburg Mission, NT, 124, 134
Herron, John, 323
Hertzog, General JBM, 96, 121
  see also Nationalist Party
Herzl, Theodor, 6
Hiatt, Les, 123, 245, **245**, 268, 271
Higgins, Winton, 282, 359

Hoberman, John, 332
Holden, Arthur, 167, 168, 171, 173
Holding, Clyde, 169, 226
Hollingsworth, Peter, 168
Holmes, Cecil, 153
Holocaust, 252, 257, 274, 296, 303,
    304, 316, 329, 336, 359
  history, 181, 247–8, 251, 278, 310
  South African response to, 52
  studies, 5, 36, 250, 256–8, 261, 274,
    279, 284, 359
  war-time newsreels, 35, 36, 41
  see also Australian Association
    of Jewish Holocaust Survivors;
    denialism; genocide, courses/
    studies
Holt, Harold, 186, 187
Horowitz, Julius, 215
Hovannisian, Richard, 278, 280
Howard, John, 317, 323, 354
Howe, Don, 167, 168, 171
Howson, Peter, 264
Huddlestone, Father Trevor, 103
Hughes, Colin, 201
humanists, South African, 54, 69, 74
  see also liberalism
Humphreys, Kevin, 242
Hunter, Ernest, 275, 276, 301
hunter-gatherer minorities,
  conferences on, 224, 245–8

ice hockey, 191, 332
Indian art (Canada), **197**
Indian values (Canada), 193, 196
Indians (Indigenous peoples)
  Canada, 188, 192, 193–6, 197, 344
  South Africa, 23, 41, 51, 58, 66

Indigenous, nomenclature of, 325
Indyk, Martin 240–1
infant mortality, 131, 142
Inkatha Freedom Party, 63
Innes, Commissioner Graeme, 314
inter-racial marriage (Australia), 136
inter-racial marriage (South Africa), 104
inter-racial sex (Australia), 136
inter-racial sex (South Africa), 75
Inuit, 190, 333, **335**, 335–6
Iqaluit, Baffin Island, Canada, 333
Iremonger, John, 288
Isaacson, Barbara (Aunt Babs), 13, **13**,
    24, 40, 90, 189
  see also Goldstein, Gerald
Isaacson, Ben (cousin), 83, 90, 103–4,
    126, 127
Isaacson, Charles (cousin), 90
Isaacson, Faiga-Ita (née Levine,
    Bobbe), 13–17, **16**, 21–2, 23, 24, 25,
    30, 35, 36–7, 347
Isaacson, Harry (uncle), 29–30, 33, 46,
    73, 81, 90, 177
Isaacson, Ian (Itz, uncle), 32, 90
Isaacson. Louis (uncle), 23–4, 25, 29,
    31–2, **31**, 33, 75, 90
Isaacson, Morris-Behr (*Zeide*,
    grandfather), 13–17, **16**, 22, 23, 24,
    25, 29
Israel
  sabbatical in, 253–9
  visits to, 217–19, 231–2, 274, 342
  see also Yad Vashem
Israel, Asher, 59, 106
Israeli consulate (Sydney), bomb attack
    on, 241
  see also antisemitism

INDEX

Israeli relatives, 106–7, 115
Issroff, Saul, 320
Italy, visit to, 259–60

Jackomos, Alick, 288
Jackson, Robert, 279
Jackson, Syd, 288
Jackson, William, 279
James, Alf, 49
Jay Creek Settlement, NT, 124
Jedwabne, Poland, 342
Jennings, Andrew, 332
Jerusalem, 251, 255, 256, 258
Jewish artists, 61
Jewish Board of Deputies (NSW), 241
Jewish community survey (Melbourne), 181
Jewish Council to Combat Fascism and Anti-Semitism, 122, 158
Jewish diversity, 322, 344–5
Jewish Higher Education Committee (Sydney), 274
Jewish unity, 6
Jewish Welfare (South Yarra, Vic), 154
Jewish writers, 4, 77, 88, 344
Jewishness, 8, 17, 47, 48, 296, 320, 322–3, 344–7
  Roman Catholic Church views on, 194, 303–4
  see also Yiddish
Jews and *apartheid*, 103, 104, 107, 273
Jones, Alan, 234
Jones, Jack, 162
Judge, Edwin, 277
Judt, Tony, 357
Jungarai, Gwoya, 135

Kakadu National Park, 221, **222**, 317, 351
  see also land rights, Australia
Kalowski, Joanna, 321
Kaplan, Mendel, 320
Kaplan, Rabbi Mordecai, 344
Karadum, Cenk, 282
Kark, Sidney and wife, 73, 141
Katie (nanny), 12
Kaunus (Kovno), Lithuania, 339
Kausman, Les, **255**
Kaye, Justice William, 167
Kazak, Ali, 296
Kelly, Jim and Bev, 336
Keperra Country Club, Brisbane, 314
Keppel-Jones, Arthur, 69–70, 72, 87–8, 189, 198, 348
KES *see* King Edward VII Secondary School (KES)
Kesteven, Sue, 223
Kiki, Albert Maori, 182
Killen, Jim, 181
Killoran, Pat, 126, 206
King Edward VII Secondary School (KES), 44, 52–3, 54
King Ranch, Texas, 266
Kingstrand hut, 145, **[CP]**
  see also Aboriginal, housing
Kintore, NT, 297
Kirby, Michael, 248, 249, 277, 315, 323
Kirkwood, Kenneth, 230
klaberjas, 67, 87
Knight, Ken, 201
Knopfelmacher, Dr Frank, 181
Konstanian-Danzig, Rachel, 338
Korczak, Janusz, 341

kosher food, 14, 20–1, 116
  see also *shtetl* food
Kowarsky, Alec and Zelda, 114
Kriel, Isaac, 59, **60**, 77, 78, 80, 101, 105, 348
Kriewaldt, Judge Martin, 121
Krige, Mr (principal, Yeoville Boys' School) 40
Krüger, DW, 98, 99
Kruithof, Pieter, 174, 175
Kuper, Leo, 70
Kupka, Hans-Joachim, 330–1
kvetching (complaining), 47, 71, 256
Kwiet, Konrad, 251, 278, 280, **281**, 331

LaBilloise, Chief Wallace, 193, 194
Labor Party, Vic, 169
Lake Nash, NT, 266
Lake Tyers Reserve, Vic, 168, 171–3, 174, 297
Lambert, Jacquie, 210, 214, 269
Lasswell, Harold, 346, 347
Lazenby, Alec, 202
legal studies (CT), 68, 72, 85, 87
leprosy, 142, 267
Levine, Dotke (uncle), 29–30, 37
Levinson, Daniel, 327
Lewis, Leslie, 123
Liberal Party
  Australian, 308
  South African, 74
liberalism, 56, 74, 86
liberals (South Africa), 69, 74, 76, 103
Liebler, Isi, 181
Liffman, Michael, 128
Lippmann, Lorna, 160, 179, 182, 183, 198, 207
Lippmann, Walter, 154, 160, 180, 183
Lithuania
  genocide, **[CP]**, 278
  history, 18, 320–1
  visit to, 337–40
Lithuanian Jews *see Litvak(s)*
Littell, Franklin, 257
Litvak(s), 3, 7, **9**, 10, 14, 18, 174, 337–40, 344, 348, 350
litvishe, 82, 338–40
Lombadina, WA, 297, 298, **299**
Long, Jeremy, 152
Long, Ken, 201
Loos, Noel, 206
Lowe, Beulah, 147

Mabo, Eddie, 206
Maccabi Games (1985), 253–5, **255**
McCorquodale, John, 160
McDermott, Lloyd, 307
MacDonald, Flora, 197
McEwen, Jock, 183
McGinness, Joe, 121, 164, 206
Mackenzie, WJM, 152
Mackerras, Neil, 204
McLean, Sue (Stevenson), 158, 160, 179, 198
Macquarie University, 225, 235–6, 237–41, 249–50, 258, 261, 271, 273–8, 282, 283–4, 288
  Politics Department, 238
  School of History, Philosophy and Politics (HPP), 237–8, 274, 277, 283
Maddock, Ken, 306
Makaratta, 246
  see also treaties, Australia, argument for

INDEX

Malan, Dr Daniel François, 36, 52, 107
  see also Purified Nationalist Party
Mandel, Shlomo, 15
Mandela, Nelson, 51, 75, 86, 95, 308
Mangope, Selina, 176
Mann, Ida, 140
Manne, Robert, 306
Maori affairs, 183–6, 328
  see also McEwen, Jock
Maori Jews, 183–4
marae, 185
'Margaret Throsby in Conversation' (radio program), 235
'Maritzburg *see* Pietermaritzburg
Marks, Shula, 248
marriage (CT), 83–4, **84**
  see also Berea *Shul* (synagogue)
Marsh, Derick, 103, 105, 107
Marsh, Jack, 312, **312**
Marwick, Max, 178, 179
Master of the Supreme Court, office of, 71–2
masters research (CT), 93, 97, 101, 109
  see also doctoral research (CT); political science studies (CT)
Mathias, Chief Jo, 195
Mayer, Henry, 235
Maymuru, Narritjin, **[CP]**
Mazrui, Ali, 345
Meagher, Edward (Ray), 167
Medding, Peter, 180
media, appearances and writing, 5, 164, 170, 173, 181, 235, 240–1, 244, 263, 285–9, 296, 318, 322–3
  radio, 164, 181, 233, 234, 235, 240–1, 318
  television, 164, 233, 234
  see also specific book titles, e.g. *Black Viewpoints: The Aboriginal Experience*; specific radio and television programs, e.g. 'A Big Country' (TV series).
Melbourne
  life in, 108, 153–5
  see also Monash Indigenous Centre (MIC); Monash University
Melmed, Ben (father-in-law), 81, 83–4, 85, 92, 176, 209, 215, 231, 233, 307
Melmed, Eddie (brother-in-law), 81, 83, 85, 178, 189
Melmed, Elsa (mother-in-law), 83
Melmed, Erica (Eddie's wife), 178, 189
Melmed, Gavin (nephew), 178
Melmed, Sandra (future wife), 80
  see also Tatz, Sandra
Melson, Robert and family, 278, 280, **281**
Menzies, Robert, 95, 122, 187
Menzies Liberal Coalition Government (1962), 157
Merrett, Christopher, 308
meshugas, 77, 82, 87–8
Meston, Archibald, 118, 134, 148, 354
  art, **[CP]**
migration studies, 239–40, 284
migratory labour (South African), 94, 97
Mi'kmaq Indians, 193, 194, **[CP]**
Miller, Mick, 121
Milton, Sybil, 278, 279
mining
  bauxite, 161

uranium, 214, 220–6, 221–7, 227–8, 229, 250, 263, 352
  see also Aboriginal, opposition to mining
Ministry for Aboriginal Affairs, Vic, 165–7
misnagdim, misnagged, 6, 7, 8, 337
missions, 118, 119, 124, 133, 134, 137, 140, 141, 142, 144, 145–9, 242, 298
  see also specific missions, e.g. Bathurst Island Mission, Nguiu, NT.
Mitchell, Justice Dame Roma, 314
mixed universities (South Africa), 86
Mkhambi, Agnes, 176
mohel see Glass, Reverend (*mohel*, 'Rev Cut Glass')
Mokwane, Johannes, 80
Monash Country Club, NSW, 239, 311, 313–5, 362
  see also *Course of History: Monash Country Club, 1931–2001, A*
Monash Indigenous Centre (MIC), 157, 158, 159, 160, 164, 175, 198, 207, 276, 319 352
  see also Centre for Research into Aboriginal Affairs (CRAA)
Monash University, 154, 155, 179, 191, 198, 204, 206, 208, 237, 264, 267
  Anthropology and Sociology Department, 179, 198
Moore, Russell see Savage, James
Moree, NSW, 297, 298
Moriarty, John, 164, 268
Mornington Island, Nth Qld, 189, 228, 297, 298

Morrow, Sylvia, 204
Moses, John, 251
Mount Allan Station, NT, 130
Mowanjum. WA, 297
Moy, Frank, 124, 151
Mucci, Michael, **CP**, 311
Muizenberg beach resort, 28–9, 49
Mullett (née Drayton), Cheryl, 312, **312**
Munungurr, Daymbalipu, 161
Murray, James, 258
Murray, Stuart, 182
Murray Bridge, SA, 299
Museum of the History of Polish Jews, Warsaw, 342
My Lai massacre, Vietnam, 261

Nalson, John, 205
Namatajira, Albert, 136
Napperby Station, NT, 162
Natal, life in, 61–110
Natal University (later, KwaZulu-Natal), 63–77, 93, 307–8, 348
Natal Witness, 66, 67, 68, 308, 351
National Museum of Australia, 311
  see also Purified Nationalist Party
Nationalist Party, South Africa, 15, 69, 74, 79, 96
Native Law in South Africa, 266
  see also Aborigines and the law, customary law
Native Policy, South African, 93–100, 108
  see also South Africa, history
Nayman, Doreen, 106, 107, 115
Nazi war criminals, 4, 105, 157, 247, 279–80

INDEX

New Zealand 327
  Jews, 320
  research on suicide, 300
  visits to, 183–6, 327–9
  see also McEwen, Jock; Maori affairs; Maori Jews; *marae*
New Zealand Jewish Council, 329
Nicholls, Pastor Sir Douglas, 165, **166**, 172, 182, 265, 356
Niewenhuizen, Miss (teacher, Yeoville Boys' School), 40
Nitch, St John B (headmaster, KES), 52, 53
Noble, WS, 119
non-White(s), South Africa, 58, 94, 177
North Australian Workers' Union, 161
Northern Territory
  research in, 116, 118, 130–47, **[CP]**, 225
Novello, Ivor, 50–1
Nuremberg Trials, conference on, 279

Obel, Mark, 87, 91
Obel, Promund, 83, 86–7, 106
O'Brien, Darren, 305
Obstacle Race: Aborigines in Sport, 276, 288–9, 361
Oenpelli Mission, NT, 224, 225, 267–8
Office of Aboriginal Affairs (OAA), 206
O'Hara, John, 326
Ohr Somayach, 274
Old Edwardians *see* Edwardians (KES old boys' club)
O'Leary, Cornelius (Con), 126
O'Loughlin, Bishop JP, 134, 164, 267
One-Eyed: A View of Australian Sport, 302, 362

One People of Australian League (OPAL), 206
Oosthuizen, Miss (teacher, Yeoville Boys' School), 40
Oribi Men's Residence, 63, 65, 67, 68, 73, 74, 75, 351
O'Shea, Paul, 304
Oshlack, Alan, 204
Oshlack, George, **255**
Ossewa Brandwag, 41, 105
Ostjuden, 6
Oxford, St Antony's College
  sabbatical in, 220, 229, 230

Palm Island Settlement, Qld, 148, 149
Panevezys (Poinevez), Lithuania, 339–40
Papertalk-Green, Charmaine, 287
Papunya Settlement, NT, 40, 124, 134, 160, 162
Parker, Robert, 119, 124, 150, 151, 154
Partridge, Percy, 121, 125, 144, 236
pass laws (South Africa), 58, 102
Paton, Alan, 74
Paton, David, 75
patriotism, 10, 57, 99, 271, 321
Peabody, George, 246
Pemulwuy, 271
Penhall, Les, 124–5, 162
Perceval, Celia, 232
Perceval, John, 232
Perkins, Charlie, 164, 268, **269**, 288
Perth, Australia, 107, 114, 115, 120, 160
Pfister, Gertrud, 332–3
Phillips, Con, 275
Piccardy, Mr (teacher, Yeoville Boys' School), 40

Pickles, Alfred, 138, 139
Pietermaritzburg, 63, 70–1, 74, 308, 348
Pilger, John, 315–16
Pink, Olive, 139, **139**
Pintupi people 134, 135
Pittock, Barrie, 121
'Play the Game', sports conferences, Copenhagen, 332, 333
Playford, John, 122
poker, 47, 65–6, 67
Poland, visit to, 337–42
political science studies (CT), 65, 69, 72, 74, 101–2
'Politics of Aboriginal Health, The' (essay), 352
Polyukovich, Ivan, 278
Ponary massacre, Vilnius, Lithuania, 339
Poor Whites, 36
Port Augusta, SA, 127, 128, 129, 233
Port Lincoln, SA, 297
Potchestfroom University, 98
Pretoria University, 63, 74
professorship (CT), 209, 264, 249
Progressive Party (South Africa), 98
  see also Suzman, Helen
Pumpenai (Pompian), Lithuania, 340
Purdue University (Indiana), 280
Purified Nationalist Party, 51, 96
  see also Malan, Dr Daniel François
Puxley, Frank, 53, 54–5

Queen's University, Kingston, 189–90, 197–8, 204, 208, 336
  see also Canada, sabbatical in
quiz kid (CT), 56, 83

Rabinowitz, Chief Rabbi Louis, 103–4
race and racism, 5, 94, 107, 181, 204, 228, 249, 284
  study of, 252, 273, 277
  see also Aboriginal Australians, protection-segregation
Race Politics in Australia, Aborigines: Politics and Law, 228, 361
race relations, 250
  Australia, 113, 134–5, 144, 155, 211–12, 213–14, 232, 354
    see also 'closing the gap' (between Aborigines and non-Aborigines)
  Canada, 213–14
  New Zealand 183–4
  South Africa, 97, 119, 210, 214
race riots, USA, 157
racial purity, 106, 136
Ranger (ERA) mine, 317, 319
  see also mining, uranium
rape sentences (Victoria), 169–70
Reconstruction Judaism, 344
Reeves, Bishop Ambrose, 103
referendum of 1967 (Australia), 187–9, 206, 247
  see also Aboriginal Australians, 'first nation people'
refugees, 108, 322, 348
Remu Cemetry, Cracow, 340
Reser, Joseph, 301
reserves see specific reserves, e.g., Framlingham Reserve, Vic
Reynolds, Henry and Margaret, 206
Rhodes, Cecil, 75
Rivonia Trial, 75
Rizal, José, 271

INDEX

Robinson, Laura, 332
Roden, Justice, 249
Roebuck, Peter, 306
Romani people, 277, 279, 336
Rosella, Joe, 38
Rosen family, 68–9, 259
Roth, Cecil, 71, 320, 345, 347
Roughsey, Dick, 213
Rowland, Sir James, 249
Rowley, Charles, 161, 188, 206
Royal Sydney Golf Club, 293–6, 305, 313, 314, 351
Royal Sydney Golf Club: The First Hundred Years, The, 293–5, 361
rugby league, 242, 298, 299, 356
Rugby League Knockout tournament, 298
Russell, Lynette, 319
Rutland, Suzanne, 294
Ryde-Parramatta Golf Club, 239
Rylah, Arthur, 167, 170

Sackstein, Hymie (uncle), 37, 50
Sackstein, Mervyn (cousin), 37, 39, 50
St George Orphanage, 36
St John, Edward, 149
St Michael's (golf course), 313
Santa Teresa Mission, NT, 137, 140, 297
Savage, James (born Russell Moore), 171
Sawer, Geoffrey, 121, 198
Schama, Simon, 344
Schmalzbach, Oscar, 248–50, 272
Schneider, Mike, 85, 178
schools *see* King Edward VII Secondary School (KES); Yeoville Boys' School
Schrire, Carmel, 224–5, 226, 245

seafood (CT), 138–9
segregation (South Africa), 58, 76, 86, 94, 119, 177
self-reliance (CT), 27, 48, 66–8
Seres, Frank, 263
Serniki, Ukraine, 278
servants (South Africa), 12, 14, 17, 26, 32, 41, 53, 58, 65, 66, 75, 91, 108
sex education (CT), 37–8, 40, 50
Shadow and Substance in South Africa: A Study in Land and Franchise Policies Affecting Africans, 1910–1960, 97, [CP], 361
Shain, Milton, 320
Shalom Institute (University of NSW), 284
Sharpeville Massacre, 102, 106, 349
Shimoni, Gideon (Gidi), 104–5, 273
Shoah see Holocaust
Shoshan, Yaakov, 255
shtetl food, 14–15, 20–1, 22, 24, 25–6, 36–7
shtetl(s), 7, 8, 18–19, 42, 137, 320, 321, 339, 348, 350
Simon, George, 183
Sisulu, Albertina, 308
Sisulu, Walter, 75, 308
Slotkin, Mrs, 88–9, 131
Smith, David, 115
Smith, Roger, 280
Smuts, General Jan Christian, 41–2, 52, 96–7, 121
Snake Bay, NT, 138, 141
snooker, 59, 81, 191, 227
soccer, 217, 332, 333
social action, 57, 285, 320, 322, 327, 347

social impact monitoring, 302–3, 318–19
social justice, 5, 28, 41–2, 87, 133, 204, 266, 286, 307
socialisation (CT), 8, 12, 177
Sociological Association of Australia and New Zealand (SAANZ), 183
sociology, 70, 179, 183, 189, 198, 238, 253
Sonyel, Salahi, 282–3
South Africa
  1976 sabbatical and travels in, 215–7
  history, 55, 93–100, 181, 316, 349
South African Institute of Race Relations, 158–9
South African Jewish emigrés, 55–6, 106–7, 108, 217, 320–2, 349–50
South African Party, 96
  see also Smuts, General Jan Christian
Soweto, 80, 216, 217, 349
Spann, Dick, 235
sports
  boycotts, 234, 239, 240, 243, 254, 265
  conferences, 332–3
  corruption in/corruption of, 241–2
  criticism, 233–4, 235, 241, 306–8, 325–6
  discrimination, 313–14
  history, 56, 57, 239, 284, 285, 306–8
  see also specific sports, e.g. boxing.
sports and Aborigines see Aboriginal Australians and sport
sports culture (KES school), 44, 53
Springborg, Robert, 241
Stanner, WEH (Bill), 114, 123, 126, 186

Starn, Graeme, 205
states of emergency (South Africa), 41, 103
Stephens, Sir Ninian, 249
Stern, Bob, 48
Stevens, Frank, 161
Stevens, Laurie, 49
Stoddart, Brian, 293, 294, 295
Stolen Generations, 171, 287, 319
Stone, John, 230
suicide, 5, 20, 27, 42, 301, 358
  of family members, 27, 29–30
  studies/research, 284, 300–2
  see also Aboriginal suicide; youth suicide
Summerhays, Father, 137
Susskind, Anne, 326
Suzman, Helen, 98
Swan Hill, Vic, 297
Swift, Michael, 179
Switkowski, Dr Ziggy, 317–19
Sydney Jewish Museum, 321

Taft, Ron, 114
Tatz, Annie (grandmother), 74, 89
Tatz, Bernie (uncle), 82
Tatz, Bessie (mother, née Isaacson), 346, 347
  during CT's primary school years **11**, 12–13, 21, 24, 28, 33, 35
  during CT's secondary school years, 45, 46, 48–9
  during CT's pre-Natal years, 66, 75, 82, 84, 85, 90
  during CT's post-Natal years, 110, 127, 176, 177, 215, 216, 233
Tatz, Brenda (cousin), 27

INDEX

Tatz, Colin, **12**, **65**, **84**, 90, **109**, **218**, **255**, **281**, 288, **360**
  Australia, life in, 113–60
  Australian Political Science Association (president, 1975–77), 205
  family life in childhood and teens, 1–60
    battered child, 23
  honours (CT)
    Honorary Doctor of Laws, University of Kwa-Zulu Natal (1997), **[CP]**, 307, 309
    honorary fellowship, AATSIS, 316
    Order of Australia (1997), **[CP]**, 307
  Natal, life in 61–110
  see also specific centres, e.g. Australian Institute for Aboriginal Studies (AIAS); fieldwork; doctoral research (CT); masters research (CT); media appearances and writing; specific universities, e.g. Australian National University (ANU)
Tatz, Karen (daughter), 110, 115, 117, 120, 177, **[CP]**, 203, 227, 231
Tatz, Kivel (grandfather), 11, 29
Tatz, Koppel (uncle), 34, **34**, 274
Tatz, Maurice (father), **11**, 12, 24, 28, 32, 35, 45–6, 48–9, 65–6, 89, 90–1, 92
  during CT's post-Natal years, 216, 229
Tatz, Pam (sister), 16, 24, 75, 90, 307
Tatz, Paul (son), 91, 105, 110, 116, 117, 177, **[CP]**, 203, 217, 227, 231, 288, 294
Tatz, Rabbi Dr Akiva (Kevin, cousin), 274
Tatz, Sandra (wife, née Melmed), 8, 124, 126, 127, 128, 137, 231, 274, 294, 297–8
  early life in South Africa and marriage, 8, 60, 77, 80–2, 84, **84**, 85, 90, 100, 109–110
  fieldwork with CT, 297–8, 299, 300, 307, 308, 315, 323, 333, 335, 342
  first job and life in Melbourne, 154, 155, 160
  life and study in Canada, during CT's sabbatical, 189–98
  life in Australia, 113, 114, 116, 117, 120, 149, 152, 202, 204, 208, 210, 225, 227, 259
    Armidale, 202, 208, 227, 228, 209
    Canberra, 115, 116, 117, 120, 124, 126
    Sydney, 234, 239, 271, 283, 289
  typing CT's doctoral thesis and assisting with writing, 100, 113, 152, 315, 323
  visits to *see under* specific countries, e.g. Canada
Tatz, Simon (son), 149, 150, 177, [CP], 203, 217, 225, 227, 229, 231, 232, 239
Tatz, Yoseph, 339
teaching *see* Aboriginal, history, teaching of; genocide, course/studies; *see also* names of specific institutions, e.g. Australian National University (ANU)
teaching profession, 72, 81, 93
Tennyson, Patrick, 181

Terre'Blanche, Eugene, 99
territorial segregation (South Africa), 95
Thiele, Steve, 263–4
'Thinking Jewish' (TV series), 5, 296
Thomas, Faith, 288
Thompson, Lindsay, 167, 172, 174, 175
Thompson, Peter, 211
Thomson, Donald, 119, 123, 167, 178
Tickner, Robert, 323
tikkun olam, 345, 347
  see also social justice
Tippett, George, 221, 317
Tirikatene, Whetu, 183
Tjupurrula, Nosepeg, 135
Toohey, Justice John, 268
Torch Commando, 54
Townsville College of Advanced Education (CAE), 206, 207
treaties with Indigenous peoples, 239
  Australia, argument for, 246–7, 353–4
  Canada, 195–6, 246
Trudeau, Pierre, 190, 196, 243
Tucker, Margaret, 168
Turnbull, Malcolm, 321
Turner, Ian, 121

Ucko, Peter 210, 211, 211, 213, 221, 223, 268, 352
umpires, 286
umpiring, 232, 233
United Party (South Africa), 51, 96, 98
university administration/administrators, 220–1
University of New England (UNE), 179, 197, 201, 204, 207, 208, 226, 227, 228, 231, 237, 238, 239

University of Technology Sydney (UTS), 261, 311,
University of Waikato, 327–8, 330, 331
University of Western Sydney, 271, 311
'Unlevel Playing Fields, "Race" and Sport in Australia' (essay), 319
uranium mining see mining, uranium
US Holocaust Memorial Museum (USHMM), 278, 279

van As, Harry, 342
van Jaarsveld, FA, 98–9
Verwoerd, Dr Hendrik, 122, 177
veterinary science, 60, 63–64
Victorian Family Council, 175
Vilna Gaon Jewish State Museum, 338–9
Vilnius (Vilna), Lithuania, 7, 337, 338
Vincent, Cyril, 38–9
Viner, Ian, 221, 223, 228
violence
  Aboriginal Australians, violence, 264, 298
  domestic, 154
  political, course in, 205
  race relations and, 56, 56, 102, 151, 252
  in sport 233, 241, 248, 252
Visser, Julian, 105
von Sturmer, John, 223, 225

Waddington, Dr Ivor, 332
Wainer, Dr Bertram, 167
Wajnryb, Dr Abraham, 278
Wajnryb, Ruth, 278
Walker, Kath (Oodgeroo Noonuccal), 121, 157, 164

INDEX

Waller, Louis, 160, 161
Walsh, RJ, 249
Ward, Dick, 267
Ward, Graeme, 317
Ward, Russell, 204
wards/wardship, 135, 155, 355
Wards' Employment Ordinance, 135, 136
Warsaw, 340
Warsaw Ghetto, 341–2
Waudby, Bill, 163
Weaver, Sally, 197
Webb, Leicester, 101–2, 114, 198
Weiss, Charlie, 162
'Welcome to Australia' (John Pilger documentary), 315–16
Welensky, Sir Roy, 76
Welfare Branch, NT, 124, 137, 141, 142, 143–4, 145, 146, 147, 151–3, 155–6, 188, 267, 352
Welfare Ordinance, 135
Wentworth, WC (Bill), 156–7, 187, 213, 224
Westropp-Evans, Robert, 231
White South Africans, 23, 51
Whitlam, Gough, 157
'Who Won and Who Cares?' (essay), 325
Whyman, Beverley, 171
Willey, Richard, 232
Williams, Cecil, 52, 54–5
Willmot, Eric, 214–15, 268, 269–71, 72
Willmot family, 270
Wilson, Alan, 294
Wilson, Sir Ronald, 306
Windschuttle, Keith, 177, 306

With Intent to Destroy: Reflecting on Genocide, 316, 362
Witt, Max, 59
Witwatersrand University, 85, 215
see also South Africa, sabbatical in
Wolmarans Street *Shul*, 104–5
Wooldridge, Ian, 244
Woorabinda Settlement, Qld, 148, 149, 298
World War II
effect on life, 6, 41
South Africa joins, 96–7
Worlds Apart: The Re-Migration of South African Jews, 321, 328, 362
Wran, Neville, 242
wrestling, 56
Wright, Richard and Sonya, 278

Yad Vashem, 256, 276, 282, 338, 342
courses at, 251, 256, 258, 273–4, 276, 282, 338, 342, 338
Yale College, 82, 83, 85, 88, 90, 92, 101
Yarrabah Settlement, Qld, 149
Yeoville Boys' School, 28, 34, 40, 44, 52, 348
Yerbury, Di, 282, 283, 288
Yiddish, 7, 18, 19, 48, 72, 337
Yirrkala Mission, NT, 161, 186
Young, Andrew, 267
Young Men's Hebrew Association (YMHA), 311, 311
youth suicide, 284, 299–300, 326, 328, 333
Yuendumu Settlement, NT, 142, 145, 162, 298
Yutar, Percy, 75, 104

Zalman, Elijah ben Solomon, 338
Zionist(s), 273
　see also Herzl, Theodor; Shimoni, Gideon (Gidi)
Zulman, Jack (uncle), 74
Zulu language, 73
Zulu nation, 63
Zungu, Christina, 91–2